The Nurture of Nature

The Nature | History | Society series is devoted to the publication of high-quality scholarship in environmental history and allied fields. Its broad compass is signalled by its title: nature because it takes the natural world seriously; history because it aims to foster work that has temporal depth; and society because its essential concern is with the interface between nature and society, broadly conceived. The series is avowedly interdisciplinary and is open to the work of anthropologists, ecologists, historians, geographers, literary scholars, political scientists, sociologists, and others whose interests resonate with its mandate. It offers a timely outlet for lively, innovative, and well-written work on the interaction of people and nature through time in North America.

General Editor: Graeme Wynn, University of British Columbia

Claire Elizabeth Campbell, *Shaped by the West Wind: Nature and History in Georgian Bay*

Tina Loo, *States of Nature: Conserving Canada's Wildlife in the Twentieth Century*

Jamie Benidickson, *The Culture of Flushing: A Social and Legal History of Sewage*

William J. Turkel, *The Archive of Place: Unearthing the Pasts of the Chilcotin Plateau*

John Sandlos, *Hunters at the Margin: Native People and Wildlife Conservation in the Northwest Territories*

James Murton, *Creating a Modern Countryside: Liberalism and Land Resettlement in British Columbia*

Greg Gillespie, *Hunting for Empire: Narratives of Sport in Rupert's Land, 1840-70*

Stephen J. Pyne, *Awful Splendour: A Fire History of Canada*

Hans M. Carlson, *Home Is the Hunter: The James Bay Cree and Their Land*

Liza Piper, *The Industrial Transformation of Subarctic Canada*

The Nurture of Nature

Childhood, Antimodernism, and Ontario Summer Camps, 1920-55

SHARON WALL

FOREWORD BY GRAEME WYNN

UBC Press • Vancouver • Toronto

20 19 18 17 16 15 14 13 12 11 10 09 5 4 3 2 1

Printed in Canada on ancient-forest-free paper (100% post-consumer recycled) that is processed chlorine- and acid-free.

Library and Archives Canada Cataloguing in Publication

Wall, Sharon, 1966-

The nurture of nature: childhood, antimodernism, and Ontario summer camps, 1920-55 / Sharon Wall; foreword by Graeme Wynn.

(Nature/history/society, ISSN 1713-6687)
Includes bibliographical references and index.
ISBN 978-0-7748-1639-7 (bound); ISBN 978-0-7748-1640-3 (pbk.);
ISBN 978-0-7748-1641-0 (e-book)

1. Camps – Ontario – History – 20th century. 2. Camps – Social aspects – Ontario. 3. Outdoor recreation for youth – Ontario – History – 20th century. 4. Outdoor recreation for youth – Social aspects – Ontario. 5. Camping – Ontario – History – 20th century. 6. Camping – Social aspects – Ontario. I. Title. II. Series: Nature, history, society.

GV195.C3W34 2009 306.4'8 C2008-907823-3

Canadä

UBC Press gratefully acknowledges the financial support for our publishing program of the Government of Canada through the Book Publishing Industry Development Program (BPIDP), and of the Canada Council for the Arts, and the British Columbia Arts Council.

This book has been published with the help of a grant from the Canadian Federation for the Humanities and Social Sciences, through the Aid to Scholarly Publications Programme, using funds provided by the Social Sciences and Humanities Research Council of Canada. The University of Winnipeg's Research Office also provided a grant for the reproduction of illustrations in the book.

UBC Press
The University of British Columbia
2029 West Mall
Vancouver, BC V6T 1Z2
604-822-5959 / Fax: 604-822-6083
www.ubcpress.ca

Contents

Illustrations

FOREWORD

Modernism in Camp: A Wilderness Paradox

by Graeme Wynn

Some forty years ago, as the environmental movement gained popular impetus and environmental history began to develop as a distinct field of inquiry, the appearance of Roderick Nash's *Wilderness and the American Mind* gave shape and direction to both of these endeavours. The book – which traced the intellectual roots of the wilderness concept and which was once characterized as the environmentalists' "Book of Genesis" – soon gained canonical status. The *Los Angeles Times* counted it one of the most influential books of the late twentieth century and *Outside* magazine included it in a list of "books that changed our world."[1]

There has been no Canadian equivalent, tracing the shifts that occurred in British North American/Canadian thinking about wild places over the long course of European settlement in the northern reaches of the continent, although several scholars have written around the edges of this topic. Among them, Patricia Jasen (in *Wild Things: Nature, Culture and Tourism in Ontario,* 1790-1914) deserves acknowledgment for revealing much about the wilderness idea while exploring the appeal of the wild and primitive in attracting European and North American tourists to Ontario in search of the picturesque and the sublime. Others, exploring the histories of

1 Roderick F. Nash, *Wilderness and the American Mind* (New Haven: Yale University Press, 1967). New editions were published in 1973, 1982, and 2001, by which time the book had gone through some twenty printings. See Bryan McDonald, "Considering the Nature of Wilderness: Reflections on Roderick Nash's Wilderness and the American Mind," *Organization and Environment* 14, 2 (2001): 188-201.

national and provincial parks, have illuminated some of the ways in which wilderness has been regarded by Canadians, but most have framed their studies as institutional rather than intellectual or environmental histories and have given limited attention to broader environmental and cultural trends. Students of literary texts, including Northrop Frye, Margaret Atwood, Marcia Kline, and D.G. Jones, have identified a distinctive set of Canadian attitudes to wilderness in poetry and fiction, suggesting (in the words of Marcia Kline) that Canadians rejected "the New World environment, [and] opted for an instrumentality that fostered their dependence on the parent civilization – thereby opening the floodgates to terror when they did have to meet the wild and natural." By contrast, on this account, Americans did almost the opposite. "Cutting themselves loose from civilization … [they] went happily into their New World," singing joyfully of the natural environment and "banishing terror" from their artistic and emotional vocabularies.[2]

2 Patricia Jasen, *Wild Things: Nature, Culture and Tourism in Ontario, 1790-1914* (Toronto: University of Toronto Press, 1995); Paul Kopas, *Taking the Air: Ideas and Change in Canada's National Parks* (Vancouver: UBC Press, 2007); Sid Marty, *A Grand and Fabulous Notion: The First Century of Canada's Parks* (Toronto: NC Press, 1984); W.F. Lothian, *A Brief History of Canada's National Parks* (Ottawa: Supply and Services, 1987). J.G. Nelson and R.C. Scace, eds., *The Canadian National Parks: Today and Tomorrow*, 2 volumes (Calgary: National and Provincial Parks Association of Canada and the University of Calgary, 1969); J.G. Nelson and R.C. Scace, eds., *Canadian Parks in Perspective: Based on the Conference, The Canadian National Parks: Today and Tomorrow* (Montreal: Harvest House, 1970). Sylvia Van Kirk, "The Development of National Park Policy in Canada's Mountain National Parks, 1885-1930," unpublished Master's thesis, University of Alberta, 1969; Ronald Clifford Arthur Johnson, "The Effect of Contemporary Thought Upon Park Policy and Landscape Change in Canada's National Parks, 1885-1911," unpublished PhD dissertation, University of Minnesota, 1972; Rick Rollins and Philip Dearden, eds., *Parks and Protected Areas in Canada: Planning and Management* (Toronto: Oxford University Press, 1993); John S. Marsh and Bruce W. Hodgins, eds., *Changing Parks: The History, Future and Cultural Context of Parks and Heritage Landscapes* (Toronto: Natural Heritage/Natural History, 1998); C.J. Taylor, *Negotiating the Past: The Making of Canada's National Historic Parks and Sites* (Montreal: McGill-Queen's University Press, 1990); Leslie Bella, *Parks for Profit* (Montreal: Harvest House, 1987); Alan MacEachern, *Natural Selections: National Parks in Atlantic Canada, 1935-1970* (Kingston and Montreal: McGill-Queen's University Press, 2001); John Sandlos, *Hunters at the Margin: Native People and Wildlife Conservation in the Northwest Territories* (Vancouver: UBC Press, 2007); I.S. MacLaren, *Culturing Wilderness in Jasper National Park: Studies in Two Centuries of Human History in the Upper Athabasca River Watershed* (Edmonton: University of Alberta Press, 2007); Theodore Binnema and Melanie Niemi, "'Let the line be drawn now': Wilderness, Conservation and the Exclusion of Aboriginal People from Banff National Park in Canada," *Environmental History* 11 (2006): 724-50. Margaret Atwood, *Survival: A Thematic Guide to Canadian*

But these arguments centred on imaginative writing are too easily made. Ways of thinking about the environment are rarely monolithic. Complex, evanescent ideas shift, sprawl, and all-too-often contradict broad generalizations about popular (or national) conceptions of nature. Without a "big picture" book based on close familiarity with a broad spectrum of sources, much remains to be understood about Canadian attitudes and actions toward wilderness and nature. In this context, Sharon Wall's thoughtful, probing, and impressive monograph, *The Nurture of Nature* is especially welcome. Although its frame and focus are tight, it makes a significant contribution to understanding the ways in which many Canadians sought to come to grips with the changing circumstances of their lives after the First World War. They often did this by looking backward toward a time when people were more intimately engaged with the environment than they seemed to be in the nation's rapidly growing towns and cities. Indeed if, as Roderick Nash suggested recently, one way of coming to terms with the complexity of nature-society relations and of realizing the possibilities of change, is by "ferret[ing] out the ... stories of the people and the causes that have made and are making a difference," this book is an important step forward.[3]

Early in the 1950s, dozens of summer camps in Ontario were providing a "back-to-nature" experience for about 150,000 children each year. Competing for campers and catering to different socio-economic groups as well as to different sensibilities, these camps varied considerably in the activities they offered, as well as in their comfort, duration, location, and underlying philosophy. But there can be no doubt that "camp," in the broadest most general sense, was a right-of-passage for a substantial fraction of Canadian children through the first half of the twentieth century (at least one in twenty, the sources suggest), and that grasping the meaning of the camp experience brings one a step closer to understanding Canada and the place of nature in the minds and lives of its citizens.

The effects, upon the young individuals who went to camp, of a more-or-less extended and more-or-less demanding summer sojourn in the "northern wilds" surely varied even more than did the camps themselves.

Literature (Toronto: Anansi, 1972); Northrop Frye, "Conclusion," in Carl F. Klinck, ed., *Literary History of Canada* (Toronto: 1965), 821-49; D.G. Jones, *Butterfly on Rock: A Study of Themes and Images in Canadian Literature* (Toronto: University of Toronto Press, 1970); Marcia B. Kline, *Beyond the Land Itself: Views of Nature in Canada and the United States* (Cambridge, MA: Harvard University Press, 1970) 53-61 .

3 "Interview: Roderick Nash," *Environmental History* 12, 2 (2007): 399-407.

Some had "the time of their lives," many endorsed the adventure by returning year after year, and some, no doubt, felt loneliness or experienced the full gamut of emotions while away from home and family. It was surely not by chance that American comedian Allan Sherman's "Camp Granada" song (to the tune of Amilcare Ponchielli's *Dance of the Hours*) struck a nostalgic chord north of the border in the late 1960s: "Take me home, oh muddah, fadduh / Take me home, I hate Granada! / Don't leave me out in the forest / Where I might get eaten by a bear / ... Wait a minute, it's stopped hailing / Guys are swimming, guys are sailing / Playing baseball, gee that's bettah / Muddah, faddah kindly disregard this letter!"[4]

In providing the fullest account to date of the Ontario camp movement, Sharon Wall is less concerned than was Allan Sherman with the immediate sentiments and reactions of individual campers to their circumstances. But her study brings us, nonetheless, to contemplate the longer term and broader implications (both personal and cultural) of this fascinating phenomenon. Whether or not they echoed the comedian's amusing satirical encapsulation of the experience of attending summer camp, the lessons, emotions, and effects of time spent in such places left their imprint upon hundreds of thousands of children. By seeking and revealing the cultural meanings of "fresh air" and "wilderness" camping, and of the activities in which campers engaged, while exploring some of the ways in which a significant number of eastern Canadians embraced nature as an antidote to the perception that contemporary circumstances were imperilling the young, Sharon Wall has produced a multifaceted study that has much to say to historians of the environment. Time and again, *The Nurture of Nature* reveals the contradictory qualities of the summer camp, even as it offers new insights into the ways in which Canadians struggled to find meaning in modernity.

One of the most striking vignettes in Roderick Nash's 1967 book is the story of Joe Knowles who "plunged naked" into the Maine woods in August 1913 to live as "a primitive man," entirely dependent upon his hands and his wits for survival.[5] Occasional notes, written in charcoal on birch bark and sent back to civilization, informed a growing audience of fascinated newspaper readers that Knowles had made fire by rubbing together two sticks, that he had fashioned clothing from strips of bark, and that he was

4 Formally titled "Hello Muddah, Hello Fadduh (A Letter from Camp)," the song appeared on an album by Allan Sherman entitled *My Son, the Nut,* released in 1963. For lyrics see "Camp Granada Song" at Boy Scout Trail, http://www.boyscouttrail.com/content/song/song-462.asp.

5 Nash, *Wilderness,* 141-51.

able to eat a varied diet of berries, trout, and venison. When he emerged from the wilderness, dishevelled but healthy in early October, public enthusiasm seemed to know no bounds. Thousands of people gathered to hear him speak at stops along the route of his triumphal train journey to Boston, where thousands more lined the streets to cheer his motorcade on to Boston Common, where 20,000 congregated to hear him speak. In New England, at least, Knowles even upstaged baseball's 1913 World Series at the New York Polo Grounds. His account of his exploits, published that same year as *Alone in the Wilderness,* reportedly sold 300,000 copies.[6]

For Nash, all of this stood as a "single and rather grotesque manifestation" of a surging public interest in "wildness," indicating that in the United States, at least, "appreciation of wilderness had spread from a relatively small group of Romantic and patriotic literati to become a national cult." Spurred by a growing sense that America's "pioneering" spirit was being weakened by the forms and trappings of modern urban life – reflected in and given shape by Frederick Jackson Turner's arguments about the consequences flowing from the disappearance of the western frontier, and resting as well perhaps on a (social) Darwinian sense of competition and "survival of the fittest" – easterners, in particular, came to venerate wilderness as a source of virility and toughness. In the northeastern United States and in eastern Canada "retreating" into the "wilderness" came to be seen as beneficial, even essential, for those worn down by the daily grind of modern life. For some this meant hunting or fishing, manly pursuits that would allow people to recapture the thrill of the chase. For others afflicted by stress, worry, sickliness, and weakness, ailments that plagued those forced to live and work in cities, remedy might be found by taking a "rest cure in a canoe." Exhaustion induced by hard physical recreation in nature would purge the ills of civilization and be rewarded by a transcendental sense of fulfillment that would revitalize the spirit and provide a sense of perspective on life. Or so believed many (including future Canadian Prime Minister Pierre Elliott Trudeau) in the late nineteenth and early twentieth centuries.

The Scots-Canadian and naturalized American citizen Ernest Thompson Seton (famous for his realistic animal stories) played a prominent role in bringing such convictions into wider circulation, and in making them of particular relevance to the raising of children and youth.[7] Living in Connecticut early in the twentieth century, Seton chose to tell stories

6 Joseph Knowles, *Alone in the Wilderness* (Boston: Small, Maynard & Co., 1913).

7 See "Blue Sky! – The Ernest Thompson Seton Pages" at http://www.etsetoninstitute.org/welcome.

about native peoples and nature to a small group of boys who had vandalized his property, rather than punish them by law. Inspired, the boys formed a "Woodcraft tribe," from which the Woodcraft Indians, and later the Woodcraft League of America developed. Seton described the early part of this story in a series of articles in *Lady's Home Journal* and they were published as *The Birch-bark Roll of the Woodcraft Indians* and *The Book of Woodcraft and Indian Lore*.[8] The opening page of the former informs readers: "This is a time when the whole nation is turning toward the outdoor life, seeking in it the physical regeneration so needful for continued national existence" and that "those live longest who live nearest to the ground, that is, who live the simple life of primitive times."[9] The latter defines Woodcraft, "the first of all the sciences," as "outdoor life in its broadest sense" and declares that "it was Woodcraft that made man out of brutish material, and Woodcraft in its highest form may save him from decay."

Others had tugged at these sentiments before. Even in the nineteenth century, North American parents worried about the influences of crime comics, pulp fiction, movie theatres, and dance halls on their children and, as Sharon Wall shows in the pages that follow, both summer camps for the sons of the relatively affluent and fresh air camps for the children of the urban poor operated before 1900. The YMCA was involved in camp work early on, and by the second decade of the twentieth century there was an almost bewildering array of organizations engaged in providing outdoor experience for the young: Boy Scouts, Girl Scouts, Camp Fire Girls, Girl Guides, Canadian Girls in Training, and so on took their places alongside the Woodcraft Indians, and all shared in some degree, a basic credo of the Woodcraft Way: "Outdoor activity is an inexpensive and delightful experience. It is a mental and physical restoration from the strains imposed by our modern existence. Camp life, although not the central focus of Woodcraft, has an honored place in the program. Adventure in the wilderness is ideal. Many of the same benefits may be obtained under less rigorous conditions."[10]

8 Ernest Thompson Seton, *The Birch-bark Roll of the Woodcraft Indians, Containing their Constitution, Laws, Games, and Deeds* (New York: Doubleday, Page & Company, 1907), 1; Ernest Thompson Seton, *The Book of Woodcraft and Indian Lore* (New York: Doubleday, Page and Co., 1912), v.

9 This 1907 phrasing is repeated verbatim on page 1 of Seton, *The Book of Woodcraft and Indian Lore.*

10 "The Woodcraft Way," part of "Blue Sky! – The Ernest Thompson Seton Pages" at http://www.etsetoninstitute.org/the-woodcraft-way.

Described in such terms, the appeal of outdoor activity and wilderness recreation (and the boundary between them was unmistakably blurred) was both nostalgic and redemptive. It harked back to earlier times and circumstances, provided an escape from the present, and offered opportunities for individuals to find, explore, and hone their strengths (or gird their loins for the challenges of daily life in the modern world). Against this canvas, the contention that summer camps "emerged as a reaction to urban, industrial culture and represented yet another manifestation of bourgeois longing for authentic experience and nostalgia for simpler times" (p. 254 herein) seems entirely coherent. Indeed, as Wall rightly acknowledges, "camps were designed as escapes from modernity in geographic, temporal, and cultural terms" (p. 14).

This is the beginning rather than the end of Wall's argument in *The Nature of Nurture*, however. Although her first chapter nicely summarizes the anti-urbanism as well as "the antimodern romanticization of nature and the simple life" upon which the camps drew, the rest of her book is given to careful analysis of different parts of the camp story, and each thematic chapter invites readers to think again about taken-for-granted assumptions, by reconfiguring and re-examining one or another aspect of the camp phenomenon. What are the implications of the class-based distinction between elite and fresh air camps? How did summer camps reflect and influence changing notions of childhood? What role did new psychological and educational principles play in structuring camp activities, and vice versa? In what ways did antimodernist sentiment influence ideals of masculinity and femininity, and questions of sexuality and co-education through the early twentieth century? What should we make of the common camp practice of "playing Indian" in relation to early twentieth- and twenty-first-century ways of thinking about race, and in the context of shifting sensibilities about Native-white relations?

Surprising and important insights flow from this approach. Although camps "embraced many facets of antimodern nostalgia" by romanticizing nature, celebrating wilderness, glorifying the simple life, and espousing "the primitive," as they "celebrated a physically and mentally tough masculinity," they were also "thoroughly implicated in the project of modernity." Camp administrators, Wall's analysis reveals, "displayed some very modern tendencies," including a strong attachment to the ideals of order and efficiency and a desire to order and organize human experience. Even as they capitalized on the perception that they offered a return to simpler, freer circumstances, camps borrowed from contemporary theory advocating "rigid and controlled approaches to child rearing." In short, Wall insists, the summer camp enshrined not simply a "rejection of modern life" but a set of complex contradictions resulting from the challenges inherent in the many negotiations of modernity taking place in and remaking early twentieth-century Canada (pages 14, 15, 253).

Similar contradictions marked the camps' and campers' engagements with nature. As Wall points out, "devotion to the ideals of order and efficiency" often led camp operators to "'clean up' the natural environment" and to engage in efforts to "rationally order and control landscapes prized for their 'wildness'" (page 14). Even when they left nature untouched, their often-extravagant embrace of pre-modern sensibilities – of wild and primitive nature – meant that camp leaders both contributed to and reinforced ideas of wilderness that rested upon the conviction that society was separate from nature. Thus to read this book is to understand that camps were hybrid phenomena. Thoroughly modern creations "born of antimodern sentiment," they attributed their "therapeutic" qualities to the opportunities they provided young moderns to experience that "intangible but much lauded entity called nature." But these claims derived their potency from pointed contrasts with prevailing notions of the city, the factory, and "progress" (page 14). Moreover, as camp leaders lamented the divorce of people from nature, and looked "longingly, if only occasionally and half-heartedly, for a bridge back," they encouraged "the construction of nature as an entity existing apart from the machinations of the human world, [as] a distinct and separate space, [as] a place one could visit, indeed should visit, to reconnect with what it meant to be truly human" (page 251). And there lies the final irony, because the celebration of earlier forms of connection between nature and society only served to reinforce the dualistic view of nature/culture so central to the modern conscience. If *The Nurture of Nature* provides no direct answers to this paradox, it nonetheless challenges us to wonder whether we can, so to speak, ever be (pre)modern, and to appreciate, again, Sharon Wall's deep and subtle treatment of the ways in which summer campers constructed their ideas of wilderness and nature in the particular contexts of their changing times.[11]

11 The oblique reference is to Bruno Latour, *We Have Never Been Modern* (New York: Harvester Wheatsheaf / Cambridge, MA: Harvard University Press, 1993).

Acknowledgments

When I was a child, I loved reading books. Looking back, I'll admit I often preferred them to people. When Sunday school friends asked me if I wanted to come over and play after church, I dutifully went and asked my mother but quietly whispered, "Say, no, Mom." I wanted to go home and read my book. To try to make me play with her, my younger sister delighted in stealing "my book" and having me chase her around the house to retrieve it. It was my usual habit to keep a book under my pillow at night so it would be "right there" when I woke up in the morning.

I can't say now that my child-self gave one iota of thought as to where a book came from or that it had actually been written by someone, who, toiling behind the pages of words, also had the help of many other people. Well, innocence is lost. I am now very aware of what is involved in making a book, at least one something like this one. In fact, my new acid test for those who tell me they might like to write one is to ask them, "How do you feel about sitting in a room alone for eight years?"

Now that the long process of book writing is over, I have many people to thank – some for concrete and practical help, some for inspiration and advice, and some, quite simply, for helping me to believe that I could get to the end of this process (and for making it a lot more fun getting there).

My first thanks go to Graeme Wynn for not only helping to get this book published but also for having it appear in the NHS series of which I am proud to be a part. From the start of my time as a postdoctoral fellow at UBC, Graeme made me feel welcome and took a genuine interest in my research and in my scholarly development. He was generous with his time, painstaking in his editing, and always encouraging to me as I worked to make this book become a reality. His sense of community-spiritedness and his willingness to mentor will not be forgotten as I move through my career.

Other individuals at UBC Press and elsewhere were helpful and accommodating during the publication process. Thanks go to Randy Schmidt for his patience in guiding me through the entire process and to Holly Keller and Darcy Cullen for friendly, prompt, and useful advice as I dealt with the technical details of publication. In terms of making this a more visually interesting book, I thank Weldon Hiebert for his careful mapmaking and the University of Winnipeg's Office of Research for funding to help cover costs of reproducing photographs in the book.

A number of people outside of UBC Press offered valuable feedback on various parts of this manuscript at different points in time. When the manuscript was in its formative stages, Craig Heron provided not only razor-sharp editing skills but also much-valued support for "oddball topics." Sincerest thanks also go to Paul Axelrod and Susan Houston for their careful reading of the text and for challenging me where they thought necessary. My warmest thanks also go to Celia Haig-Brown and Molly Ladd-Taylor for positive feedback and constructive criticism. Special thanks go to Veronica Strong-Boag not only for agreeing to come a long way to serve on my defense, but also for supporting my bid for a postdoctoral fellowship which, in part, allowed me the time to finish this book. Members of the once-active Toronto-based Consumer History Reading Group must be thanked for creating an intellectually stimulating environment and for reading and commenting on parts of this work. Among others, these included Amanda Crocker, Sarah Elvins, Allan Gordon, Jeet Heer, Steve Penfold, Peter Stevens, and Joseph Tohill. Thanks also are due to Gillian Poulter and to Cecilia Morgan who have also read parts of this manuscript and who have been sources of encouragement and intellectual support at various points throughout this project.

In terms of conducting the research that led to the content of this book, I have a number of individuals to thank. In the very early stages of my research, historian and camp enthusiast, Bruce Hodgins, at Trent University, was generous with his time and helped give me a broad picture of the early summer camp landscape. In Toronto, Wendy Macdonald of the Family Service Association and staff at the Upper Canada College archives were extremely helpful in allowing me access to camp records and in locating former campers to be interviewed. Staff at the Ontario Camping Association also offered access to historical sources and help in locating interviewees. In their own ways, Bob Christianson, Dale Callendar, and Fred Okada of Bolton Camp gave me a more personal take on the fresh air camp experience. Dorothy Walter, formerly of the Ontario Ministry of Education, generously shared with me records of Bark Lake Camp as well as her own experiences with the camp. Finally, thanks go to Bernadine Dodge and Jodi Aoki at the Trent University Archives and to staff at the United Church/Victoria University Archives for archival assistance.

In terms or making this a richer study, I would like to thank interviewees in a special way. Their willingness to share their (often) much-treasured memories of camp with a relative stranger will always be remembered. Because of them, I believe this is a more valuable study than it might have been. When finished our interview, one interviewee told me: "I've now talked more about camp to you than I have to anyone in the last forty years." I am very grateful for that and I hope that she, and others, will feel it was worth the time spent.

Although no one can write your book for you, in my case, it certainly helped to have supportive colleagues, friends, and family along the way. For a number of years now, several good friends have been a lifeline of support for me. Catherine Carstairs has always been ready to analyze any piece of history (and, more importantly, life) with me. Janet Miron has (for some reason) always believed in me, and Marcia Ostashewski has been ready to listen to my woes and trials (book-related and otherwise!) and to actually make me feel better. In their own ways, Fiona Miller and Steve Penfold also helped me to believe that I could finish this book. Further along the way, Lara Campbell, Tasha Riley, and Michelle Swann provided friendship and distraction from book-writing at just the right times. For helping me hang on to the goal of finishing a book during the first crazy years of teaching (and for bonding with me in new "northern" climes), I have a number of people to thank. Katrina Srigley, Rob Teigrob, Peter Cook, Mark Crane, Hilary Earl, and Angela Failer helped me to survive while working seven days a week in North Bay. In Prince George, Loraine Lavallee, Josée Lavoie, and Lisa Dickson always kept life interesting. Jonathan Swainger made me feel I really could do this. Holly Nathan let me drive her truck and was the friend I got to know in the nick of time. Finally, this book is partly responsible for landing me back in the city, Winnipeg, where I first started out and where I gained a whole new slew of colleagues who welcomed and encouraged me as I undertook the final stages of the book-writing process.

My final thanks go to my family, whose support has been consistent and much valued throughout this long process. My heartfelt thanks go to

Ramona Wall and Glenn De Baeremaeker for providing generous hospitality (whether in Scarborough or in the Muskoka's) and frequent escapes from academic work. Rachel Wall provided escapes of a different sort, with telephone calls at the right moment conveying her constant support. The Winnipeg contingent of my family, for much of the time, was far away, but for parts of this process was much closer than they ever would have imagined. To Heather and Steve Peter (and the loveable Kirstin, Dylan, and Jessie) I owe a great debt of thanks for keeping up my spirits, for endless encouragement, and for the right amount of red wine on cold Winnipeg winter evenings. Finally, to my parents – Sieg and Teenie Wall – I am forever in debt not only because they brought me into this world but also because they taught me books were wonderful things and even kept them in shelves around the kitchen table. (My mother would say because there was nowhere else left to put them!) Later in life, they let me live in their basement to finish writing this one. In their own distinct ways, they have taught me the power of critical thinking even though they haven't always agreed with my conclusions.

I can't imagine anyone would want to keep this book under their pillow at night or dodge social engagements to finish reading it, but if anyone gets a fraction of the satisfaction that I found in some of my childhood books, it will have been worth the effort.

- An earlier version of Chapter 4 was previously published as "Making Modern Childhood, the Natural Way: Psychology, Mental Hygiene, and Progressive Education at Ontario Summer Camps, 1920-1955," in *Historical Studies in Education/Revue d'histoire de l'éducation* 20, 2 (2008): 73-110.
- An earlier version of Chapter 6 was previously published as "Totem Poles, Teepees, and Token Traditions: 'Playing Indian' at Ontario Summer Camps, 1920-1955" in the *Canadian Historical Review* 86, 3 (2005): 513-44. It is reprinted by permission of University of Toronto Press Incorporated (www.utpjournals.com).

The Nurture of Nature

Introduction

To be modern is to live a life of paradox and contradiction.

– *Marshall Berman,*
All That Is Solid Melts into Air

Thousands of Canadians are familiar with the image of Pierre Elliott Trudeau, sun-tanned and buckskin-clad, canoeing solo through the glass-like waters of a nameless Canadian river, flanked by luminous autumn foliage. The image is from the 1994 video-biography of this colourful and controversial former prime minister, a man who was eulogized at his funeral for "lov[ing] the outdoors, like so many Canadians."[1] Fewer Canadians are aware that, at the age of ten, Trudeau was immersed in a full summer of outdoor recreation at Camp Ahmek in Algonquin Park, one of Ontario's most prestigious summer camps. Already at this young age, Trudeau was adept at mastering contrasting elements of the modern experience. According to his biographer, other campers at this elite camp "were astonished by this thin kid from Montreal who vied with them at diving and canoeing while quoting Baudelaire at the same time."[2] This (and other) back-to-nature experiences of Trudeau's childhood apparently left their mark. At the age of twenty-five, Trudeau offered his poetic homage to the outdoors in an essay entitled "Exhaustion and Fulfilment: The Ascetic in a Canoe":

> What fabulous and undeveloped mines are to be found in nature, friendship and oneself! The paddler has no choice but to draw everything from them. Later ... he will be astonished to find so many resources within himself ... How does the trip affect your personality? Allow me to make a fine distinction, and I would say that you return not so much a man who reasons more, but a more reasonable man. For throughout this time, your

> mind has learned to exercise itself in the working conditions which nature intended. Its primordial role has been to sustain the body in the struggle against a powerful universe. A good camper knows that it is more important to be ingenious than a genius.[3]

To this way of thinking, the canoe trip was not just a venture into nature but a journey back to the "real self." "Ideally," Trudeau wrote, "the trip should end only when the members are making no further progress within themselves."[4] Canoeing was a transcendental experience. "It purifies you more rapidly and inescapably than any other," he concluded. "Travel a thousand miles by train and you are a brute; pedal five hundred on a bicycle and you remain basically a bourgeois; paddle a hundred in a canoe and you are already a child of nature."[5]

Despite his youthful idealism, in his adult life, Trudeau was not successful in escaping either modernity or bourgeois culture. On the contrary, while in office, his governments did their best to modernize Canadian legislative and constitutional frameworks. Indeed, this prime minister played a significant hand in initiating a range of modern, liberal reforms, from the liberalizing of laws governing divorce, homosexuality, and birth control, to the repatriation of the nation's Constitution and adoption of the Canadian Charter of Rights and Freedoms. Clearly, this nature-loving prime minister was also an avid devotée of modern liberalism who applied the test of reason to all things political, attacking tradition – in social values, in parliamentary procedure, in constitutional relations – and exalting the status of the individual above any "special interests." Here was a prime example of the paradox and contradiction of being "modern."

This is not a study of Trudeau; it is a study of what his case broadly symbolizes – that is, attempts to find meaning in modernity through antimodern leisure-time pursuits, specifically, the summer camp. Outdoor recreation was only one among many antimodernist responses to the nature of modern life in Canada. Since the late nineteenth century, antimodernists had been lamenting the pace and direction of cultural change, the humdrum and monotonous regularity of modern living, and the impact of what they called "overcivilization." Canadian historians have charted how their search for meaning and for more intense experience shaped the nature of English-Canadian imperialism, artistic nationalism, wildlife conservation, and big-game hunting, among other things. In early twentieth-century Nova Scotia, a growing aversion to the impact of industrial modernity spawned what historian Ian McKay has termed a "quest of The Folk" – a search for identity and meaning in a premodern incarnation of Nova Scotians. Folklorists and cultural producers claimed and popularized an image of an unpretentious fisherfolk as the province's true cultural identity. This image essentially denied the history of industrial development in Nova Scotia, but what did this matter as it also proved to be the goldmine that fuelled modern tourism in that province?[6]

The summer camp shared several characteristics with this broader array of antimodern phenomena. As much as it seemed a rejection of modern society, the camp was ultimately part of that society, helped individuals to adjust to it, and, at times, even fuelled the culture of commodification and consumption that lay at the heart of modernity itself. After all, camp may have provided one kind of escape, but this was usually at a cost – sometimes a high one. Ultimately, camp offered children escape from the city, but it may also have sapped desire to change the environments they were (presumably) escaping. In fact, camp directors frequently replicated the dynamics of social life "back home" and routinely saw the isolated setting of camp as ideal not for extending children's freedom but, rather, for furthering adult control. In this sense, Trudeau's belief in the use value of the canoe trip and its transformative potential echoes the modern functionalist approach of many summer camp administrators – an intriguing phenomenon, when one considers that the camp was most often marketed for its antimodern virtues. From another perspective, the camp can also be seen, like other antimodern phenomena, as the attempt by everyday individuals to create meaning and purpose in areas of their life still deemed within their control. Even children themselves wielded their own kinds of control within the camp setting. This book, I hope, shows something of both realities and also sheds light on the broader contours of Canadian society and culture in these years.

The summer camp emerged as a result of broader social and cultural developments; key among these was increasing scepticism regarding the impact of urban life. As early as the 1870s and 1880s, bourgeois observers across the nation began voicing their concerns about the negative impact of urban growth. For a nation that had defined itself largely in agricultural terms, rural depopulation was regarded as serious cause for concern.[7] As Paul Rutherford argues, "the Canadian response to the urban fact, especially to the appearance of the 'big city,' was generally unfavourable."[8] In the critiques of those who denounced urban growth, the city was alternately characterized as dirty, immoral, cold, and indifferent; it was also seen as the site of a host of temptations, including excessive drinking, prostitution, and all sorts of other consumer products and entertainments.

Young working-class women – drawn to large cities by the increasing opportunities for paid labour – were thought to be particularly imperiled by the fact of urban life in terms physical, sexual, and economic.[9] While some were drawn there for its pleasures, others agonized over its risks. For those who could not escape its daily grind, the city was blamed for inflicting the psychological pain of an increasingly stressful pace of life. The end result was what professionals termed "neurasthenia," more popularly referred to as "Worry: The Disease of the Age."[10] The general sense of crisis shared by these (mainly) middle-class observers spurred them on to initiate a host of reforms intent on improving everything from public health and social welfare to town planning and municipal governance.[11]

While some sought to improve the city, others sought to escape it, and a range of back-to-nature solutions was the result. As social and environmental historians have shown, the view of nature implicit in these solutions represented a distinct departure from earlier ones. Indeed, in the mid- to late nineteenth century, when it first became fashionable to think of nature as benevolent and health-giving, such a stance represented a reversal of centuries of thinking about the human relationship to the natural world. Europeans who colonized the New World were certainly no nature-lovers; they brought with them fundamentally Judeo-Christian notions of wild spaces as hostile and alien, wilderness regions to be tamed and subdued by the artful human hand. As Bill Cronon points out, "To be a wilderness was to be 'deserted,' 'savage,' 'desolate,' 'barren,' in short, a 'waste,' the word's nearest synonym."[12] North American pioneers had similarly ambivalent attitudes towards the natural environment, with which they struggled on a daily basis. Not surprisingly, those who worked for years to clear stubborn stumps from recently reclaimed land, those dependent on the vagaries of climate and weather for their subsistence, were not inclined to regard nature as the benevolent Mother Earth that later generations would venerate. The more holistic views of Aboriginal peoples apart, the statement by nineteenth-century literary figure, Anna Jameson, that "a Canadian settler hates a tree," was perhaps overly dramatic but likely expressed an essential truth.[13]

In the intervening decades, Europeans and Euro-Canadians alike began expressing more positive views of nature. In fact, changes in thinking were evident in the long-settled Old World long before they emerged in the New World. As Raymond Williams has shown in the British context, nostalgia for "the country" – for the good old England of a simpler time – dates back some four hundred years.[14] More specifically, the emergence of European Romanticism as a reaction against Enlightenment rationalism shaped new tastes for the sublime and for "wilder" natural landscapes in the eighteenth and early nineteenth centuries. This new appreciation for nature in its less ordered manifestations had its impact on both sides of the Atlantic. Well-to-do nineteenth-century North Americans consumed their own versions of the sublime at sites like Niagara Falls, while also taking more placid enjoyment in pleasure cruises through the Great Lakes.[15] The trend towards more positive assessments of nature accelerated with industrialization and the routinization of work as "Mother Nature" was valued increasingly for her therapeutic qualities.[16] In Ontario, as elsewhere, this resulted in the taste for nature-based recreation, the "rest cure in a canoe" becoming popular as a remedy for urban anxiety and stress. For those who could afford it, big-game hunting, canoe-tripping, cottaging, and resort holidays were all fashionable uses of summer leisure time.[17] For times when total escape was not viable, citizen groups and city planners alike sought to bring nature to the city with Garden City initiatives in Europe and City Beautiful campaigns in North America.[18]

Worries about urban living were magnified when middle-class observers considered modernity's impact on the young. Typically, they feared that children steeped in consumer culture might become incapable of enjoying life's simpler pleasures or of understanding the importance of physical exertion and hard work. Paradoxically, having fought to limit the most extreme forms of child labour, middle-class Canadians now worried about how children would use their expanding hours of leisure time. In their eyes, children were especially vulnerable to the lure of consumer culture. Anxious parents and educators worried about the impact of crime comics and pulp novels, movie theatres and youth dance halls, and some worked to prohibit or restrict access to these.[19] Indeed, to Canadians in the first half of the twentieth century, children seemed to need protection from the very culture that surrounded them.

Restricting and regulating children's exposure to consumer culture was one response to changing conditions; providing recreational alternatives was another. In the late nineteenth and early twentieth centuries, a network of child- and youth-oriented institutions emerged across Canada and the United States that sought to provide "wholesome" outlets for children's leisure time. Beyond the playground movement, which sought mainly to provide spaces for supervised children's play, other youth organizations designed more ambitious programs to fill children's leisure time. Concerned to counter the ill effects of city living and to infuse young men's leisure habits with a more spiritual tone, the YMCA established itself in both the United States and then Canada in the late nineteenth century. As David

MacLeod argues, by the 1870s, the Y was shifting its emphasis to adolescent (and middle-class) boys. By the early twentieth century, the Y was collaborating with the Protestant churches to deliver the Tuxis and Trail Ranger programs, designed in hopes of keeping older boys involved in the church. More critical of organized religion, but equally concerned about modernity's impact on youth, Ernest Thompson Seton had established his hugely popular League of Woodcraft Indians just a few years earlier. Aside from attracting thousands of urban boys to its recreational program in the first decade of the century, it is generally recognized as the inspiration for the Boy Scouts movement, which affected millions more. (In fact, Seton upbraided Robert Baden-Powell, the Scouts' founder, for essentially "stealing" his ideas.) Baden-Powell, however, took these ideas and shaped them according to a more militaristic and imperialist bent.[20]

A number of these institutions had their female-oriented counterparts. The YWCA developed shortly after the YMCA and had similarly religious aims and views of urban life. The female counterpart to the Scouts, the Girl Guides, emerged in Britain in 1909 and quickly spread to North America. In 1915, the Canadian Girls in Training was founded by some who thought the Girl Guides offered an excessively British model for Canadian girls, one many also considered too competitive, authoritarian, hierarchical, and secular. Established mainly by YWCA women, in consultation with those involved in girls' work, the CGIT had a more clearly religious mandate than the Guides; groups were formed out of Sunday school classes and came under the control of the individual Protestant denominations. The organization was also influenced by ideas of "new womanhood" and by modern educational principles, as Margaret Prang has demonstrated. Targeting adolescents in particular – and using summer camps to do so – it was quite the interwar success, drawing over 250,000 Canadian girls to its program during this period.[21]

Taken together, these youth-oriented institutions had a major impact on the life and leisure activities of thousands of Canadian children and youth. Organizations targeting boys aimed to prop up flagging urban masculinity, those targeting girls sought to keep urban girls appropriately feminine, and each was also shaped variously by religious, nationalistic, and imperialist values. Whatever the varying approaches of these institutions, they shared the worry that modern childhood and youth were in peril, that children needed to be treated separately from adults, and that leisure-time institutions, under adult control, might help to bridge the developing gap between the generations.

Roots and Branches of the Summer Camp Movement

Both in its aims and its membership, the summer camp movement grew out of this background of recreational innovations for the young. (Indeed, back-to-nature programming was on the agenda of a number of youth organizations.)[22] To a greater degree than other recreational institutions, the summer camp combined fears over modern childhood with the expanded faith in back-to-nature solutions. It was also a mainly North American phenomenon. While Germany, Britain, and Australia experimented with open-air schools in the early decades of the twentieth century, and a few European countries experimented with summer camps, residential summer camping was (and remains) a predominantly North American activity.[23] The earliest camps were found on both sides of the Canada/United States border, in a broadly contiguous area encompassing the New England States and Ontario (with a few early camps also founded in Quebec and Nova Scotia).

American camps were the first to emerge. In 1861, private boarding school headmaster, Frederick William Gunn, began taking his students on two-week camping trips away from the school in Connecticut. These loosely organized trips evolved, over the next sixty years, into a network of very profitable ventures known as the Keewaydin camps. The first opened in Maine in 1894 and was relocated to the Temagami region of Ontario in 1904. While some refer to Gunn as the "father of American camping," others argue that his early camp-outs were not the true precursors of organized summer camping. In the latter view, the establishment of permanent campsites (and not the simple act of "going camping") marks the true beginning of the summer camp's history, and a number of these were established in the 1870s and 1880s, some ten or twenty years before the first permanent Keewaydin camp. Most of these were private camps for boys that catered to upper-class clientele. Among them was New Hampshire's elite Camp Chocorua, running from 1881 to 1889. There, young gentlemen-to-be learned to share in the quasi-military democracy of this "Boys' Republic." By 1900, some twenty private camps were in existence, all but one in the Northeast.[24]

The first fresh air camps for the urban poor emerged in New York City. As Leslie Paris explains, the New York Children's Aid Society began sending children to a summer house on nearby Staten Island as early as 1872. Other New York institutions targeting the urban poor followed suit, organizing a range of summertime day excursions and longer vacations not far from city limits. Settlement houses, run by churches and other charitable organizations that sought the integration of immigrants into North American urban life, also established camps. These offered a combination of recreation and education for moral uplift at little or no cost. Assimilationist and even anti-immigrant sentiment was strong at these camps; administrations typically saw their contributions as "Americanizing" immigrant and racial others. By 1897, Peter Schmidtt claimed that seventeen American cities had established similar ventures for the urban working class, serving over 500,000 mothers and children each summer.[25]

Organizational or agency camps for the middle class formed a third group of American camp ventures. The first of these, Camp Dudley, was established by the New York YMCA in 1885. Y camps multiplied quickly thereafter; twenty years later, some three hundred were operating nationally. Aside from the Y, other groups were prominent in camp work, including the Boy Scouts, Seton's Woodcraft Indians, and the Sons of Daniel Boone. Initially, the development of camps for girls lagged considerably behind that for boys, but it was given a boost with the formation of the Girl Scouts and the Camp Fire Girls in the second decade of the century. As Paris describes, because they were non-profit and, hence, charged lower fees, agency camps offered recreational opportunities for many more children than did private camps. On the other hand, as the years went on, many also resembled private camps in their striving to offer an increasing range of amenities. All told, American camps of these three types reached "a staggering number of children," as Peter Schmidtt puts it; David MacLeod estimates that, by 1924, over seven hundred private camps and roughly five hundred agency camps were welcoming American children.[26]

In Ontario, the first camps fell into the same categories of private, fresh air, and agency-run. The very first Canadian camp was established in Nova Scotia in 1889, when the Truro YMCA set up camp in Chance Harbour. Four years later, the Ottawa YMCA founded Camp On-da-da-waks on the Ottawa River. In 1894, the Toronto City Mission established the first fresh air camp on Lake Ontario near the town of Bronte, and fresh air work was given an added boost in 1901 with the establishment of the (still-existing) *Toronto Star* Fresh Air Fund, which helped these camps stay afloat. Private camps soon followed. Camp Keewaydin, relocated from the Maine site, and Camp Temagami, both on Lake Temagami, were established in the opening years of the twentieth century. In fact, since early in the century, the two have vied for the title of "first" and "oldest" private camp. Sorting out exactly which camp was first is a somewhat complicated matter and, perhaps, not the most important point. More interesting is the fact that both camps saw the title of "first" as something valuable, something historian Alan Gordon argues also operated in the realm of national heritage sites.[27] Clearly, camps were meant to be appealing because they took people back in time, returned children to "a simpler life." The notion that one was the "first" could serve as a valuable marketing tool. Whoever was first, others soon followed. By 1920, at least nineteen camps were known to be operating in Ontario: eleven private camps, five fresh air camps, and three agency camps.[28]

As far as the history of Ontario's residential camping is concerned, the pre-First World War period differed in some important ways from the later period, upon which this book is primarily focused. During these years, camps were few in number and operated outside the context of an organized camping movement. Religious impulse was often the main influence in their founding and organization. Typically, camp amenities were few, educational influences were minimal, programming followed fairly simple patterns, and bureaucratic tendencies were rare. In terms of the types of children served, the range was limited; according to the Ontario Camping Association, before the First World War, the typical camper was usually an adolescent boy.[29]

From a smattering of camps established in the late nineteenth and early twentieth centuries, a recognizable camping movement emerged during the interwar years. One basis of this movement was growth in the total number of camps. Between the First World War and the Second World War, at least sixty-three camps were established in Ontario. While agency camps were said to be "springing up all over,"[30] fresh air camps were thriving, and new private camps were also on the increase.[31] In 1933, the directors of six or seven private camps came together to form the Ontario Camping Association (OCA), a central event in the shaping of an Ontario camp movement. As an organization, the OCA organized conferences, distributed literature, and, generally, coordinated collective action to raise the profile of residential summer camping in the province. As Meg Stanley explains, though the OCA encouraged camps to raise their own standards of camping, it was not, officially, an accrediting body until 1965.[32]

From the start, this Ontario movement was closely linked to the American one, with the OCA being a chapter of the American Camping Association (ACA), which was established in 1910. OCA members attended American conferences, read American literature, and evinced a "great feeling of fraternity" with the American movement.[33] Even after the founding of the Canadian Camping Association in 1936, both it and the OCA remained sections of the ACA.[34] Clearly, while this book focuses on Ontario, the summer camp was a North American phenomenon.

From these interwar roots, the Ontario camping movement truly flourished in the postwar period, the early years of which this book also explores. Numbers of OCA-affiliated camps grew from twenty-three in 1939 to 146 in 1955. Of these, almost 40 percent were established in the ten short years between 1945 and 1955.[35] Records of the Ontario Ministry of Education, which began licensing camps in 1941, also suggest that this was a period of significant growth.[36] The OCA was clearly optimistic about the future and began declaring the "new order of things" in 1946, the same year it first established a permanent office with one full-time staff member.[37] The OCA's *Bulletin* now claimed that camps that "twenty-five years ago ... continued to expect applications right up until the day camp opened" were now sometimes turning away parents months before the summer's start. In their view, this surely indicated that parents had accepted camping as "a most necessary part of a child's education."[38] In the same spirit, two prominent camp educators announced the camp's "coming of age within the educational and social welfare structure of (North) American life."[39]

National statistics also suggest that summer camps were booming in the 1950s. In 1952, *Saturday Night* magazine claimed that "between 5 and 7 percent of all Canadian children attend a summer camp," while in the pages of the *Financial Post*, a young Peter C. Newman quantified this at 150,000 children by 1954.[40] Newman, who sought to capture any trend of national significance and who would later make his name documenting the workings of the Canadian business and political elite, commented on the financial potential of the summer camp phenomenon. In his opinion, "Canada's summer camps are today more than fun. They've become big business."[41] Claiming that these "outdoor fun palladiums" had their tents "full to the flaps with bookings," he ventured that 1954 "promises to be the best in Canadian camping history." Ontario camps accounted for a good deal of this growth, and OCA members felt themselves to be riding the recreational wave of the future.

Writing the History of the Summer Camp

In the United States and, to a lesser extent, in Canada, a literature tracing the history of the summer camp has begun to emerge. For those involved in the movement, the goal in writing its history has been largely to trace early developments and to give "credit" to its early founders.[42] On the other hand, scholarly treatments with a more analytic bent are also appearing, and a number of distinct themes have begun to emerge. The significance of the camp's natural setting and deconstructions of the notion of "wilderness" in the American context have drawn the attention of historians Leslie Paris and Michel Smith as well as architectural historian Abigail Van Slyck. Influenced by the questions and perspective of environmental history, Smith's study of American camps focuses on the camp as a special place, a unique environment in which to shape children. Smith also underlines the persistent understanding of "nature" and "culture" as distinct and separate entities that endured throughout the twentieth century. Paris's study is especially strong in setting the camp within a broad cultural context and in exploring the close connections between urban and camp communities. Indeed, taken together, these works explore not only the physical but also the cultural landscape of camp. Paris and Van Slyck offer analyses of the rituals of summer camp, with Paris being particularly adept at showing the tensions between some of these – which relied on the incorporation of consumer culture – and the camps' commitment to a rhetoric of nostalgia. The shaping of modern childhood at camp and camp as an educational innovation are other emerging themes of these works.[43]

Within these works (and others) the racialized aspects of camping are also receiving attention. Camps' "Indian" programming and (in the American setting) traditions of "blackface" minstrelsy at camp have been analyzed for what they implied about racial "Others" and about the broader racial politics of the twentieth century. In terms of ethnicity, the camp's role in North American immigrant and Jewish communities is also being explored. One of the first book-length studies of summer camps, Paul Mishler's *Raising Reds,* examines a collection of radical (leftist) summer camps, concluding that they were useful in "Americanizing" new immigrant groups while, at the same time, affirming the "differentness" of these children and fostering the preservation of their immigrant cultures. For their part, Nancy Mykoff and Leslie Paris take up the theme of ethnicity and cultural transfer at camp in the context of American Jewish communities.

When it comes to gender, girls' camps and models of femininity have received increasing attention. Perhaps because the link between youth, recreation, and masculinity has been explored in earlier studies of the YMCA and the Boy Scouts, recently, the construction of girls' relationship to nature and physical fitness has been the more intriguing question. Susan Miller's American study focuses explicitly on girls' camping, as do a smattering of articles in the American and Canadian context. All seem to agree that girls' camps recreated, but also sometimes challenged, traditional notions of femininity or, at the very least, provided girls with challenging outdoor experiences.[44]

This book draws on previous work, tracing the history of the summer camp in the Canadian (and, specifically, Ontarian) context. At many points, it suggests similarities with the American movement. Most important, it endorses similar conclusions concerning the camp's implication in modernity and its ambivalence regarding questions of escape, isolation, wilderness, and roughing it. It also pays special attention to tensions within the camp movement, in particular, how the issue of modernity was negotiated at camp. Ultimately, I conclude that, as in most contexts, modernity was neither wholly resisted nor wholly embraced; rather, camps were hybrid institutions. They embraced many facets of antimodern nostalgia. Romanticization of nature, celebration of wilderness, glorification of the simple life, and fascination with "the primitive" were all important aspects of camp life, which also typically celebrated a physically and mentally tough masculinity, reinforced traditional compartmentalization of experience by gender, and valued community, belonging, and a "natural" spiritual experience. In a real sense, then, camps were designed as escapes from modernity in geographic, temporal, and cultural terms.

Yet, camps were also thoroughly implicated in the project of modernity. Camp administrators, for one, displayed some very modern tendencies. Most obvious was a devotion to the ideals of order and efficiency that resulted in efforts to "clean up" the natural environment and to rationally order and control landscapes prized for their "wildness." Even when they strove to leave nature untouched, they contributed to the creation of another modern construction – namely, "wilderness" – and reinforced the dualistic view of nature/culture so central to modernism. Adherence to modern ideals of childhood and child-rearing at camp also reveals an inclination to order not just space but also human experience. That childhood should consist of a set of homogenous and, significantly, happy experiences, unconnected to the world of productive labour, was a fundamental premise of camp life. Professional expertise was relied upon to guide an understanding of children and to mould healthy personalities, while long-respected and informal approaches to child-rearing were regarded with suspicion.

Born of antimodern sentiment, the summer camp was ultimately a modern phenomenon, a "therapeutic space" as much dependent on the city, the factory, and "progress" to define its parameters as on that intangible but much lauded entity called nature. In short, the summer camp should best be read not as a simple rejection of modern life but, rather, as one of the complex negotiations of modernity taking place in mid-twentieth century Canada. If camp was an escape, it was never more than a temporary one. As camp literature frankly acknowledged, "Our ... children are not going to be bushmen all their lives; they are going to come back to be city dwellers."[45] Outlining the limits of this antimodern, primitivist adventure, another observer explained, "There is ... no reason why civilized people should either return to the savage state or that they should necessarily acquire the primitive arts of life for which modern living provides few outlets. There are undoubtedly, however, substantial values to be derived from occasional or frequent returns to the primitive."[46] In essence, the summer camp was another instance of what historian Ian McKay calls "modernizing antimodernism."[47] At the same time that it romanticized a natural, simple life of community and connection, it was also implicated in, and even celebratory of, some of modernity's central organizing principles.

This study, then, is not a romantic or hagiographic account of the rise of summer camps in Ontario. It seeks to understand the *meaning* of the summer camp phenomenon by addressing several broad questions: why and under what conditions did the summer camp emerge? who founded camps and what types of children were accommodated? how did relations of class, gender, and race play out in camp programming and in the daily life of camp? what relationship did summer camp administrators have with emerging ideologies of childhood promoted by child psychologists and educational professionals? To answer these questions, this study relies greatly on the ideas, programs, and practices of camp founders and administrators, but it also tries, where possible and with the aid of oral history, to look at camp through the eyes of campers themselves. At camp, as elsewhere, adults wielded power over children and youth, but that control was never total. Campers helped shape the meanings of camp, and camps also need to be studied from the camper's eye view.

This study also remains mindful that youthful experience, like any other, was forged out of the existing frameworks of class, race, gender, and sexuality, all of which are products of culture, however deeply embedded and seemingly natural. Still, these cultural products had powerful effects on the lives of individuals. Social class shaped the nature of choices parents faced when contemplating sending a child to camp; it also shaped the nature of camp amenities and programming. For their part, boys and girls did not experience camp in the same way, nor were they meant to. Programs were deeply gendered, informed by a fundamental belief in the different abilities of each sex. Failure to conform to dominant gender ideals could mean being labelled "delinquent," a "he-man," a "sissy," or a "tomboy," depending on the role from which one deviated. Aboriginal staff members, for their part, were aware of other aspects of difference; in particular, the social distance separating themselves from those campers and staff labelled "white." Even had they believed that no such thing as "race" existed, their everyday experience would repeatedly have told them otherwise.

Age is clearly another important facet of experience (and of power) that I take into account. The compartmentalizing of human experience according to broad phases of the human life span has gone on, in some way, for centuries; however, as Howard Chudacoff argues, real "age consciousness" was a development of the late nineteenth and, especially, twentieth centuries. In the leisure-time setting of summer camp, as in the educational and medical settings Chudacoff explores, the importance of age was again emphasized and specific age norms reinforced. Summer camps, like schools and children's hospitals, were premised on the notion that children deserved distinct treatment from adults, but it was also believed that this treatment needed to be tailored to fit the needs of children of different ages. Age-specific programming and special treatment of youth were both part of summer camp agendas.[48]

This, then, is a history that analyzes structure and power. Power operated at the level of structure to perpetuate and sometimes contest norms of age, gender, sexuality, class, and race. It also contributed to the colonization of space and place, and it was reflected in appeals to professional expertise and in the appropriation of Aboriginal culture. Power also played out between identifiable groups: children and camp staff, camp staff (including Aboriginal workers) and administrators, administrators and parents, and, sometimes, between different groups of campers themselves.

Systems of power may operate everywhere, but they operate in unique ways in distinct contexts. The focus here is Ontario. In the first half of the twentieth century, summer camps operated across the country, but Ontario was unique both in the number of its camps and in the vibrancy of its camping movement. Even the founding of the Canadian Camping Association (CCA) in 1936 did not represent a true nationalizing of the movement; Ontario camp directors were its central players for some years to come. A decade after its founding, one of its members, Mary Northway, admitted that its board had been "composed of Toronto people for ten years" and that "the rest of Canada was rather 'honourary.'"[49] One of its main objects, "to function in localities where there is no local association,"[50] pointed to a lack of comparable organization in other parts of the country. Other sources confirm that Ontario dominated the history of camping. In 1960, the *Toronto Star* estimated that "about 70% of Canadian camping is done in Ontario."[51] While summer camps certainly emerged in other provinces, historians interested in the movement have come to think of it as a "peculiarly Ontario phenomenon," a situation that persists to the present day.[52] Ontario's special role can also be linked to the central theme here; that is, the camp's fundamental connection to conditions of modernity, which were often most advanced in that province. In short, then, my study is a regional one, based in Ontario. In many ways, it is also a study of urban values and culture. Camp, by definition, took place outside large urban centres, sometimes as far away as the Muskoka, Algonquin Park, and Temagami regions. Yet, it was largely urban Ontarians – many of them Torontonians – who filled the roster of campers and who took up positions within the movement. While studying these urban Ontarians, I consciously avoid confusing Ontario with Canada, a mistake often made by nationalists, politicians, and historians alike.[53]

Certain individuals and directors stand out as key members of this camping movement, and their names come up frequently here. All had their strongest connections with private camps. Taylor Statten, founder of the upscale and widely known Ahmek and Wapomeo camps in Algonquin Park, was the most prominent individual involved in Ontario camping. Born in 1882 to an upper-middle-class family in southern Ontario, Statten became involved with children and youth in both recreational and educational capacities. At the age of twenty, he signed on as a voluntary worker with the Toronto Central YMCA in 1905, becoming the full-time secretary of boys' work and, in 1912, the Y's national boys' work secretary. While active in the Y for roughly twenty years, Statten became widely known in Canada as a captivating public speaker and for his part in developing the Canadian Standard Efficiency Test (CSET), a series of tests and awards used by the Trail Rangers and Tuxis groups and designed to develop boys' intellectual, spiritual, physical, and social capacities.[54] Due to his growing reputation, Statten was approached in 1924 to join the staff of the newly reopened Pickering College (a private boarding school for boys). Statten agreed, becoming Pickering's director of character education and, according to his biographer, the first vocational guidance counsellor in Canada. Clearly, the various aspects of Statten's professional career fed into his camp work. Through the Y, Statten launched his first experiments with camping, while his work at Pickering College brought him into contact with boys of the privileged classes, many of whom he later brought to Camp Ahmek, which he founded in 1921. He stayed on as director of Ahmek until his death in 1956.[55]

Several others who became important players in the summer camp movement in Ontario had similar prior experience with youth organizations and with the educational system. A.L. Cochrane and A.S. Clarke – founders of the first boys' camps in Temagami in the opening years of the century – both held positions at private schools: Cochrane at Toronto's Upper Canada College (UCC) and Clarke at the Gunnery School, a Connecticut preparatory school. Both were effective in linking school and camp work and in recruiting campers from among their students. Both also started life outside of Canada and shared the perspective that Canada was the place for true wilderness adventure. There, however, the similarities ended. Cochrane, born in England in 1870, ran away from home as a teen to join the British army. Somehow, he found his way to the "right" circles, for when he arrived in Canada in 1894, he came with a letter of introduction to the distinguished historian Dr. Goldwin Smith. With these connections, he landed his position as physical education instructor at UCC, where he taught until 1921. According to one of his daughters, Cochrane had "quite a military bearing and a very nice English accent which went over quite well at UCC." In her view, "they took him on because he was such a nice English gentleman, [laughing] not because he knew anything much."[56] She also saw his "craving for wild life" and his desire to immerse himself in the outdoors as somewhat at odds with his military background and position at UCC. Nevertheless, he apparently combined these interests well, staying on at UCC for twenty-seven years and, for almost twenty of them, also directing Camp Temagami (also known as "Cochrane's Camp"), which grew "beyond all expectations." In the 1930s, he was named honorary president of both the Ontario Camping Association and the Canadian Camping Association.[57]

By contrast, rather than a "nice English gentleman," American A.S. Clarke, founder of Keewaydin Camp in Temagami, is remembered by some as "a born salesman." Attending the Gunnery School (run by American "father" of camping, William Gunn) as a child in the 1880s, Clarke went on to Harvard Law School and eventually served as a probate judge and as a representative in the Connecticut legislature. Throughout much of this same period, Clarke ran Keewaydin, a camp with a somewhat "macho" reputation, where boys spent much of the two months of summer out canoe tripping. As a business, the camp was quite successful, allowing Clarke to take on camp work full-time in latter life.[58]

Prominent women camp directors also came from relatively privileged backgrounds, but uniquely for them camp work represented the rare chance for personal independence and an economic alternative to marriage. Mary S. Edgar, who founded Glen Bernard Camp near her hometown of Sundridge in 1922, was also involved in the YWCA, the CGIT, and the Girl Guides. A contemporary and friend of Statten's, Edgar was, at heart, more a literary than an organizational type, who expressed herself in poetry and storytelling at camp and, later, as the first editor of the CCA's *Canadian Camping Bulletin* in 1949. While growing up the daughter of a general store owner in northern Ontario, Edgar left to complete her high school education at Havergal College, a private girls' school in Toronto, which named her honorary trustee later in life. Unlike the directors of many camps, Edgar founded Glen Bernard in the community in which she had grown up, and she kept up good relations with that community throughout her years as camp director. According to former camper and staff person Mary Northway, "she knew everyone in the village and in the outlying farms," and she kept the camp connected to the community through charitable ventures, camp performances, and her practice of buying local supplies.[59]

Mary Hamilton, founder of Tanamakoon in Algonquin Park in 1925, was, like several others, also intimately connected to educational circles in Toronto. A friend of both Edgar and Statten, she began her professional life teaching physical education at a number of Toronto's private girls' schools before becoming head of physical education at Toronto's Margaret Eaton School. The school played an important role in providing female physical education instructors across Toronto in the interwar years. Hamilton's founding of Tanamakoon was envisioned as an extension of her work at the school. In the 1930s, a decade after taking on the school's principalship, she had camp counsellor training added to the course in physical education. Like other camp directors with school positions, she created tight links between camp and school, arranging for students to apply their skills as new counsellors at Tanamakoon for the two months of summer.[60]

Dr. Mary Northway, though something of a second-generation pioneer, held a similarly important place in the early history of Ontario camping. Her camping "career" began as a camper at Edgar's Glen Bernard in the 1920s, and it continued on as she became program director in the 1930s and, finally, the co-director of her own camp in the 1940s. During these same years, Northway also pursued higher education, ultimately obtaining a PhD in psychology from the University of Toronto. There, she had the distinction of being one of the favoured students of renowned psychologist William Blatz. Once she completed her dissertation in 1938, Blatz took her on as lecturer at the prestigious Institute of Child Study. Northway's accomplished academic career drew on her life-long interest in camping. Her doctoral research consists of a case study of children's social relationships at camp and was researched at Glen Bernard, the camp of her own childhood and youth. By the 1940s, Northway filled a number of different roles, including professor of psychology, camp director, and Ontario Camping Association committee chair.[61]

In exploring the history of these individuals, their camps, and the wider camping movement, this book draws on the literature and (where possible) records of private, fresh air, and agency camps. Taken as a group, their founders were urban and middle class, but, as elsewhere, they served sets of quite contrasting clientele. Private, for-profit camps, often located in the desirable Muskoka, Haliburton, Algonquin, and Temagami regions of the province, formed what I refer to as the "elite" of the Ontario camping community. They catered to a well-to-do, upwardly mobile, middle- and upper-class clientele. At the other end of the social spectrum, fresh air camps provided subsidized camp holidays for the poorest sector of Ontario's working class. So that they might do so, these camps were usually located just outside of large urban centres. Camp Bolton, located just outside Toronto and the largest of its kind in the province, here provides a case study of the fresh air experience, while published fund-raising appeals of the *Toronto Star* Fresh Air Fund offer a broad picture of fresh air camps in general. The third group, agency camps, were run by a host of youth organizations and churches. These were fee-charging but also non-profit camps that were scattered across the province. They served a broadly middle-class (though also, at least partly, working-class) clientele – those not wealthy enough to afford fees at upscale private camps but not disadvantaged enough to be considered for the subsidized fresh air experience. Here, camps run by the CGIT, several camps run by the YMCA, and a counsellor-training camp run by the Ontario government provide a window onto this type of camp; the first two also provide examples of the influence of religion in early twentieth-century Ontario camping.[62] These three types of camps – private, fresh air, and agency – did not represent hermetically sealed categories of experience (some children, for instance, might have attended a YMCA camp one year and a private camp the next), but they do point to the broadly class-segregated nature of the camp phenomenon.

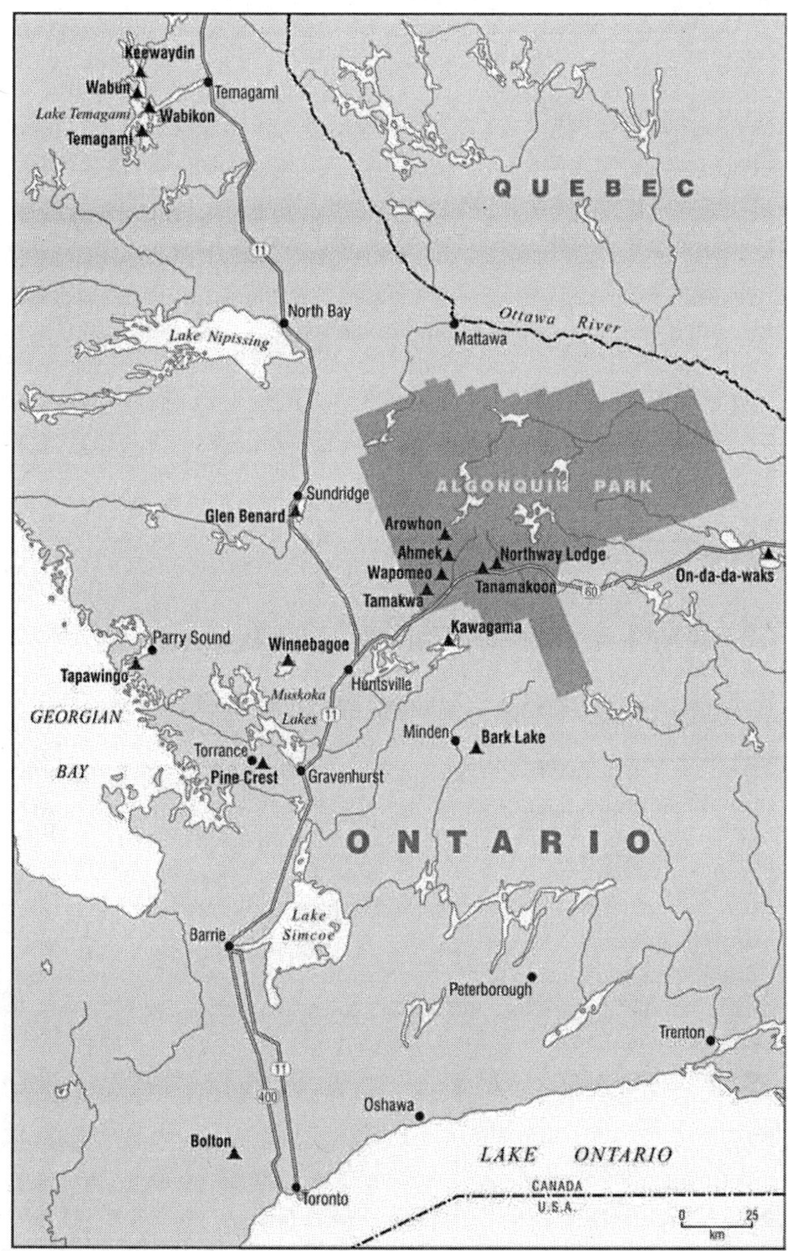

Location of camps mentioned frequently in the book

In the case of individual camps, the nature of source material varies. Published sources include brochures, camp manuals, academic publications, and newspaper articles. In addition to records of individual camps, a broader view of the camping "movement" was obtained by studying the records of the Ontario and Canadian camping associations. Finally, in order to understand the gendered dimensions of camping, this study considers boys', girls', and coeducational camps.

While published sources tell us a lot about the perspective of camp administrators and promoters, I also explore the daily life of the camp as it existed beyond the pages of the published report. I consulted unpublished records of individual camps, including administrative reports, correspondence, and committee proceedings. Directories of member camps published by the Ontario Camping Association also supplied broad statistical information on the number of each type of camp as well as on their fees and locations. In addition, I rely on interviews carried out with former campers and directors. A substantial number of interviews, undertaken in the 1970s and 1980s by members of the OCA, are on file with the Trent University Archives, and I draw upon a number of these. Additionally, I conducted interviews with eighteen former campers and two former directors/camp owners expressly for this study. The majority were Toronto people; two grew up in the United States and attended camps in Ontario.[63] A majority (though not all) interviewees attended camp in the 1940s and 1950s, which helped balance out print sources (which were more abundant for the interwar years). Interviewees also offered a perspective beyond that of camp administrators and their published (and often self-congratulatory) accounts. Recollections of on-the-spot campers were useful not only in confirming (or sometimes dispelling) impressions gained during the course of archival research but also in offering glimpses into the "culture of childhood" at camp. Like all sources, oral history is not infallible. On the other hand, memory – its faultiness included – has something to tell the historian. How individuals choose to tell the story of their lives is also a part of our ongoing history, a reality I have tried to integrate into this book.[64]

This book traces significant changes and continuities in Ontario's camping history. Over the years from 1920 to 1955, changes occurred not only at the statistical level but also within the gates of individual camps. These took place at many levels, altering the look and feel of camp life, camp accessibility, the nature of camper populations, and the organization of camp programming. In the early histories of most camps, the desire to bring order to wild nature affected the spatial and physical dimensions of camp life, while, over the years, improvements in transportation infrastructure brought people more easily to camp. Technological innovations were, in many cases, gradually integrated into camp life, while, in others, camps were shaped by their conscious rejection of modern amenities. The emergence of academic psychology and new educational pedagogy altered the thinking about and execution of camp programming. Campers were organized into increasingly age-specific categories, and administrators more prominently considered their emotional and educational needs. Finally, changing notions of gender and sexuality prompted the emergence of coeducational camping, while changing racial politics and notions of cultural "respect" influenced the decline of "Indian" programming.

Summer camps were affected not only by broad social and cultural changes but also by important moments in Canadian economic and political history. The Great Depression, the Second World War, and the postwar economic boom all had real impacts on summer camps, which were never as isolated as their literature claimed. While new camps continued to appear during the 1930s, at existing private camps enrolments fell, while fresh air camps faced growing wait lists of needy children and declining budgets with which to accommodate them. An abundance of labour power was one positive outcome of the Depression for summer camps, but this situation was completely reversed during wartime. During the Second World War, the King government's decision to provide all-out support for the "mother" country also affected camp life. As the state sought the total mobilization of available labour power, all camps suffered from labour shortages. Fresh air camps, largely dependent on charitable donations for their survival, suffered from lack of funds due to competition with wartime fund-raising. For their part, camp administrators responded to the hard years of depression and war by promoting the camp as ever more useful with regard to protecting children from the harsh conditions in the outside world. In postwar years, general economic affluence did for individual camps what it did for the camping movement on a grander scale. Agency and private camps were increasingly sure of attracting campers; due to the opening of international travel, some came from increasingly distant corners of the earth. For the first time in their history, fresh air camps felt that material deprivation was a less pressing issue for its clientele. As material security was more taken for granted, emphasis on campers' emotional security and personality development intensified at all types of camps.

Clearly, life at camp changed over the course of the early twentieth century, but there were also important continuities, often the very things that kept campers coming back year after year and generation after generation. Administrators might alter camp landscapes and add to the list of comforts available, but camps throughout this period would be seen as fundamentally natural spaces, spaces that offered a physical, emotional, and geographical contrast with daily life. Over the years, parents – rich and poor – welcomed the temporary break from child care that camps afforded and, at the same time, saw their children as profiting from the experience. To children, camp was a fun, challenging, and occasionally miserable experience. Some looked on camp life as a trial to be endured; many others enjoyed their camp holidays and looked back on them with fond memories. For these children, activities were novel, canoe trips were exciting, and friendships brought a sense of community often treasured long after childhood. Indeed, camps offered community to modern individuals in a number of different forms. While campers are more likely to remember the personal aspect of community, camps also built community on broader levels. Private camps strengthened ties between children of the middle and upper classes, ties that fostered not only friendships but also broader social connections to elite social circles in Canadian society. Agency camps kept youth connected to church and religious organizations and fostered a sense of Christian community that encouraged a social gospel orientation towards the wider society. Perhaps less successfully, but with no less energy, fresh air camps worked to make community between distinct classes. Indirectly, they also offered a space for working-class Ontarians to foster their own distinct sense of community. Finally, throughout the period under study, camps were persistently (if not strictly) divided by class and, for much of it, by gender too. Even as coeducational camping emerged, the belief that boy and girl campers required different treatment was another continuity of camp life.

This book examines these changes and continuities in the history of camp life in six thematically organized chapters. Chapter 1 begins with an exploration of anti-urbanism and the antimodern romanticization of nature and the simple life that lay at the root of the camp phenomenon. It also considers the geographically divided nature of the camping movement as well as the extent to which the natural environment was reordered and the camp program rationalized in contrast to the rhetoric of "wildness" and "freedom." Chapters 2 and 3 explore the class-segregated nature of the Ontario camp phenomenon. Their primary focus is the two ends of the class spectrum: Chapter 2 focuses on the nature and function of the elite camp experience and Chapter 3 on the history of fresh air camps and their impact on working-class campers and communities. Along the way, the middle-class experience of agency camps is also explored. Chapter 4 returns more directly to a consideration of the modernizing aspects of the summer camp in assessing its contribution to a new notion of childhood and the espousal of psychological and educational principles. Chapter 5 considers the gendered nature of the camp experience, how antimodernist sentiment influenced ideals of masculinity and femininity, and issues of sexuality and coeducation, which became the modern educational norm. Finally, Chapter 6 takes a look at the role of Indian programming and the popularity of "playing Indian" at camp, offering a consideration of its relationship to Native-white relations and the category of "whiteness" in early twentieth-century Ontario. Each chapter is a reconfiguration and re-exploration of the contradictory nature of the camp phenomenon, of both its avowed antimodernism and its seemingly inescapable modernity.

My particular analysis of the camp experience might have come as a surprise to the original founders of Ontario's camps, quite possibly to the thousands of Ontario citizens who attended summer camp, and perhaps, even today, to some of those who agreed to be interviewed for this book. For all that, I hope that former campers will find in its pages a recognizable recreation of the camping world that so many of them anticipated each year, experienced each summer, and remembered, often long years after childhood. If my analysis leads frequently to conclusions concerning the social relations of power, and if my investigation of camp's modern elements exposes a less often contemplated side to the movement, this is not to cast the story in a conspiratorial light. It is meant to remind us that, in liberal capitalist societies and under conditions of modernity, the seemingly innocuous realm of leisure is shaped by the same relations of power, and problems of identity, authenticity, and meaning, that we are led to believe are left far behind when we pack up our bags, head out of the city, and get "back to nature."

I

Back to Nature: Escaping the City, Ordering the Wild

Modernity as an idea is difficult to pin down. How the forces of modernity changed the physical landscapes of Canadian societies is a more straightforward matter. In early twentieth-century Ontario, as elsewhere, modernity meant changed space. More than that, not just space itself but thinking about spatial use was transformed. The lure of industrial employment caused massive shifts in population from country to city, a consequent "emptying" of rural areas, and a seemingly unending transformation of urban landscapes. Technology transformed the streets of burgeoning cities, with a clutter of telephone cables, streetcar wires, and an ever-increasing number of automobiles. Other technological innovations and the growth of consumer and youth cultures gave birth to new urban spaces: the pleasure garden, the dance hall, and the movie theatre, to mention just a few examples. Attempts to cope with the negative aspects of urban change spawned yet other spatial transformations. Innovations in transportation (first streetcar, then car) made suburban development possible, allowing some to escape the noisy, crowded, and polluted world those innovations were partly responsible for creating. Urban parks offered bits of cultured nature, temporary escapes from the pace and activity of the rest of the urban scene.[1]

Thinking about space changed too. As Keith Walden and others have noted, increasing numbers and scale encouraged "more intensive differentiation of space," where uses were increasingly separated, one from another, in contrast with the integrated and heterogeneous preindustrial walking city. Urban living was an increasingly anonymous experience, where personal appearance did not always tell you "who was who" and who could be trusted. Ordering the environment spatially was one response meant to give meaning to this potentially chaotic social world. "Middle classes," Walden argues for the late Victorian period, "became more inclined to quarantine problematic social groups, isolate unpleasant activities and insulate their own territories from competing sources of power."[2] With their world thus neatly (though never fully) ordered, it was but a small step to categorizing spaces into good and bad, "healthy" and "unhealthy." Where something (or someone) was located was now seen as providing essential information. A street in the slums, even if one had never been there, could be assumed to be crowded, dirty, and dangerous. A visit to a well-tended park in a middle-class neighbourhood could be assumed to put one in a state of relaxed calm. For those of antimodernist leanings, spaces of modernity were viewed with suspicion and concern. Many viewed "the city" and many urban spaces as bad, unhealthy spaces. While urban parks and playgrounds might temporarily counter the ill effects of city living, many believed that only spaces outside the city's limits were truly good and healthy.

The history of the camping movement in Ontario provides one example of this dichotomous thinking about space and of generating spatial solutions to perceived social problems. It also offers another example of the enthusiasm for "the natural," which had been shaping middle- and upper-class sensibilities from the late nineteenth-century onward. That natural spaces were good was one of the fundamental assumptions of the camp movement as a whole. From this perspective, nature seemed to offer everything the city lacked: tranquility, purity, and character-building opportunities. To the same degree that "the city" was condemned in this literature, nature was extolled.

This praise of the natural world was delivered in general terms, but camp enthusiasts also articulated a particular vision of "life in the woods" as their antidote to urban life. The summer camp – as their answer to the problem of urban "artificiality" – was first and foremost geographically rooted in the setting of nature. If nature was the stage, the set design was to be minimal; architecture was to be as natural as possible and activities were to centre around the healthful arts of "the simple life." Whatever the rhetoric, however, the stance taken vis-à-vis modern culture was ambivalent rather than simply critical. In this sense, what is telling about the summer camp phenomenon is not only its lofty goals but also its limitations. Even as "the natural" was regularly glorified, on the ground, camp administrators had a hand in "improving" it. Increasing material comforts were part of the unfolding story of twentieth-century life; camps could never wholly resist them. When it came to social class, camps never succeeded in transcending the dynamics of the society that surrounded them. If all children were thought to benefit from "direct contact with Mother Earth," children from different economic backgrounds generally found themselves attending camps in geographically distinct parts of the province.

Summer camp was, in many ways, a world apart – removed from the city, centred in nature, and offering a set of novel activities and experiences. On the other hand, the truth is that a general faith in order and efficiency, technological advances, and class divisions shaped camping experiences much as they did life at home. This chapter examines the dual nature of the summer camp, the pull of both modern and antimodern, especially as it relates to the natural landscape.

Escaping the Metropolis: The Camp as Alternate Space

Anti-urbanism was nothing new in the interwar period, but the nature of city living was. For the first time, during these years, urban living became the dominant Canadian experience. The forces of modernity acted at different rates on different parts of the country, however, and central Canada was most rapidly transformed. The pace of industrial capitalism in Ontario meant that, by the interwar years, it was the most thoroughly urbanized province. In 1921, when 47 percent of all Canadians were urban dwellers, the number in Ontario was close to 60 percent. By 1951, when the national average reached 62 percent, in Ontario the figure was already 10 percent higher than that.[3] While "the city" might be the object of derision and scorn, a majority of Ontarians had – willingly or otherwise – accepted it as their home. For a good many, that home was Toronto, whose population tripled from roughly 208,000 to 675,000 in the first half of the twentieth century.[4] More probable than not, many who were critical of urban life were not likely to live anywhere else. The facts were that most Ontarians were now urban dwellers and that they were living in cities that had larger populations than ever before. In these cities, Ontarians encountered an expanding array of commercial leisure options. While Victorian and turn-of-the-century bourgeois observers feared the social impact of the saloon, the roller rink, and (even) indiscriminate tobogganing, twentieth century onlookers feared alarming new temptations such as dance halls, movies, and American crime comics.

Camp founders, like so many others, were influenced by the anti-urban sensibilities of their day. Like other bourgeois observers, their tendency was to demonize the city as crowded, unhealthy, and the site of an expanding landscape of commercial entertainments and independent youth culture. Indeed, anti-urban rhetoric was the stock-in-trade of the camping movement in Ontario. In contrast to Victorian Canadians, this brand of anti-urbanist was more likely to characterize the city as "artificial" than immoral – an affront to nature rather than to God. As a Fresh Air Fund promoter stated in 1924, "We often hear it said that city people do not live natural lives and there is much of truth in the statement."[5] Fundraisers for more illustrious camps shared remarkably similar views. In 1931, the editor of the Camp Ahmek newsletter, ruminating over the emergence of the summer camp, argued that it was "the increasing artificiality of city life with its standardized customs and habits of living, with its ready-made appliances for performing all the tasks of the modern home, that has brought into prominence the institution known as the summer camp."[6] Clearly, if the twentieth century saw the increasing social prestige of science and technology, it also witnessed a growing counter-cultural pessimism regarding the social impacts of these advances.

Whether rescuing young unfortunates from urban slums, shaping future leaders out of youthful elites, or reinvigorating church and youth work, camp administrators shared a mistrust of urban life. In their eyes, the city was an especially dangerous place for children and youth. Promoters of fresh air camps for the poor were particularly dependent on a narrative of urban space as artificial and unhealthy. The picture they painted was one of a looming metropolis of concrete and steel, of hot pavement and tenement buildings. This rhetoric persisted throughout the interwar, war, and postwar years, though it could be expressed differently according to the times. In 1941, the *Toronto Daily Star* expanded on the city's shortcomings, borrowing wartime imagery to heighten the intensity of its appeal:

> No barbwire bristles on the boundaries of Toronto ... But Toronto, nevertheless, is just one huge and stifling concentration camp to many youngsters who live in its heat all through the summertime. Children like to feel green grass under their bare toes, like to swim and fish, like outdoor fun and sunshine. They don't find much of all these in the city. Hot pavement burns their feet. Horn-tooting traffic shrilly orders them off the street, sometimes knocks them down. There's not much fun and fresh air.[7]

In the postwar years, the *Star* continued with its critique of urban life. In 1946, it stated: "Ronald and Donald are two in a family of nine children. They hate the city. Just a few months ago a baby brother died. The doctor said it was T.B. – but their mother said it was the city. 'The city killed him,' she said, 'and if we don't get away it's going to kill all of us.'"[8] Increasing automobile use, considered a sign of progress by many Canadians, was deemed another threat to the poorest of the poor, especially to children, who were threatened by the dangers of increased traffic.[9] Overall, the city emerged as a space completely outside nature, its polar opposite. Article titles such as "No Trees or Grass in Sight" and "No Trees, No Grass, No Fun, You Can Give Kiddies All Three" were typical fare in the pages of the *Star*.[10] At times, the argument was made that not only was there not *enough* nature in cities but that what was there was not of the right sort. Medical experts were sought out to bolster these claims in the *Star*. "It would do ... more good than medicines," a Toronto physician declared regarding the benefits of an out-of-city holiday in 1935. "You don't get the right kind of sunshine in cities."[11] During the same year, another article urged potential donors to send children to camp, where "stars look like real stars."[12]

Private camp literature shared this anti-urban bent, though it was expressed in slightly different ways. When it came to middle- and upper-class children, worries centred not around squalid conditions and crowded housing but on the city's harmful consumer culture and "mechanized" way of life. If the physical well-being of middle- and upper-class children could generally be taken for granted, their spiritual and emotional welfare could not. Taylor Statten, founder of the upscale Camp Ahmek and Camp Wapomeo, believed that camp life was so necessary precisely because it provided "an outlet for all sorts of yearnings and pent-up emotions" that the city and its "gilded palaces of amusement" could not.[13] In 1935, Statten, himself a product of small-town Ontario, lamented the passing of rural society and contemplated urbanization's impact on modern boyhood:

> With the trend of our population from the country to the town, it is no longer possible to keep the boys busy during vacation time, raking hay, hoeing corn or even weeding the backyard garden. The dynamic energy with which every active, red-blooded boy is charged must find an outlet. If the energy is not directed and turned to account, it will certainly lead the boy into mischief and quite often into evil ways that will follow him through life. The streets of every city offer no end of dark corners which boys, left to their own devices, will frequent.[14]

Agency camp literature also made its anti-urban and antimodern outlook known. Though it did not give specifics, a YMCA camp director's manual referred to the "ills of civilization," no doubt assuming his audience understood these implicitly. At CGIT camps, "Morning Watch" exercises, meant to guide girls' solitary spiritual development, suggested in 1940 that one of the city's pitfalls was the lack of quiet. Referring to the sound of a bird singing or a chipmunk chattering, it suggested that "such a tiny sound would never have lived at all" in "city, town or village," a significant indictment for those who saw stillness as a prerequisite for spiritual connection.[15] The "evil" that Statten mentioned lurking in urban spaces was interpreted in more explicitly religious terms by the CGIT. In the pages of *The Torch*, the organization's journal for girls, one writer wondered in 1933 whether "the attraction of trashy literature and movies and radio have deadened [the girls'] capacity for spiritual response," adding that "the Christian community" had to address such problems if it wanted to succeed with youth.[16]

Clearly, "the city" was often the lightening rod for criticism of a host of social developments, as it had been in earlier decades. Behind tirades against towers of concrete and hot pavement lay a more general apprehension about technological change, modernity's homogenizing tendencies, and the loss of individual initiative. Already in childhood, it was thought, Canadians were becoming soft, habituated to technological comforts and alienated from "real" experience. "Children today, especially in large cities, have little opportunity for really creative living," one camp director lamented in 1941. "Lights go on at a switch, heat comes when a knob is turned ... [and] drama means sitting in the movies."[17] Certain observers suggested this trend was rooted in new conditions of work. In 1939, in terms sharply critical, camp literature warned: "The mechanization of industry, the corporate form of business, and the rapid increase of routine activities in general seriously threaten to submerge initiative, self-expression, and creative effort in the great masses of people."[18] In the postwar years, as fears regarding mass society and the rise of the "organization man" increased, Canada's acting director of physical fitness, Doris Plewes, went so far as to say that "the assembly line" and the "routine of business" and "even the professions" were responsible for "confinement of persons" and "curtailment of expression."[19]

If such passages took on quasi-socialist tones, for the most part, the proposed solutions pointed in more conservative directions.[20] In essence, this camp literature implied that the pathway to a better life was via the wise use of leisure. While Shirley Tillotson examines the postwar period for interest in leisure as the one remaining realm in which citizens could experience true democracy, the history of camping suggests such viewpoints had earlier roots.[21] As early as 1928, Camp Ahmek's counsellor handbook described modern society as "mechanized," "corporate," and "routinized," lamenting that "the only chance for the majority to secure the sense of self-respect and dignity that comes from the use of their abilities and creative capacities will be in avocational and leisure-time experience."[22] State bureaucrats who welcomed the establishment of summer camps in the postwar period later echoed these sentiments, stating that the only solution to finding a "fuller life" was to "live in our leisure ... in a word, [to] turn to RECREATION."[23]

Typically, for those who made this argument, the problem of leisure was cast as one of poor choices, a stance that reflected a broader distrust of popular culture. In the view of camp promoters, when left to their own devices, much of the public was inclined to partake of the shallowest of entertainment options. Activities that came in for particular criticism were those that failed to demand *involvement* of the participants, as other historians of leisure have pointed out.[24] Radio, movies, even spectator sports were to blame for offering the most passive of pastimes and for spreading what Camp Ahmek literature referred to as "the disease of bleacheritis." In 1928, it was argued that, rather than involving themselves in "active, self-propulsive types of leisure pursuits," "multitudes today are almost entirely dependent upon amusements that are supplied for them, which they take sitting down – watching, riding, or listening."[25] All in all, the realm of leisure, which promised such satisfaction, was more often seen as impoverishing than enriching the lives of modern Ontarians. "Having fun," it seemed, could be a matter of serious concern.

Getting Back to Nature

In addition to its anti-urbanism and implicit critique of consumer culture, the summer camp phenomenon was part and parcel of the broad revisioning of the human relationship to nature that had been under way since the mid-nineteenth century. Like promoters of other wilderness and nature-based experiences, camp administrators promoted their particular back-to-nature activity as the healthy antithesis of modern urban life. In promotional brochures and in the pages of staff manuals, they constructed nature as an unquestionably positive and life-enhancing force, a realm to be sought out and embraced, never feared. They also commonly equated nature with "real life" and the city with a wholly artificial existence. What city children needed, they argued, was a space apart, a miniature world that existed outside the limits of modern urban living. From this perspective, camp space was valued for two reasons: first, for its distance from the taint of "artificial" consumer culture and, second, for its link to all that was natural. In Camp Ahmek's literature, camp was extolled for providing upper-class youth with "fresh strength with every contact with Mother Earth,"[26] and the wilds of Algonquin Park were extolled for offering "a cure for most real and all fancied ills."[27] Even more emphatically, a writer for the *Toronto Daily Star* insisted that "a good dose of outdoors cures almost anything."[28] For children of the inner city, who regularly endured the worst of urban conditions, connections with nature were believed to have near enchanting effects, as suggested by another *Star* appeal in 1924:

> Spirited away from the city's heat and their own unsettled environment, these children would at once enter a delectable fairyland where every activity would be a solace for tired, undernourished bodies. Under the magic influence of cool lake breezes during play time and sleep time worry's problems would quickly be erased from their mental slates.[29]

Camp was offering not simply recreational choices, this literature seemed to insist; contact with nature was considered a prerequisite for physical, emotional, and spiritual health. To this way of thinking, outdoor experiences were meant for more than the privileged few. "Every child has an instinctive yearning to get back to the natural and to the simple fundamentals of the green earth," one *Star* writer asserted in 1920, while, in 1943, another described "the inner longing for the country" that presumably resided within every youthful soul.[30] Camp, then, was no superfluous luxury. In Camp Ahmek's 1939 private camp counsellor handbook, the language of necessity, and not choice, was used to describe the summer camp's origins:

> If the camp had not been invented, we should now have to create it, such need there is today of the steadying offices of direct contact with the earth: the constancy of evening and morning, the sureness of brooks and tides, the firmly planted trees, the upholding hills. Is it not well for us all early to find a close relationship with the earth, our long home? ... A camping experience may be valuable if it does nothing more than to help a child enjoy being a first-hand part of roads and trails, fire and water, sunrise and dusk.[31]

For agency camps with, often, more explicitly religious agendas, the benefits of the back-to-nature experience were understood in highly spiritual terms. Organizations like the YMCA and the CGIT shared their society's generally positive attitudes to the natural world – to "God's great outdoors" as they might call it – but, for them, camp life had even more strictly functional purposes. Getting children to camp was seen not as an end in itself but as a way of counteracting what many saw as youth's growing disinterest in religion. As A.W. Milks, YMCA Camp On-da-waks director, put it, "In no other place are boys so susceptible to spiritual influences as at camp," a statement many assumed applied equally to girls.[32] Echoing the "nature-as-temple" perspective common in this period, CGIT camp literature frequently reiterated that nature had an awe-inspiring effect on teenaged campers, drawing them naturally closer to God. According to a 1929 camp report, "nature surroundings" created "reality in worship ... which does not seem to exist even in church." So powerful was nature's influence deemed to be that its religious message frequently required no articulation. Continuing the discussion of nature-based "worship," the same camp report explained: "Often in the evening we gather together informally to watch the sun sink into the west. Sometimes we sing hymns ... but more often we sit in silence, awed by the great beauty."[33] For youth who didn't make automatic connections between nature and godliness, a 1955 poem in one CGIT camp newsletter reminded them how much time Jesus himself spent outdoors, arguing that he "would [have made] a great camper."[34]

The belief in nature's powerful, even subliminal influence was the backdrop against which all summer camp projects were launched. Whatever goals a camp held, so the thinking held, they were more likely to be achieved in a natural setting. Almost unaided, nature was assumed to have an inherently educative impact on youthful characters. Nature, so it seemed, wiped children clean of all negative influence, allowing ambitious educators of both secular and religious bents to imprint their new messages on the childish slate.

Living the Simple Life

Summer camps had much in common with other nature-based holidays, but they were also unique. In the minds of administrators, camp was not simply one more outdoor leisure option, one more opportunity to relax at the lakeside. In the American context, camps were sometimes explicitly marketed as an alternative to the pampered resort holiday.[35] On both sides of the border, camp was regarded as an experience that touched children in a way that other outdoor recreations could not. It was not just the simple fact of being "out of doors" that accounted for the transformation in young campers. If this were true, the pleasure trip, the resort holiday, or even the city park would, presumably, have done as well. Uniquely, the summer camp promised sustained and direct contact with nature, unmitigated by comforts and technological buffers. It was a point of pride that, at camp, nature was not simply viewed from a deck chair or passenger seat or treated as some kind of passing wilderness picture show. Instead, it was there to be wrestled with as one learned to paddle stern over choppy waters, boil water over an open fire, or build an impromptu lean-to in anticipation of a rainy night on the trail. In short, camp offered lessons in the arts of the simple life. Much more than contact with nature, camp promised immersion.

In an era, then, when the public consciousness was assaulted with the promises of comforts and the wonders of all manner of consumer products, camp promoters simultaneously preached the gospel of simplicity and appealed to Canadians to discover the joys of "roughing it." In this they manifest yet another desire for the "simple life," what historian David Shi has shown to be a recurring if minority tradition in comfortable North American society. The meaning of the simple life was never fixed, however. Depending on the context, Shi tells us, simple life advocates showed "hostility toward luxury," "a reverence for nature," "a desire for personal self-reliance," "a nostalgia for the past," and "an aesthetic taste for the plain and functional."[36] All of these also shaped camp life.

In the architectural realm, simplicity was clearly the watchword. In one sense, architecture represented the antithesis of camp life. By definition, it was human-made, constructed, rather than natural, one of the crowning achievements of civilization and not nature. References to the "great outdoors" implied a critique of life "indoors" and the containment of humanly designed structures. In the world of camping, the response to this apparent contradiction was the adoption of one of the earliest forms of human shelter, an almost anti-architectural structure known as the tent. By definition, it was movable and reduced the distance from the outside world to a minimum, a space where changes in weather and transitions from day to night had immediate and unavoidable effects. At a number of camps, tents (as opposed to cabins) were the only form of shelter provided for campers in the earliest years. In some cases, tents and cabins were used side by side, occasionally out of necessity but sometimes with the former reserved as a special treat for those considered up for the challenge of truly roughing it.[37]

As camps sought to establish permanent sites and to secure steady clientele, the use of buildings was eventually seen as unavoidable. By 1931, aside from sleeping cabins, Camp Ahmek boasted a new dining hall (with seating for four hundred), several camp offices, a carpenter's shop, an Indian village, a medical centre, a theatre, a post office, and a "hotel" for visiting parents.[38] Still, in the planning of camp buildings, aesthetics was an important factor. Camp literature stated explicitly that buildings, as much as setting and program, should reflect the ethos of natural simplicity that purportedly infused all of camp life. Simple, however, did not mean unplanned. Far from ad hoc or arbitrary, camp buildings and space were quite consciously designed to enhance experience of the natural in quiet, understated fashion. As Mary Northway recalled of Glen Bernard Camp's design: "It was very simple ... We lived in wooden cabins with open windows – no window panes, no glass – with mosquito netting across them."[39] In 1946, an OCA Camp Bulletin put in writing the principle to which many camps had long been adhering: "Our buildings and furnishings ... should be of such a type as to blend with their environment. They should be of such character as to contribute to the health of the camper but not so as to make him soft."[40] Such recommendations translated into a general preference for the rustic and the rough. The log cabin-style structure, preferably "with the bark on," as noted at Ahmek,[41] was one of the most popular choices where it could be afforded.

In their attempt to design "natural" buildings, summer camps were not striking out in an entirely novel direction. In fact, the taste for "rusticity" – which also surfaced at parks and resorts – had roots that went as far back as the eighteenth-century English landscape garden and the Romantic taste for blending architectural structure with wild space.[42] Invocation of the rustic represented "an attempt to bring the outdoors within," as writer Craig Kilbourn puts it, to express fundamental harmony with nature, a goal especially attractive to urban-weary upper middle-class society.[43] In much the same way, camp architecture in Ontario "toed the line between nature and culture, wildness and civility,"[44] as Barksdale Maynard argues with regard to the American camp.

Drawing on earlier traditions, summer camps worked to have architecture suit their unique purposes. If materials used in the construction of rustic buildings sought to bring nature within, other architectural features promised to draw one's focus outwards. Even when indoors, the camper was meant to feel part of the surrounding environment. Paneless windows

Craft building, Bolton Camp, c. 1940s. Using logs "with the bark on," the craft building at Bolton was one example of the natural architectural style adopted at many camps. The abundance of windows was meant to draw the eye outward. *Copyright Family Service Association of Toronto.*

– with only screens to keep out the bugs – reduced the barrier between inside and outside, while porches and verandahs encouraged the contemplation of nature, even if from comfortable, protected locations. The design of one cabin at Ahmek illustrates this attempt to blur the line between indoor and outdoor spaces. An official history of the camp explains:

> This structure, built at the lake's edge, was of the standard Adirondack pattern, with a sloping roof and an overhang over the doorway and window area. The flooring was flagstone and there was no glass or screening in the windows, nor was there a door to close. This was great for those who liked to rush out of bed in the morning and do a swan dive straight into Canoe Lake, just one yard from the door.[45]

Outdoor theatres and chapels were other popular features that sought to maximize contact with the surrounding landscape. Theatres provided shelter and stage for performers, while audiences were entertained completely al fresco. Outdoor chapels ran on the same basic principle and were common at many camps, even those with less explicitly religious goals. Many were not buildings at all but merely designated space, geographically distinct from the rest of the camp. Frequently situated on hillsides or islands, they often included, as at Ahmek, nothing more than "a rustic pulpit and rude benches" arranged in amphitheater fashion. From such vantage points and with these minimal furnishings, it was believed that these chapels allowed the presence of the sacred to be more keenly felt. Here "nature as temple" took on both literal and metaphoric meanings. To heighten the sense of listening to nature's spiritual messages, a CGIT camp manual advised that "a tradition of 'no-talking' from the time the campers pass a certain spot on the path to the chapel will add to the reverent atmosphere." Some of nature's annoyances could also be avoided, it was suggested, by finding a spot that eliminated the possibility of "sun in the worshippers eyes" and excessively strong winds.[46]

Outdoor chapel, Camp Tanamakoon, c. 1920. Camp "chapels" were often not buildings at all. Instead, as pictured here, they made use of the natural surroundings to create the appropriate feelings of awe. *Algonquin Park Museum Archives #3151 (George May).*

The theatre at Camp Ahmek, c. 1940. Campers couldn't get much more "into" nature than when attending outdoor theatres like this one, where the audience followed the action from the vantage point of their canoes. *Algonquin Park Museum Archives #3131 (Hugh Colson).*

Camp Tanamakoon girls, c. 1940. Another example of the outdoor theatre at camp. *Algonquin Park Museum Archives #3148 (George May).*

In the effort to create a natural aesthetic, placement of buildings was also regarded as a factor of strategic importance. Above all, the goal was to avoid a regimented or too orderly look. Looking back on the early years of Camp Tanamakoon, Director Mary Hamilton explained that cabins were "scattered on either side of [the main lodge] along the shore wherever there was open space" since, as camp administrators claimed, "we prized our trees and never wantonly cut them down."[47] Though this could not be said of all camps, even at the highly manicured and sprawling Bolton Camp, efforts were made to create a natural aesthetic. "There are four dormitories and a few tents," a 1941 report explained, "but by far the larger number of us live in cheerful, airy cabins – not set out in rows, but arranged engagingly here and there to take advantage of a good view, or perched high above the winding creek."[48] Above all, nothing was to appear orchestrated or unnatural. Buildings were meant to look as if they – like the trees from which they had been constructed – had sprouted from the earth around them.

A backward-looking longing for "simpler days" guided not only the camps' use of space but also their programming. Typical programs emphasized skills that were considered to be basic to human survival and that promoted valuable self-sufficiency. Since the ability to transport oneself wherever one might need to go was considered fundamental, many camp programs placed strong emphasis on instruction in swimming, canoeing, and hiking. The compulsory "morning-dip" was something of an institution at many camps, while "nature hikes" were undertaken at even the most "citified" locations.[49] Once campers reached their destination, other skills were required. Woodcraft – everything from axe-handling and fire-starting to outdoor cookery – was deemed essential know-how. Adding a domestic spin to their description of these skills, Tanamakoon's literature argued that their female campers learned "almost anything one must know how to do in order to be at home in the woods."[50] The need to understand the natural environments in which campers moved also translated into lessons in nature lore, another camp staple.[51] Ultimately, many camp administrators would likely have agreed with Ontario's director of education, who stated explicitly in 1947: "[Camping] brings the boy and girl back to the fundamental problems of humanity – the problems that have faced man from earliest times – the problems of shelter, food and transportation." He elaborated:

> The hut or tent is once again the shelter that wards off the elements ... On overnight trips, the camper learns the art of travel on foot, with his pack on

> his back – or by canoe with his own strength providing the motive force. He learns the urgency of co-operation at the journey's end, in setting up his camp ... and he learns the joy of satisfying the hunger his exertions have induced with food he has earned by his own efforts.[52]

Without question, the canoe trip represented the pinnacle of this search for simple living and, for many, the essence of the summer camp experience. The canoe trip was considered simple because it reduced life to two primary concerns: movement and survival. Paddling and portaging moved one along; making and breaking camp, collecting wood, starting fires, and campfire cooking provided the means of survival. Canoe trips were also "simple" in another sense. Here, no one was a specialist; rather, all campers were to take pride in being self-sufficient generalists, each sharing equally in all tasks. Pride of accomplishment also came from surviving the more unpleasant aspects of the trip. As historian Jamie Benidickson has noted, for the canoe-tripper there could be "something intensely satisfying about lying in a damp sleeping bag, sipping hot tea" in the context of an adventure that promoted self-sufficiency.[53] In this sense, experiencing discomfort – the difficulties of the simple life, if you will – was definitely part of the package, as Ahmek camper James Buchanan remembers of the 1950s:

> On some of these canoe trips, you swore that you would never go on one of these trips again. These portages were absolutely murder ... carrying a seventy-pound pack before these prefabricated foods came out – it was rough ... [But when] you got back to camp, or back home, whether or not one [went] back on a canoe trip in one's life, you thought of it as a positive experience.[54]

Physical isolation was another factor that was thought to "simplify" camp life. Camps varied in their isolation from urban centres, but, by definition, camp was something of an isolated world. Administrators were well aware of, and openly commented on, the camp's delightful removal from the larger society. As one put it, looking back, "There were two parts of life: camp in the summer and the city in the winter and they didn't overlap."[55] Taking the antimodern view, accessibility, here, was regarded in negative terms; in short, the harder to get to, the better. Elite private camps in Algonquin and Temagami were the winners here. In the interwar years, a trip to Algonquin was a full day's train ride away, with an additional two-mile walk into Camp Ahmek.[56] By 1950, the ride had been

Camp Temagami boys, c. 1930. Portages during private camp canoe trips were often strenuous activities – especially when they lasted up to two miles – but they also built up boys' pride and sense of manly accomplishment. *Courtesy Upper Canada College Archives.*

shortened, but only by three hours.[57] Temagami was even harder to reach. Though the Temiskaming and Northern Ontario Railway reached the town by 1904, this still entailed a ten-hour ride from Toronto. For American campers, who made up the bulk of the clientele at a number of Algonquin and Temagami camps, journeys were even longer.[58] Complicating the trip in for all Camp Keewaydin campers was the camp's island location, a factor that also affected travel to other camps, including Temagami and Wapomeo.

The island camp held a particular allure for outdoor administrators, enamoured as they were with the positive qualities of isolation. In such locations, the separation from society and from technological comforts that many camps espoused took on added geographical dimensions. To those interested in child psychology and development, this naturally bounded space represented the perfect laboratory for the testing of new theories. On the other hand, given the hard-to-reach location of many camps, the island metaphor was an apt one even for those not literally surrounded by water, as camp directors were sometimes aware. "Once you got to camp you were isolated as on an island," Mary Northway claimed of Glen Bernard near the northern town of Sundridge (by no definition an island). "Very little visiting from parents, very little going away from camp except by canoe ... no radios, certainly no television, no movies. The whole life for the month ... was entirely centred on camp."[59]

While all camps could claim a certain degree of isolation, or at least separation, from the broader society, fewer could claim rights to "wilderness," another valuable camp asset. To their advantage, a number of (mainly private) camps were located in areas many considered predominantly "wild." In 1919, Taylor Statten described the Algonquin Park region, the site of his future camping enterprise:

> The Park is a paradise of virgin wilderness, containing nearly fifteen hundred lakes. When you step from the train, you feel at once the "bite" in the air – redolent with balsam, pine, and spruce. This great reserve of nearly four thousand square miles abounds with wild life and the Lakeland breezes which sweep over it are impregnated with life-giving fragrance, filtered through millions of acres of pine woods.[60]

Another camp enthusiast recalled of the Haliburton area of the 1940s: "[It] was untouched in those days. It was a wilderness,"[61] though certainly this was partly the work of memory. On the other hand, "wilderness" is a subjective term and, what one considers "wild" is very much in the eye of the beholder. In the first half of the twentieth century, part of what defined an area as "wilderness" was the perceived lack of human presence. However inaccurate, this sense of human absence instilled camp canoe trips with a special edge of excitement. Campers testify to the fact that, while out tripping, "we'd see nobody,"[62] or, as another Temagami camper puts it, "It was very unusual having anyone else camping on the same island as you. Or on the same lake."[63] When the Ontario government purchased the Bark Lake property, only 130 miles northwest of Toronto, it was noted happily that the site was "rather ideally situated for camping in that there are no summer cottages anywhere on the shore."[64] In fact, the issue of visibility was of central importance. Seeing wilderness, in fact, was always, in part, an exercise in self-deception. Ultimately, it didn't matter so much that others shared use of the space as, simply by keeping them out of sight, one could retain the much coveted feeling, if not reality, of isolation. The most glaring example of self-deception was the blatant erasure of Aboriginal presence on the land. Although, at some camps, references were made to sites as having previously been "Indian land," at others, like Camp Temagami, administrators used postcolonial rhetoric to describe surrounding areas as "newly discovered," "practically unexplored," and containing numerous "unnamed" lakes.[65]

In Ontario, wilderness was also defined by its relation to "northernness." As cultural geographers and historians have shown, however, "North" was as much a region of the mind as of geography.[66] In Canada, though North has been used extensively to give definition to our national identity, it remains a notoriously difficult concept to pin down.[67] A quick glance at any school atlas reveals that what Ontarians of this period had come to designate as North – the Algonquin, Temagami, even Muskoka regions – was not far from, in fact was even south of, much of the nation's southern border. It was also a good seven or eight degrees south of official North at the sixtieth parallel and even further from the edge of the treeline, which is fundamental to any Inuit definition of North. However, as scholars have demonstrated, space and society are not separate entities; rather, the construction of geographic space is conditioned by social relations. Geography, in short, is another "way of seeing," and generally it is the powerful who are doing the looking and, thus, whose perspective matters.[68]

In the case of the camping movement, it was Toronto that served as the reference point from which all other points were measured. To be "North" in Ontario, as historian Daniel Francis points out, has often meant simply being "anywhere north of Toronto."[69] The camper's idea of North was slightly more discriminating; Bolton fresh air camp, located just north of Toronto, was not considered northern. Typically, it was canoe trip camps – ranging from one hundred to three hundred miles north of the city – that were considered truly "northern" camps. Ahmek literature routinely referred to itself as "the homeland of the north,"[70] while Mary Northway spoke of Glen Bernard as "the far northland."[71] Beyond camping circles, others echoed this view of camp space as northern space. In 1944, the *Globe and Mail* reported on the Drew government's consideration of more sustained support of summer camps:

> It is not sufficiently understood that we have in Ontario an almost unbroken chain of lakes stretching from Ottawa to the Manitoba boundary. There is no other holiday area like it in the world ... The children of Ontario will have the opportunity to live in the fresh air of the northern woods and build up their bodies in these healthful surroundings.[72]

Implied in the glorification of Canada's "northern woods" was an implicitly positive view of the North – one significantly at odds with other contemporary views. As Karen Dubinsky demonstrates, constructions of northern Ontario were generally negative, and, in the early twentieth century, southern Ontarians were inclined to view the region as a "wild and immoral netherland," the home of uncultured immigrants, working-class radicalism, and sexual immorality. In the face of alarming rural depopulation in the South, the North was subject to much the same negative stereotyping as the city.[73] What the camp phenomenon suggests is that competing images of the North could be held simultaneously. In the first negative view, the North was constructed largely in terms of populace: who was there, the work they did, the ways in which their social world was organized. In a second, more positive view, the North was pure landscape: rugged Shield territory, empty space except when urbanites chose to descend upon it. From this perspective, the North invariably meant parkland, summer, and leisure. In this frame of mind, one gave little thought to lumber or mining operations or even, for that matter, winter. If socialist-minded immigrant loggers might be cause for concern from one's urban vantage point, they were conveniently forgotten when most near at hand.

As alluded to above, to some extent, the state shared not only ways of thinking about the North but also camp administrators' antimodern understanding of the needs of children and youth. In practical terms, the question of state support for summer camps emerged during the Second World War. During this period, increased state intervention in Canadian society, coupled with concern over the national lack of fitness revealed by wartime recruiting, had the effect of drawing the summer camp into the state's broader discussion of youth, recreation, and the public good.[74] The Canadian Youth Commission, which emerged as a result of this nationalist preoccupation with health and wartime fears of delinquency, endorsed state support for the summer camp as a worthy educational and recreational activity in 1943.[75] Likewise, the National Council on Physical Fitness recommended "one month's camping every year for all of Canada's ... children"[76] and established its own camping subcommittee in 1944. At the provincial level, the Ontario government offered concrete support to non-profit camps with the establishment of a system of grants to summer camps in 1945 and, three years later, with the founding of a counsellor training camp. By 1955, roughly 350 camps were receiving provincial support. At the training camp at Bark Lake, teenage campers were trained in woodcraft and canoeing skills and, in exchange, were expected to give two years service at non-profit camps.[77]

State support of summer camps should not, however, be exaggerated. Antimodern belief in modernity's impact on children seems to have been shared, but ensuring concrete measures of support was a seemingly difficult matter. For one, federal-provincial wrangling over jurisdictional control resulted in the disbanding of the National Council on Physical Fitness.[78] Provincial funding, for its part, was never extensive; monies were allocated on a per capita basis at rates so low that the average camp likely received no more than $130 per year. The Bark Lake training camp for counsellors likely did more to influence the culture of camping by helping with problems of labour recruitment. Yet, with no method of enforcing the service requirement, and with only limited numbers accommodated each summer, the camp's true impact is difficult to assess.

Ultimately, the state's handling of the issue reflected more general concerns about the level of state intervention appropriate in a private realm like recreation. As Shirley Tillotson and others have noted, with the war against fascism still fresh in mind, the spectre of too much government meddling in such an area easily awakened liberal fears of the erosion of democratic values.[79] Indeed, the Ontario Camping Association showed a persistent ambivalence to "interference" from the state. In its case, it seems the independent-minded, antimodernist bent of most camp directors didn't fit well with the idea of the state's "taking over" its movement. As Mary Northway, academic psychologist and OCA research and education chair, put it, the great danger was not political but bureaucratic. "The great danger of the world today," she argued, "is not any particular political 'ism,' but the bureaucracy that can so easily arise under any form of government or institution."[80] Once again, the camp enthusiast extolled simplicity, this time, over the potential evils of bureaucracy.

Ultimately, the focus on simple living was a touchstone of camping throughout these years. This focus persisted, perhaps even intensified, in the postwar years. In the pages of the Ontario *Camp Bulletin* and elsewhere, "simple" was plainly de rigueur. In 1946, the bulletin hailed Camp Ahmek for "helping boys to live the simple, rugged life of the outdoors" and Northway Lodge for offering "a place where girls live the simple life." The writer elaborated, commending Northway Lodge, an Algonquin camp for wealthy American girls, for providing only the solid camping fundamentals of "swimming, sailing, canoeing, out-tripping and ... just living close to nature. "To some," it was noted, "Camp Northway might seem severe; to others, a chance to recapture reality."[81] Here, lack of amenities was a badge of honour, not the cause for embarrassment it might be back home. Even if "simplicity" could sometimes also be good for the camp budget,[82] lack of amenities and the feeling of "roughing it" were certainly essential parts of camp life that created an exciting environment for many campers.

The Geography of Class

As the exploration of camps' relative "northernness" suggests, class was an important aspect of the geographic location of camps. To a great extent, it determined who landed in "wilderness" locations "up North." As Roderick Nash points out in the American context, true gentlemen had been enjoying wilderness since the early nineteenth century.[83] Given the cost of gaining access to wilderness, one can see why a "gentleman's" budget would certainly have been useful. Distance translated into pricey train fares and, in later years, the expense of hours of highway travel. In terms of fashionable wilderness areas in Ontario, getting there was one thing, staying there another. A stay at exclusive inns like the Algonquin Hotel would have been possible only for the wealthy few. By the 1920s, the regions of Muskoka, Algonquin, and Temagami had already become exclusive favourites of the wealthiest class of Ontarians as well as of a significant contingent of American tourists.[84] Camp founders and clients often had prior experience of these regions at exclusive hotels, lodges, and privately owned cottages. More than a decade before founding their camps, the Statten family took a trip to Algonquin Park and became so entranced with the "rich greenery" and the "smell of pines" on Canoe Lake that Statten arranged to lease the spot for the family's summer home.[85] Other staff and campers had similar experience of these areas that predated their camp involvement and that give their reminiscences a certain proprietary air. As one Ahmek enthusiast, Ron Perry, recalled of the 1920s, "We roamed all through Algonquin Park. I think we got in every lake and every cranny of that wonderful part of the country."[86] It was likely due to upper middle-class familiarity with these areas that camps Temagami, Keewaydin, and Arawhon foresaw no trouble in attracting clients not only to their children's camps but also to their lodges for visiting parents.

To camp owners who were targeting an elite clientele, the regions of Algonquin, Temagami, and Muskoka were natural choices. The Danson family's choice to relocate Camp Winnebagoe from the Rouge River, just outside Toronto, to the Muskoka region in 1933 was explained in terms of the desire to be up with "the bigger camps," but this was as much a statement about reputation and prestige as about scale. A 1946 Winnebagoe brochure made this connection explicit:

> Camp Winnebagoe is situated in the heart of the world famous Muskoka region ... 135 miles from Toronto on provincial highways ... It is a beautiful estate of several hundred acres – high and dry natural woods – virgin pines, cedar, birch and maple, on the shore of enchanting Skelton Lake. It has a most interesting shoreline broken up by inlets, bays and rivers, and meets with beautiful High Lake which is also part of the Winnebagoe estate ... For many years this particular location has been chosen as the playground and summer resort of the most discriminating in Canada and the United States.[87]

Camp, of course, was not solely an elite enterprise, though many campers never knew the scent of Algonquin pines or the sparkle of northern lakes. Indeed, the summer camp phenomenon was marked by a distinctly classed geography. The children who spent ten days at fresh air camps run by the Neighbourhood Workers' Association, the Hebrew Maternal Aid Society, or the Downtown Church Workers did not travel for hours to far off "northern" space, however one defined that geographical entity. Most often, they found themselves headed for sites just outside their city in regions that no one would have dared to call "wilderness." As a 1920 Fresh Air Fund appeal put it, children like "Reddie" – a poor resident of Toronto's "slums" – would be amazingly fortunate to enjoy not the lakes of the "far-off north" but, rather, "the fabled and fabulous green lands full thirty miles from Dirt Street."[88] Nine years later, the fund appealed again to prospective donors to help send "poor kiddies" to camp, "away from the heat and noise and turmoil of the city to the real open spaces of southern Ontario."[89] In contrast to long trips to northern camps, the trip to Bolton fresh air camp began with a short, one-hour train ride from Union Station in the heart of downtown Toronto and ended with a shorter drive in the back of large flatbed trucks. "We were packed in like parcels," is how one camper remembers it.[90] No surprise that the landscape, flora, and fauna at these camps differed from that of their northern cousins. As the *Star* noted of the twenty camps it supported, "there are no moose, no bears."[91]

Without question, concern with curtailing expenses determined the rural placement of fresh air camps, which were designed to accommodate large numbers of campers. While upscale northern camps typically accommodated between one and two hundred campers per season, many of whom stayed at camp the entire summer, fresh air camps typically

View of Bolton Camp, c. 1920s. The landscape ideal at Bolton was clearly more rural idyll than wilderness escape. *Copyright Family Service Association of Toronto.*

moved campers in and out every ten days. The largest, Camp Bolton, accommodated an average of nearly four thousand campers per summer. In these cases, rural settings close to urban centres only made economic sense, a fact that shaped the nature of fresh air camp programming. Promotional rhetoric also differed, with fresh air administrators frequently drawing on rural rather than wilderness imagery to fuel their appeals. Repeatedly, *Toronto Star* journalists, writing on behalf of the city's Fresh Air Fund in the 1920s and 1930s, spoke of the "wonderful trip to the country," of the "glories of the country" and "the sunshine of the country, where birds and cows and horses make life worthwhile."[92] They frequently lamented that poor city children were completely unfamiliar with the most common rural scenes. A 1929 appeal bemoaned the fact that, for many, their only knowledge of barnyard animals was gleaned from "glimpses of ... stockyards" and pictures on condensed milk cans.[93] A 1937 appeal marvelled: "Country Scenes Amaze Boy, Saw Robin for First Time" and "Living Near Lake Ontario, Tots Have Never Seen It: Cow Is Mystery."[94] While lack of familiarity with the bovine species seemed to invoke particular alarm, according to a 1935 appeal, this ignorance was typical of urban working-class children:

> Down the street was a nine-year-old girl who knew about the country only what she had read and heard. Asked if she had ever seen a field of wheat she said, "Do you mean that high stuff?" No, she'd never seen any. She had never laid eyes on a brook or a stream, a frog, a berry bush, a vegetable garden, a farm house, a dirt road, a horse or a cow grazing [again with the cows!], fresh milk in a pail, a hen with chicks, eggs in a nest, a woods, a tent, wild flowers – in short, she's lived nine summers in the heat of a squalid, ugly street.[95]

With this appeal to popular rural nostalgia, the fund made its case for the fresh air experience, a camp holiday of distinct geographic proportions.

In terms of their location, agency camps differed from both private and fresh air camps. As outgrowths of children's organizations with roots in small towns and cities all across the province, these camps tended to be more geographically scattered. Like fresh air camps, they were situated in the general vicinity of the populations they served. For example, children from the Orillia YMCA camped at Camp Summerland on nearby Couchiching Lake; those from Peterborough's YMCA found themselves at Camp Kawartha on one of the Kawartha Lakes; and those from the Kitchener YMCA camped at the Ki-wa-y Camp just twelve miles outside of town. It was the same with Girl Guides who attended residential camps: those from Ottawa camped at Camp Woolsey on the Ottawa River; those from the Georgian Bay area camped on the banks of Lake Huron; and those from Hamilton camped on the eastern tip of Lake Erie. Certain organizations – often Toronto-based and charging higher camp fees – were able to set up camps in some of the more desirable areas (like Muskoka). For the most part, however, if agency camps were to be found "up North," it was in order to serve the clientele of local northern towns. When, in 1924, the Ontario Girls' Work Board, administrator of the CGIT camps, urged the purchase of some "Northern camp ... for this year," the aim was to provide camping for local girls, not to provide novel experiences for girls from more southerly parts of the province.[96]

Effectively, the North was a space to which only a minority of campers had access. In the first half of the twentieth century, the North as holiday space, as a space to escape worries and cares, existed mainly as a reality for upper middle-class and wealthy Canadians. For members of the urban working class (who simply could not get there) or of the small-town working and lower middle class (for whom the North was the site of home and work), the space had little, or different, meanings. For the better off, at least one of its meanings – exclusivity – was clear. By 1956, these geographical realities were apparent to the authors of *Crestwood Heights*, who provided a sociological analysis of postwar suburban culture. They stated simply:

> Summer camps, like clubs are ranked by status. Those camps catering to wealthy children are generally some greater distance to the north, and are equipped with elaborate permanent buildings ... flotillas of canoes, rowboats, and sailboats, and stables of riding horses. At the other end of the scale are the camps sponsored by urban welfare agencies which are apt to be much closer to the city, with fewer permanent buildings ... less elaborate recreational facilities, and a conspicuous policy of "back to nature" – though, even then, not too far.[97]

In light of these findings, the argument of cultural geographer Rob Shields, that the North has played a "mythically central but politically marginal" role in Canadian society, could be qualified.[98] In fact, the North's political marginality has seasonal dimensions. If southerners cared little about what went on there during the cold months of winter, their attitudes were quite reversed when the summer's heat drove them to the comparative cool of Temagami, Algonquin, and Muskoka. During that season, at least a minority of southerners cared very much about legislation affecting leasing agreements on northern lakes, the nature of logging practices, and the extent of Native entitlements to hunt and fish. Ultimately, the choice of these areas as the site for elite recreation determined that social distance from "the masses" took physical, geographic form. Class inequalities clearly shaped the use of natural space, much as they did urban development. In the end, "getting back to nature" could mean vastly different things, depending on which side of the tracks one called home in the city.

Complexities of the Simple Life

Camps, then, were not as far removed from urban realities as long train rides might have one believe, and they would become less so as time went on. This held true as much in the physical ordering of camp life as it did in the geographical placement of camps. The settings of camp life certainly contrasted with those children regularly encountered, but were they as "natural" as promoters insisted? As environmental historians have demonstrated, under conditions of modernity, nature, even "wilderness," is very much a human construction. "Nature," William Cronon puts it quite simply, "is not nearly so natural as it seems."[99] Likewise, Alexander Wilson argues that technologically advanced societies tend to romanticize nature as an untouched quasi-sacred refuge at the same time as they increasingly manipulate so-called natural landscapes.[100] Others have demonstrated that, even under the guise of "protection," natural spaces have been significantly altered.[101] Despite the increasingly engineered quality of what we call nature, the modern tendency is also to dichotomize nature and society and to ignore the fundamental interrelations between the two realms. As Anne Whiston Spirn states, "Calling some landscapes 'natural' and others 'artificial' or 'cultural' ignores the fact that landscapes are never wholly one or the other."[102]

This kind of subtlety was rarely at work within the camping movement, where the dichotomy of artificial/natural served as a convenient touchstone. The truth was, of course, that camps were never situated on completely "natural" or "untouched" space. If this is easy enough to see with regard to areas just outside urban centres, where Bolton and other fresh air camps were established, it was also true of more distant areas like Muskoka, Algonquin, and even remote Temagami. Wilderness, it seemed, was always slipping out of one's grasp. In Muskoka, for instance, American demand for lumber had already significantly depleted timber stocks by the 1880s.[103] During the same period, efforts were made to construct the region as a new agricultural frontier. Though never successful, the attempt left its mark on the land in the form of a network of colonization roads and a small but significant population. What really transformed Muskoka in the twentieth century was the influx of tourists seeking cottage and resort holidays. As early as 1915, the area already boasted fifty commercial lakeshore hotels and over six hundred cottages on its three major lakes.[104] Although little has been written on the subject, recreational uses of the land intensified between the inter- and early postwar years, so that by this period, the area was already considered too "civilized" for some. With growing numbers of cottagers, hotel visitors, and the local service infrastructure that grew up to cater to them, the landscape could hardly be called wholly "natural."[105]

Further north, Algonquin and Temagami landscapes were also affected by human intervention during the early twentieth century. In both areas, outdoor recreation was only one among several profit-oriented uses of these spaces, which the province had declared forest reserves in 1893 and 1901, respectively. While each claimed valuable stands of timber and wildlife, Temagami and the surrounding area was also the site of some of Ontario's most valuable mineral deposits and sources of hydroelectric power, resources that were mined with increasing intensity as the century progressed.[106] Given the potential profits of Algonquin and Temagami, it was not surprising that the state opted to put the interests of resource industries first. As Gerald Killan points out, the philosophy that guided policy in both areas was "wise use," not "preservation."[107] From the earliest years, this led to conflict between resource industries and recreationalists, often centred on unwelcome changes in the visual landscape.[108] Efforts in 1912 to redesignate Temagami as parkland were ultimately unsuccessful, revealing, again, the state's commitment to economic interests. By the interwar and, certainly, postwar years, if these areas were not supporting large urban populations, neither were they pristine or untouched wilderness.[109]

As with the regions in which they were situated, the sites of many camps revealed evidence of human impact before and after their establishment. Taylor Statten's Camp Ahmek, situated on Canoe Lake in the southern portion of Algonquin Park, provides an interesting example. Even the official camp history, contrary to Statten's own impressions, states that "Canoe Lake was not a pristine wilderness in 1912 when Taylor and Ethel Statten first visited its shores."[110] On the contrary, the northern edge of the camp had been "the focal point of logging on [the] Lake" since 1897, which, in its heyday, supported a population of some seven hundred residents.[111] The physical remnants of this logging history were easily seen in the early years of the camp's establishment. At one end of camp lay "a very large pile of bark," while "a spur line of the railroad" ran down from the mainline to the camp's waterfront.[112] At other camps, pollution was already an issue in these early years. YMCA camp director W.A. Milks warned those starting new camps: "The danger of river or lake water is caused by sewage pollution from towns and cities," suggesting that some had found out the hard way.[113] And as camps themselves brought hundreds, sometimes thousands, of youngsters out of the city each summer, the landscape felt the inevitable impacts. In postwar years, garbage and litter could become unsightly problems. In 1941, at the YMCA's Camp Pine Crest, the waterfront staff reported: "The waterfront area ... should be cleaned. On a calm sunny day anyone can see just about everything but the Cat's Pyjamas within a few feet offshore – tins, bowls, scrap iron, coat hangers, tooth paste containers – this would take ten men a full day to do properly."[114] The advice of one camp manual to bury tin cans in the ground while out tripping was evidence that some camps considered their environmental impact but that more attention was given to the visual than to long-term effects.[115]

What is particularly intriguing about a camp's physical and spatial development is that many of the changes that were effected were initiated not by outsiders but, quite consciously, by camp administrations themselves. In theory, camp literature spoke frequently of respect for all things natural and a desire to keep sites in their "natural state." As one camp director claimed: "We kept it very simple – not a bush cut down."[116] What was "natural," however, was clearly in the eye of the beholder. As Michele Lacombe has argued, bourgeois recreationists seeking escape from city stresses also took pleasure in ordering "wild" landscapes.[117] For many, as long as the changes one made were "for the better," they could be counted as "natural." In 1946, it was approvingly noted of one camp administrator that, "while she has improved on the outdoors, she has not disturbed it."[118] Like parks, highway viewpoints, and even forests, camps were clearly human constructions, "built landscapes" designed to suit the needs of their recreational populations.[119]

"Improvements" were the first order of business at many camps, though this was defined differently according to the context. While some administrators sought to tame spaces deemed unruly, others worked to create "wildness." In order to accommodate their programming needs, camp administrations at many camps cleared large areas for activities and for buildings, removing "surplus trees" as one director put it,[120] and sometimes kept up "lawns" to manicured perfection. At the Statten camps in Algonquin Park, resort-like sandy beaches were not natural phenomena but, rather, the careful creation of camp managements. In 1931, it was observed that "an unattractive, stumpy sand lot" had been "converted into a beautiful Florida beach," with the addition of more than eighty truckloads of "nice even granulated sand."[121] On the other hand, especially at fresh air camps located closest to "civilization," administrators sought to avoid an overly domesticated look. In the early 1920s at Camp Bolton, for instance, trees had to be planted to create "forests" out of previously agricultural land.[122]

A closer look at Camp Bolton, run by the charity-minded Neighbourhood Workers' Association, suggests that efforts to create wildness coexisted with those to "tame" the spatial environment. There, in the gently rolling landscape of the Albion Hills, some thirty miles northwest of Toronto, the same impulse for order and efficiency that guided social service work informed the attitudes of fresh air camp administrators. The site itself, referred to as a "natural park" and praised for its "great natural beauty," in truth required the efforts of many human hands to keep it that way.[123] From the start, camp planners saw the need for "improvements." The year 1923 saw the filling in of the pond and "the grading and seeding of playgrounds"; 1924 brought "the building of a bridge, the lowering of the grade behind [the main lodge], [and the] constructing [of] a ditch"; and 1925 saw "the sodding and cribbing of river banks."[124] By 1926, a full-scale "programme for beautification," requiring employment of a landscape gardener, was under way. As the official camp history acknowledged in 1938, nature, unaided, could not always be counted on to create beauty. It might just as easily give birth to chaos and disorder. Administrators candidly remarked on the degree of planning and forethought required to transform Bolton into a pleasing, "natural" space.

> The planting of trees, shrubs and flower gardens, the preservation of old trees ... and the placing of the buildings so that they would seem at home in their surroundings, has gone steadily forward. The present unity, on which so many visitors remark, is to a large extent due to this and to ... capable and thoughtful planning ... Each year new areas are redeemed from the wild, weed-ridden state, and made to blend into the beauty of the grounds.[125]

Over the years, dozens of locals were employed as groundspeople whose task was the "redeeming" of wild nature. Indeed, visitors commented on the wonderful results of their handiwork. In the eyes of one 1937 guest, the grounds were "unbelievably lovely, with their beautiful lawns and immaculately kept buildings. The whole thing is so beautifully ordered."[126] The *Bolton Enterprise* concurred with this view, noting that "the grounds are always beautifully landscaped and the whole camp managed to a degree of efficiency which does not stand even comparison."[127]

Just as camp landscapes were not always as "natural" as camp rhetoric insisted, camp life and programming were not always as "simple" or as "rough" either. Children were interested in the novel outdoor experiences of camp, but they were also interested in having fun. Having interesting, even challenging experiences on canoe trips was one thing; but most campers did not want to be uncomfortable all the time. At all but a minority of camps, tents were gradually phased out, reserved mainly for overnight and canoe trips. Though sleeping cabins were generally designed according to the "rustic" ideal, camp brochures also assured parents that they would be comfortable. Clearly, when children should be made comfortable and when they should "rough it" was something of an ongoing

Landscaped setting of Bolton Camp. The manicured perfection of the lawns at Bolton Camp was a far cry from the "wilderness" ethos of most private camps. *Copyright Family Service Association of Toronto.*

decision. More in keeping with the former, the Ontario Camping Association (OCA) explained in 1946 that girls at Camp Wapomeo were "housed in double log cabins, each with lounge and fire place," conditions the OCA considered "exceptionally good."[128] Winnebagoe's promotional literature boasted that "every modern healthful comfort and device that trained judgment can secure has been provided ... Screened-in sleeping bungalows and cottages provide the maximum comfort and rest on hot summer nights."[129]

Proving to parents that camps were safe places to send their children was another factor that limited the willingness to take "roughing it" too far. In the early interwar years, camping was still new to many parents, and directors worked to quell potential fears. Bert Danson recalls of the early 1930s, when his mother started up Camp Winnebagoe: "In those days you had to sell people on sending their children to camp ... [It was], 'what do you mean, send them away without their parents, won't they cry?' ... It was just foreign to people."[130] Assuring parents that physical risks would be minimized was part of making this "sell." In 1928, Taylor Statten claimed "health and safety" as his camps' primary objective. Ten years later, references to safety occurred four times on the first page of the Camp Wapomeo brochure.[131]

Into the postwar years, as camps became a widely accepted part of the recreational landscape, the emphasis on safety continued and, perhaps, intensified. In 1947, the YMCA, for its part, worked at improving the safety standards at its camps, one official noting quite rightly that "one drowning can set a camp, and indeed all our camps, back for many years." Promotional literature now constructed even the landscape as hospitable to urban youngsters. Especially at northern private camps, tensions were ongoing between efforts to entice campers into rugged wilderness adventures and the desire to assure parents that physical risks would be minimized. A postwar brochure for Camp Temagami, the camp that boasted its "pioneering" spirit, explained carefully to parents: "In front of the camp is a spacious bay, *well protected* on all sides from strong winds, making an excellent and *safe course* for the practice of aquatics. The water here is *shallow, with a firm sandy bottom*, and as the bay is *constantly supervised* ... a novice may learn to swim, or manage a boat or canoe, under *close supervision* and without going beyond his depth."[132] If child-rearing followed a more "permissive" model in postwar years, as historians have argued, camp literature also suggests an increased protectionism as well, a trend that continued into the late twentieth century.[133]

If safety was increasingly on the minds of twentieth-century parents, they were likely relieved that the much-lauded isolation of camps was gradually reduced over this period, creating yet another gap between the image and reality of camp life. In all truth, complete isolation had never been the goal of any administrator, whatever the rhetoric of camp literature. As Susan Miller, borrowing from Leo Marx, notes in the American context, the real goal was to find a "middle landscape" somewhere between civilization and the harshest realities of nature. In Ontario, once-remote areas became increasingly accessible with the extension of provincial highways and telephone lines in the late 1920s and 1930s. By 1927, the Ferguson Highway connected Temagami with North Bay, bringing the region within a day's drive of Toronto,[134] while, in the early thirties, the construction of Highway 60 into Algonquin Park did the same for that area. Then as now, the building of highways sometimes ignited controversy. In the case of Algonquin Park, several groups, including the Ontario Anglers'

Association and the Ontario Society of Artists, were opposed to the building of Highway 60, while most of the residents were in favour of the planned extension.[135] Typical of the tensions in the camp movement, the Taylor Statten camps seemed torn on the question. In 1931, the editor of the Ahmek newsletter noted: "The road through the Park would give the Camps better transportation arrangements, but at the same time it would be sure to spoil some of the semi-primeval loveliness of the Park."[136] In the end, the road went ahead, with the camps remaining neutral on the issue. Improved telecommunications were another element that helped minimize the camps' isolation. In 1937, Bolton Camp, hardly isolated from the start, boasted that "telephone communication exists between all [parts of the] camp and with Toronto," while a guest at the camp claimed the institution was outfitted "with all the modern equipment of a city."[137] The ironies were everywhere. In 1946, the same Winnebagoe brochure that celebrated cooking over "the open camp fire" and sleeping "under the star-ornamented canopy of heaven" also proudly declared: "Modern communication systems, such as direct telephone and telegraph connections, make contact with [the camp] as simple as if it were in your own city."[138]

Campers themselves were always a factor in shaping the culture of camp, and this minimized isolation in another sense. Throughout these years, it was a nearly impossible task to keep camp life entirely isolated from changes occurring in the broader culture, even those elements of popular culture so often criticized in camp literature. Not all campers, it seems, were content with just living the "simple life" or "getting back to nature." Campers who were particularly attached to their comic books and records often found ways to bring them to camp. The authors of *Crestwood Heights* commented on the attempt to limit the influence of mass culture at postwar private camps: "Radio and daily newspapers at one camp were for the sole use of the supervisory staff. Some children complained that they missed television. One mass communication tool, however, could not be screened out of any camp observed during the research – campers clung tenaciously to their comic books!" This tendency was noted at other camps. In the case of teenagers, directors sometimes found it easier to adapt to emerging youth cultures than to try to prohibit their expression. Dancing was one activity that dominated youth attention from the interwar years on – one that was often criticized by those involved in youth work but one that influenced camp life nonetheless. Directors at some camps planned evening dances, perhaps another attempt to hold the attention of older campers. After one failed attempt to select the music that interested campers, Bert Danson, postwar director of Camp Winnebagoe, singled out two of the "popular, older" campers to buy the records, instructing them: "I want you to buy the records the kids will like." Finally, home movie-making technology also affected camp life, as Leslie Paris demonstrates in the American context. In the United States and Ontario, it seems, movies served as a marketing tool to bring in new campers, as a handy form of entertainment for campers on rainy days, and as a way of fuelling alumnae memories and loyalties.[139]

One of the offshoots of the "modernization" of many camps in the 1940s and 1950s was a renewed determination among others to reclaim "real" camping. For example, in a postwar brochure, Camp Temagami billed itself as "one of the few real backwoods camps, [which] aims to keep alive the pioneer spirit." The sense that some camps were now truly "authentic" and others not truly worthy to be called camps was also evident in Mary Northway's praise for certain "roughing it" style camps in 1946:

> These camps have contributed a good deal because they have insisted that the core of camping is camping. They have emphasized the simple, outdoor living and enjoyment of the activities of the outdoor world and have minimized city frills ... I visited Miss Case's camp ... She has retained the virtue of simplicity – a rare asset in these days of "Bigger and Better" this, that, and everything.[140]

Defining the truly authentic camp was never a simple matter. For some camps, retaining the tradition of tenting was important. In 1941, Northway Lodge, an American girls' camp in Algonquin Park, claimed its "pioneer spirit" was due to the fact that all of its campers still lived in tents. Likewise at Bark Lake, the province's counsellor-in-training camp, it was boasted that "all the campers lived under canvas" until at least as late as 1958.[141] For other camps, it was sticking to the old staples of the camp program and avoiding the addition of too many "citified" activities that proved a camp's authenticity. According to postwar Camp Temagami literature, what made it a real camp, and also increasingly unique, was its ability "to specialize in ... general forms of campcraft that may not be possible nearer civilization."[142]

For many private campers, canoe tripping was central to their notion of "real" camping. Canoe-trip campers saw themselves as the "real" campers, in part because their "real" skills were "really" used. From their perspective, there was no point in learning to canoe if you weren't going to leave the camp waterfront or, likewise, to learn to chop wood if you were never to start a fire. The canoe trip allowed campers to put these skills to use. At the same time, it encompassed all that was deemed most healthy about camp life: heightened isolation and immersion in nature, the development of top-notch skills and endurance, the need for both self-reliance and cooperation, as well as the formation of close friendships. At Camp Ahmek, which retained its emphasis on canoe tripping into the postwar period, the tripping experience was described as the antithesis of urban living: "It is a completely new way of life for the city-bred person," a 1962 guide to programming claimed. "From dawn until bedtime the tripper is learning to exist comfortably and safely, without the conveniences of home and away from the pressures of an organized society."[143]

Campers themselves often treasured their experiences at their "pioneering" canoe-tripping camps. As modern conveniences and comforts became more widespread in the postwar period, the thrill of doing without seemed only to increase. Living with kerosene lamps in crude communal-style cabins was exciting to children who took their warm, well-lit, and private single-family dwellings for granted. Many campers, like the camp literature, raved about the experience of tripping, often the highlight of camp and the source of their most vivid memories. Shirley Ford, Glen Bernard camper in the 1940s, much preferred tripping to the more regimented life in camp:

> We would get trucked off to Algonquin Park and then we would set out. We would be 10 days in the wilderness catching fish ... paddling ... portaging, and singing ... I loved the canoe tripping because it [took us] away from demands. If we wanted to stop, we could stop and cook a meal, and have a skinny dip, then sing around the campfire. And if we wanted to paddle up til dusk we could. We just did ... It was lovely because you were free and out in the world of creation.[144]

Other campers remember not just "lovely" but also distinctly distasteful aspects of canoe tripping. Being able to deal with the tough, unpleasant conditions, however, was also part of what made the experience memorable for campers, even years later. Kathryn Wirsig openly admitted her dislike for certain elements of tripping but, in 2001, still looked back on it as fully worthwhile. "I went on many canoe trips of varying lengths," recalled this Wapomeo camper. "Often the paddling was tough, the days long and the food yucky [sic], but the experience was wholesome and developed character."[145] Even in the earliest years, camp life had never been static, and yet, later on in life, these camping "alumnae" sometimes had difficulty watching as their camps continued to change in the late twentieth century.

To their eyes, increasing comforts altered the experience dramatically. Former Ahmek camper David Bawden admitted in our 2001 interview that: "It is hard to think of the camp having electricity in every cabin. I think that would spoil it somewhat for me now."[146] Even at Bark Lake, only established in 1947, ex-campers had the feeling that "much of the real camping flavour [was] lost" in later years.[147] In a 1973 interview, staff member Gord Wright explained why he chose not to revisit the camp:

> The reason I haven't been in since is I heard they've almost made motels or hotels out of it. I think if people have to go to the outdoors and build hotels ... it's just too posh. You miss the early days of the last tents, a leak here and there ... a bit of wind ... all added to the adventure of the young people. I've seen too many examples ... where that happened ... some wealthy citizen decided he had to put electric light bulbs in the tents. Well the first thing the lads did was screw out the bulbs and have it dark.[148]

Ultimately, the distinction between "real" camps and "modern" camps was exaggerated since, at every camp, there were tensions between anti-modern, back-to-nature ideals and the seductive lure of the comfortable and the modern. If the establishment of Ontario's summer camps was, at root, a geographical and spatial solution to the problem of "the city," this chapter also reveals just how difficult it was becoming, under conditions of mid-twentieth-century modernity, to truly isolate one thing from another: nature from culture, country from city, the simple life from a host of urban complexities. If the modern tendency was to spatially segregate, the modern reality was a constant blurring of boundaries, with even back-to-nature enthusiasts being influenced by the impulse to order, the expectation of comfort, and the seemingly irrepressible influence of technological innovation. However isolated or wild campsites may once have been – usually long before the founding of summer camps – as modern urbanites moved out into the woods, they couldn't help but bring their essential "modernity" with them, a fact that shaped their experiences there and that ultimately wrote itself on the landscape. In the end, camp enthusiasts helped to modernize the wilderness while realizing their back-to-nature fantasies.

However, to campers themselves and to all who grew to love their summer homes away from home, the fact that the summer camp did not truly challenge the terms of modern urban living was of little concern. That the movement itself was not animated by a genuine back-to-the-land sentiment and, in fact, was not even as ambitious as the European Garden City movement – both of which sought a fundamental reshaping of the spaces of daily life – went largely unnoticed. Camp was about learning to "live in one's leisure," about finding spaces of temporary rejuvenation, new sites for adventure far removed from the everyday. At this limited task, the movement seemed generally to succeed. In doing so, it also revealed another fundamentally modern tendency, what Anthony Giddens refers to as the "sequestration," or compartmentalization, of experience.[149] Accordingly, camp would continue to be thought of, throughout these years, as a quintessentially natural experience, an escape from the thoroughly artificial life of the city. Camp was often remembered as a distinct and special place, far removed from the ordinary spaces of childhood, yet somehow bearing an authenticity that the latter lacked. As one grown camper put it, looking back on her camp years: "Back then there was still that pull to the simple and the real. What was simple and real was the outdoor life."[150]

2

Socialism for the Rich: Class Formation at the Private Camp

In 1939, Taylor Statten, founder and director of two of Ontario's most illustrious summer camps, had the following to say about this modern recreational-educational institution in the woods:

> The camp furnishes an admirable laboratory for practice in th[e] democratic ... way of life. It possesses most of the elements of the normal community, but in simplified form ... Here may be found different racial, religious, national, and socio-economic groups ... [T]he contacts with representatives of different races, religions, nations, and socio-economic levels are direct and personal. It is easy to see the manual laborer, the skilled worker, the Jew, the Catholic, the Protestant, as persons, even as friends, whose needs and welfare are as important as one's own.[1]

In truth, while this may have fit well with contemporary democratic rhetoric, it fell far short of describing the camp world. The reality was that children of vastly different socio-economic groups did not mix at camp; they found their class standings solidified, not challenged, by their camp experiences. Statten's own private camps, Ahmek and Wapomeo, catered to a select and discriminating clientele: the most humble being an ambitious sector of the aspiring middle class, the most comfortable being well-connected families of wealth and standing. In 1928, Statten himself declared of his campers: "These children come from the best of homes. Their parents and grandparents for generations back are from 'good stock'

Camp Tanamakoon canoe trip, c. 1920. Canoe tripping was an essential aspect of programming at private camps and their settings were well-suited for this purpose. *Algonquin Park Museum Archives #3162 (George May).*

... Some day he may be one of our most honoured citizens."[2] A closer look at the history of private camps reveals that this was, by far, the more accurate description.

Not just at Ahmek and Wapomeo but also at other private camps children of relative privilege were immersed in the "lessons of class" that were also taught at the private school, the fraternity, the social club, and the board room. Uniquely, however, this outdoor education was lauded for cultivating the toughness, resourcefulness, self-confidence, and team spirit deemed necessary to groom future leaders, whether of professional, political, or industrial varieties. Along the way, bonds of class friendship – often of life-long duration – knit these camping communities together. The relationships formed there were the source of enduring friendships, romances, marriages, and valuable social connections. For many at these private institutions, camp was a unique and long-treasured experience, a haven of warmth and community, standing in stark contrast to the perceived coldness and impersonality of modern life.

Seen in a broader perspective, the history of private camps points to the fundamentally class-segregated nature of the camp movement in Ontario. Children of all classes attended Ontario camps in these years, but, generally speaking, they found their way to different sorts of camps.[3] This chapter examines the experience of those at the upper end of the social scale – children of the upper-middle and upper class who sent their children to private camps. It considers the questions: who attended these camps? what was the nature of camp programming? and what were the immediate and longer-term impacts of these experiences? To emphasize the distinctiveness of these camps, in this chapter I make comparisons with agency camps, while in the following chapter I delineate the unique character of the fresh air camp. What becomes clear is that the private camp, in its programming, amenities, clientele, even location (as we've seen), did not depart from but, rather, reflected trends in the broader society. Though modernity seemed to promise wealth and broad social improvements for all, in truth, industrial and technological progress coexisted with ongoing class oppression and social division. Distinct class cultures were one of the results. Private camps, like elite suburbs or exclusive social clubs, provided yet another escape from heterogeneous class mixing; they provided no escape from modernity, and certainly not from its class cultures.

Creating an Exclusive Community

In the writing of Canadian history, analyses of class have revolved almost exclusively around two players: the working class and the middle class. Working-class histories have centred on accounts of workers, organized labour, and, more recently, working-class family economies. Frequently, these histories contain discussion of the middle class, but, typically, the composition of that class is left somewhat vague. Other treatments of class culture in Canada have also been crafted, quite usefully, around the dichotomy of working-class and middle-class cultures. In these discussions, it is frequently noted that the working class was never culturally homogenous, while "the middle class" is often rendered in somewhat monolithic terms. One wonders whether everyone from respectable school teacher to millionaire industrialist can usefully be subsumed under the rubric of middle class. Is there perhaps a need for explicit discussion of a world beyond the middle class, for consideration of the fact that even respectable professionals could seek social mobility and entry into yet more prestigious social circles, and, indeed, that such circles existed?[4]

Studies of elite culture in Canada have frequently been conducted by those outside the historical discipline. In 1965, in his widely read *Vertical Mosaic*, sociologist John Porter made careful efforts to describe the nation's economically stratified society. Other sociological and journalistic studies, in essence, concur with Porter's notion of the pyramid – with a broad base of working and middle-class Canadians at the bottom and a small collection of elite families at its top – as a useful image of the Canadian class system. They also agree that the powerful in this country are not an isolated or unconnected collection of individuals but, rather, "an interacting social entity." In *The Canadian Establishment,* journalist Peter C. Newman argues that the cohesiveness of this group owed more than a little to childhood conditioning at elite institutions:

> Perhaps because it comes so early, when personalities are still malleable, no influence is more cohesive, no bond more lasting, than time spent at the private schools and other institutions that instill Establishment values. Those early impressions, absorbed through willing pores, set lifetime priorities, prejudices, presumptions, and above all personal partnerships. At a subconscious level, they perpetuate the idea that privilege exists and that it should be exercised ... One meets the right people. The latticework of connections begins to form, stretching all the way to the Order of Canada ... honourary degrees, and other rewards that may eventually follow.[5]

Others agree that childhood has been an important time for the shaping of class tastes and attitudes. In one of the few historical studies of elite culture, Jean Barman argues that the private school was both statistically and culturally significant in the backgrounds of an important minority of elite adults in early twentieth-century British Columbia. At these schools, Barman suggests, character building was of central importance. Developing character was thought to require several things: a controlled environment, contact with the right people, and "systematic reward and punishment."[6]

Private camps, like private schools, formed one more piece in the "latticework of connections" that fostered elite culture in Ontario. This was noted not only by the sociologists who published *Crestwood Heights* but also in the pages of Porter's *Vertical Mosaic.*[7] Camps, like schools, offered an environment of select contacts for those of privileged backgrounds and the hope of improved life chances for those in search of social betterment. In fact, in Ontario, many private camps had close connections to private schools. In some cases – as with Camp Temagami and Camp Keewaydin – camps were the summertime projects of private school staff, who found it easy to recruit campers from among their student populations. The connections Taylor Statten fostered between Camp Ahmek and Pickering College have already been noted. In much the same way, A.L. Cochrane was well placed, as physical education instructor at Upper Canada College, to attract student campers to Camp Temagami. From his position at the school, Cochrane published camp updates, year-end reports, and regular ads in the pages of school publications.[8] In a brochure from what appears to be the early postwar years, the administration made the private school connection plain: "Camp Temagami has the unique distinction of being officially recommended and endorsed by both UPPER CANADA COLLEGE and the UNIVERSITY OF TORONTO SCHOOLS," the promotional literature virtually shouted.[9] At a number of private "American" camps, including Keewaydin, Northway Lodge, and Tamakwa, links to private schooling were solidified by the hiring of teachers as counsellors and camp staff. Already salaried employees, free for the summer and as well versed as any in child psychology, teachers looking for backwoods adventure made ideal candidates for staff and counselling positions. Potentially, they also ensured an even tighter connection between the goals of camp and school.[10]

In other cases, connections with private schools were less formal but equally strong. Many private schools acted informally as "feeders" for camps, often thanks to student word of mouth. According to one Glen Bernard camper, September schoolgirl chatter back in the halls of Bishop Strachan was enough to fuel new interest in the camp. "That's how camps grew," Jane Hughes explained in our interview in 2000. "We'd all talk about it, and say what a wonderful time we had and next year there would be a few more. Word of mouth. No commercial advertising."[11] Although this last is clearly overstated, Hughes's comments capture an essential truth – namely, that private camps relied heavily on the reports of campers (and talk between parents) to attract new clients.

These practices assured camps of a constant clientele with particular school-camp connections intensifying over time. Indeed, of Camp Temagami, alumni now claim: "Camp Temagami virtually became [Upper Canada College's] summer session."[12] This statement likely comes close to describing the relationship between other private schools and camps, at least for a portion of the students. Glen Bernard Camp, for its part, was known to recruit from Havergal, Branksome Hall, and Bishop Strachan girls' schools, while Keewaydin drew its campers almost entirely from exclusive American preparatory schools. Other anecdotal evidence also suggests a close relationship between private schooling and elite camps. In the words of Bert Danson, son of Winnebagoe's founders, "the private camps were really for well-to-do people, people who used to send their children to private schools." When asked about the presence of public school girls at Glen Bernard camp, ex-camper Marjorie Royce replied, "Not so many, no. [They] couldn't afford it, I think."[13]

Indeed, throughout the early twentieth century, fees were telling indicators of a camp's target clientele and provided important clues as to probable class backgrounds of campers. At fresh air camps, run by charitable organizations and churches, fees were minimal or non-existent, the whole purpose being to provide holidays to those who could not afford them. Agency camps were non-profit, but they were also not charities, and, thus, more substantial fees were unavoidable. As the director at Camp Pine Crest, one of the oldest YMCA camps in Ontario, put it in 1951, "The operation of a camp for boys requires money. Pine Crest serves boys whose parents can afford to pay for the services rendered." One 1947 brochure estimated that fees at Y camps averaged approximately ten dollars per week. In 1949, the average fee at twenty-eight organization camps listed with the Ontario Camping Association was $13.59 per week. Both suggest that these camps were targeted at a middle-class clientele.[14]

If agency camps were pricey when compared with the fresh air variety, they were certainly reasonable when set against the private camps. Quite simply, the fees charged at many private camps ensured that only the wealthy or, at least, financially comfortable, would consider them. As early as 1904, Keewaydin was charging $95 for a month's stay and $225 for a two-month trip to James Bay. In 1929, Ahmek and Wapomeo were charging $250 for an eight-week stay, making camp more costly on a monthly basis than the most expensive private schools.[15] In 1949, the average private camp fee was $32.88 per week, more than twice that of the typical agency or organizational camp.[16] Averages, of course, hide the degree of variation. At some of the most expensive private camps, fees were three to five times those of agency camps. Keeping these camps more out of reach of the merely middle class was the fact that one- and two-month stays were often the only option. As Douglas Creelman remembered of the mid-1940s at Keewaydin, "at that time you came for the full eight-week session. There was no alternative."[17] For a full two-month stay, nineteen of forty-nine private camps were charging $300 by 1949, with Ahmek charging $350 and Keewaydin, Winnibagoe, and Wabikon as much as $400.[18]

If fees effectively kept some people out, other methods were used to draw the "right" people in. In some camp brochures, "prestige lists" – compilations of the names of campers' parents – were used as one way of indicating the quality of the clientele.[19] In 1922, the Statten camp administration boasted: "Among the parents who have already enrolled their boys for this year are Lady Eaton, Col. F.H. Deacon, Dr. Wallace Seccombe, Dr. Coon, Senator Hardy of Brockville, and many of the leading business and professional men of Toronto."[20] Eliciting endorsements from well-known supporters was also popular. In this vein, a 1950s Temagami brochure included recommendations from both J.G. Althouse, provincial director of education, and popular radio personality (and former camper) Foster Hewitt.[21]

As at the province's private schools, then, *who* the private camp gathered together was as important to the project of class formation as *what* its programming taught, as parents were well aware. According to Leslie Paris's study of American summer camps, "choosing a camp was a performative act of social reproduction, a means of announcing one's allegiances, desires, and ambitions through one's children"[22] – a description that was never so accurate as in the case of this select group of camps. Camps were not unlike other class-specific institutions of the upper class, where simple attendance was a marker of social status and where it was taken for granted that one would be mingling with those already cut from the same cloth. In case any were not fully aware, the Statten camps' newsletter reminded its readers in 1931: "The high calibre of everybody on Canoe Lake allows us a choice of the best."[23] Declarations of this sort might also attract those hoping to elevate their status by mingling a few rungs up the social ladder. For those middle-class families willing and able to come up with the fees, camp might provide the friendships and connections that could open new doors.

In class terms, then, the populations assembled at these camps were relatively homogenous. Generally, their roots were in the upper, upper-middle, and aspiring middle classes. They were predominantly private school educated and also broadly Anglo-Protestant in background (some camps claiming a minority of Jewish campers, and several others a predominantly Jewish clientele). When, in 1940, camp enthusiast and psychologist Mary Northway summed up the nature of the camp population at Glen Bernard Camp, her frank remarks served as a fairly apt description of the private camping community as a whole:

> The majority of its campers come from one city, but smaller places in the province and a few in the United States are represented. The camp population is derived from a relatively narrow economic stratum of society, ranging upward from the upper middle class. Racially it is also a highly selected group, consisting almost entirely of Canadians or Americans of the Nordic race ... All conventional branches of the Protestant faith are represented;

> there are a few Roman Catholics, but no Jews. Politically, the groups represented are of traditional Conservative or Liberal parties, with a few mildly socialistic-minded present. The educational background of the campers is that of private schools (two-thirds of the group), and the public and high schools in the "better" parts of the cities. The camp society is, therefore, highly homogeneous in background. The spread is small in age, home, wealth, creed, race, or school.[24]

Were children aware of these shared roots? It is hard to know. Certainly, later in life, some were aware that, as campers, they had been moving in relatively privileged circles. As Douglas Creelman remembered it looking back in 2000, the population at Keewaydin was definitely "upper class." "Oh yes, very much so," he stated emphatically. "The camp was not cheap and you're talking about a commitment." As one of the rare public school students at Keewaydin, Creelman was perhaps more class conscious than some others. For many children, it is likely that class was not a concept given concerted or explicit attention. Many would possibly have shared the sentiments of a Wapomeo camper, who admitted: "I never knew or cared where anybody came from except my buddies from Toronto. I think I lived in a little contented bubble with no special interest in where people came from." No doubt this partly reflected childish self-absorption, but it also, arguably, reflected a Canadian blindness to the class-stratified nature of social life. Lack of concern in this regard was the prerogative of those who took contentment for granted. Even this camper from the late 1920s and 1930s, however, admitted that difference would have been noticed: "Certainly, the campers were a homogeneous lot," she commented, "no blacks, no French, and certainly no poor kids."[25]

In terms of their geographic origins, private camp clientele were also unique. Certainly the largest proportion of Ontario's private camp population hailed from larger urban centres: first Toronto, and then Hamilton, Ottawa, and Montreal. American campers were also prominent at the most reputable Ontario camps. As with the well-to-do north of the border, wealthy Americans (particularly from Ohio and the New England States) had been looking to the Algonquin, Temagami, and Muskoka regions as holiday and resort areas since the late nineteenth century. For many, their image of Canada rested almost solely on its recreational possibilities. As historian Tina Loo has observed, this country represented the optimal blend of wilderness and modernity: the first making it attractive, the second reasonably accessible. Many first experienced Canadian "wilderness" during childhood stays at summer camp. At several upscale institutions, ex-campers estimated that Americans made up anywhere from one-quarter to one-third of the total camper population. Wapomeo ex-camper Elizabeth Shapiro recalls that, by the late 1930s, "there were enough campers from the New York area to warrant a separate car on the New York to Toronto train."[26] At some camps, American children were not just a minority of the campers; it was a matter of common knowledge that certain institutions were essentially "American" camps, with the overwhelming preponderance of both campers and staff hailing from the United States throughout this period. Of ten "American" camps that could be identified, all shared the characteristics of these elite camps; that is, they were privately run, charged high fees, and were located in the most desirable regions of Temagami and Algonquin Park.[27]

Counsellors were another important component of the reputable private camp community. At many private camps, the preference was for university graduates or students in the process of attaining degrees. More than that, Ahmek literature boasted in 1928 that many of its staff had been accepted at "the *foremost* universities and professional schools." Even as such staff was more difficult to come by in postwar years, Tamakwa claimed that its counsellors represented "the cream of the [American] colleges," while a Temagami brochure explained: "Camp counsellors are chosen with great care. Our Senior Counsellors ... are either university students or graduates." Given the interest in attracting American customers – or perhaps only because they were already campers – sometimes a sizeable minority of these were American graduates. At Camp Ahmek, Americans formed more than 20 percent of the 1931 staff, while at American-run camps like Keewaydin, they formed the overwhelming majority.[28]

One way of ensuring a steady supply of suitable counselling staff was through the introduction of counsellor-in-training (CIT) programs in the interwar years. In this way, senior campers were carefully moulded into staff (often while still paying camp fees). In 1931, Statten referred to the "increasing number" of former campers among his counselling staff, some of whom had attended for "seven or eight years before holding a position." In his words, "Counsellors of this variety are a real asset, since they have grown with the camp and are intimately associated with its aims and development."[29] Though very youthful staff were sometimes the source of discipline problems at camp, at the very least, administrations were assured that CIT's shared the class values and background of the majority of the camper population.

At times, private camps took pains to secure not only respectable middle-class youth and young adults but also renowned and accomplished individuals with near celebrity status. According to Keewaydin's official history, it claimed "an impressive roster of staff," which drew further on the American prep school for its popular athletic coaches as well as for recruiting a number of famous singers. While Winnebagoe was happy to claim George Young, an Ontario marathon swimmer, among its staff, Arowhon boasted that it had "most of the Canadian Olympic team coming and going from camp," in particular, its swimmers and divers. Other camps followed suit, with famous golfers, musicians, artists, and naturalists among the star-quality staff.[30]

Roughing It in the Woods

Once at camp, children of relative privilege were immersed in camp programming, which reinforced the class culture of home and school. Private camp directors, like private school administrators, viewed their work as more than the mere shaping of children: theirs was the task of grooming social leaders. As with private schools, "character" was their buzz word. "Character is contagious," the Statten camp literature informed its counsellors in 1928: "Our lives will radiate influences which shall help to mould the characters of some of the most promising citizens of our land."[31] At Temagami, a similar sense of purpose prevailed, with administrators claiming in late season in 1920: "New problems were solved and such experiences gained as develop character and assist in making our citizens of the future, men of ability and resource, as they have proved themselves to be in the past."[32] Certainly, character building also went on at other camps; the difference here was that well-turned-out campers were expected to become not just good citizens but, potentially, skilled leaders.

As with all camps, setting was key, but here, nature was prized for providing the backdrop for a unique class drama. Directors who secured sites in exclusive locations were convinced that both setting and population were of the highest quality. They assumed that exposure to nature – an unquestioned good – would bring out the best in the best. At Camp Ahmek it was asked in 1931: "Why is it ... that camp-made friendships are so permanent?" The answer being that, "in the busy, happy two months during the summer we see people as they really are and not as the artificiality of the city makes them."[33] In one way, this was standard camp thinking. However, due to the kind of clientele they attracted, to the unique demands and opportunities of their programs, and to their access to "real" northern "wilderness," private camps saw themselves as firmly in a category all their own.

Camps of all sorts promised back-to-nature escapes, but it was at private camps that immersion in nature and desire for "roughing it" were key. Camp activities were celebrated for their ruggedness, their demand for active involvement, and their cultivation of leadership skills. For many private camps, canoe tripping was the centrepiece of simple life programming. Even more so than other activities, the canoe trip was regarded as an important character-building experience and, by extension, the ideal training ground for raising those "most promising citizens" that directors envisioned their campers would become. Above all, it was meant to be a cooperative enterprise, a journey in which all shouldered the load and in which team work was essential. While trip guides and counsellors took ultimate responsibility for campers' safety, campers generally shared the tasks of paddling (bow and stern), portaging, setting up camp, and cooking. Leaders, it was assumed, would come naturally to the fore.

Upscale private camps were not the only ones to offer campers the joys of canoe tripping, but their emphasis was unique. Fresh air camps simply did not have the resources – geographical or otherwise – to feature canoeing in their programs, but agency camps for middle-class clientele were not always as constrained. At least two camps run by the YMCA administrators in the 1950s – Pine Crest for boys and Tapawingo for girls – claimed that canoe tripping was an essential aspect of their camp programs. A 1953 study of Ontario YMCA camps revealed that five out of seven included canoeing among the roster of activities.[34] One cannot assume, however, that instruction in canoeing meant participation in canoe trips or, where it did, that trips were of very long duration. In early postwar years at Pinecrest, only a minority of boys went out on trips of more than a couple of days. During the summer of 1951, Pinecrest could claim only a total of seventeen trips that had been organized, though this number climbed into the thirties several years later. During the same period, the Y's Camp Tapawingo, which claimed tripping was "a major emphasis in camp," stated only that girls spent at least one night on trips away from camp.[35]

Contrast this with the situation at a number of private camps. At Ahmek and Wapomeo, where tripping was considered "the most important department of our camp life" and as the real "roughing it" aspect of programming, it was reported that over 235 trips were organized during the summer of 1930. Due to the fact that private campers generally spent much longer at camp, this meant that many participated in more than one trip per summer. For girls and boys alike, these trips could be as long as a week or more. Private campers were also typically initiated into trip life at younger ages and challenged to develop much broader competencies. While the YMCA's Camp Pine Crest assured parents that "counsellors paddle stern on all trips," and referred to their youngest campers as "little fellows" who were "not physically equipped to 'rough it'" on canoe trips, the Temagami-based Keewaydin welcomed boys as young as ten years of age. At this remote American-run institution, in-camp programming was virtually non-existent. Ex-camper and staffman from the 1930s and 1940s, Robert Foster, recalls: "Our staff and campers [were] out on canoe trips most of the seven-week season ... 13-15-year-olds ... typically went on a three-day warm-up trip, then three 11-day trips. Campers over 16 commonly took three-week and even seven-week trips, the latter usually to James Bay."[36] While Keewaydin was unusual in its almost sole emphasis on tripping, trips of several weeks were not unknown at other camps. Children at many private camps clearly had the chance to develop proficiencies and to experience adventures in a way that those at agency camps did not.[37]

Canoe instruction, Camp Tanamakoon. Before heading out on wilderness canoe trips, private campers – girls as well as boys – were expected to be proficient in all the fundamentals of canoeing. *Algonquin Park Museum Archives #3140 (George May).*

In a context of advancing technologies, not only canoeing but even traditionally elitist activities like sailing and riding could be sold as simple life activities – ones that cultivated noble self-sufficiency and pure enjoyment of one's natural surroundings. Note the antimodern description of sailing in Camp Ahmek literature in 1931:

> What a sport in this modern age of science and invention, with speed boats that go a hundred miles an hour ... In a sailboat, the wind may drop and we shall be doing splendidly if we cover a couple of hundred yards an hour ... Where then, does the fun come in sailing? The methods of the sportsmen are seldom the quickest and frequently they are exceedingly old-fashioned. The quickest method of racing boats is not by means of sails and wind but it is the way, really the only way followed by sportsmen and sailors. There is the thrill of it all – the sails straining, the crews hiking and the spray flying, as every muscle and all the skill one possesses is summoned to bring your dinghy across first.[38]

Clearly, the truly dignified "sportsman" valued quality of method and craft over speed. It is not hard to see what the lesson was for later life, whether for business or the professions: strive hard, put your "all" into something, and you will succeed. Even more, you will come out on top, a true leader. At Winnebagoe it was riding that was credited with fostering self-sufficiency and lusty appreciation of the outdoors. In 1946, a brochure from the camp stated:

> Overnight riding trips are a thrilling adventure. After a pleasant ride through new trails, and the destination has been reached, the riders take care of their own horses. They water them, then unsaddle and unbridle them, and turn them loose to roll and romp. After a filling meal, cooked over the open camp-fire and songs, chatter and stories are ended, each camper bundles himself in his blanket roll and is soon fast asleep under the star-ornamented canopy of heaven.[39]

If these activities had a certain masculinist appeal, others, which instilled old-fashioned respect for hard work, were geared to female campers. In "the weavery" at Wapomeo it was girls who were encouraged to develop a sense of accomplishment and traditional craftsmanship. While weaving was also taught at some fresh air camps, at this upscale camp, Taylor Statten insisted that girls develop "a thorough understanding of the hobby."

Riders from Taylor Statten Camp. Riding was one of the activities that marked private camps as a cut above the rest. *Algonquin Park Museum Archives #5062 (Mary Clare).*

To this end, he purchased "spinning wheels, carding equipment, a huge old-fashioned loom (1822 vintage) and weaving equipment of all sorts." Taking his purist vision one step further, the camp history states, "he even contemplated importing sheep into Algonquin Park to provide the wool."[40]

Taken together, the preference for training leaders in the rugged outdoors, the adamant appreciation of premodern pursuits, and the general romanticization of wilderness suggest that the antimodern impulse that animated the camping movement as a whole was most intense in the private camp setting. While all camps nurtured a back-to-nature fantasy, this manifested itself in class-specific ways. For those well accustomed to the luxury of modern conveniences, doing without was apparently novel enough to be considered good fun. Not surprisingly, it was those for whom comfort, even luxury, provided the backdrop to their daily experience that "simple living" held such a mystique. Put simply, if comfort was the norm, putting up with discomfort or lack of amenities could sometimes be exciting. In the early 1930s, when many Canadians were living far from comfortable lives, young Elizabeth Shapiro found Wapomeo, which was "free of all civilized amenities like flush toilets, running water, or electricity," to be "exciting and different."[41] One young Arowhon camper from the

1940s and 1950s expressed similar intrigue with the simple life: "I loved the outdoor aspect of camp," she stated. "I loved roughing it. The cabins were minimalistic – a cold water sink, screens with roll-down tarps [that] protected us from the outdoors. I adored it!"[42] Contrasting as it did with comfortable home lives, then, the comparatively Spartan nature of camp life captivated the imagination of many a fortunate youth.

"Smoothing It While You Rough It"

While private camping was about "roughing it," it was also about smoothing the way for campers' future success. Not surprisingly, those who prided themselves on their physical travels "off the beaten path" also had high expectations of the cultural and social aspects of camp programming. At most private camps, on-site programming still held an important place and was planned with thoughtful consideration. With regard to both out-trip and in-camp activities, then, the idea was to set oneself in a category beyond the merely average. Music programs offer a telling example. At all types of camps, campfire sing-alongs were central and bonding events; at these camps, music meant this and much more. At Camp Ahmek and Camp Wapomeo, where "the development of appreciations"[43] was listed as one of the primary objectives, a taste for high-brow culture was energetically fostered. "Music holds a very high place," the camp literature explained, "as a character kindling agency. That is *good music*. There is a type which stirs the lower desires and calls us back to the jungle. Camp is the greatest place on earth for developing *an appreciation for good music*."[44] Parents were assured that activities included "evenings devoted to the work of Schumann, Brahms, [and] Schubert" performed by "distinguished pianists and soloists" and, on occasion, musical quartets.[45] Likewise, at Winnebagoe, "talks on period music" by "a recognized authority and successful musical director" were said to be "a great influence in the aesthetic development of campers."[46] Children at private camps were also encouraged to develop their own musical abilities via private piano lessons, individual voice training, and, in one case, membership in the camp's brass band.[47]

Sports fuelled a similar level of class culture. Sailing and riding have already been mentioned; tennis, golf, and synchronized swimming were also options at some camps (though Ahmek alone distinguished itself with the Mock Fox Hunt).[48] As with more rugged activities, the acquisition of skill was only one objective, the other was socialization into a culture of exclusivity. To this end, at Ahmek boys who learned to sail and who had passed the requisite tests were inducted into the "Ahmek Sailing Club" with special rights of admittance to the sailors' clubhouse, where campers could store gear, hold sailors' meetings, or dip into the library of "sea stories and pirate yarns."[49] At Glen Bernard it was membership in the "Yacht Club" that held weighty "prestige value," while elsewhere it was excellence in riding and jumping that garnered one special attention.[50] With all of these activities, bourgeois sensibilities could be developed as almost incidental benefits, as hinted at in Winnebagoe's 1946 brochure:

> There is something romantic and intriguing in directing a willing mount to take you through the winding woodland trails. There is a thrill in the hasty retreat of a startled hare or the flight of the birds alarmed by the thud of the horses' hoofs. Here our campers have the opportunity to study nature and trot lazily through ever changing scenes with new surprises and new thrills awaiting at every turn in the road.[51]

Children of privilege learned that the natural world, like the social world, was there for them to consume, there to offer them "new surprises" and "thrills." The feeling of mastery here – of the horse and of nature in general – was likely deemed a beneficial influence for those who would be expected to prove "mastery" in other realms.

It was tacitly understood that one of these future realms might be political, a consideration that also shaped programming at private camps. While camps of many stripes spoke of the need to mould campers into responsible citizens, the way in which grown campers might make their contributions to democracy was imagined uniquely at private camps. In a general sense, campers were taught the lessons of active (but also, respectable) citizenship. Tanamakoon, for instance, reminded campers that the good citizen not only votes but also "keeps the law," "backs up his representatives," and "criticizes constructively."[52] In 1939, counsellor manuals at Ahmek spoke confidently about initiating the child's political education:

> The camp ... should provide practice for campers in sharing in the obligations and responsibilities as well as in the privileges of an organized community. For the older campers there should be considerable opportunity for practice in the technique of thinking, which might serve to protect the individual against propaganda, prejudice, and pressure groups. The camp ... should also develop in campers a larger understanding of, and loyalty to, democratic principles of social life and organization. With older campers,

> the camp should seek to develop increased sensitiveness [sic] toward major social problems and to stimulate or strengthen the desire to work for a better social order.[53]

Overall, it was hoped that children shaped by such a process would be active participants in the political process. One even senses a progressive tone here, though, significantly, campers were encouraged to be law-abiding and suspicious of "pressure groups" (who might they be?) as they worked for "a better social order."

Considering that at least some private campers were expected to become more than just "good citizens" and to shape the direction of democracy itself, at these camps induction into the political process also took more direct forms. Several camps organized camper councils – comprised of democratically elected representatives – and allowed them a hand in minor aspects of camp administration.[54] Grafting their lessons in democracy on to the Indian theme, administrators at Tanamakoon divided children into four tribes, each tribe electing a "little chief" by secret ballot. "Little chiefs" were ordered, among other things, to take charge of the opening proceedings of Council Fire, which, in an interesting twist of cultural fusion, were "conducted ... in parliamentary style." Girls at Glen Bernard also elected "chiefs," a role considered "a very great privilege of a senior camper."[55]

Ahmek literature offers the most detail regarding the workings of "cooperative government" at camp, with this camp becoming something of a leader in its early adoption.[56] After "abolishing" the office of program director in 1924, the latter was replaced by a complex system of camper councils, created from the amalgamation of campers' "duly elected representatives." Once again, the Indian theme was invoked, with democracy presented as the age-old wisdom of the first "Canadians."[57] The system divided the camp into six sections (by age) and started each day with meetings of each "tent group" (or cabin). Representatives of these – "sagamores," or "little chiefs" – met in "sectional councils" with sectional directors to discuss daily programming issues. "Sachems," or mayors, of each section – elected by the entire section – together with members of the administration, formed "the camp cabinet," ranked as "the highest official legislative body within the camp" and the group charged with consideration of program policy and general administration.[58] In the spirit of progressive pedagogy, it was claimed that, through this system, "campers learn more concerning the nature of law and regulation, concerning respect for the opinions and interests of others ... than by any amount of academic instruction."[59] Clearly, these were thought to be important matters with which private campers should become familiar.

Less formal aspects of programming were also calculated to have a lasting impact on young campers. Not only what one did – whether playing in the band or riding horse – but how one did it, even what one wore, were regarded as crucially important. Whatever the image of life in the woods as free and easy and unfettered by convention, the reality was often quite the contrary. Parents, quite simply, expected camps (like schools) to teach children how to function socially in the right circles. When asked, in 1920, what they wished their children to learn at camp, parents of Ahmek and Wapomeo campers replied: "To be more courteous and mannerly," "[to] improve table manners," and – mentioned more than once – "[to] correct defects of posture." (One truly ambitious parent suggested: "Get an inspiration to study French and Latin"!)[60] Camp memories of the 1940s at Glen Bernard point to similar parental motives. "My mother and father decided we needed a little bit of polishing," Helen Stewart recalled laughingly, "that we needed camping, we needed to meet more girls, people."[61]

Camp administrators strove to meet parental expectations in this regard. Some placed considerable emphasis on developing the social skills needed to mix in polite company. Certainly, at Ahmek, living the "wild life" was no justification for lapses in social convention, as instructions to counsellors revealed in 1928:

> Table manners at camp should be better than they are at home ... There is not only no excuse for a slump from courtesy and gentlemanliness at table when a boy leaves home and comes into the woods, but there is a duty and a privilege on our part to send boys home more thoughtful and more responsive to these amenities than when they came to us.[62]

Respect was also expected when addressing one's superiors, a contrast with the presumably democratic nature of camp. In the early years at Tanamakoon, girls were instructed to address counsellors as "Miss So-and-So" rather than by Christian names. In 1939, Taylor Statten still regarded it as "one of the traditions of our Canoe Lake Camps" to continue what he considered "the old English custom of saying 'yes, sir' and 'no sir.'"[63] To parental demands to improve posture, administrators at Tanamakoon responded with the institution of "Pine Tree Day." Apparently, the geographical landscape could be put to any number of symbolic usages, as the director's recollections reveal:

> The pine tree was a symbol of good posture. Campers nominated campers whom they believed deserved to be singled out as showing sufficiently good posture for the pine tree poster. During the week a secret committee of counsellors would keep an eye on those nominated and make a decision as to whether they were ready or not. Those who failed to come up to the mark were taken aside and shown where they had fallen short.[64]

Dress was also important. Mimicking the private school tradition, in the early years at some camps, children were expected to appear in uniform at least some of the time, a not always pleasant or comfortable experience.[65] Whether in uniform or out, campers were expected to adhere to respectable standards of dress. In 1939, Statten explained that, "for meals, Ahmek campers do not wear sleeveless shirts, and Wapomeo campers do not wear 'halters.'"[66]

Teaching privileged youngsters correct comportment in polite society also included providing a certain degree of creature comforts. Indeed, those camps most taken with antimodern escapes were also those most likely to provide modern indulgences. More than likely, they merely re-created the luxuries children had come to expect at home, a common trend in middle- and upper-class wilderness recreation since at least the nineteenth century.[67] Indeed, the same camps that claimed the real backwoods flavour also competed in providing the best accommodation, food, equipment, and staff care. Detailing the quality of one's food and kitchen staff was common in the pages of private camp brochures. For its part, Ahmek frequently boasted of the high quality of its food, which was served up by "one of the best and highest-paid French chefs in the north country." Also at Ahmek, boys who roughed it out on canoe trips were rewarded with "warm water in the wilderness" upon their return to camp and after the addition of hot showers in 1931. Higher staff/camper ratios at private camps also ensured wealthy parents of closer individual attention and quality care for their children. In 1949, these camps reported an average of one counsellor for every 4.5 campers, while some places, like the American-run Northway Lodge, boasted as many as one counsellor for every three campers. Clearly, attracting a cultured clientele in this business meant exhibiting an intuitive understanding of when austerity was called for and when comfort and care were the key. In this sense, Taylor Statten's advice to trippers to "smooth it while you rough it" apparently applied as much to the entire project of private camping as to the canoe trip itself.[68]

The comfort level of private camps appears all the more stark when compared with that of agency camps, where campers were well taken care of but were not exposed to extensive luxuries. Camp food was one example of adequate but not luxurious care at the agency camp. One YMCA camp manual included a suggested grocery list of sixty-six items, and, of all of these, the closest mention of meat came in the form of three entries regarding sardines, "fat back," and "empire bacon." In a sample menu in the same manual, meat was never served more than once a day, usually at lunch and typically as part of a low-budget casserole such as beef stew, shepherd's pie, meatloaf, or pork and beans. Suppers were generally meatless with high carbohydrate concentrations of fried potatoes and bread (served three times in one week), creamed potatoes and "cheese loaf," scrambled eggs and corn bread, and macaroni and cheese.[69] In terms of special treats, boys at Camp Pine Crest in the 1940s were treated every two weeks to a one-hundred-mile steamer ride through the Great Lakes, but parents were asked to pay extra for this. When it came to staffing, at YMCA camps counsellors were often forced to divide their attention between eight or more campers. In 1947, camp educators were somewhat alarmed at the findings of a study of twenty-five Y camps across the country. Staff-camper ratios varied from between 1:5 to 1:16, with thirteen camps reporting more than eight campers for every counsellor. These numbers improved slightly by 1949, when OCA data showed twenty-seven agency camps reporting an average of one counsellor for every 6.7 campers. Still, the contrast with private camps was clear, offering yet another example of the differences between private and agency camps.[70]

In the end, as with any good finishing school, the point of becoming polished at private camps was to shine in the right company. The wish of Helen Stewart's parents that she "meet more people" was surely shared by others. Important contacts could also be made in urban contexts, but, for many, the camp setting represented the chance to develop truly lasting bonds. At a personal level, these bonds meant a great deal to ex-campers, but they also had more practical uses later in life. The Ahmek faithful who penned this 1931 article on "Friendship" for the camp newsletter was aware of both aspects:

> Under ordinary circumstances we often meet people, work with them, play on teams with them – but yet a chance meeting later in life means nothing more than a few minutes of reminiscing. But let two old campers meet after a lapse of time and the story is different. Immediately they are on common ground, without any strained politeness or unnaturalness ...

> such friendship is a thing, the value of which becomes more apparent as we get older. When we are out in the business world or attending a university it becomes vital. We live and work for it; it is the thing that carries us over the difficult paths.[71]

In the end, all of these factors – a sense of shared backgrounds, the ability to "rough it" in "wilderness," access to good equipment, and acquaintance with the same rules of etiquette – helped not only to bond together members of these select camp communities but also to convince them that they were a cut above the rest.

Reputation and loyalty were also a matter of broader proportions. Private camps fostered pride in their individual institutions, but they also fostered a broader sense of community with other camps they considered their equals. Between a number of select private camps contacts were frequent and bonds were tight. Not only did private camp directors share camping "know-how" at informal get-togethers, but they also visited, exchanged staff, and considered one another close friends. It was friendships between the directors of seven or eight private camps that, ultimately, formed the basis of the Ontario Camping Association in 1933. Not surprisingly, in early years, the organization worked mainly in the interests of private camps. Their competitive claims aside, this group of camps in many ways saw itself as an elite camp community. To fuel "spirit," each thought of itself as "the best," but within the broader camp movement these camps also regarded some, and not others, as true camping colleagues.[72]

This points to an important fact about class identity formation, as true in the camp setting as in any other. Fostering strong bonds with some is always part of the project; as Stallybrass and White argue, exclusion of others is also essential.[73] This took place on multiple levels at camp. To foster exclusivity in the physical sense, camps claimed exclusive title to often desirable parcels of land. More than one private camp in Ontario was involved in conscious battles over land. In the opening years of the century, there was some controversy about removing the Temagami islands from the protection of the Temagami Forest Reserve, a move that ultimately allowed for the establishment of the area's camps, resorts, and cottages. Though Toronto legislators initially fought the move, founders of both camps Temagami and Keewaydin claimed space as squatters on Crown land. Keewaydin's official history describes the move in near heroic terms: "It was a bold stroke," Brian Back states, "to build in defiance of building restrictions within the reserve."[74] In Algonquin Park, private camps also fought to retain access to what was, in essence, Crown land. In the late

1920s, Taylor Statten sought the expansion of Camp Wapomeo onto a second island on Canoe Lake. One Ahmek enthusiast admitted in his history of the camp that the island in question had been "a very popular public camping site," one that "park authorities were reluctant to close ... down."[75] Nevertheless, even if "with a great deal of difficulty," director Taylor Statten eventually prevailed; the public campsite was removed and Wapomeo won its island lease in 1928. Twice more in their history – in the 1950s and 1970s – Algonquin Park camps struggled successfully to retain access to what was officially public land. The government's plan in 1973 to bring the whole of the park back "to a wilder condition," to transform it into "the average man's wilderness," was, apparently, not to be.[76] According to one director, this was never truly a possibility; the collective power of these camps ensured the retention of their leases. Eugene Kates, founder of Camp Arowhon in 1934, looked back on this period in a 1985 interview:

> I never hesitated to spend money developing the camp. I never believed there was any real possibility of camps like [Ahmek, Wapomeo, Arowhon, and] Tanamakoon being kicked out of the Park. Our political clout ... is so strong between all these camps ... We have such strong alumni combined ... There's a limit to what a government can do. And the government is dependent on the mass of people most of the time but the influential people are much more important in a smaller thing like this than the masses.[77]

Whether others recognized it or not, these camps saw themselves as a group of "influential people" – a kind of camping elite – much of the time content to remain isolated at out-of-the-way institutions but also unafraid to act publicly to advance its interests when necessary.

Exclusivity, to be sure, was a matter of more than physical dimensions; it was also a way of thinking and feeling about insiders and outsiders. Different sorts of camps were always considered somewhat outside the fold. The fact that, before the Second World War, the Ontario Camping Association had difficulty attracting fresh air and agency camps to its cause perhaps points to a lack of connection between different types of camps.[78] At the same time, even within privileged private camp communities, it seems that "outsiders" emerged. As children would discover in later life, even within exclusive circles, one could find oneself closer or further from the coveted centre. At camp, the same elements that helped foster a sense of solidarity – shared class background, education, or ethnicity – could be the basis for the marginalization of those who lacked these common bonds. As one of the rare public school students at Camp Keewaydin, attended mainly by American prep school students, Douglas Creelman was sometimes painfully aware of being out of place in the 1940s. "When you're nine or ten, that was hard," he confided. Explaining that he encountered some "wonderful people," he also admitted that there were "many in the group I found despicable people – snobs."[79] After camp, Creelman had no contact with fellow campers, a rare thing in this setting in which many others formed life-long attachments. In other cases, the bonds between consistently returning campers could easily have been experienced as "cliqueishness" by those attending for only one summer.

Jewish campers were another category of potential "outsiders" at private camps. In the interwar years, anti-Semitism was still commonly and, sometimes, stridently voiced, publicly as well as privately.[80] As ex-camper Joan Moses explains of her childhood growing up in Toronto in the 1930s and 1940s, "there was an enormous discrimination in those years and, if not as overtly [sic] among the privileged classes, it was certainly very much so below the surface."[81] In the American context, Jews were typically barred from attendance at Christian camps, but this was never the case in Ontario.[82] Still, the reality of anti-Semitism meant that attendance at primarily non-Jewish camps was not always a pleasant experience. Looking back in the 1970s, Bert Danson recalled that, before the early 1930s, "there were no camps for Jewish children. There were just the regular camps and Jewish children went to camp there too. Sometimes the kids had a good experience, sometimes they didn't." No doubt for such reasons, Sadie Danson, Bert's mother, sent him to a Jewish camp in the United States when he was growing up. On a more formal basis, Danson herself acted as a representative for two Maine camps, directing affluent Jewish families from Toronto and Montreal to these American camps. It was not until the early 1930s that Jewish organizations in Ontario began to open their own camps, the first ones being their version of fresh air camps for the underprivileged. Agency camps – run by Jewish labour and youth organizations – also appeared. To attract clientele from the more affluent portion of the Jewish community, Danson started her own private camp, Winnebagoe, in 1933. Like other camp founders, Danson and her husband had already been active in Jewish youth work in Toronto. After the founding of Winnebagoe, other private camps targeting the Jewish community appeared in the 1930s and 1940s. As in the American setting, Jewish camps of all kinds offered spaces free from anti-Semitism (sometimes even with kosher kitchens) as well as the opportunity to strengthen one's sense of identity and ties to a wider ethnic community. At the same time, private Jewish camps filled much the same role as did the other private camps studied here, helping to bond together members of a privileged class. The class-conscious goal of providing spaces for elite escape was evident in Winnebagoe's promotional literature: "Camp Winnebagoe caters to a select Hebrew clientele," a 1946 brochure states, "and since its inception has gained and retained the unqualified endorsation [sic] of some of the finest families in Canada and the United States."[83]

The Outside World Intrudes

The hard times of the Great Depression had distinct, if varying, effects on camps in Ontario. Overall, the number of Ontario camps continued to increase throughout the 1930s, though this didn't mean that camps were having an easy time. One of the things that makes compiling accurate camp statistics difficult is that, during any period, as new camps opened, others closed. While private camps were something of the elite of the camping community, financial pressures surely affected them in the 1930s. With fees providing the main source of camp budgets, any decline in enrolment was directly felt. Although statistics from individual camps are hard to come by, there is evidence that at least Keewaydin, Ahmek, and Wapomeo found their enrolments contracting. However valuable it seemed in good times, in hard times, camp may well have been viewed by middle-class families as an expendable cost. One thing that helped private camps remain open was that, if clients were scarce, labour was not. A history of Camp Ahmek suggests that staff in these years was easy to come by, with many apparently "happy to work simply for room and board."[84]

For those children whose parents could still afford the expense, private camp may have afforded increased isolation from Depression-era hardships. Although even fresh air camp administrations sometimes spoke of being isolated from the Depression at camp, for private campers, who lived much of their lives isolated from real economic insecurity, the camp may have served a negative function of further distancing them from the harsh realities of this period. One camper, looking back on the 1930s at Ahmek, sounded almost smug about how easily the troubles of the world could be forgotten at camp. "I never felt in those days ... that the camp ever suffered from the Depression. You never had the feeling that the world was down, down, down. Once you hit Canoe Lake ... we [sic] were all having the greatest time in the world, the outside world was shut off and camp carried on in a very upbeat situation. It was a very happy, happy place."[85] Camp, in this case, may well have made children happy, but one wonders here how much the camp was succeeding in creating those "better citizens" who worked for a "better social order" or, even, who were all that conscious of the social conditions around them.

The Second World War seems to have had more impact on private camps than on agency and fresh air camps. For one, the state's reach into the personal lives of its citizens was intensive, in contrast to its reluctance to intervene during the 1930s. State-organized mass mobilization of labour, resources, and funds devoted to the war effort all had their impact on summer camps. The most significant repercussion was undoubtedly labour shortages. Young adult men formed the backbone of administrative and counselling staff at most boys' camps, and their relative absence was keenly felt. The Ontario Camping Association felt strongly enough about the situation that members wrote to the Selective Service in Ottawa in 1943, "suggesting that the OCA might be put in a definite category."[86] With labour shortages throughout Canadian society, one doubts whether the state would have prioritized camp work in this way, though the outcome of these actions is unknown. We do know that, in many cases, camps were forced to do what other Canadian businesses were forced to do: rely on younger or predominantly female labour. For private camps, this might have meant hiring high school and not university students, as less illustrious Y and fresh air camps had long been doing. Such students were not difficult to attract; their summer breaks coincided nicely with the camp season, the work was potentially more enjoyable than the alternatives, and camp wages – though always meagre – might more easily be saved in a setting in which there was little to buy. Even in this situation, however, some private camps liked to feel they were one step ahead of the pack. Looking back, Bert Danson claimed that Winnebagoe was able to select not just any high school students but those from the "best" neighbourhoods and schools.[87]

Private camps were also influenced by heightened levels of patriotism throughout Canadian society and, accordingly, encouraged (or compelled) campers to make various wartime contributions. From the Statten camps, Statten's daughter and wartime administrator, Adele Ebbs, reported that campers (presumably girls) were sewing and knitting for the war effort, just as women and girls were doing back in the cities. The Statten camp administration also took steps towards conservation, adjusting the materials used in camp handicrafts as well as "eliminating bread and butter at noon dinner" and "restricting bacon and jam at some specified meals." Given the state of things in the broader society, these don't sound like overly stringent measures. Interestingly, one American camper recalls that, during the Second World War, "the food was much better at [Ahmek] than [what] we were able to obtain in the States."[88] Senior campers were called on to make the most substantial contributions. In the mid-1940s, the province set up the Wartime Rangers Program, which drew on the labour of capable youth at Algonquin and Temagami camps. Boys and girls alike were asked to perform the duties of park rangers for the duration of the conflict. Under the program at Camp Tanamakoon, girls "checked visitors' licences ... undertook fire protection, the maintenance of portages, and the construction of docks, fireplaces, shelters, and new campsites" over a four-mile stretch of river and portages.[89]

The years following the war were generally good ones for the life and growth of private camps in Ontario. The title of Peter Newman's 1954 article on the success of Canadian summer camps – "Junior's $10 Million Adventure in the Pines" – really was referring to these camps. In postwar years, private camps met with a steady supply of campers, while conveniences and amenities seemed only to multiply. Efforts to enhance the dining experience and to assure parents of the quality of camp food provide just one example. In 1946, a Winnebagoe brochure stated that the camp kitchen was handled by "an expert chef and dietician," while postwar promotional literature from Ahmek explains that "railway express and refrigerator truck service from Toronto" brought in daily shipments of all manner of fresh food. A detailed description of the food served at Tamakwa in the 1950s suggests a clear contrast with both the fresh air and the agency camp:

> Prepared by a devoted staff of sixteen people ... [the food] has to be good ... Bread and milk is delivered fresh daily. Fruit and vegetables are brought in from Toronto twice weekly. Beef, veal, butter, cheese, fish, eggs and poultry arrive each week and are stored in large walk in refrigerators. Ice cream is served on an average of four times each week. All baked goods, cakes, pies, rolls, biscuits, cookies and pastries are baked in our modern bakery – including birthday cakes and special award cakes.[90]

At this and at least several other prestigious private camps, campers could also expect their dining experience to be enhanced by the "waiters and waitresses," sometimes "maids," who attended to their needs. Quality of food and the dining experience were clearly considered markers of class, a fact that was starkly illustrated by another incident at Ahmek. According to one history of the camp, on one occasion, a bear was caught and killed and bear meat turned up on the dinner menu. However, the camp administration seemed all too aware that, as Tina Loo explains, eating game meat in the twentieth century was considered a mark of low class standing. In this case, the business manager felt that the bear meat could be consumed but only if served alongside "the very best spring lamb" since he "would not have it said that the camp was living off free food from the Park."[91]

In postwar years, as previously, amenities of all sorts reminded campers at an unconscious level that people of their sort were deserving of the best. At their simple life pursuits, campers exerted themselves with the aid of fleets of canoes, sailboats, and rowboats, while, at an increasing number of camps, they treated themselves to hot showers to soothe whatever aches their exertions induced.[92] Into the postwar years, amenities increased at many private camps; by the 1950s, Tamakwa was boasting a "sailing fleet of fourteen boats," sixty-eight canvas canoes, equipment for waterskiing, three asphalt tennis courts "near the edge of the lake," an archery range, basketball and volleyball courts, and shuffleboard. At riding camps, not only the campers but even the animals came in for quality treatment. Winnebagoe brochures boasted that stables were "equipped with electricity and running water throughout" and that horses were fed only "the finest of hay and the highest grade of crushed oats."[93]

Improving amenities was all part of the larger goal of building the reputation of one's camp, something that mattered deeply to both administrations and campers in postwar years. Superlatives were the lingua franca of this select camping community: claims to being first, best, oldest were ongoing.[94] Some campers developed attachments and a sense of loyalty to camps that rivalled loyalties to universities and colleges. In the 1950s, one American ex-pat and former camper at Camp Kawagama put it this way: "In the States ... when you meet someone you always ask, What college did you go to? In Canada, it's, What camp?!"[95] At Ahmek, references to camp as a beloved "northwoods alma mater" suggest that others saw this parallel. It seems possible that announcing that one had attended a camp of renowned reputation acted as real cultural capital later in life, a badge from which others could deduce one's relative status. One wonders whether sociologist Wallace Clement's comment that "to participate in [elite] club life is to be known by those who count" might equally be said of these camps.[96]

As private camps' foundations grew more solid and their reputations assured, they also attracted increasing numbers of international campers in postwar years. As they had done before the war, Americans continued to make up a substantial and influential portion of these. Though a minority at most camps (except those run by and for Americans), they made their presence known. In postwar years at Winnebagoe, American campers were able to convince director Bert Danson to fly the American flag alongside the Union Jack. In these years of general affluence and increased consumption, American campers sometimes also set the fashion tone for other campers. Of Camp Kawagama, Geraldine Sherman recalls, "the best boys and most fashionable girls came from Buffalo." She describes the city's postwar reputation in the minds of Canadian campers, who were dazzled by its opportunities for consumption: "[It] existed in Ontario mythology as a stylish mecca for shopping and Sunday drinking. Kids from Buffalo set the sartorial standard. One year, they came with white wool Adler socks, madras plaid Bermuda shorts and little white dickies. The following year, it was no socks, khaki cut-offs and neckerchiefs. It was hard to keep up."[97] New predominantly "all-American" camps also continued to be founded in Ontario in the postwar years as Americans considered their own wilderness increasingly hard to find. Camp Tamakwa, founded in the postwar period, explained that its highest concentration of campers were from the cities of Detroit and Buffalo (along with Toronto).[98]

Certain Ontario camps also boasted clientele of more exotic origin, especially with the opening up of international travel in postwar years. In 1950, a Statten camps brochure claimed that campers were drawn from not only a number of eastern seaboard states but also from points as far away as "Europe, South America, Mexico, the West Indies and Hawaii."[99] Three years later, in his journalistic exposé of the economics of camping, Peter C. Newman noted that "regular attendance from South America is the boast of many Canadian camps."[100] The recently founded Tamakwa was also proud to claim clientele from around the world. In no particular order, a postwar brochure explained that campers hailed "from places as far removed as New York and California and Sault Ste. Marie, Ontario, and Rome, Georgia and many places in between."[101] Such campers likely made up only a small portion of the overall camp population, but success in attracting even a few such far-away clients was offered as more evidence of the high calibre of these enterprises.

When considering distinct groups of campers in the postwar period, Jewish children represent another interesting case. Certainly, in the wake of the horrors of the Holocaust and with the rise of notions of cultural pluralism, postwar years saw increased discussion of "respect" for "ethnic" communities.[102] How much this altered the experience of Jewish North Americans is another question. We know that in the postwar period, the

Jewish community continued to patronize distinctly Jewish camps throughout North America. In fact, a number of new, predominantly Jewish camps were founded in Ontario in the immediate postwar years. On the other hand, Jewish campers also continued to turn up at predominantly non-Jewish private camps in postwar years. Some, apparently, felt quite comfortable there. Interviews with former campers suggest that Jewish campers enjoyed their stay at predominantly non-Jewish camps, but they also suggest that these camps were sometimes used as a way to integrate into the cultural mainstream and to distance oneself from what some still considered to be the socially undesirable label of Jewish. As others have argued of elite private schooling, James Felstiner now believes that his parents sent him to summer camp as a means of cultural "integration," a way to ensure that others would see him "more as American than Jewish."[103] He himself thrived on his camp experience and later counted Ahmek as, "after my parents ... the most significant positive influence on my life."[104] Feeling at home, however, was not something to be taken for granted. One ex-camper who attended Wapomeo in the late 1940s expressed a relieved gratitude when "no big deal was made of my being Jewish," though she confided she never knew whether this wasn't due to her WASP-sounding name – "Blake" – which her father had changed (from "Bloom") for just such reasons.[105] Indeed, other evidence suggests that, even as Jewish children were admitted to these camps, administrators sometimes regarded them as a group apart. Taylor Statten's daughter, Adele Ebbs, recalls having "a lot of Jews in camp," some of them on staff. When one such senior staff member complained about the lack of Sabbath observance for Jewish campers, nothing was done, but, in Ebbs's words, "They didn't seem to mind."[106] She also remembers the year she had "so many 13-year-old Jewish girls" at Wapomeo that she put them all in one cabin, something that also happened at Ahmek.[107] She felt it necessary to apologize to the father for this situation, adding, "I presume the reason you send Rebecca to camp is because we are a Gentile camp otherwise you would send her to a Jewish camp." The father, perhaps feeling some irritation, responded: "Don't be silly, I send her to Wapomeo because it is the best camp." Incidents such as these reminded Jewish campers and staff that, even when they themselves felt right at home, others might not be viewing them in precisely the same light.

The sense that there were clear insiders and outsiders at these private camps continued into the postwar years in other ways as well. Building impressive reputations sometimes also involved distancing from those who had not. Private campers' sense of superiority extended in a number of directions. An air of friendly competition always existed between members of different private camps, with campers being keenly aware of the fine distinctions between their camp and the next. Statten camp alumni still claim they can spot one of their own simply by observing their canoeing skills. The art was to "paddle 'Indian style,'" one former Wapomeo camper explained in 2000, "which is not taking your paddle out of the water and bringing it down but a smooth stroke where you hardly raise your arm. And we always kneeled in the canoe. You never [sat] on the seat."[108] Administrators encouraged this self-conscious approach, instructing children that they functioned as ambassadors for their camps when out tripping. "The name of Camp Wapomeo should be upheld by our own trippers," they were reminded in 1963. "In this way it will gain the respect of others and be an example to those who have not had the same opportunity for training, experience and expert leadership."[109]

When these camps thought of setting "an example" for others, however, it was more likely campers who had never attended a private camp that they had in mind. Interviews suggest that the private camp community as a whole was highly conscious, for instance, of the contrast between fresh air camps and their own. With few amenities and barely outside the reach of large urban centres, fresh air camps made no claim to "the North," to "wilderness," or to the "roughing it" camp experience. Bert Danson, postwar director of Camp Winnebagoe, gave his opinion of fresh air camp directors in 1973: "Many of [them] were ... 'do-gooders' who wanted to help these poor unfortunate children. They really had no knowledge as to how to run a camping program ... They just got the kids out of the city, to a country setting where the children could swim ... play baseball and have campfires. Basically, that's all."[110] Private campers who had experience of both settings agreed that the two types of camps were distinctly different. "There's no comparison at all," Marjorie Royce explained of private Glen Bernard (where she was a camper) and Bolton fresh air camp (where she later worked as a counsellor). When asked to elaborate in our interview of 2000, she admitted the main difference was "the wealth, of course ... They didn't have canoeing or sailing or anything like that."[111] Breaking into these select communities as an outsider was not always easy, even if one had the money. In certain cases, returning campers were given priority over others. In 1949, the Ahmek administration explained that new campers were not permitted to apply until after mid-December, the aim being to "protect" former campers "from disappointment."[112]

Anyone connected with camping in these years knew that not all camps were alike, a fact that sometimes generated tensions in the camp movement. There is evidence, for instance, that agency camps may have sometimes resented the outlook of private camp administrations. In 1954, when rumours circulated that the YMCA's Camp Pine Crest was a subsidized venture, the administration was highly offended. The director's response to the situation revealed not only an insistence on being seen as distinct from the fresh air institution but also some tensions with their private camp cousins:

> We have found that in a number of homes ... parents have been informed through Camp [K...], that Camp Pine Crest was a subsidized operation. In each case this interpretation raised concern in the minds of the parents involved about sending their boys to Pine Crest, as they are not anxious to have their boys' camping supported by the community ... It would seem to us quite unethical for an organized private camp to stress the fact that another organizational camp was subsidized in an effort to enlist campers.[113]

From the perspective of the cultural historian, camps of all types shared some common features. For those living at the time, however, it was often the differences that were most keenly felt.

Assessing Impact

More than any other type of camp, private institutions were likely to have an impact on the children who attended them. One reason for this is, quite simply, a matter of time. As we've seen, during the first half of the twentieth century, children at private camps frequently spent their entire summers at camp, much longer than the time campers spent at either fresh air or agency camps. At Bolton fresh air camp, ten days was the typical time allotted to those fortunate enough to make it on the camp rolls, the idea being, of course, to provide holidays for the largest possible number. Agency camps, for their part, typically set their fees according to weekly increments, revealing, at the very least, that parents had the option of sending children for just one week – something private camps rarely offered. Though evidence from the YMCA's Camp Pine Crest and the YWCA's Tapawingo suggests that the typical camper stayed approximately three weeks in the early 1950s, at many other agency camps, stays were likely shorter.[114] Clearly, Taylor Statten's statement that children spent more hours under adult supervision at summer camp than they did during the entire year at school generally applied only to these private camps. Compounding the private camp's influence was the fact that many campers returned year after year. During the 1920s it was estimated that, each year at Ahmek, more than half of the boys were return campers. Similar situations prevailed at other private camps. At Temagami, it was noted in 1924 that "the majority of the 'old crowd,' staff and boys, [are] returning"; a Winnebagoe brochure explained in 1946 that "the vast majority of the campers return from year to year"; while a camper at Keewaydin during the 1940s and 1950s recalled, "It was a pretty stable population."[115]

For children who spent long weeks at camp and who returned year after year, the camp's impact could be significant. The weakening of what, in some cases, must have been already distant parent-child relationships was likely one of the results. Especially for private school students, spending much, if not all, of the summer at camp and the rest of the year at boarding school must have reduced the importance of "home" even further in their experience. Outside the realm of promotional literature, well-to-do parents were, in fact, frequently reproached for using camp as a convenient dumping ground for their children. Directors were quite candid in noting that parental motives for sending children to camp did not always coincide with their own. Winnebagoe's director, Bert Danson, admitted: "A lot of kids went to camp because their parents wanted to get rid of them ... get them out of the way so they could spend more time on the golf course."[116] The assumption that children were unwanted intrusions on the summer schedules of wealthy parents was commonplace in these years, as even grown children later recognized. "A child was a bit of a nuisance around the city," is how Mary Northway looked back on the years of her own childhood in the 1910s and 1920s.[117] In her eyes, camp represented "the ideal solution for *them* as to what to do with a twelve-year-old only, very spoilt child while they played golf and looked after the family business."[118] Shirley Ford, a Glen Bernard camper from the 1940s, agreed: "Most of the kids who stayed for two months were boarding school kids ... You don't want a thirteen-year-old hanging around so they go to boarding school, they go to camp."[119]

In this regard, camps quite unintentionally helped shape the nature of affluent childhood. Administrators, it seems, faced something of a catch-22. On the one hand, they were critical of parents' lack of meaningful contact with their children; on the other, they regarded their own influence as highly beneficial. By offering lengthy camp stays, these camps inadvertently increased the child's distance from home. Parents, for their part, were apparently confident that staff at camps with the right reputations would provide adequate care for their (sometimes very young) children. Suggesting yet another parallel with private schooling, as Northway again put it, "parents trusted the people who were running the school or camp."[120] If administrators and campers' parents did not always share the same motives, their relationship was symbiotic, with each having an interest in getting children to camp.

While reducing the influence of the familial home, the private camp also created a special "home away from home" for its campers. In this spirit, administrators worked actively throughout the year to create a sense of camp community and to sustain connections that would ensure return customers. To this end, reunions, fall picnics, and cabin group parties were successfully organized. During the winter of 1930, Wapomeo campers in Toronto, Guelph, and Montreal (in the latter case, described as "a crowd of young ladies – the elite of [the city]") reunited to "renew camp friendships."[121] Tanamakoon and Glen Bernard also arranged mid-year get-togethers, luncheons, and teas for their girls, while Ahmek literature described a whole host of ways that year-round loyalties were fostered in 1929:

> The memories of camp life are kept alive throughout the year by such things as: reunions of campers; regular meetings of tent groups, where enough members live in one community; correspondence between boys and between counsellors and boys; the regular edition of the camp paper; the availability of movie films taken in the camp, and in many cases contact with "the Chief" [Taylor Statten].[122]

Keeping up year-round connections ensured that the opening of each new summer session largely entailed the meeting of old friends and only a few introductions to strangers. Often, bonds made early in one's camping career endured for many years. Of her more than ten years at Wapomeo starting in 1927, Elizabeth Shapiro remembers, "I was cabinmates with a group of girls, mainly from Toronto and we were a real clique who remained together summer after summer."[123] Likewise, in our interview in 2000, Shirley Ford explained, with regard to the good friends she made at Glen Bernard in 1942, "I went through my camp life with them."[124] In the minds of such children, camp was more than just summering vacation space: it was the site of intense friendships, a fact that bonded them all the more to their "northwoods" summer homes. At Ahmek, it was said that campers like these took "sophomoric pride in being 'old campers' and [were] eager historians and interpreters of Ahmek's past and future."[125]

One of the greatest shows of loyalty was the decision to return as a counsellor, a not unusual occurrence at private camps. At Tanamakoon, it was estimated that, on average, counsellors returned for two or three summers, but there were also "many who stayed on five or six, some even for ten or eleven."[126] Statistics for other camps were not easy to come by, but impressionistic evidence suggests that it was not children alone who developed fierce attachments to these micro-communities in the woods. Certainly, the establishment of CIT programs helped to formalize the transition from camper to staff. Serving as staff once past the years of childhood was, for many, an ideal way to pursue their love relationship with camp for many more years. When James Felstiner, who attended Ahmek for four years during the Second World War, began to think about summer work in 1953, his desire to work with boys meant, as he put it, that "Ahmek was the only place I considered." Later a successful lawyer and judge, in 2001, he still looked back on camp work in the 1950s as "perhaps the happiest work I have ever done."[127]

For some, the intensity of feeling was heightened by the finding of more literal love relationships at camp. In addition to young crushes and teenage flirtation, romances – some leading to marriage – were a common phenomenon at these elite institutions, another route to the solidification of class ties. This may well have been true of other less prestigious camps, but here lengthy stays and annual returns were particularly conducive to the formation of solid bonds. Most commonly these romances were between staff members, but for campers who grew from childhood to adolescence and sometimes early adulthood together, it was also natural to look for life partners from among the camp population. As Winnebagoe's director recalled, for those who returned year after year, sometimes from ages eight to sixteen: "They knew each other throughout the years. Some of them were boy-girlfriends at 14, 15 and they carried on their romances."[128] Before the Second World War, Winnebagoe was unique among these early camps for being coeducational, but staff members of the opposite sex still came into contact at other camps. As more camps turned to coeducational programs in postwar years, more options presented themselves for heterosexual romance. The very fact of one's presence at any of these camps more or less guaranteed one's respectable class and family background, a precondition for a well-made match.

Administrators evinced a certain acceptance, even tacit encouragement, of such liaisons, certainly among counsellors and staff. While Winnebagoe administrations sometimes frowned on overt displays of affection among such couples – for example, discouraging hand-holding – generally speaking, prohibitions against boyfriend-girlfriend attachments did not exist at this camp. Far from it, Joan Moses, who attended Winnebagoe in the early 1940s, admitted: "They promoted them, in a way." And this may also have been true at other camps. Indeed, at Winnebagoe, no effort was made to control the behaviour of counselling staff once off duty. Postwar director Bert Danson freely informed his staff: "In the evening, when you have your time off, that's your time off. What you do ... is none of my affair."[129] As Elizabeth Shapiro recalls, spending leisure hours together was also common practice among male and female counsellors at Ahmek and Wapomeo in the 1920s and 1930s. Such time spent together clearly aided in the development of close bonds. So much so, it seems, that the relative frequency with which counsellors paired up at Winnebagoe elicited a certain mock criticism. The reminiscences of Danson – expressed in heavily gendered terms – are illustrative:

> Let's be honest. A lot of girls went there looking for husbands. Strangely, a lot of them found husbands there too. As a matter of fact ... we were just reminiscing about how many Winnebagoe romances there have been over the years. There have been quite a few. We don't say to the girls, "Come to Winnebagoe and find a husband," but it has happened.[130]

Whatever the case as to who was "hunting" whom, the evidence confirms that "many matches were made" at these camps. In some cases, as at Temagami, such couples were willing to share that typically private institution – the honeymoon – with the entire camp community.[131] Camp memories and family histories could, in such ways, become intimately entwined.

Identification with private camps went beyond the days of youth in other ways. Where camp marriages resulted in children, camp loyalty could be quite literally "reproduced," with ex-campers sending offspring back to the camps of their youth. In such cases, camp often claimed a central place in the family history, alongside traditions of loyalty to schools and universities. In camp histories, these children were proudly referred to as "second-generation campers" and "the first grandsons of the camp."[132] Even for those who never found true love there or sent children back in turn, it was not uncommon to develop life-long attachments that manifested themselves in a number of ways. At Ahmek, the alumni newsletter produced a substantial following, claiming six hundred "paid up subscribers" in 1931. In the same year, editor Ron Perry was happy to state that "the campers, counsellors, 'old boys' and 'old girls' seem to enjoy the issues and are prepared to back up the magazine with subscriptions."[133] Many "alumni" – as they were tellingly called – reconnected more literally with their camps, returning for visits in adult years. Administrators at Ahmek helped to formalize these with the institution of "September Adult camp," which functioned as an annual camp reunion for many "old boys and girls." The life-long friendships such initiatives nurtured were a feature not just of this but of many select private camps. Looking back in 2000, one camper at Arowhon during the 1940s and 1950s was unequivocal about the importance of camp and the friends she made there:

> Some of the best days of my life were spent at camp. I was, don't forget, an only child. This was like having so many sisters – it was wonderful ... [T]he camaraderie is a lifelong memory ... Many of the friendships I made at camp have lasted until this day. I am in touch with a few on a very regular basis, others, more infrequently, some hardly ever, but could call any one of them in their city and bring back the past immediately. Camp, especially Arowhon, has had a profound influence on my life.[134]

James Felstiner, who describes Ahmek as "a vital force" in his life, states simply: "The friends I made at camp have been and continue to be our closest friends."[135] It seems that Felstiner and others had caught what some called "Ahmekitis," a disease "as easy to catch as an Algonquin trout and as hard to shake as a highway motor cop." In 1931, the editor of the camp newsletter elaborated on the nature of this unique affliction:

> Its symptoms are unmistakable. A boundless energy, physical and mental "pep," and the development of a state known to authorities on personality as "poise" ... There is really no cure for the affliction ... Many persons, apparently cured, have suffered complete relapses. These usually occur on or about the first day of Spring. Poking one's nose into [the camp newsletter] or receiving a large manila envelope marked with the magic words "Taylor Statten Camps" simply brings the illness on again with all its original violence.[136]

Those at other camps experienced a similar intensity of feeling. Nancy Shore, a 1950s Kawagama camper, admitted later in her life: "I would love to see that space again. I try to tell [my husband] about camp, and he just doesn't get it. That's when you know there are things in your life that are yours alone."[137]

Other now-grown campers have been drawn back not so much to the camps' physical space as to the geographic regions in which they were located. Their lives continue to be marked by the taste for "wilderness" and for outdoor adventures that these formative experiences first instilled. In the early 1970s, when Camp Temagami was shut down and the island sold off into smaller lots, one of its alumni, Ralph Barford, considered buying one. Deciding against it, he nevertheless made several return trips to the area, introducing his sons and, later, grandsons to the joys of Temagami tripping.[138] For her part, as an adult Joan Moses still considered a gentle canoe ride the only way to experience the natural world, whether with others or all on her own. "I hate motor boats," she explained, adding, "I love the peace and quiet and the individuality of canoeing."[139]

If attachment to these forest communities was meant to make future life easier for ex-campers, a glimpse at their later lives confirms that *something* was indeed smoothing the way. Like private schools, camps were never shy in outlining and taking partial credit for the successes of their alumni, especially where that involved notoriety of one kind or another. Administrators were especially proud of the politicians who emerged from their midst. Though clearly this occurred years after the experiences of childhood, some credited camp with first developing the skills that facilitated entry into the political realm. At Tanamakoon, Director Mary Hamilton claimed: "Some ... gained mastery of their shyness, others were grateful for their start in public speaking."[140] Whatever the case, Temagami claimed later prime minister John Turner among its ex-campers – an association of which Turner himself was said to be "very proud" – while Ahmek boasted the likes of Pierre Trudeau and David Lewis among its alumni.[141] Interestingly, Trudeau's biographers explain his appearance at Ahmek as "part of the gentrification process that the Trudeaus underwent" and as the ten-year-old Pierre's "first protracted encounter with the world of the Canadian upper-middle class."[142] Whatever the role camp played in shaping Trudeau's suitability for, and choice to enter, politics, having such important figures among its camp alumni didn't hurt its claim to be turning out "men of ability" and the "most promising citizens."

Private camp alumni also succeeded in other realms of Canadian society, claiming positions of relative prestige and influence. As administrators were not shy of informing the public, prominent Ahmek families included the Eatons, Westons, Molsons, and "members of the Labatt brewing empire family."[143] Of Winnebagoe, Director Bert Danson explained that "we have so many prominent people today who were campers of ours," among them "multi-multi-millionaire" Murray Koffler, two judges, and a brain surgeon "down at the Toronto General."[144] In general terms, Temagami boasted that "Cochrane's campers are to be found around the world."[145]

Camps made the most of such examples, but we are safe in assuming that not every camper became a millionaire industrialist or political success story. Still, even those of the merely aspiring middle class likely left their camp years more polished, socially "connected," and better prepared, perhaps even more likely, to lead lives of privilege. In a general way, ex-campers credit their experiences with developing valuable confidence and leadership skills, as administrators hoped. "I believe the effects on me were long-lasting," Elizabeth Shapiro asserted of her time at Wapomeo in the 1920s and 1930s, "the friendships, the happy memories, the confident feeling that I could cope with most every adverse event."[146] Another Wapomeo camper agreed: "Camp gave me confidence to accept leadership for the rest of my life."[147] Camp forays in democracy clearly helped some to build this solid base of confidence, if not always political careers. Susan Morgan recalls being chosen "by secret ballot" as a "Colour War" captain at the end of camp season as "the ultimate affirming experience ... I'm sure people who get elected to Parliament don't feel better than I [did]."[148] In all of these cases – of the later publicly prominent or the merely privately contented – it would clearly be naïve to suggest that camp alone gave children the tools to succeed. It was, however, one more instrument in the tool kit that laid the foundation for early twentieth-century upper-class formation.

In the fall of 1987, in the pages of Hamilton's major daily, J.F. Conway described the seemingly novel emergence of a summer camp for "capitalist kids."[149] In his wry account, entitled "Why Can't Summer Camp Just Be, Well, Summer Camp?" Conway described the "corporate training" offered at one $2,000-per-week Palm Beach camp, where, aside from acquainting themselves with bourgeois sporting activities, campers explored the intricacies of the stock market and closed their days with "five-course dinners." The point of comparison, as the title suggests, is clearly with the good old "more modest and traditional ... camp" of the author's own youth, where camp life presumably entailed nothing more than good fun in the sun, a few memorable cabin raids, and the acquisition of several new pen-pals.

Clearly, what Conway didn't know when he wrote his article was that the use of the camp as a tool of class formation was nothing new in the late twentieth century. On the contrary, private camps had been shaping bourgeois and upper-class culture for more than a half century before he put pen to paper. Conway can, perhaps, be forgiven his ignorance since, in the late twentieth century, such institutions in Ontario were not typically shouting their exclusivity from the rooftops. They were more likely to go quietly about their business, counting on past histories and carefully worded brochures (and fee scales) to draw in the appropriate campers.

Whatever the concern with appearances of inclusivity, the shaping of a sense of shared interests, values, and experiences – in short, of a class culture – was both object and, to a great extent, outcome of the private camp experience. Far from escaping the bounds of civilization, for many, the backwoods experience reinforced lessons of class learned back home in upscale urban neighbourhoods and elite private schools. Along the way, it also helped shape a class taste for a very particular, pared down wilderness experience – the antidote to high-pressure jobs and the strains of modern social and economic success. Indeed, in their enthusiasm for back-to-nature, "roughing it"-style camps, Canada's privileged classes showed that they were both directors, in many ways, of modernity's forces and the quintessential antimodern consumers. As young campers indulged in unique outdoor adventures, surrounded by campers of similar class backgrounds and guided by those who sought to raise the next generation of social leaders, they would not only learn these lessons but would be bonded to, and supported by, others who had learned them as well. These tight friendships, whatever they meant personally, also, if unconsciously, functioned as strong class solidarities. If these camps consisted of any real egalitarianism, it was a democracy of elite peers, a kind of socialism for the rich. Whatever the boasts of individual achievement and hard work, the reality was that the future success of these youth was dependent on a host of social connections, insider information, and acquired skills. In the early decades of the twentieth century, the private camp was one site in which these connections were fostered and such skills acquired; for a minority of youth, the private camp experience provided a unique and important aspect of their class formation.

3

"All they need is air": Building Health, Shaping Class at the Fresh Air Camp

On 23 July 1925, the *Toronto Daily Star* quoted one happy camper who offered his opinion of the fresh air camp he attended:

> Any boy who comes to this camp is made as happy as possible ... There is system and organization at every turn ... The boys sleep in tents, which are in two even rows ... When it is time to get up [the director] ... blows a whistle about six-thirty in the morning. We are given about ten minutes to get dressed and find our soap and towel. He then blows another whistle and we line up in groups ... We then walk down to the lake for a wash ... At eight we line up for breakfast and march to the cookhouse for our plate of food ... After breakfast we have physical exercise, games and the camp is cleaned up by the boys ... [At the end of the day] we are lined up again for evening prayer and about half past nine we are all in bed.[1]

This article was only one of hundreds that had been singing the praises of the fresh air camp and bemoaning the plight of Toronto's poor in the pages of the *Toronto Daily Star* since 1901. Appeals like these were a major tool in the fund-raising efforts of the *Star*'s Fresh Air Fund, whose object was to send deprived "slum kiddies" to camp. As widely proclaimed, fresh air camps were meant to provide healthy, enjoyable holidays for children (and mothers) who endured the worst of urban conditions. Fresh air camps were more than just fun, however. Their clear concern with order and regimentation, as revealed above, points to objectives that existed at only an implicit, perhaps unconscious, level. Even while offering recreational

Campers at Bolton Camp taking a break, c. 1920. Because children like these generally spent only ten days at fresh air camps, Bolton Camp, the largest of them, was able to accommodate thousands of children each summer during the interwar and postwar years. *Copyright Family Service Association of Toronto.*

good times, camp programming was calculated to infuse working-class culture with middle-class values. Interestingly, this did not mean that most children or their families experienced camp as an unwanted intrusion. Whatever its true authorship, the above article points to a fundamental truth: namely, that children went to fresh air camp intending to have "as happy [a time] as possible," many finding their expectations fulfilled. Not all who attended these camps were as enthusiastic as the young author above; some even avoided being sent there. Still, a good many mothers and children welcomed these camp holidays, savoured their two weeks at camp, and sought out ways to return. This chapter explores their experience, tracing the fund-raising of the Toronto Star Fresh Air Fund as well as the history of Ontario's largest fresh air institution, Bolton Camp.

The fresh air phenomenon represented a different world of camping from that of the private or agency camp. Most obviously, it served a completely different clientele. Fresh air campers were the objects of charity; they and others were well aware of this fact. The inclusion of mothers and infants at certain fresh air camps was another obvious and telling difference, highlighting the unique objectives of the fresh air institution. The point here was not simply to socialize children but to rehabilitate a class. Directors of private camps may have sought to influence the running of the upper-class home and agency camps to bring new influences to bear on the middle class, but they had only indirect ways of achieving this. Fresh air camps, on the other hand, by also accommodating mothers at camp, multiplied the ways in which they could influence the working-class family. In the case of both mothers and children, the class gap between administrator and camper shaped the nature of programming, while the charitable nature of these camps set limits on the fun they could provide.

Fresh air camps differed from private and agency camps, but, like their more illustrious cousins, they exhibited ambivalence towards the fruits of modern culture. In this case, however, this did not manifest as hostility towards modern comforts or as a desire for "roughing it" experiences. Fresh air camp workers and supporters were bothered, instead, by the very existence of their target clientele, the under- and unemployed urban poor. This class was considered not only as a blight on the landscape of modern industrial progress but also as one of its direct results. Poor children were understood to be modernity's most vulnerable victims, those who exposed, in the starkest manner, the dark side of modern economic growth. And yet the fresh air camp was not simply antimodern in its outlook. As fresh air administrators sought to alleviate the stresses of urban poverty, they relied on the principles of modern social work to guide them. Industrial efficiency may have created their problems, but efficiently modern social service work might now solve them. More than this, the appearance and flourishing of fresh air camps bolstered the quintessentially modern belief that life should include regular and gratifying bouts of leisure, even for the nation's poorest citizens.

The summer of 1901 was a sweltering one in Toronto. Many were unbearably uncomfortable, but the young were hardest hit; several infants died. During the course of this immobilizing heat wave, Joseph Atkinson, editor of the *Toronto Daily Star* and local philanthropist, conceived of a plan to help these most vulnerable of Toronto's citizens to escape the city's heat. With a number of nearby camps already in operation, Atkinson set about establishing a central fund to raise monies for their assistance.[2] From that point on, the *Toronto Star* Fresh Air Fund used the paper to make its daily appeals throughout that summer and every summer after that, up until the present day.

Atkinson's initiative was not conceived of in a vacuum. The fresh air camp's focus on physical welfare was in keeping with broader concerns with public health, which emerged in the late nineteenth century and gained momentum in the interwar years. Indeed, since the establishment of the province's first department of health in 1882, the issue had come to be seen as a matter of not only individual but also national well-being, with children regarded as the movement's logical starting point. School medical inspections were one of the early initiatives undertaken. In addition to provincial initiatives, the federal government attempted to do its part in 1920 by establishing the quasi-public National Council of Child Welfare, which focused a good deal of its efforts on health-related matters. As a broad movement, public health initiatives did much to improve the lives of Canadians. Though some question the bourgeois perspective of health promoters, Neil Sutherland argues that, "of all the reform efforts for children ... the public health movement had the most immediate, the least ambiguous, and the most precisely measurable positive effects."[3]

Concerns over public health had both their modern and antimodern aspects. Improving health conditions for the mass of the people was very much a modern initiative. In earlier centuries, almost everyone had been forced to accept disease, weather, and poor housing conditions as unavoidable aspects of life. The belief that health should and could be improved was reflective of the more general belief in human perfectibility and progress. Still, there were antimodern aspects to child health initiatives, not least because the modern industrial city was proving unhealthy in so many respects. This view shaped fresh air movements in Europe, England, Australia, and New Zealand. Indeed, from the late nineteenth century to the mid-twentieth century, Western medical opinion strongly advocated the curative properties of fresh air, a view that inspired changes in hospital architecture, the development of new spas and resorts, and experimentation with open-air schools.[4] Located in bucolic country settings, these schools were frequently designed under medical direction, allowing education to occur in open-air settings.[5] In Canada, precedents also existed for this back-to-nature charity work. As early as the 1880s, with the inauguration of the Children's Aid Society (CAS), individuals like J.J. Kelso began taking groups of children on day excursions to the Toronto Islands. During the same period, the CAS's belief in the curative properties of fresh air and nature was also revealed in its preference for rural foster homes for dependent and neglected children.[6]

If Ontario fresh air camps were not unique in their orientation, they were so in scope. The achievements of the *Star*'s Fresh Air Fund offer one way to measure the growth and expansion of the fresh air enterprise. From its humble beginnings – in its first summer, raising $1,000 to send children on nearby day picnics – the *Star* intensified its efforts so that, by 1918, it was raising sufficient monies to send over 1,800 children to camp and "twice as many" by the following year. By 1922, the fund was assisting seventeen camps and, by 1928, thirty. In terms of the numbers accommodated, the 1920s also saw substantial growth, when between six thousand and seven thousand children, mothers, and babies were sent to camp each summer. Over the next twenty-five years, the *Star* helped send between nine thousand and thirteen thousand children to camp each summer. While total numbers are difficult to gauge, the *Star* itself estimated in 1936 that the fund had aided over 500,000 children (and mothers) since its inception. Even if we allow for the fact that a certain number of these were return campers and that others were only sent on day picnics, the extent of the fund's reach appears impressive indeed. Clearly, in the interwar, wartime, and early postwar years, the fresh air experience was one that touched significant numbers of Ontario's working class.[7]

The Institutional Environment

In the strictest sense, fresh air camps of all varieties were the outgrowth of early twentieth-century charity work. Many of these works were conducted by religious groups, offshoots of the array of denominations functioning in the province at the time. For instance, in 1922, the list of groups receiving support for their camps from the *Star*'s Fresh Air Fund included, among others, the Methodist Deaconess Home, the Church of England Deaconess Home, the Presbyterian Fresh Air Commission, and the Salvation Army. Non-Protestant religious groups, including the Catholic Boy Life Council and the Hebrew Maternal Aid Society, were also recipients of the fund's aid. In addition to these, a number of secular organizations, including the University Settlement House, the Central Neighbourhood House, and the Neighbourhood Workers' Association, ran camps that were supported by the *Star*'s fund. Apart from receiving the odd donation from the City of Toronto, the fund itself was fuelled entirely by private donations. Bolton Camp, run by the Neighbourhood Workers' Association from 1922 onwards, was by far the largest camp supported by the fund and, according to the camp itself, the largest fresh air institution on the continent. Given Bolton's proximity to Toronto, it is likely that a large proportion of the fund's campers hailed from the province's largest city.[8]

The fresh air camp phenomenon was rooted in the philanthropic tradition; it was also influenced by the emergence of professional social work. Again, antimodern solutions were devised using very modern tools. As Marianna Valverde points out, the transition to "scientific philanthropy" – what she defines as a blend of both traditional charity and emerging social service principles – was well under way by the eve of the First World War.[9] While Valverde's work demonstrates charity's influence on the emerging welfare state, the history of fresh air camps reveals that principles of modern social work also shaped twentieth-century charity. Indeed, fresh air work adopted a number of principles from the toolbox of scientific philanthropy, including a belief in the value of social investigation, detailed record-keeping, and the usefulness of categories of "deserving" and "undeserving" poor.[10] In 1920, the fund assured its public that: "Before the name of any child is listed to be sent to a camp ... the conditions surrounding the child's daily life are thoroughly investigated."[11] To help in this task, the Fresh Air Exchange was established in that same year, with its main objective being the ferreting out of "cheaters," those who weren't truly needy by the fund's definition, or who tried to get to camp more than once in a summer.[12] This kind of thinking represented the persistence of Victorian attitudes towards the poor; on the other hand, the establishment of a central registry of this sort was regarded as a boon for scientific efficiency:

> To this office will go all the names of children who are to go to fresh air homes. Here they will be checked and looked into to see there is no duplication and that only those coming within the objects of the fund are allowed to go ... it is expected it will be a perfect working machine and a clearing house for all applications ... The social workers are co-operating closely in the work.[13]

The strictest objectivity of those carrying out these duties was both valued and assumed. Appeals routinely constructed these workers as hard-nosed and practical, an implicit contrast with the supposed bleeding-heart charity workers of a previous era. Like the professional social workers James Pitsula has described, in 1940, these workers were portrayed in the *Star* as "technician[s] of human relations"; from their "cold and practical files," it was said, they "painstakingly prepare[d] the lists of children."[14]

Exposing the undeserving and keeping an objective distance tell part, but not all, of the story of fresh air camp work. Like social work itself, this work also revealed evidence of more progressive views on poverty. Clearly, workers who regularly witnessed the inadequate living conditions poor families faced couldn't help but feel compassion for aid recipients. In some cases, this allowed workers to get beyond an individualistic approach. Reflecting what Gale Wills has labelled the "minority radical tradition" in early social work, real efforts were sometimes made to explain that the poor were not to blame for their unhappy lot, as in this 1924 *Star* appeal:

> When you think of the word "underprivileged" in its relation to the children who are sent on summer vacations ... you must not run away with the idea that the parents are at fault. There may be many cases where there is reason to believe the parents could do better by the children than they do, but for the most part the children are underprivileged on account of circumstances beyond the control or beyond the comprehension of father and mother.[15]

A 1934 appeal was even more to the point. "Not all poverty ... in Toronto is due to inherent incompetence of the parents," though the writer was apparently aware that some were sceptical.[16] Over the years, and during periods of generally harsh attitudes towards the poor, this view revealed itself from time to time as *Star* writers showed a sensitivity to the issues of unemployment, illness, and inadequate housing. Given the broader social and political climate, this attempt at viewing the broader picture should not be overlooked, even if was not the opinion that always prevailed.[17]

The Neighbourhood Workers' Association (NWA), which ran Bolton Camp, provides a useful example of these broader trends. Though officially established in 1914 "as a charitable organization for the giving of the basic necessities of life to those in need," its mandate expanded under the influence of both a professional social work orientation and the simple desire to help. As stated in their own literature, the NWA sought "organized planning of the city's social work services," as was typical of early social work initiatives. Over the years, its work represented that blend of material assistance and lessons in self-help that marked social service work in general; it aided with distribution of municipal relief, provided used clothing and Christmas hampers to the needy, and ran a year-round clothing and sewing centre for mothers as well as educational and recreational clubs to entertain and "to provide healthy family interests." It was also involved in efforts to improve living conditions in more substantive ways, claiming to have played a major role in pushing for workmen's compensation, mothers' allowances, and unemployment insurance.[18]

In 1922, the NWA established Bolton Camp as one more recreational initiative to both entertain and provide new and "healthy interests." By choosing a location just outside Toronto, the association ensured that as many campers as possible would be accommodated at the lowest possible cost. From the start, both children and mothers (typically, with infant children) were welcomed at the camp. Making one's way to camp involved several steps. First, one had to attract the attention of social workers or otherwise get one's name on the lists of potential campers for the season. After that, one could expect to be "investigated" to establish one's neediness and, finally, if accepted for camp, to undergo a medical exam. Once at camp, one could expect to spend the next ten to twelve days doing what were considered typical "campy" activities. Though never offering fancy luxuries, Bolton was like other camps in providing instruction in swimming, arts and crafts, outdoor games, and introducing children to the joys of campfires, cook-outs, and "Indian" programming.

When the NWA founded Bolton Camp, it envisioned it not as an isolated recreational initiative but, rather, as part of the larger fabric of social service work in Ontario, as did the founders of other fresh air camps. Bolton may have been a separate space, but it was very much part of the NWA's overall mission – one more front in the battle on urban poverty. For example, work to reunite campers back in the city was explained in 1933 as efforts to "carry on some of the ideas developed at camp" and, ultimately, "to build together ... more closely the summer work and our winter programme of activities."[19] The *Star* offered a very similar explanation of the fresh air camp's purpose in 1924, describing it as "an integral part of the year-round work of the various welfare agencies," a place where "old social problems are met and mended in [a] new setting."[20]

Whether at the NWA or elsewhere, children figured prominently in this fight. Children, as far as public fund-raising went, were the members of the working class guaranteed to elicit sympathy. In contrast to possibly "shiftless" and "lazy" parents, who too often succumbed to bad attitudes, drink, and desertion, children were defended, again and again, as the innocent victims of circumstances beyond their control. In 1930, one writer admonished: "Don't blame the kids! Children are in no way to blame for the crowded, unsanitary, poverty-crushed, ill-smelling homes in which they find themselves."[21] In 1929, as if to underline the generational contrast, *Star* articles made a point of stating of unemployed fathers: "The *Star*

Fresh Air Fund is not worrying about the man," and, "The man can look after himself."[22] At the same time as many bourgeois onlookers blamed poor parents for their plight, new cultural attitudes towards children made more pitiable victims of their offspring. As in the case of Mothers' Allowance, maternal education campaigns, and early social work initiatives, camp was firmly defended as "in the interests of the children."[23] Only in such an atmosphere could the *Star* confidently declare in 1928: "Because the *Star* Fresh Air Fund is for the benefit of children, we have no hesitation in pleading its case."[24] Children, it seemed, were emerging as the one unquestionably deserving category of the poor.

Building Health, Elevating Tastes, and Adjusting Attitudes at Camp

Once public sympathy had been aroused for poor children trapped in urban squalor, how was summer camp promoted as the necessary corrective? Quite simply, in the interwar years, poor health was named as the most pressing problem of urban children and improving health as "one of the fundamentals of fresh air work."[25] Children with health problems, the public was repeatedly assured, topped the list of fresh air camp applications. Fresh air camps were by no means alone in their emphasis on health. Camps of all sorts were touted as healthy recreational options, and concern for health was part of many camp programs. Medical inspections before coming to camp and regular health inspections once there were common. Promotional brochures at all manner of camps routinely advised parents that medical staff was either on hand or nearby and that medical opinion was treated with unqualified respect. At the private camp Wabikon, the director warned staff in 1952: "You should never diagnose or offer treatment! We have a clinic and a competent medical staff. Consult them promptly at the first sign of something unusual ... no one doctors themselves, no one takes medicine OF ANY KIND without approval of the 'Doc.'"[26]

A vital difference, however, between fresh air camps and others was that most children at private and agency camps were relatively healthy already. Literature from these camps promised the enhanced health benefits of their programs, but they also spent a good deal of energy simply convincing parents that their children would not suffer a net *loss* of health at camp. Dozens of children living in close quarters could be the source of outbreaks of various sorts, while new activities undertaken raised the risk of accident. Parents of these campers clearly worried about the welfare of their children at camp and often hoped (especially with boys) to see them gain in strength and resourcefulness. As a group, however, they did not turn to camp as a primary way of addressing their children's health problems.

By contrast, from the start, the modus vivende of the fresh air camp was to raise the often low standard of campers' health. Documenting the unhealthy circumstances of poor families as well as the life-changing impact of camp was the bread and butter of the *Star*'s public appeals, especially in interwar years, when the biggest problem facing young campers was simple malnourishment. "Undernourished, underweight ... undersized ... [and] unfortunate" one 1920 appeal grimly alliterated, while another quantified the extent of the problem in 1935: "Approximately eighty per cent are underweight on arrival."[27] Linked to the lack of adequate nutrition, campers were found to exhibit a host of ailments and, sometimes, life-threatening diseases. In 1930, attempts to document the ravages of inadequate nutrition resulted in the following list: "diseased tonsils ... decayed teeth ... rickets ... enlarged glands ... anorexia nervosa ... rheumatic fever ... ear infections ... anemia ... lung conditions ... [and] skin disease."[28] While diphtheria and chronic bronchitis were also mentioned, when it came to disease, cases of tuberculosis – the scourge of poor families in the interwar years – were most frequently cited. In certain dire cases, health was so precarious that the possibility of deaths at camp could not be ruled out.[29]

In response to the prevalence of these ailments and diseases, camps promised the healing power of fresh air, something the city was understood to be lacking. Modern cities were the sites of industrial progress, but, as the *Star* put it in the 1920s, they also spawned "dust and grime and rank atmosphere,"[30] creating air they described as "an almost opaque compound of nauseating potency."[31] The notion that city air was suffocating the poor sometimes seemed to eclipse the reality of any other problems. The case of little, pathetic "Florrie," "pale and underweight," was typical. "The thing she supremely needs," it was summed up succinctly, "is fresh air."[32] Other appeals implied that Florrie was no special case but, rather, that "Every hour of the day, scores of little tots ... are literally starving for nothing more than fresh air."[33] Choice of this term as the primary descriptor for these camps was hardly accidental; it nicely described both the physical element and also the notion that a change of pace – a "breath of fresh air," so to speak – was all these children needed.

In addition to fresh air, campers were guaranteed sunshine and good food, other weapons in the fight against ill health and disease. In contrast to present-day fears, in these years, sunshine was regarded as almost wholly benign. "Sun tan is to be commended, provided there is not overexposure,"

Babies outside at Bolton Camp. Fresh air camps truly lived up to their name, offering even the youngest of campers their time out in the open. *Copyright Family Service Association of Toronto.*

declared Toronto's medical officer of health in 1932. Far from detrimental, sunshine was regarded as essential treatment for a number of childhood diseases, including bronchitis and rickets. Good food also had a role to play. Camps took great pride in providing children with large doses of fruit, vegetables, eggs, and other dairy products. However inconsequential we might now regard this brief change in diet, the Fund was clearly convinced that, by feeding campers well, it was providing a vital service. "Even two weeks of good food make an enormous difference in the physical [and] mental condition of the little victims of unemployment," it was confidently stated in 1922.[34]

Of all the foods available to campers, milk held special pride of place. The public was frequently reminded that milk was in generous supply at these camps. In 1928, it was stated that "rich milk for the babies is insisted upon" at one camp, while Bolton administrators proudly declared that no limit was placed on its consumption. Clearly, milk was valued for providing a relatively cheap source of protein, but it also took on symbolic importance at this camp. Milk was, in one sense, nature's perfect food, the infant's lifeline to survival. Never mind that milk consumed at camp was not of maternal origin; it nevertheless symbolized the fresh air camp's nurturing role. More than this, though "whiteness" came in for some (usually) mock questioning at camps, many positive connotations were also still associated with it.[35] Bolton's "milk circle" for the nursery-aged campers points to the powerful role milk played in the fresh air camp setting. "Milk is a very important part of the morning programme," the 1943 report explained. "The children sit in a circle on the grass, stories are read and songs sung before the milk is passed around. After it is over, the children, one by one, put their glasses on the tray and go off back to the toys." During that same summer – when total milk consumption tallied in at 38,660 quarts – the report went on to explain that milk was served "at mid-morning and mid-afternoon to campers who ... required extra nourishment."[36]

If fresh air camps envisioned something of a maternal role for themselves, they also sought the stamp of medical approval. As with other aspects of the camp project, those who sought antimodern escapes also valued the approval of modern experts. Fresh air institutions in Ontario, as elsewhere, were happy to claim the backing of the medical (and other) professions. "Not we alone," a *Star* journalist claimed in 1932, "but doctors, nurses, [and] social workers are unanimous in declaring that two weeks' holiday in the out-of-doors, with good, substantial, appetizing food and healthy surroundings, would revive and restore them to good health again."[37] The presence of medical personnel on staff at these camps further reinforced the image of a medically sound enterprise being under way. While camp doctors – certainly nurses – were common at many camps during this time, the role played by fresh air camp medical staff was unique. At Bolton, for instance, nurses were instructed not only to care for the medical needs of children while at camp but also "to study the individual case" and report back to the Department of Public Health or "other interested organizations" with regard to any physical conditions that became known at camp.[38] As with charity and social work more generally, camp intensified the statistical gaze focused on the poor, one that could be put to potentially controlling ends. Medical professionals were powerful individuals; their views on things mattered. When prominent neurologist Wray Barraclough commented on poverty's impact on children, there were likely many who took his words to heart.

> Holidays and change of air would not have much bearing on the intellect or mind of children who are mentally defective ... [However,] [t]here is

> the class of children ... who have become dull-witted and slow because of poverty and accompanying circumstances ... A vacation, new surroundings and environment for these types would be decidedly a good thing.[39]

Doctors like these may have had the best of intentions, but class values also shaped their interventions, and those of other professionals, at camp. Teaching working-class campers not only what to eat but also how to eat in the proper way, is one example. "Twenty per cent of our people never sit down to a meal at all," a Toronto social worker connected with the camps noted with disapproval. "They snatch snacks standing. There is little attempt at setting a table."[40] To social workers of this era, family customs and rituals were not a matter of tradition or taste but, rather, in their eyes, integrally linked to health and well-being. In their view, lives lacking in "regularity" and "right habits" could never be considered truly healthy. As the Bolton literature asserted in 1935, "The routine at camp is, in itself, an education – the regularity of meals, the kind of meals served, the systematic rest hour, and the definite plans for retiring."[41] While trying to be helpful, camp administrators often found it hard to avoid a paternalistic approach. Bolton's Annual Report of 1935 revealed not only a genuine concern for health but also the typical middle-class prerogative to assess and instruct. "Camp presents a splendid opportunity for teaching health," was the sunny conclusion. "Workers and campers live in close proximity, so that ... workers may observe the food and health habits of campers, and many suggestions can be passed on."[42]

To the general public, fresh air camps were sold as providing fun and improving health for poor working-class children, but a closer look reveals that the organizations that ran them also had other goals. As Margaret Tennant argues of fresh air camps in New Zealand, "It was easier for both doctors and lay people to intervene in children's lives in the name of health than under any other rubric," allowing camps to become "training grounds for children who did not fit contemporary ideals."[43] Likewise in Ontario, mothers and children may have come to camp in the name of health, but, once there, they were also a captive audience for middle-class reformation of their habits, character, and outlook. This was rarely a matter of explicit policy, nor was it necessarily, or generally, successful. Still, the attempt to remould working-class culture at camp was another reminder that camp life was deeply influenced by, and not divorced from, broader cultural trends.

One of the most basic "lessons" the fresh air camp taught was that not all camps were alike. While one United Church fresh air institution claimed its activities were "modeled after those of a private camp," at the typical fresh air camp, there were also many points of difference. In fact, at the camp in question, the list of activities included "instruction in swimming, life saving, rowing, handicrafts and games."[44] Programming with a so-called "Indian" theme was also common at fresh air camps, as elsewhere. Significantly, at neither this United Church camp nor at Bolton was there any chance of canoe tripping, riding, sailing, or tennis, a fact determined by both geography and resources. Without even a lake, swimming instruction at Bolton took place in cement "swimming tanks," and, as one report stated frankly, "Bolton is no place to teach fancy diving."[45] The same keep-it-simple principle applied to camp sports, which usually meant baseball – a low-budget, play-anywhere sport – and other simple, inexpensive games deemed suitable for girls.[46] As at private camps, music was an important aspect of programming, but here campfire sing-a-longs were the usual fare, with no mention of private lessons or quartets of professionals entertaining while one dined. When it came to food, one could expect simple fare. Before 1950, meat – what historian Ellen Ross describes as "a particularly eloquent signifier of class" – was conspicuously absent from fresh air camp menus.[47] Clearly, as administrators of fresh air camps planned their programs and amenities, cost was always uppermost in mind. One did not come to fresh air camp expecting hot showers and French chefs, water-skiing, or tennis. Considering the expense of these things, it is not surprising that one Bolton administrator – previously on the payroll of Taylor Statten's private Algonquin camp – was fired for "trying to make Bolton too much like Ahmek."[48]

Fresh air camps did not offer luxury, but they rarely idealized "roughing it." On the contrary, *Star* appeals frequently lamented the already rough living imposed on too many working-class families. In early years, lack of running water and electricity were noted deprivations, but recreational amenities gradually got added to the list. "There isn't any radio or victrola," a 1930 appeal sadly stated: "No electric refrigerator, no vacuum or automatic dish-cleaner. Only the bare necessities."[49] Working-class children were in need of many things, as fresh air administrators saw it, but instruction in simple living was not one of them. In 1940, the *Star* couldn't have put it more plainly: "It is good for families from well-to-do homes to rough it in the country, but we feel that these children from underprivileged homes should have as many of the niceties of home living as possible."[50] As administrators were well aware, for such children, lack of amenities was not intriguing camp play but everyday grim reality. Where roughing it occurred, it was more often a matter of necessity, not choice. As one observer noted

Swimming at Bolton Camp, c. 1950. Amenities at fresh air camps were a stark contrast with those at private camps. Here, Bolton campers enjoy a swim in the camp's "cement swimming tanks." *Copyright Family Service Association of Toronto.*

of the lack of electricity at a Baptist fresh air camp in 1940. "There is nothing to do but go to bed at dark or else sit a while in the starlight or about a beach fire, then go to bed by flashlight."[51] Likewise, during the same year, when campers' cots were so closely packed in at one camp that there was no room to kneel down and say prayers, it is doubtful this was anyone's idea of living the healthy, simple life.[52] The contrast with private camping couldn't have been more stark. No one idealized the material deprivation these children endured; on the contrary, it was hoped that camp could provide a taste of modern comfort.

Fresh air camp administrators wanted to offer their campers a modicum of comfort, but they also wanted to teach them lessons to take home with them. For example, while arts and crafts were a staple of most camp programming, here, they were seen as having unique value. "These occupations serve to employ the minds and hands of the campers," a Bolton report explained of the program in 1935. "They teach skill and dexterity and develop creative powers and initiative."[53] Lack of initiative was a deficiency typically attributed to poor working-class families, while the need for "skill and dexterity" pointed to the kind of work that administrators conceptualized for their grown-up (male) campers – namely, manual labour.[54] If this was not expected to make them wealthy, it was meant to divert attention from potential sources of dissatisfaction. As the same report asserted, "The handicraft work at Bolton Camp this summer has illustrated admirably that 'busy folk are happy folk.'" Considering that many Bolton campers came from homes with out-of-work fathers – potentially disgruntled collectors of relief – keeping "working folks" busy was considered a commendable feat.

Fresh air campers were meant to learn other lessons, both social and cultural. Music programs may have been simple, but their objectives were complex. Bolton's annual report for 1937 boasted that campfire sing-a-longs were encouraging a taste for "decent music" and developing sound spiritual values. To do so, it was clear that working-class tastes needed some readjustment:

> Perhaps some stranger to camp might say, "Oh, but these folk – their souls are filled with jazz and sentimental tunes, and church plays a small part in their lives." Experience shows that these souls are hungry for decent music ... To see shiny-eyed girls and boys around a campfire, and hear them singing lovely, funny, gay, clean-worded songs; to see tired mothers sing much the same ones ... is to realize that music is in every heart and only wants a chance and that songs live forever in the minds of those who learn them.[55]

As at other camps, formal programming was only one method of teaching new lessons. At Bolton, even dining rooms could have their "educational aspects," as a 1936 report explained. Children, at dinner, could develop "social ability [and] self-control," as one four-year-old was commended for doing. This camper noted of his less enlightened dinner companion, known for seeking out the largest piece of bread, "It's rude to pick isn't it?"[56]

One of the things meant to help campers in their cultural re-education was the positive example offered by camp staff. Camper/counsellor relations were centrally important at all camps, but here the relationship took on unique class dimensions. Fresh air camp counsellors, like those at other camps, generally came from middle-class families. In 1924, the Bolton literature boasted that all counsellors were "from good homes and all religious environments."[57] Other references, to counsellors from "college halls, private schools, and collegiate institutes" and to counsellors as "these *young ladies* from the universities and colleges and schools," made their class origins more or less clear.[58] Through these middle-class recruits, administrators hoped to transmit new values to campers. As far as health was concerned, nurses were responsible for formal instruction, but it was counsellors who were to monitor its daily application, ensuring that teeth were brushed, that hands were washed, and that campers avoided "eating too rapidly" and wearing the same clothing "day and night."[59] More than simple monitors of habit-training, however, counsellors of respectable backgrounds were to be living, breathing inspirations to working-class children. In contrast to campers' often "lazy" fathers and "ignorant" mothers, counsellors would provide examples of right values and living. In 1930, the *Star* made it clear where it stood when comparing the influence of counsellors and working-class mothers and fathers. At camp, it was claimed, children would "find and learn to love men and women leaders who are to them what their own parents should have been."[60]

Behind all fresh air camp programming and staffing, administrators had one overarching goal: to foster class harmony. Administrators recognized that their campers represented the poorest of the poor, those who might be expected to develop dangerous class resentments. They knew that disappointed children could grow into disgruntled adults, taking with them into adulthood a mistrust of, and antipathy towards, more privileged classes. Preventing these class resentments from developing was one good reason, the *Star* offered in 1943, for sending even "perfectly healthy boys and girls" to camp:

> [They] need some help too or they will develop an illness of their own. A hard one to cure. It is only natural for them to form warped opinions and grow up with the wrong outlook if they are left year after year to swelter in the hot city while other children ... spend their summers at cool resorts ... While health might be impaired by continual confinement ... it is also their mental attitude that we must watch. Children will form their own opinions based on things that happen to them. And these are the things they will never forget.[61]

Concern with refashioning working-class attitudes was a subtext that ran through camp programming and planning. If young campers could be moulded into courageous and hard-working adults, happy with the simplest pleasures in life, then, it was believed, they would not think to criticize those better off than themselves. As one appeal put it, "Two weeks of bliss would restore their love of life and their belief in society."[62] Life wasn't fair, but a gift of two weeks fun and fresh air in the country might soften the edges of this harsh social reality.

"I never been nowhere": Mothers off to Camp

At a number of fresh air camps, and certainly at Bolton, work with mothers was considered an important part of the overall mission. At the camps that accommodated them, mothers made up roughly 20 percent of the camp population.[63] As novel as this might now seem, in the first half of the twentieth century, working-class mothers were frequently the targets of reform efforts on behalf of charity, social work, and the state. Indeed, mothers were seen as a good place to start in reshaping working-class families. During the interwar years, mothers' allowance and maternal education campaigns were instituted, presumably, to raise the standards of child care across the country, while, during the postwar years, reception work with immigrants frequently targeted mothers for improvement of their child-care and home-making skills.[64]

In the pages of the *Star*, mothers, like children, were frequently depicted as poor, hapless victims and deserving of a fresh air camp holiday. According to countless appeals, mothers were threatened by the ravages

Mothers make the last leg of the journey to Bolton Camp, c. 1920s. After riding the train from Union Station in Toronto, campers headed for Bolton Fresh Air Camp rode the last few miles in the back of large flat-bed trucks. They may have been "packed in like parcels," as one former camper recalls, but they certainly seemed happy to go. *Copyright Family Service Association of Toronto.*

of ill health, depressing and unsanitary conditions, and the unemployment of primary wage earners. True enough, as those charged with maintaining the good health and spirits of the rest of the household, mothers were forced to withstand additional strain. "Mothers bear the main burden of the poor," one 1933 appeal began: "If you find children in a poor home, it's more than likely you'll find a mother who is in worse shape than they."[65] Despite cultural prejudices against it, wage work was often the only alternative for the poorest of the poor. Due to the dual pressures of child-rearing and wage-earning, and to their well-known tendency of placing their nutritional and material needs behind those of the rest of the family, such women were regarded by some as most in need of a holiday that involved relaxation and good food.[66] Following the logic of self-help, however, part of what made such women admirable in the eyes of their benefactors was their refusal to see themselves as entitled to aid. One deserted mother of five, forced into wage labour, was praised for her heroic attitude. "She doesn't complain, nor ask for help," ran the *Star*'s glowing description.[67] When it came to deciding where to direct limited sources of charity, victims who quietly coped, and not those who protested their circumstances, were clearly most appealing to middle-class sensibilities.

Fresh air appeals were contradictory in their depictions of mothers, however. Alongside images of martyr-like women – effective fund-raising tools, perhaps – were other less flattering images. For every hard-working, neatly dressed, and self-respecting mother, many more were apparently lazy, unkempt, and without shame. As in other contexts, social workers were critical of mothers who had too many children or who took on wage work, whatever the circumstances. Even when occasionally praising the individual mother, visiting professionals couldn't help but make unfavourable, if implicit, comparisons to the majority of less commendable poor women, as the 1923 assessment of one deserving case revealed:

> The house was clean, very different from many of the very poor homes into which one enters, which are so often dirty and heavy smelling. But this house had an actual sweetness about it which was refreshing after visits to a succession of dismal little dens that were offensive both to eyes and nose. It was at once apparent that here was a home, not merely a sort of lair. Yet the woman apologized for the untidiness ... this was no slattern with tously hair bunched under a soiled mobcap but a neat woman in a print dress with greying hair tied in a tidy knot behind.[68]

Working-class women were criticized not only for poor home-making skills but also for poor mothering. One 1940 critique foreshadowed postwar concerns with affection and the psychological nurturance of children. "The mother has made a cripple of her," it was said of one girl with a pronounced limp. Her homelife of "constant bickering" and, later, divorce was blamed for her condition. "All she needs to restore her to mental and physical health is to be with normal people for a while," the *Star* confidently asserted.[69]

Mothers of all classes were the target of such criticisms, but as scholars have noted, it was the practices of working-class women that were most often subject to the scrutiny of outsiders. Fresh air camp offered yet another site for intervention in this realm: camp programming for mothers was designed in direct response to their perceived failings. To address problems of poor house-keeping, Bolton offered prizes for the best-kept cabin not only to children but also to mothers. Staff made routine visits to mothers in their cabins, where, it was said, "adjustments regarding their living conditions and hints as to better house-keeping methods" were made. To combat maternal ignorance in other realms, from at least 1936 on, Bolton offered cooking classes or "instruction in simple dietetics." These were not meant to impart culinary expertise but, rather, to teach women how to stay within working-class budgets. Lessons typically stressed "economy," offering simple instructions in using fruit and vegetables and, in one case, "the use of left-over food." At other times, the scales between instruction and indulgence tipped in the other direction. Lessons in "beauty culture," for instance, reflected the desire to entertain but, at the same time, encouraged class notions of beauty and hygiene. "The worker stressed the importance of cleanliness and neatness as the basis for beauty," a 1936 report explained: "The women were taught to shampoo and finger wave their hair ... They discussed the method of washing and ironing clothes ... The use of make-up and nail polish was considered, emphasizing that in both it was important not to be glaring." The observation that these classes sometimes led to "startling results" underlined the belief that, whether caring for their homes or themselves, working-class women were clearly in need of a little help.[70]

Of all the habits administrators sought to reform when it came to their adult campers, child-rearing practices were the primary target. Ultimately, instruction in cooking and cleaning was merely an elaboration of the more fundamental goal of fresh air camping for mothers – namely, "education for motherhood," to borrow a phrase.[71] As with the state's

Bolton Camp, interwar years. Much as they did at Well Baby clinics in the city, mothers at Bolton practised their child-care skills under the guidance of the public health nurse. *Copyright Family Service Association of Toronto.*

maternal educational campaigns, baby care was deemed all-important. At fresh air camps, public health nurses performed much the same functions as they did in the city, teaching mothers the arts of feeding, bathing, and general health and then watching over their shoulders as women practised what they learned. As in other settings, maternal ignorance was assumed. Bolton's Annual Report for 1936 informed the public as to how this ignorance was being combated. First, on teaching the value of fresh air: "Many of them are afraid the babies will catch cold if they are left outside. Of course, it's a fallacy, and we teach them so." At feeding time: "Many mothers don't even know how to turn a milk bottle upside down to get whole milk. It's a simple thing, but it's a fact that everybody doesn't know how." And finally, in impressing the need for cleanliness: "I have seen many instances ... where mothers have, for the first time in their lives, learned how to wash their children in the proper way."[72] For those with older children, discipline was an issue the camp also sought to address. Mothers at camp were not only reminded not to be over-indulgent but also, indirectly, to curb their tendency to yell and nag. While some new mothers may have welcomed the advice, one wonders how the average woman responded to the suggestion that she take direction from the "Camp Mother" concerning "the problems and characteristics of her [children]." The idea that, after only ten days of observation at camp, this outsider would offer mothers "a clearer understanding" of their own offspring was no doubt offensive to some.[73]

Apart from what the camp might offer them, mothers at camp could also be useful from the administrators' point of view. Because fresh air camps were essentially charitable ventures, economizing was always a priority. On a purely practical note, bringing mothers to camp appears to have lessened the workload of the (mainly) volunteer staff. While it was said of mothers at the City Mission Camp, "Their only duty ... is making their own beds,"[74] during the 1930s at Bolton, mothers were encouraged to help out with dishwashing, to "share in the cooking" during cook-outs, and to offer their talents in sewing to aid fund-raising efforts.[75] At other camps, their work was apparently vital. "A certain number of mothers are always taken ... to help with the work at the camp, the cooking, bed-making and so forth," it was stated of an unnamed camp in 1939: "Only mothers who can really work at the camp are taken, only a very few of the best. No sick ones."[76] True enough, mothers generally enjoyed large chunks of time away from the responsibilities of child care, but these were not total. For instance, babies and toddlers at Bolton shared cabins with their mothers and not counselling staff.

If we might now wonder how mothers felt about what the camp had to offer, this was not a priority at these institutions. Ultimately, mothers were the recipients of aid, which emphasized children as its true target. A 1940 appeal put the camp objectives plainly: "All this work with the mothers," it was stated, "is just another way of making a better life at home for the small children, who are really the chief interest of the fresh air work."[77]

Responding to Changing Fortunes

If, as labour historians have documented, the 1920s were difficult years for Canada's working class, they were good years for the fresh air camp in Ontario. In fact, there was a direct relationship between increased neediness and the fortunes of the fund. Accordingly, in these years, the *Star*'s Fresh Air Fund was extremely successful in raising increasing amounts of funds. From its humble beginnings, raising just over a thousand dollars in its second year of operation in 1902, the fund induced the public to donate over $7,000 in 1916 and, by 1921, a whopping $41,000.[78] Numbers of children sent to camp rose accordingly. From its early beginnings accommodating a couple of hundred mothers and children each summer, by the 1930s, Bolton Camp alone was accommodating over one thousand campers per session, with the summer comprised of at least four sessions.[79] Waiting lists were common; already in early June of 1922, the *Star* claimed that there were "1300 applications on file at the central office."[80] In 1924, it was claimed that "Toronto's fresh air work has been steadily growing for the past six years ... [T]he value of such work has so appealed to the public imagination that money has been forthcoming to more than quadruple the activities."[81]

Even with the onset of the Depression, the fresh air camp movement continued to thrive. Like private camps, fresh air camps were affected by hard economic times but in distinct ways. While the rolls of private camps dwindled, fresh air camps felt pressure to accommodate an increasing number of needy children. True enough, under financial constraints, some camps were forced to close or to reduce operations. The fund in general, however, and Bolton Camp in particular, continued to do well throughout this period. Donations from the general public continued to roll in, suggesting that, if many blamed the unemployed for their condition, the plight of their children still elicited sympathy. The fortunes of the Fresh Air Fund held steady as it took in between $28,000 and $30,000 each summer. According to the *Star*, this resulted, in 1931, in "more children at camp than any previous year of the fund's existence." While noting financial pressures, the administration at Bolton Camp also seemed upbeat and confident. The annual report declared 1932 as "the very best in Bolton Camp History," while the minutes of the Camp Committee recorded that, in 1934, the camp itself was in "the best condition in its history." The Bolton administration recognized that not all "social work activities" were faring as well but stated: "fresh air work emphatically seems to be one of the things which the public believes in and wishes to support."[82] Apparently, addressing child welfare and offering back-to-nature solutions was a winning combination as far as eliciting public support went. In this sense, fresh air camps for children paralleled Depression-era back-to-the-land solutions for their parents, both indicating an ongoing suspicion of urban society and culture.[83]

Working-class people were well aware of the popularity of the Fresh Air Fund and, during the Depression, some pressured it to do more than provide "kiddies" with camp holidays. As Linda Gordon has found in the context of American social service agencies, working-class people were not passive recipients of aid; rather, they were active agents who sometimes lobbied for intervention not envisioned by charitable organizations or the state.[84] In the case of 1930s Toronto, the fund was surprised to find poor families requesting everything from extra clothing for the children, to help with the rent money, to prevention of evictions and, even, to finding jobs. On one unique occasion, a public health nurse approached the *Star*, requesting a hospital bed for a child with cancer; on another, a grandmother sought a country burial spot for her unfortunate granddaughter.[85] In 1932, the *Star* described the stream of needy people who waited on the leather bench outside the Fresh Air Fund office, ready to solicit aid for all kinds of problems:

> Now it is a man who is to be deported, seeking clothing so that he might go back to his old home town looking a little bit respectable; now it is a mother holding high her child's shoes, the soles of which are entirely through ... Maybe it is a mother pleading that some special food might be provided ... maybe some lonely widow eager to acquire a sewing machine ... maybe some foreign-born man and wife who don't quite understand the procedures of the new country.[86]

Clearly, the fund had an interest in limiting such requests, but it wasn't always wholly unresponsive. On the one hand, fund writers sometimes felt compelled to list the problems it was *not* meant to address. Readers were reminded in 1931 that the fund could not "give an idle man a job or pay his rent."[87] Still, it occasionally did act, appealing for used clothing, paying the week-end rent on one occasion, and, indeed, finding a country cemetery plot to ensure the unfortunate deceased girl would not be "condemned forever to the hopeless hell of cities." Even fathers were not entirely ignored; the fund couldn't promise jobs, but it did organize two week-end camp visits for them in 1936. Whatever their effectiveness, these pleas revealed that working-class people were not simply passive recipients of middle-class benevolence; they actively pushed the fund to act in their own best interests.[88]

This type of self-assertive action was not, however, what fresh air camps necessarily sought to encourage. Indeed, it was during the Depression that the *Star* clarified that it was attitudes and outlook that were its primary targets of change, not the economic circumstances of the poor. As a *Star* appeal stated in 1933, "The biggest thing a fresh air camp can do is to give people new attitudes towards life and themselves."[89] If two weeks of fresh air could not deliver them from a life of hardship, it could nevertheless give working-class people the tools to "keep on fighting," to "develop personal pride," and to enjoy life "without even fine homes or money."[90]

Ultimately, the fund made clear that, as a charity, it saw its role as eliciting sympathy for the disadvantaged, not providing a structural critique of poverty. In 1930, when many around the world were beginning to see that economic downturns were, in fact, symptomatic of capitalist economies, the *Star* plainly stated: "Social problems can't be categorized. A whole series of contributing factors makes it almost impossible to lay a finger upon the sole root of the trouble."[91] Another appeal stated: "It isn't poverty in the bulk that is the tragic thing. It isn't the mass of men without jobs, mothers deserted by husbands, children neglected and unkept [sic]. Not that. The appealing thing ... is the individual instance of hardship ... [and] it is for [this] ... that the *Star* Fresh Air Fund exists."[92] Indeed, one can't help but wonder whether the fund felt the need to contain what its appeals had the potential to unleash – that is, mass sympathy for the plight of the poor and general questioning as to poverty's root causes. More risky still, one might empower the poor themselves to think of their situations as unjust, engendering a sense not of gratitude for charity but of entitlement to aid. The public was reminded more than once over the years that fresh air camps could only "alleviate" stresses and "transplant" children for a short time; they could not "unlock the shackles" of poverty but only "assuage the wounds the hard edges make."[93] In short, the fresh air camp was in the business of providing escape, not of "fuss[ing] and fum[ing] and ... criticiz[ing] the things which make such conditions possible."[94] It was meant, above all, to help people cope, and that is what it was best able to do.

Fresh air camps, like others, were also influenced by Canada's entry into war in 1939. Interestingly, while this was a boon for the rest of the economy, the Second World War brought more difficult times for fresh air institutions. Most significantly, donation-dependent fresh air camps now had to compete with wartime charities for public contributions. From the fund-raising highs of the Depression years, annual funds raised fell to approximately $20,000 in the summer of 1940 and to as low as $13,000 by 1944.[95] Fund-raising pitches in the *Star* were now moved from the front and early pages to later sections, with war news demanding centre stage. Those running individual camps also faced new wartime challenges with the introduction of rationing and the ubiquity of labour shortages. At Bolton Camp, the rationing of gasoline meant fewer visitors in camp, while food rationing added "considerable work" to the task of keeping campers fed.

To deal with the problems of securing labour, which were said in 1943 to be "formidable," the Bolton administration was forced to rely on elderly men as groundskeepers and on increasingly inexperienced male counsellors, some as young as fifteen years old. The domestic labour of mothers, which had always been helpful, became more so, as in 1942, when it was said that they "helped out considerably in the kitchens."[96]

Still, despite the challenges, the Fresh Air Fund and camps like Bolton persisted in their efforts, arguing that "War or Peace – They Need Help." Suggesting that support for the Fresh Air Fund was still high, in August 1940, the Toronto Children's Zoo and the Canadian National Exhibition each donated one night's proceeds to the *Star* fund, while, in July 1941, a highly successful Toronto businessmen's fund-raising carnival agreed to split its funds equally between the *Star* and war charities. War may have brought fewer donations to camp coffers but it also brought renewed purpose. Fostering citizenship took on added importance during wartime when patriotic feelings ran high. A Bolton report, no doubt written after the outbreak of war, conceded in 1939 that: "In the midst of destruction it is hard to think of the quiet constructive things – the things that have to do with a child's health and the shaping of his future," but quickly added that, "these things, at long last, are the only things which really matter."[97] Bolton was also asked to make more direct contributions to the war effort; for three summers in the early 1940s the Department of Defence asked to make use of the camp for cadet and officer training, requests that, the camp admitted, "could hardly be refused in time of war."[98]

When considering their camper populations, fresh air camps also expressed new concerns about the home conditions of working-class children. These concerns fit with what historians have already documented about worries over family life during wartime, especially the perceived connection between married women in the wage labour force and increasing rates of juvenile delinquency. Camp literature and fund-raising appeals showed similar concern for absent fathers and mothers "exhausted by factory work" in war industries. As always, the children were the real concern as, too often it was said, they were packed into "crowded day nurseries" or, worse, left unattended and "roaming the streets." Though fresh air camps saw themselves as helping boys to "go straight" as early as the 1920s, it was in the war years and immediately after that references to juvenile delinquency increased in the pages of the *Star*. As was typical of the period, "delinquency" could include a range of behaviours, from petty thefts at outdoor fruit stalls and toy stores to the even more innocuous "crimes" of using "bad language" and, in one case, swimming without a bathing suit at the

Toronto beaches. (Luckily, in this 1947 case, a "policeman of understanding" passed this "delinquent" on to the *Star*'s Fresh Air Fund and not the juvenile court.) Although poverty and material conditions were sometimes alluded to in terms of causes, "summer boredom" was also blamed. "They just steal because they are so bored," the *Star* reporter stated in August 1941. And, assuming that being deprived of outdoor summer fun was reason enough for delinquent behaviour, he went on: "Naturally, they can't go out and play golf, they don't play tennis, the lakefront often is weary miles away and they may not have a swimming suit. They can't get jobs, these youngsters, so they steal."[99]

Fresh air camps were meant, then, to address the problem of delinquency and, indirectly, to "conserve and strengthen family life," the official wartime mandate of the Neighbourhood Workers' Association, which ran Bolton Camp. To this end, fresh air camp administrators made special efforts to accommodate servicemen's families and the children of working mothers. In the early 1940s, Bolton was proud to keep track of how many such families it was helping, boasting, in the summer of 1941, that 1,007 campers (mothers and children) were from servicemen's families. For these campers, like others, the natural setting of camp was meant to soothe tired nerves and rejuvenate mental health. Fresh air and green fields were helpful in this, but, more broadly, camp was about making "fine contacts," forming "new interests," and catching glimpses of "a better way of living" that would set potential delinquents on a new path. Ultimately, change of environment was, again, seen as key: "A boy who has had a few weeks in the country is more amenable. He's easier to deal with."[100] As for mothers, the camp claimed to offer them "an oasis in a war-torn world ... a little world all its own, where all things became new."[101]

In the affluent postwar years, both the Fresh Air Fund and Bolton Camp continued to thrive. Indeed, the success of the fund directly affected Bolton. In 1947, when the fund set $25,000 as its fund-raising target, a full $13,000 – over 50 percent – went to assist campers at Bolton Camp.[102] Bolton's size alone explains why it was so generously supported by the fund. Most other fresh air camps, accommodating usually not many more than one hundred campers at one time, paled in comparison with the one thousand-plus accommodated at Bolton. The relative prosperity of these years, though not shared equally between all classes, also seemed to affect the population and administrators at fresh air camps. When a 1949 fresh air appeal bemoaned the fact that young "Jimmy" "has no bicycle or catcher's mitt – none of the paraphernalia that even poor boys collect,"[103] it was meant to indicate how unlucky this boy was. At the same time, lacking recreational equipment was certainly a different level of deprivation than lacking proper food and shelter, as many "Jimmys" of the interwar years had done.[104]

To some degree, the affluence of these years also influenced the objectives of camp, which saw some shift in emphasis. With general improvement in standards of living and new medical breakthroughs, health was, in some ways, a less pressing concern. In a brief history of the Neighbourhood Workers' Association, the organization noted that: "Originally, people came to [us] because of economic need. But from the war years on, more and more sought help as well with personal and family problems."[105] Bolton Camp literature also intimated that educational priorities and the development of mental and psychological health were at least as important as were the physical health objectives. While, as the next chapter shows, this development had been under way since the mid-1930s, an educational focus seemed more realistic in years when, broadly speaking, standards of living were rising for all Canadians.

The contrast shouldn't be too sharply drawn, however, between the relative importance of health objectives before and after the war. Even in the more affluent postwar years, and as educational objectives were given increasing attention, the health of all fresh air campers could not be taken for granted. The health benefits of camp were still regularly announced, suggesting that, even in the era of TV and turntables, for the very poor, the material struggle for survival was ongoing.[106] While Franca Iacovetta points out that images of Canada as a land of plenty abounded in state literature of the postwar period, in reality, there were still many for whom proper nourishment was not a taken-for-granted condition.[107] In 1946, the *Star* was still quoting children who, apparently, were not getting enough to eat. "Can we go to camp?" ran one 1946 petition. "It isn't the fresh air ... we've plenty of that ... But I was thinking how wonderful it would be to get three square meals a day."[108] Other appeals noted that poor nutrition could still be linked to illness among its camper population. "Rickets is a class disease," the *Star* journalist wrote in 1948. "It is poverty's horrid child ... [I]n every one of these cases [it] could have been prevented had the proper foods been available."[109] And, if diphtheria and tuberculosis were less common in postwar years, new and frightening threats – like polio – also emerged.[110] As in earlier years, fresh air camps continued to battle with health issues, but their ultimate goal – to influence the values and culture of working-class families – remained constant. In 1949, to the question, "What good is only two weeks of [camp]?" the *Star* responded not by stressing health or material well-being but, instead, by stating: "A great gain has been made if the tenement-house child has become thoroughly dissatisfied with his lot."[111] You might be expected to have a "happy time" at camp, but you were also meant to go home less content with the domestic status quo.

Evaluating Impact: "A really happy time"

Given the somewhat amorphous nature of fresh air camp goals – improving health, elevating tastes, transforming attitudes, even providing good fun – assessing impact is a challenging task. How does one determine whether children were "healthier" after ten days at camp, whether campers formed a taste for "better" music, or whether mothers truly adapted their child-rearing techniques? In the short, ten- to twelve-day stay at fresh air camp, it was unlikely that either children or mothers were going to make wholesale lifestyle changes. Fresh Air Fund writers were clearly aware that there were limitations to what one could achieve in two weeks. From the other side of the question, one wonders, did children and their mothers want to go to camp? Did they want to go back? How were fresh air camps regarded in the broader working-class community?

From camps' perspective, physical changes were the easiest to determine. As Tennant argues in the New Zealand context, weight gain promised to give "a measurable, statistical demonstration of the health camps' success, one that was easily publicized [and] widely understood."[112] Indeed, at Ontario camps, "weighing in" became something of a ritual, as it was at British open-air schools. Reports from Bolton and daily *Star* appeals frequently cited average (and even total) weight gains per summer. In 1925, it was stated of Bolton campers: "Last year the average gain in weight was two and a half pounds. Many of the children gained four, five, or six pounds. One child held a record of eight pounds in twelve days."[113] In 1935, the public was informed that over 90 percent of campers put on weight and, in 1938, that "some 1750 pounds more of live boy and girl leave camp each party than came in."[114] Hard data such as this perhaps satisfied the social service compulsion to quantify; however, as reliable evidence of true health, it is harder to assess. It is now commonly accepted that weight gain of such rapid proportions may, in fact, not be recommended, as even camp administrators eventually acknowledged.[115] On the other hand, in 1922, Bolton was embarrassed to find that campers had suffered a net loss in weight, and so the issue was downplayed altogether.[116] The possibility of fighting and curing disease in ten to twelve days seemed

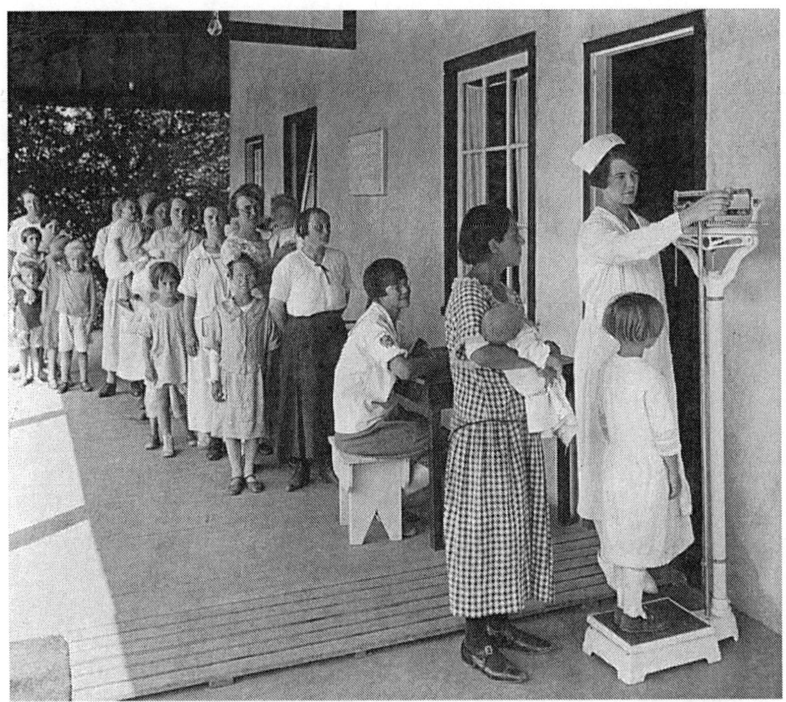

Weighing in, Bolton Camp. During the interwar years when working-class children were frequently undernourished, weighing in was a regular ritual at Bolton Camp. Evidence of weight gain was a concrete achievement that fresh air camps used to publicly demonstrate their effectiveness. *Copyright Family Service Association of Toronto.*

even less likely. Certainly, it is doubtful that "skyshine" ever cured rickets, as Toronto's medical officer of health once claimed in 1932.[117] Advice concerning inoculation may have aided in breaking down suspicion concerning such practices, but, again, this is hard to determine. In the end, if one considers that general health is a matter of ongoing and stable conditions, it is hard to see how two weeks of camp could have made much difference. If adequate meals were considered a welcome, even rare, treat, their long-term health impact was likely only negligible.

Fresh air camps may have been more successful with other goals, influencing mother's child-rearing practices among them. As was the case with other maternal education campaigns, urban women, now more isolated from female networks of support, were sometimes truly grateful, especially as new mothers, for the advice of public health nurses regarding baby care and child-rearing.[118] One mother, described in 1926 as having "absolutely no idea of how to ... train her four tiny children" later stated: "Oh, Miss, but the Nurse *is* nice ... she doesn't talk at you, like some do. She just kind of shows you how."[119] Claims were also made of reformed housekeepers serving proper meals in tidy houses. In 1924, the public health nurse had this to say concerning one apparently transformed housewife:

> Her house and the surroundings were blots in the landscape of an otherwise tidy little street. The nurses hinted very strongly that when she went to camp she must not disgrace the Health Department ... She not only saved us from humiliation but ... Bolton Camp had such an effect on her that all her buried housekeeping instincts were revived and she won the prize for the best kept tent ... [C]onditions at home are [now] very much improved.[120]

In the hopes of detecting change, small acts could be read as having large symbolic importance. In a 1924 report, when one mother turned in "a rather grimy 'comfort'" that her two-year-old had been sucking, the case was lauded as indicating "the changed point of view." On another occasion, a social worker was satisfied to find a mother and her children, just returned from camp, happily "sitting down to a meal" when she made her unannounced visit.[121]

Still, it was difficult to know how far such changes went and whether they could safely be read as a transformation of working-class attitudes. Fund-raising appeals certainly sought to put the best face on the work of camp, although their glowing praise (and perfect grammar) raises some question as to their authorship. Other evidence suggests that campers sometimes greeted fresh air projects with at least a little suspicion. Organizers noted, with some impatience, that mothers, and even children, were not always eager to sign up for a spot at camp. Extending holidays to working-class mothers meant domestic work for fathers left behind. Some fathers may have resented this; mothers sometimes expressed hesitancy because of this.[122] Child labour could be equally critical to working-class family economies, a factor that may have affected their attendance at camp.[123] Other worries concerned the nature of the experience itself. Especially in early years, when fresh air camping was still relatively new, wariness was likely more pronounced. Indeed, in 1922 – the same year Bolton Camp opened – the *Star* detailed the misgivings of some working-class women:

> We were repeatedly told by these tired-out mothers that it was too great an effort to get the family ready to go; and that anyway they were sure there

> must be a "catch" in it somewhere – that it couldn't mean that they could go and not have to work probably harder than they would have to do at home; and that the children would worry them to death, because they probably would not be allowed to make very much noise; and a thousand and one other objections.[124]

These misgivings might also have masked a more general reluctance to accept what was regarded, throughout this period, as charity. From the perspective of working-class families, accepting a fresh air camp holiday could be considered yet another "hand-out," signalling personal failure and engendering feelings of indebtedness. The case of one brave mother, who asserted in 1938, "I am not ashamed of sending my children to camp,"[125] suggested that others still were. In other cases, mothers' promises to repay camp debts "when I am in a position to do so" – and the fact that certain others did – indicated an uncomfortable awareness of being caught on the wrong side of charity's ledger sheet.[126] As late as 1946, the Bolton administration disparaged the fact that "some people have been hesitant about making application ... thinking [this] is a camp for those families who are on relief," reiterating, for public benefit, that a majority of campers paid some fee.[127] Campers, themselves, were seemingly well aware of this and of the shame of accepting "hand-outs." "Oh, yes. My parents would pay," one interviewee was quick to clarify. "It wasn't a free thing."[128] On the other hand, resistance to charity sometimes broke down for the same reasons that it was offered; that is, because of the children. Suggesting that new notions of childhood were being solidified across class lines, fathers admitted the need to "pocket one's pride" for the children's sake. One mother stated, "My first thought is for them, poor little things."[129] Charity was not really charity, it seemed, if accepted on behalf of those who could not be expected to help themselves.

Suspicions, however, could also turn out to be justified, as some discovered once at camp. Mothers at Bolton, for instance, were not unaware of class bias and of what sometimes felt like condescension on the part of middle-class staff. In 1939, the reference to certain problems "of social distance" having been "worked out," in fact, betrayed the existence of class tensions. The "problem," it was explained, "does not arise to any extent ... between boys and girls and staff" since "children are accustomed to having their teachers in school giving them leadership. But the problem becomes somewhat different when you are dealing with adults." Asserting that they had always been careful "to eliminate condescension and the accentuation of social differences," administrators insisted they had tried to "remove from the minds of the mothers the idea that they were in a subservient position."[130] Whatever their admirable efforts, administrators could find that even generosity could be the source of tension. In this respect, the portions and types of food that so delighted young campers were not always appreciated by mothers who were unable to accommodate these tastes at home. As the *Star* itself admitted, "A child who has had two weeks' regular meals is not likely to be very enthusiastic about being given a slice of bread in the morning and then told to stay outside until another slice falls due in the evening."[131] It is possible that lessons in "beauty culture" may also have been met with any number of objections. One can only guess as to how displaced persons and survivors of Hitler's concentration camps felt when asked in 1950, "And when was the last time you mothers had your hair done?"[132]

The overall impression is that fresh air institutions lacked the camp spirit and sense of unity typical of many private and agency camps. While length of time at camp had a part to play in this, class differences quite possibly raised barriers not found elsewhere. Counsellors themselves served generally shorter periods of time; a Bolton report stated that 75 percent came for only one two-week session.[133] For their part, some mothers retained a generally wary attitude even once at camp. Administrators couldn't help but notice a certain "reserve" among their adult campers, a typical feature of interclass relations, and what social scientist James Scott might call a natural part of their "public transcript."[134] This working-class reticence bothered middle-class philanthropists, who were troubled when giving charity opened literal doors to them – facilitating visits to working-class homes – but failed to give them emotional access to the poor.

If mothers and children brought some reservations with them to camp, it was equally true that, for many of them, the fresh air experience was a popular and much sought-after commodity. *Star* writers regularly described children with "shining" eyes begging parents for a chance to go to camp and wan-looking waifs who turned up at *Star* offices to personally request that they be selected. Waiting lists were typical at the headquarters of fresh air establishments. In June of 1935, Bolton Camp was already filled up for the summer, with the phone said to be ringing off the hook with those hopeful of cancellations. Mary Murphy, Bolton camper from the late 1940s and early 1950s, expressed her feeling that "a lot of kids in Toronto were pleased to have that camp."[135] She herself thoroughly enjoyed her stay, admitting, somewhat guiltily, her resentment at having to leave early one year when her mother broke a leg. Leila Warnock, another postwar camper, thinks back on the holiday aspect of Bolton with fondness, explaining that "the only other place in Toronto where we used to get away was over at ... Centre Island."[136] Clearly, the camp's goal of "giv[ing] burdened and underprivileged people a really happy time" was met in many cases.[137] Numerous adult ex-campers were grateful many years after for the fund's generosity. Their stories were offered up in the *Star* as living proof of the fresh air camp's beneficial effects. In articles with titles like, "He Was at Camp Once Now Saves to Send Others," the Star related stories of poor kids who had made good, were duly appreciative, and were now willing to pay back their debt to their middle-class benefactors.[138]

For sometimes slightly different reasons, many mothers were as avid about camp as their children. If some could be reluctant and wary, other mothers actively appealed to get their families to camp. These women wrote letters and sometimes marched down to *Star* offices, citing ill-health, inadequate nutrition, and the psychological stresses of poverty as reasons they should be chosen for camp.[139] Of those selected, many also wrote letters upon their return, praising the meals (and the fact that some one else made them!), the freedom from constant demands of child care, and, above all, "the rest," as so many put it. "I have been married for 25 years and the holiday you gave us last year was the first rest I have had in all my married life," stated one grateful mother in 1935.[140] Some wept upon leaving, others begged for extended stays.

It is not hard to understand the intensity of these responses when one considers the daily working lives of these women and what camp offered by contrast: two week's escape from (most) cooking, cleaning, and some child care; the prospect of light entertainment; the potential for camaraderie; and physical distance from home, the site of all too many stresses. Even mothers who stayed behind at home were clearly grateful for a week of reduced child care. "I am writing to ask," one mother explained to the *Star* in 1922, "if you could send my four little ones away for a week before they go back to school ... I thought if the children got away it would give me a chance to get rested up a bit ... I have had so much worry in the past year."[141] Not surprisingly, in the depths of the Depression, the Bolton administration noted the gratitude of mothers and children alike: "We have never had a year in which the expressions of appreciation and enjoyment of the campers was so evident and outspoken," it was noted at the end of the 1932 season.[142] When individual women made such claims as "I have never had anyone care for me and have always been used to serving others" or "[After] pinching and screwing to get enough to eat, you sure do appreciate what people do for you [at Bolton]," the stories rang all too true.[143]

For mothers and children who valued the camp experience, there were a number of specific attractions. One of these, without question, was food. In contrast to long traditions of complaints about food at private and agency camps, fresh air camps represented, for its underprivileged clients, the rare chance to eat well for an uninterrupted ten to twelve days. As one of the more flexible aspects of the family budget, food (unlike rent, for example) was one of the easiest places that corners could be cut. For children from such families, food was one of the highlights of camp. "We ate. We ate like crazy," was the recollection of one interwar camper: "I couldn't do up the top button on my pants when I got home."[144] For young Mary Murphy, 1940s camper, food looms large in her memories of Bolton. Remembering the hot porridge and "especially [the] brown sugar" – an unheard of luxury in her family of ten – she explained, "I thought I had died and gone to heaven. I never wanted to leave."[145]

Not only did they feel themselves well fed, campers also had fun. Swimming period, arts and crafts, and Indian council rings could have their hidden purposes, but they also, quite simply, entertained. The urge to "show kiddies a good time" was at least one of the bases on which the fund appealed to donors and, no doubt, the one on which many contributed. Even mothers were deemed to be deserving of a little fun. To this end, Bolton provided afternoon teas, garden parties, and evening programs of "games, singing and [folk] dancing" for its adult campers.[146] In 1940, the City Mission Camp declared that their mothers "spen[t] most of their time lying on the beach in the sunshine, resting," while Bolton asserted that "mothers can have fun too ... perhaps learning how to sketch, or in the craft house learning to weave or knit."[147] Reflecting the broader shift to more hedonistic attitudes to leisure, whatever its didactic purposes, camp also provided agreeable and engaging experiences for mothers and children, the stuff of which good memories were made.[148] More than simply fun in themselves, camp activities also allowed women to meet others with similar experiences and to experience the comfort of working-class friendship. This was apparently the case for one mother, "seven years on the dole." "Unwilling to associate with others in her own position, too ashamed and too proud to try to mix with former friends, she had gone through those seven years alone," a Bolton report explained in 1944. But ultimately, as the administration saw it, "the informal friendliness of Camp, a chance to talk things over with others who had been through that same valley ... all helped her to relax the springs of self-control and reserve wound too tight."[149] When Bolton made special efforts to accommodate soldiers' families during the war, other mothers stated they found "great comfort" in "meet[ing] others with our own interests, namely our men overseas."[150] In contrast to relationships formed at private camps, these friendships likely did not persist much beyond the days of camp, but the memory of them may have helped women to carry on in hard circumstances.

Fathers and other members of the working-class community were aware of the fresh air camp's popularity and made their own contributions to the cause. In 1933, one father, grateful for the chance to send his children to camp, offered to do furnace repair work "free of charge" to anyone who made a donation to the fund.[151] The group of fathers who stayed at Bolton briefly in 1936 also proved themselves eager to be regarded as more than the objects of charity. Having little in the way of monetary capital, they made generous offers of free labour to the camp. The result was a one- and two-week work camp for fathers, arranged for the following spring.[152] At that time, twenty-five men provided services around the camp, in exchange for room and board. Other groups made contributions of their own, as when, during the depths of the Depression, Toronto A&P workers purchased eighty-four acres of land adjoining Bolton to help extend the camp's work, and, in 1935, the International Brotherhood of Carpenters donated a "fully equipped" children's playhouse.[153]

By the early 1950s, there is reason to think that working-class Torontonians regarded the Fresh Air Fund as something of a sacrosanct institution. In 1951, a telling incident occurred in the midst of a municipal election campaign. In July of that year, a *Globe and Mail* cartoonist dared to compare the hopes of the local Labour candidate, Ford Brand, to those of a poor child pleading to be sent to camp. With captions like "Make Fordie's Dream Come True" and "Has Never Been to City Hall: You Can Help Him off Hot Pavement," the paper raised the ire of a number of tradeunionists.[154] So angered were the members of the Toronto and District Trades and Labour Council that they insisted on publicly defending not only Labour's candidate but also the Fresh Air Fund itself. They passed a resolution, declaring fresh air camps to be "worthy projects [which] are supported to the strongest possible means by citizens of this city."[155] In the article covering the affair – "Labor Calls Criticism of *Star* Funds Despicable" – the message was made clear that fresh air work was no laughing matter. Ultimately, fathers, mothers, and other working-class citizens had come to take their own pride of ownership in this holiday institution and, by their actions, intimated that the fresh air camp was more than the domain of bourgeois philanthropy.

As much as fresh air camps may have felt delightfully distant from the daily experience of poor women and children, the depiction of these institutions as providing isolated environments, as with all camps, was misleading. Fresh air camp was not a separate world but, rather, one intimately connected to the work of urban social service organizations, to traditional charity, and to modern social work. In fact, the fresh air institution was perhaps the camp most wedded to the promises of modernity. Their staff of doctors and nurses promised improved health; their social workers promised more regulated lives; and modern technology promised tight connections between rural camps and the urban organizations that spawned them.

In the antimodern setting of nature, fresh air camps pursued their very modern agenda. Above all, they sought not simply to entertain the poor but also to *change* them. This was not necessarily a matter of conscious intent, nor did it always succeed. Still, it was a significant subtext of the fresh air experience. If, as labour historians and others argue, the working class was constantly being remade throughout the twentieth century, the history of the fresh air camp suggests that one element influencing its constitution was working-class interaction with modern charity and social work. While businesspeople and politicians aimed to control workers on the job and through legislative measures, charity volunteers and social workers fought to win the hearts, minds (and habits) of their children at the local community centre, YMCA, or, as we have seen, camp. This is not to suggest that administrators, staff, and youthful counsellors were not genuine in their attempt to show campers a good time, but only to point out that even such an innocuous goal was influenced by the class perspective of those who pursued it. It was precisely the nature of middle-class culture that the lines between health and habit, manners and morals, were generally indistinct. When middle-class people took to the country to show "slum kiddies" a good time, bourgeois values and perspectives were not left behind at home.

Working-class campers, for their part, did not come to camp as blank slates of experience upon which charity effortlessly wrote its message. They came to camp because they enjoyed it, and they supported it in their adult years because they wanted others to share the experience. Indeed, for campers young and old, fresh air camp was a welcome, happy, and much anticipated treat, novel enough to seem, indeed, like a world apart. If some felt occasionally patronized by camp administrators, this didn't stop thousands from seeking out the experience and, sometimes, returning for more than one summer. Ultimately, both the limitations of the fresh air camp and its powerful and often positive impact on individual campers are evident in the comments of one grateful mother. Once returned to her unchanged and difficult home circumstances in 1922, this Toronto woman still felt camp had a role to play: "Now when I am tired out and can see nothing but dirty children, clothes to wash and meals to get, I just sit down, close my eyes and see those lovely hills and trees, and I feel like a different person."[156] Whether she – or her children – were different in the way that camp administrators hoped they would be remains an elusive question, but no one could dispute that fresh air camp had made an imprint on this woman, as it did on thousands of other working-class mothers and children.

4

Making Modern Childhood the Natural Way: The Camp Experiment with Psychology, Mental Hygiene, and Progressive Education

In a radio broadcast of April 1947, Dr. J.G. Althouse, Ontario's chief director of education, praised the summer camp for all it had to offer the children and youth of the province. In his comments, he lauded the camp's natural setting, commended the simplicity of its programming, and extolled the old-fashioned self-sufficiency it engendered. In a sentence, he summed up what many regarded as the camp's most vital attribute. At summer camp, he explained, "The complications of our modern way of life are largely removed."[1] In understanding camp life as offering a possible flight from modernity, Althouse was not alone. Camp administrators from the late 1920s through to the mid-1950s promoted the summer camp as both a much needed escape from modern, urban living and the pathway to a world of natural, premodern simplicity.

Idealizations such as these were meant to convince the public, but they shouldn't fool the historian. Summer camps were situated in the seemingly constant world of nature, but their administrators also prided themselves on keeping abreast of the most recent psychological and educational trends. While the notion that outdoor living was "good" for one dated back at least as far as the mid-nineteenth century, during the middle decades of the twentieth century this idea was elaborated and refined by those influenced by the emerging discipline of psychology. During these years, promoters of camp life regarded it as providing the ideal environment for fostering psychological health and well-being. They also argued that the camp was unique in its ability not only to preach the ideals of progressive education, but, more important, to apply them.

Al Helmsley, park naturalist, conducting nature hike with girls from Camp Tanamakoon, 1951. Administrators believed that camp activities educated children in a hands-on way, a possibility that seems to be likely here as Tanamakoon girls are introduced to the leopard frog. *Algonquin Park Museum Archives #888 (MNR; Al. P. #2)*

In essence, the summer camp had a dual face. What many people saw when they looked at the camp was a retreat from the modern world. As social theorist Anthony Giddens argues, under conditions of modernity, nature is typically "constituted independently of human social activity," allowing many to think of it (wrongly) as a world apart.[2] Those who ran and administered camps often shared and sought to capitalize on this perception, but, ultimately, their actions helped to narrow the distance between the two supposed "worlds." If "getting back to nature" had at least the air of good old-fashioned simplicity about it, when it came to thinking about "the child" who was to be transformed by this experience, summer camp openly declared itself part and parcel of a very modern project. For, as Giddens also argues, one of the defining features of modernity is that "expert systems are not confined to areas of technological expertise. They extend to social relations themselves and to the intimacies of the self ... The doctor, counsellor and therapist are as central to the expert systems of modernity as the scientist, technician, or engineer."[3] Whether or not counsellors or therapists always achieved their desired ends, in the natural setting of summer camp, as elsewhere, reliance on their expertise marked a significant shift in systems of cultural authority.

This chapter explores the impact of educational psychology and progressivism on the Ontario summer camp. An examination of camp literature and programming reveals that reliance on emerging psychological and educational expertise shaped thinking about the benefits of camp and also about the nature of "the child" and "childhood" as a category of experience. At the same time, the class background of campers shaped the application of psychological ideas in different ways at different camps as actual children were encountered and managed. As far as camps' educational mission was concerned, they were possibly more successful than schools in delivering progressive education, although there were also limits to the progressive experiment.

Modern Theories in a Natural Setting

The emergence of the summer camp took place amidst important changes in thinking concerning child development in North America. In the late nineteenth century, emerging notions of children as dependent and as in need of protection resulted in the introduction of public and, later, compulsory schooling, the establishment of separate children's institutions, and struggles to eliminate child labour.[4] Into the twentieth century, the modern notion of childhood that these changes implied was further bolstered by the force of scientific and professional expertise. Common sense understandings of children as living a distinct stage of the human experience were solidified by explicit theories of child development emanating from newly established departments of psychology.[5]

The emergence of psychology as a distinct discipline was closely tied with what was known, in North America, as the mental hygiene movement. Like eugenicists of the period, this movement initially endorsed a largely hereditarian view of mental deficiency, a stance that shaped early academic psychology in important ways. From this perspective, "immorality," laziness, and even criminal tendencies were thought to be inherited traits and, thus, largely untreatable. As a result, these early proto-psychologists necessarily saw the scope of their work as limited. Rather than seeking cures or therapies, they confined themselves to the classification and segregation of mental "defectives" already present in the population, the prevention of their reproduction, and attempts to secure tougher immigration legislation to keep others out. If the "defective" could not be cured, professionals could nevertheless direct some attention to the healthy. Accordingly, national committees for the promotion of mental hygiene – constituted, Sol Cohen explains, by "reform-minded academicians, social workers, physicians and psychiatrists"[6] – were established in both the United States and Canada in 1909 and 1918, respectively. It was these bodies that, as historian Mona Gleason puts it, "brought psychology out of the laboratory and into the public spaces."[7] Thanks to funding from the Canadian National Committee for Mental Hygiene, psychology was able to detach itself from the study of philosophy and emerge as an independent discipline, with the first Canadian Department of Psychology established at the University of Toronto in 1926.[8]

During this same period, psychology underwent a broad shift from hereditarian views to environmentalist ones. According to the new wisdom, personalities were not born – they were made. From the psychologist's viewpoint, this clearly held greater promise in terms of intervention and treatment and, accordingly, a much broader scope for professional development. Imbued with modern optimism regarding improvement and perfectibility, psychologists now embraced the belief that one's environment was key in shaping mental health. Since early experiences were taken to be formative, the child and the earliest environments of childhood became the focus of much psychological investigation. Prevention emerged as the new watchword as researchers shifted their priorities from the exploration of the pathological to discerning the patterns of "normal" and "healthy" development. Children were understood to pass through distinct stages on their way to fully adult personalities, a notion with roots in Darwinian theories of evolution but one also elaborated upon by twentieth-century psychology.

The shift towards an emphasis on child psychology took place for more than just academic reasons. As Brian Low and others argue, funding for psychological research, specifically from the American Laura Spelman Rockefeller Memorial Fund (LSRM), was central in shaping the priorities of the mental hygiene movement and early academic psychology. According to Low, the Rockefeller Foundation was interested in funding mental hygiene projects as "a design for improving future society by altering the psychological conditions of childhood within families, schools, and communities."[9] Low further argues that it was a particular type of child-rearing model that Rockefeller hoped to encourage: what historians refer to as the "permissive" model, what proponents at the time referred to as "the mental hygiene point of view," and what, by the 1950s, was accepted by educators, the helping profession, and the general public as common sense. According to this view, personality development (and disorders) occurred primarily in childhood, making it imperative that the school, as its primary educational goal, pay close attention to this development. Since psychologists who aligned their research with these priorities had the best chance of obtaining financial support, work in the area of child psychology mushroomed, including research into physical growth and maturation, mental development and testing, laboratory research involving children, and observational studies of children in more natural, everyday settings.[10]

In the interwar years, no one epitomized the environmental view more precisely than renowned American behavioural psychologist John B. Watson. Like others of his time, Watson turned his back firmly against hereditarian views as he trumpeted the malleability of personality.[11] Indeed, for Watson and later disciples like B.F. Skinner, the child was something of a Lockean "blank slate": "in the baby, there are no instincts," Watson once put it. The task of the child psychologist then, was not to peer too deeply inside the child but, rather, to control child behaviour. In interwar Canada, this "scientific" approach, which promoted rigid scheduling and intensive habit training, found its way into child-rearing manuals, maternal advice literature, and institutional programming for children in various settings.[12]

Not all, however, shared this structuralist view of child development. In contrast to Watson, Freudian psychologists gave more credit to the internal world of the child and to the desires and motivations that lay behind observable behaviour, guided by what they saw as the immense power of the subconscious. From this perspective, the infant was not a human tabula rasa but, rather, a being containing essential "drives" that predated the conditioning efforts of psychologists and parents. Accordingly, more emphasis was placed on understanding the child as an individual with unique emotional needs rather than on the application of methods of behaviour control. Dr. Benjamin Spock, whose *Baby and Child Care* sold millions of copies in the postwar period, was largely responsible for popularizing this approach.[13]

In Canada, the work of William E. Blatz, a prominent child psychologist of the period, represented a blend of these two perspectives (as did much of the educational psychology associated with the mental hygiene point of view). On the one hand, Blatz sought to counter the "inefficiency" of most family homes; at his Institute for Child Study, the day nursery incorporated the same habit-training, unbending routine, and detailed record-keeping favoured by the behaviourists. We should "take them all away if we could," was his comment on the advisability of removing children from the parental home, revealing, like Watson, an unabashed confidence in the expert approach.[14] On the other hand, Blatz was also influenced by Freudian ideals. He rejected the use of coercion of any kind and objected to interference with children's natural inclinations. This "free-choice learning," as he called it, acted as an important counterpart to the "conformity learning" of daily habit-training. Finally, Blatz revealed a vital interest in the emotional world of the child, elaborating his theory of security, to which he held children were always aspiring. Blatz's research was conducted within the context of a discipline dominated by the mental hygiene perspective. His Institute of Child Study, like so many North American innovations in child psychology, was funded by the LRSM. In particular, his work fit with what Pols describes as "the natural history model" of child development research. Proponents of this model were doubtful as to the usefulness of laboratory-based research, arguing that this setting was artificial, foreign to the child, and, thus, not likely to replicate the everyday behaviour that psychologists sought to observe.[15]

Widely known for his role in overseeing the upbringing of the Dionne Quintuplets, Blatz was less well known for his involvement with summer camping. For a time, during the interwar years, he served as on-site psychologist at the well known and respected Taylor Statten camps in Algonquin Park. In 1942, his connection with camping was formally recognized when the Ontario section of the (then) American Camping Association enlisted him to deliver lectures and stimulate discussions with groups of counsellors.[16] Ultimately, Blatz's interest in camping was no surprise. For those who favoured the "natural history" approach to development research, camp represented yet another site in which observation of everyday child behaviour could be carried out. One might argue that Blatz also had indirect influence on Ontario camps through his student, Dr. Mary Northway, who, as we've seen, was heavily involved with Glen Bernard Camp and also the Ontario Camping Association.

"As Far Removed as a South Sea Island"

William Blatz's appearance at summer camp was not something that would have made sense in the early years of Ontario's summer camp history. At the turn of the century, when the first camps in the province were being established, the camp was understood in different terms. Indeed, the common wisdom within the camping movement was that, before the 1930s, camp objectives were conceptualized in mainly recreational terms. Camp directors who felt themselves to have advanced beyond this early phase looked back on these early years as a time when camp was advocated primarily as good clean fun and not much more.[17] According to this narrative, camp objectives became more sophisticated in the interwar years, a claim substantiated by a review of the camp literature. Particularly from the 1930s onwards, the camping movement articulated its goals in the language of educational psychology. This was no accident; as we've seen, many camp directors had both direct and indirect connections to educational circles and to the emerging psychological discipline.

Operating within these milieus, camp directors were influenced by the dominant educational psychology of their time. In particular, camp literature echoed psychology's focus on the environment, something that came easily in a context in which uniqueness of setting was the primary selling point. Camp administrators of all types shared the belief that human beings were capable of change and that their environment was the key factor in effecting it. While proponents of mental hygiene were, by Cohen's description, "dazzled by the school's potential"[18] as a site for the observation (and alteration) of child behaviour, outdoor educationalists were even more hopeful of the camp. Camp was not only a distinct place in the geographic sense, but it was also considered to provide a fundamentally new environment, with all the connotations of experimentation and potential progress this conjured up. In this lay its power, as promoters agreed. In the literature of fresh air camps, this was made abundantly clear. As one promoter saw it in 1924, working-class children were "building for the days to come under a very great handicap indeed. One word explains it all and that word is 'environment.'"[19] Another put the situation more positively in 1942: "Children usually grow up according to their environment and at these fresh air camps many are introduced to a new life."[20] Camps of different types may have conceptualized this "new life" in different terms, but they shared an understanding of what made the camp environment so valuable: first, its fundamentally "natural" character, and second, its isolation.

Administrators were well aware of, and frequently delighted in, the camp's removal from the larger society. This isolation entailed distance not only from consumer culture but also from competing educational influences, including the home. The authors of *Camping and Character* stated openly in 1929 that it was the setting in which "erratic parental discipline can be avoided and ... mental hygiene methods ... carried out without prejudice or interference."[21] Clearly, when seen in light of the psychological aims of the movement, this physical removal took on added importance. Isolation was what every psychologist sought, the necessary condition for the controlled experiment. For those who favoured the natural history model, camp seemed to offer a nice balance of the two. Without placing them in the artificial laboratory setting, camp founders created the conditions for "a constancy and thoroughness of observation ... which cannot be secured in many other situations," as *Camping and Character* recognized. "In camp ... the entire day may be carefully observed and recorded."[22] Psychologist and camp director Mary Northway elaborated on the camp's usefulness for child study in 1940:

> The summer camp offers an ideal field for research for the social psychologist. It is an isolated, constant, temporary group, as far removed from the ordinary roads of social intercourse as a south sea island. Camp suddenly comes into existence when a group of individuals, cut off from the ties of their normal societies, are thrust together in one geographic community, and a new society is created. While camp lasts, it is an isolated community; and it may be considered a society in miniature.[23]

It would be a mistake, however, to see the two essential aspects of the camp environment – nature and isolation – as unrelated. As camp educators saw it, it was precisely the combination of the two that made the camp superior to other children's institutions. Camp isolated children more completely than either schools or clinics, places where most psychologists tested theories of intelligence and aimed to shape child development. And yet, as two camp enthusiasts put it, while camp offered "complete environmental control," it also offered opportunities for "personal fulfilment of emotions and interests."[24]

In short, camp was supposed to be both psychologically beneficial and fun. According to a 1933 report from Bolton Fresh Air Camp, in terms of fostering healthy "self-development," camp offered children, "greater opportunity ... than if they were at the most expensive Summer Hotels."[25] The clear implication was that "over-civilized" luxury and comfort prevented honest connection with the natural world. Summer camp, by contrast, offered life-changing experiences involving direct contact with nature. The healthiest modern children, then, would be shaped in this seemingly premodern setting.

One of the qualities camps were praised for fostering was independence, something Blatz and his contemporaries saw as a key marker of maturity. In effect, camp was to act as a way station between childhood and adulthood, a space in which children could achieve "emancipation" from parents. Especially at private camps, where children, sometimes as young as four years old, spent the eight weeks of summer, increased independence was an inevitable by-product. As Camp Ahmek's counsellor handbook explained in 1939, "'Untying apron strings' is a popular way – [and, clearly, also a gendered one] – of expressing this function. This process of emotional weaning and the establishment of habits of independence ... must be complete before an individual has achieved psychological adulthood. Even in a month or two, the camp can frequently accomplish very valuable results in helping campers to 'grow up.'"[26] In this same spirit, the Camp Ahmek administration discouraged counsellors from demanding "blind obedience to authority" from their campers.[27] Camp was meant to build confidence, helping children to think for themselves and stand on their own feet. As in the wider world of psychology, shy children were regarded as in particular need of improvement. Staff members were instructed to use "careful observation" to root out the "timid or seclusive [sic]" camper, while camp bulletins glowed with reports of "happier and more self-confident" children who, previously, had been "quiet and withdrawn."[28]

At camp, as elsewhere, the ultimate test of the healthy personality was the ability to work well with others and, especially, one's peers. Though clearly ordered by adults, camp was regarded as a world made for children, a mini-community in which their needs were paramount and in which they were to learn, above all, from each other. There, children neglected, coddled, or perhaps without siblings at home were forced to live alongside others on an ongoing basis, a matter for praise in the camp literature. Camp enthusiast and doctor of psychology Mary Northway stressed in 1939: "It is highly important that a child learn to be at home with his own contemporaries. Acceptability by older people or by younger children in no way makes up for failure to get along with one's own age group."[29] This focus on "peers" – what Chudacoff describes as an emerging "age consciousness" – was echoed throughout the camp movement.[30] On a practical level, age grouping of campers became a pedagogical imperative. It was clearly with pride that a 1938 report stated, "The programme of Bolton Camp has grown by studying the needs of each age and sex group and planning for these accordingly."[31] A year later, the camp had divided children ranging from infants to sixteen years into at least six separate categories, each with its own distinct program, a pattern repeated at private and agency camps of this period.[32]

Typically, peers were understood to be children of the same age group; at the summer camp, as we've seen, peers were also grouped by class. The fact that camps of different types were established for children from different economic backgrounds also shaped the nature of psychology's impact at camp. At private camps with typically hefty fees, resources were available to hire on-site psychologists and to undertake extensive psychological testing. Lower camper to staff ratios also allowed counsellors and other staff to pay more careful attention to individual campers and to apply principles of child psychology to their work.[33] Middle- and upper-class parents might also have played a role. In the interwar years, parents of this sort were more likely to seek out the camp for its socializing potential than were, say, parents of the poor, who appreciated fresh air camps mainly for providing out-of-city holidays and a break for overworked mothers. As early as the 1920s, the private Camp Ahmek was aware that well-to-do parents sent children to it so that they would "learn to play and become less reserved," "to gain more self confidence and overcome shyness," and, "one of the most common suggestions," to learn to "mix readily with others."[34] More cynical opinions suggested that wealthy parents also appreciated having children off their hands for the summer, but it seems they also expected them to come home better people.[35]

In a number of cases, private camp directors and staff were, themselves, trained psychologists who looked to the world of camping as a summertime outlet for their expertise. The case of Mary Northway has already been mentioned. Her academic training in psychology clearly influenced her approach to campers, witness her Watsonian belief that she was working with "the most powerful and plastic material in the world, namely, children."[36] In her eyes, good camp workers were produced by combining experience with children and "technical knowledge of child development." Elsie Palter provides another example of a trained psychologist turned camp director. After founding Camp Kawagama with her husband in 1945, she prided herself on keeping a psychological profile of every camper who passed through the camp gates. With a box of index cards kept well into old age, Palter was apparently still analyzing her campers many years after their camp holidays.[37]

Of private camps in Ontario, Taylor Statten's Camp Ahmek stands out for its early, most intensive, and thorough-going application of psychology to the realm of camping. Indeed, one might regard the Ahmek administration as one of the "early adopters" of ideas that would become widely accepted elsewhere in later years.[38] No doubt this process was helped along by Statten's connection to two social scientists, Hedley S. Dimock and Charles E. Hendry, who undertook observational studies at the camp in the 1920s, resulting in a number of publications over the years. The most widely read of these publications was *Camping and Character*, what some would come to think of as the "North American bible of camping." Ultimately, the (over three-hundred-page) 1929 study amounted to the camp's public statement on the fruitful union of psychology, education, and camping and was tellingly subtitled "An Experiment in Character Education." While admitting to difficulties in the precise measurement of "character," the authors nonetheless stressed the importance of applying "the most rigourous scrutiny and techniques," asserting that "the summer camp must participate in th[e] endeavor to develop and apply more scientific methods to test its results." In a chapter entitled "Appraising the Results," life at camp read like a formal psychology experiment, complete with references to "measuring devices," "empirical judgements," and "standard deviations," replete with charts and graphs.[39]

Dimock and Hendry gathered information for their study in a number of ways. First, there were the medical exams, two or three "tests of proficiency" in camping skills, and other tests assessing campers' general intelligence, knowledge, and values. More covertly, counsellors rated campers according to the camp's "Behaviour Frequency Rating Scale," which included fifty-four different aspects of behaviour. Children were also the subject of more descriptive "behaviour observation reports" and "weekly progress reports" on their general conduct and camping skills. Finally, even parents were asked to assess their child's social, emotional, and psychological progress before and after camp, another way of furthering the parent education goals of mental hygiene.[40] Clearly, record-keeping and analysis were central to this project, as stated in the camp's counselling handbook in 1939: "In the business world records and accounting as a means of judging results are taken for granted. Because the camp is not dealing with tangible outcomes, such as automobiles or biscuits, for example, is no reason for not attempting some accounting of results. We believe that persons and their development are of great importance, worthy of adequate records, and of the best techniques of appraisal."[41] What solidified and further facilitated psychology's impact at Ahmek was the establishment of the camp's own "Department of Psychology" in 1930. Like the many child guidance clinics springing up across North American cities after the First World War, the department allowed a set of bona fide professionals to hone their strategies for the measurement and recording of psychological data at camp.[42]

What sort of "character," one might wonder, were these professionals measuring? The list of items on the Behaviour Observation Scale gave some indication. Rather than the older nineteenth-century focus on sobriety, thrift, and Sabbath-observance, or on a list of "immoral" habits, the scale aimed at detecting defective personalities and indications of "maladjustment." Counsellors were expected to rate campers on their "resourcefulness," "initiative," "leadership," and "friendliness" as well as "stubbornness," "timidity," "fearfulness," and "overbearing attitude." While "character" could be detected in such things as the willingness "to observe rules and regulations" and to "contribute well-considered suggestions to the ... group," lack of adjustment was apparent in tendencies to "blush easily," "grouch [and] find fault," and "seek the limelight." In essence, character and well-adapted personalities were one and the same. Both were now matters of near scientific dimensions, as the camp's interest in decoding "laws of personality" suggested. With their focus on the child's "fundamental urges, drives or motives," such laws implied, as many psychologists were doing, that there were really no "bad" children, simply those who used maladaptive means to achieve their emotional ends.[43]

Ultimately, the "psychological gaze" at Ahmek was broad indeed. The typical child was evaluated and assessed at every turn, whether by formal testing or simply while enjoying the life of camp. In addition, more difficult, misbehaving youth could expect individual visits to the camp psychologist, a scenario that allowed the gaze to become even more personal and direct. *Camping and Character* provided an overview of a few of these "problem campers," who had behavioural problems such as "lying," "stealing," "temper tantrums," and "poor eating habits." At Ahmek's Department of Psychology, camp psychologists observed, diagnosed, and treated campers as they saw fit. In the course of this process, every problem and personality was refracted through the prism of psychological expertise, as the description of young Albert, diagnosed "neurotic," reveals: "During the interview with the psychologist, Albert was chewing gum, biting his nails, scratching, and constantly moving around. His fears included water, snakes, the dark, and lions. He dreams ... about spooky things ... Bed-wetting persisted until he was seven. When made to hold his hands quietly in his lap, his facial muscles were affected, indicating the definiteness of his neurotic condition."[44] Clearly, what many might consider typical childhood habits and fears could be cause for professional intervention and treatment at the hands of psychological experts.

At Ahmek and other private camps, administrators developed a psychological critique not only of their campers but also of the well-to-do family and homelife. While private campers were frequently viewed as the leaders and upstanding citizens of the future, administrators also worried about the potential problems inherent in conditions of privilege. Here, camp psychologists anticipated the negative assessment of the wealthy family offered by *Crestwood Heights* authors in postwar years.[45] In *Camping and Character*, the case was made that material abundance posed its own unique challenges to healthy development:

> The boys who attend private camps come largely from the homes of the business and professional classes. Their adjustment needs probably differ from the adaptive needs of boys in other kinds of camps ... This does not imply for a moment that boys who come to private camps are better adjusted socially than the attendants at other camps. A parent's fortune may be a boy's greatest misfortune as has been repeatedly pointed out by psychiatrists.[46]

Put another way, "spoiling" was the ever-present danger in privileged families. As Mary Northway observed in 1937: "Bella was the youngest of six in a wealthy family. Very early she assumed the role of 'spoilt youngest' and used it to rule the family and gain her own ends ... She loved attention and used subtle tricks to secure it."[47] Observers at other camps were equally critical of parents who relied on material rewards as behavioural motivators. Director Mary Hamilton concluded what many also believed, that, "in our aim to make youth a happy time for children, we are prone to become indulgent rather than wise."[48] The result was the "postponing of independence" and undisciplined personalities, unfit for leadership roles.

If wealthy parents were accused of giving too much in a material sense, when it came to the question of proper love and attention, they were often faulted with a lack of generosity. In *Camping and Character*, absentee parents drew special attention. Mothers, in particular, were charged with neglect of their duties, too often leaving children in the hands of alternate care-givers. In the case of "problem camper" "Ezekiel," it was stated: "His crudeness of dress and eating habits are largely accounted for by his home situation, where the responsibility is divided between the mother, maids, and a sister. This probably means that he does just about whatever he wants." Another mother who came in for criticism was described as "a woman of culture [who was] ... away from home considerably" and who was in the habit of leaving her boys with either the housekeeper or their grandmother. Wealthy fathers, for their part, were blamed for being overly absorbed in business success and in out-of-town travel as well as for, in their pursuit of social prestige, giving children poor role models. Clearly, while historians have told us much about the professional critique of the working-class family, it is interesting to note that, under psychology's gaze, wealthy families also came in for criticism.[49]

As the objects of this intensifying gaze, children at private camps responded in various ways. Reactions to on-site psychologists were sometimes distinctly negative. In this respect, the experts at Ahmek encountered some challenging cases, campers like "Freddy," who left his psychological assessment "in a humiliated ... but rebellious mood" and "Ezekiel," who, only hours after his session to improve his attitude, was found "flick[ing] a large sticky piece of chewing gum into the camp mother's coiffure."[50] Even those not in any way singled out for observation sometimes bristled at the psychologist's presence. Indeed, while completing their fieldwork, the authors of *Camping and Character* were felt by some to be hindering children's full enjoyment of camp. "The two men 'got in the way' of campers doing their daily activities," states one history of the camp. "There were forms to be filled out and evaluations to be made every day which interrupted the normal flow of the program. From a campers' point of view, the two men were 'outsiders' and did not appear to be the type of people to easily fit into a camp situation."[51] Such responses were not entirely unique. At Glen Bernard, Mary Northway was forced to admit that her own research met with some resistance, despite her personal history with the camp. During the second phase of her research, she confessed there were several campers who refused to participate, indicating that the questions were "too personal." Asking participants to identify their "least favourite camper," for instance, generated "considerable resentment."[52] On the other hand, some campers who had trouble fitting in sometimes appreciated the individual attention of the professionals.[53] The important point here is not so much whether the expert gaze was appreciated or not but, rather, that it provided the yardstick by which mental health was now measured.

At agency camps run by youth organizations and religious groups, psychology also had its influence. Due to their relatively low fees, these camps did not have the resources to develop departments of psychology, but camper populations were small enough to allow for a fair deal of individual attention. In 1940, at the YMCA's Camp Pine Crest, this translated into "hundreds of hours" of "personal counselling" provided not by trained psychologists but by counsellors and, in some cases, the director.

Administrators showed great faith in the value of this talk therapy, with camp reports detailing the progress of individual campers upon receiving personalized attention from staff.[54] Campers were praised for learning to share in cabin clean-up, for accepting an outcast camper, or just generally for getting along with others. Administrators at agency camps, like those at private camps, stressed the importance of detailed record keeping as a way of counting their successes (or failures). As at Ahmek, information for records was solicited from parents, counsellors, and other staff. In 1951, at the Y's Tapawingo for girls, at least some campers went through extensive "intake interviews," which included questions about parent-child relationships, children's work habits and interests, as well as attitudes towards "race and religious prejudice, snobbishness ... boys, and sex."[55] Like private camp administrators, those at agency camps were self-conscious about how they differed from camps of the past in this regard. As a brief history of the Y's On-Da-Da-Waks put it somewhat smugly, "Record-keeping was not a strong point with the early directors of Camp O."[56] By contrast, by 1949, Pine Crest's administration was asserting that "records are invaluable in estimating the success and value of camp program and should therefore be very carefully kept."[57] At the same time, these camps tried to balance Watsonian-style record keeping with a more Freudian interest in the individual child. Canoe trips, for instance, were to be planned "to fit *the campers*," while those keeping reports on the camp were expected to remember that "the most vital part of a camp concerned [the] boys, and what effect the camp had on their lives."[58]

This situation was both similar and different at fresh air camps in the province. Certainly, there was no question of on-site psychologists or departments of psychology at camps of this sort. Even if the hiring of professionals had been feasible (which it was not), with thousands of campers each summer (compared to, perhaps, two hundred at the typical private or agency camp), it would have required a small army of psychologists to offer the same level of attention as was given at private and agency camps. Furthermore, the short ten-to-twelve-day stays typical at fresh air camps allowed little time for observation, let alone diagnosis and treatment. Finally, one wonders to what degree psychological assessment was thought appropriate for working-class children. The actions of misbehaving poor children – boys in particular – did not go unnoticed, as we've seen, but they were more likely to win them the label of delinquent than neurotic, with the goal being to "reform" them through social workers rather than to "treat" them through psychologists.

Still, even at the low-budget, charity-run Bolton Fresh Air Camp, psychological theories had their impact, and these years saw an increasing interest in campers' emotional and psychological well-being. While fresh air camps had initially recommended themselves to the public for their health benefits, concerted efforts were made in the late 1930s to convince the public that their mandate went far beyond providing nutrition and combatting disease. "In terms of physical health [a camp holiday] means much," it was declared as early as 1931, "but no one will ever be able to estimate the benefits to mental health this outing ... means."[59] Though camp promoters were not the first to make such claims, their emphasis on using nature as a tool in early personality development rather than simply as a fresh air tonic was unique. By 1944, administrators at Bolton declared that physical well-being was now taking a back seat to other concerns, that, in fact, "the health influences ... although very important in themselves, are subordinate in value to ... other factors."[60]

Fresh air camps also showed the influence of modern theories of childhood in their emphasis on play. When camp promoters spoke of "the natural desire of every normal child for recreation,"[61] they were drawing on the wisdom of psychologists, sociologists, anthropologists, and educational and recreational theorists from the 1880s onward. These experts agreed that, more than the mere pleasure it provided, play in its organized and supervised form could instill values of sexual purity, discipline, respect for authority, and, more broadly, the ever-sought-after "character."[62] But, as promoters of fresh air camps noted, for working-class children, the problem of play was also a spatial one. Modernity meant many things in early twentieth-century Ontario; one of these was the changing nature of urban life. In an age before environmental controls, the intensification of industry and the fact that some of the poorest workers lived closest to places of work meant that their children found themselves in spaces many considered unsuitable for play. In the pages of the *Toronto Daily Star*, Fresh Air Fund promoters bemoaned the fact that, even in the hot days of summer, the most accessible options for poor children's play were cramped backyards, nearby back lanes, or – the bourgeois nightmare – the streets. On the other hand, many "baby breadwinners" were not playing at all, and this, too, the *Star* documented: "Two Little Girls Support Mother and Family of Six," "Eight-year-old Girl Works to Help Support Family," "Two Young Girls Support Family of 5 on $15 week." These were only some of the headlines that sought to elicit public support in the 1920s.[63] The implicit message was clear: to be a child was to play, to be an adult was to work. From this perspective, even unpaid contributions to the family economy were considered an affront to childhood's fundamental nature. "This child has practically lost her childhood," a 1923 article said of one eleven-year-old. "She is an old woman in effect. She never gets out to play ... Instead of dolls she has real babies to look after. Instead of 'playing house' she has had to get meals for a family."[64] As late as 1940, the fund was still occasionally bemoaning the problem of child labour, when twelve-year-old boys were acting as "m[e]n of the house" rather than "flying model airplanes." Camp promised to right this situation, if only temporarily. Readers were assured, "with your aid he'll be a boy for ten days."[65]

Partly thanks to camp, the belief in a child's right to play was becoming twentieth-century common sense. In essence, this was an elaboration of the notion that children deserved protection from wage labour. Working-class families might (and did) sometimes defy this way of thinking, but statements like those above showed that they would face increasing criticism if they did so. Children, it was now agreed, were entitled to something adults could never hope to regain: a carefree phase of life, free from worries, work, and unpleasant emotion. "Sadness Creeps into a Young Life at a Time When Nothing but Happiness Should Abound," the subtitle of a 1922 appeal, demonstrated just how rosy the theoretical notion of childhood had become.[66] According to the *Star*, "normal childhood" now included "pleasant play in pleasant surroundings, good food that is not pinched and stinted; clothes that are at their very least well-fashioned enough to prevent self-consciousness and shame ... and toys to hold the imagination." Those without these, it was stated, had "but ... small chance of reaching normal healthy manhood and womanhood."[67]

Ultimately, the fresh air camp was one more institution through which middle-class ideals of childhood and child-rearing were spread to working-class families. In this sense, camps contributed to the broader cultural transformation of the meaning of childhood. Crucial to this way of thinking was that children were not just smaller versions of adult psyches. "Children are neither vegetables nor miniature men," Mary Northway asserted in 1939, while, of Director Mary Edgar it was said, "She felt very strongly that children should be children."[68] These seemingly banal statements spoke volumes concerning the shift in conceptions of childhood. They highlighted the notion that children had needs, interests, and abilities distinct from those of adults – beliefs not so firmly held by previous generations.

Camps of all kinds helped construct new notions of childhood, but they also distinguished between childhood and youth. Like educators, psychologists, and others interested in the young since the turn of the century, camp administrators shared the notion of adolescence as a unique and distinct time.[69] Youth were regarded as occupying a distinct developmental space, advanced beyond the realm of childhood but not yet fully adult. At camp, age-graded programs tailored activities to youth's perceived interests, while camp's spatial organization often allowed for increased independence of its teenaged campers. At Camp Wapomeo, girls over fourteen were housed on an island separate from the main site of the girls' camp. Teenage boys at Camp Pine Crest – labelled "Pioneers" – were treated with similar distinction. While younger campers were confined to cabins, these teenaged, more experienced, boys slept in tents "on their own campsite."[70] The focus on adolescence as the period of sexual awakening was also reflected at summer camps. In postwar years, as we've seen, administrators believed that teenagers were "most interested" in the new coeducational programming, and, thus, mixed-sex activities were directed mainly at them.[71]

Giving older campers unique treatment and special privileges was one way of encouraging the transition to camp staff – a transition that many camps hoped youth would make. True enough, counsellors were frequently university and even high school students, not much older than the oldest campers. In one way, this was simply necessity, but counsellors' youthfulness was also constructed as an advantage, a factor that would facilitate the intimate bond between "teacher" and "student" favoured by progressive educators. Despite administrators' best hopes, however, adolescent campers and relatively immature staff also presented unique problems at camp. Interviews with former campers reveal stories of those who planned secret trysts after dark and who had to be "pulled out of the bushes" by patrolling staff. Young counsellors, for their part, could be distracted from their work by camp girl- and boyfriends. Sometimes they were simply eager for outside excitement. In their visit to camps, the authors of *Crestwood Heights* observed in postwar years that "the greatest difficulty with counsellors ... is to keep them on the camp site after duties are over" and to prevent them from "go[ing] into town," "do[ing] stupid things," and drawing the criticism of disgruntled locals.[72] Clearly, the idea that youth was a time of both opportunity and potential peril was reflected in the history of Ontario's camps.

In theory, both childhood and youth were constructed as categories beyond class. Thus, while adults who enjoyed material comforts and holiday pleasures were to count themselves "lucky," all children were understood to be "deserving" of their rightful portion of good times. In this modern view, the condition of childhood denoted not only satisfaction of needs but also the creation of good memories. Childhood was a time not only to *be* happy but also to look back on with fondness, much as an idealized conflict-free past figured in antimodernist thinking about collective experience. Childhood was to function as "the good old days" of every individual, the time before "now" when all was placid stability and calm. Again, compared with the outlook of earlier generations, this signalled a paradigm shift of radical proportions.

Psychology and the Camp in Changing Times

Psychology affected the summer camp throughout this period, but time also played a role in influencing the nature of its impact. The idea of camp as isolated from the rest of society, though never wholly true at any time, was shown to be even less so in the years of worldwide depression and war. Nevertheless, the rhetoric of isolation continued. As we've seen, private campers often felt disconnected from the Depression at camp. Likewise, at fresh air camps, the Depression seemed to deepen the feeling that camp could offer escape from society, with the presumed isolation of camp life and its psychological benefits taking on added appeal. Bolton Camp saw its work as "still more essential and valuable," offering mothers and children a short respite from the strain of constant worry and daily troubles. In triumphant tone, a 1933 report declared the camp as "one area exempt from the Depression":

> I do not mean that the finances were not affected ... Quite the reverse. There had to be a concentration upon financial problems never before known ... But all this was not apparent in the life of the Camp. As one entered its gates, that oppression and mental worry which have been universal for four years seemed to be left behind. The mothers and children coming from families which have known more than their share of these problems and worries became conscious that this was an area where, for a brief time at least, they could feel security and peace and happiness.[73]

The Second World War presented camp administrators with different challenges. We've already seen how these affected financial fortunes and the availability of labour at summer camps. In the private camp literature, however, there is also evidence that administrators worried about the war's potentially harmful psychological effect on campers. At the Taylor Statten camps, the war strengthened the citizenship-building mandate, but it also caused debate over whether impressionable young minds should be exposed to the realities of military conflict. In response to a student questionnaire of 1942, administrator Adele Ebbs initially emphasized that "camp should not be isolated as Utopia from world events ... [Campers] do have to return to their own communities ... and one of our main aims is to make them better citizens."[74] Still, when asked directly if she believed in supplying campers with regular updates of current events, her answer was "No." Her real objection seemed to lie with the psychology of the matter. "The issue can be over-emphasized if care is not taken," Ebbs explained, arguing that children could be "easily over-stimulated." Ultimately, she sought to instill practices of good citizenship among campers, to contribute to the war effort, but only if this could be done while "keeping the emotional side under control." This all fit well with the notion of childhood as a protected time, the idea that "children should be children" and that certain types of knowledge were not suitable for their consumption. Still, camps differed on the question. Shirley Ford remembers Director Mary Edgar reading out headlines and short articles on war news at Glen Bernard, suggesting that ideas were not uniform as to the information with which children could be expected to cope.[75]

The treatment of youth during the war provides, again, some contrast to this picture. Even Ebbs conceded that it might be appropriate to organize discussions about the war for older campers if they "showed interest" and if discussions were "well led." Likewise, at Northway Lodge, the Algonquin camp for older (mainly American) girls, the director made a point of reading *New York Times* articles on the war to her campers. In her view, "we did not want to separate ourselves from the world, especially in war times." The CGIT, whose sole focus was adolescent girls, took a similar approach, reminding its campers, "you have to see the world as it is," not surprising of an organization originally founded to provide an outlet for girls' contributions during the First World War.[76] And it was senior campers at private camps who were asked to make the most extensive wartime contributions in terms of replacing the labour of park rangers. This differential treatment suggests, again, that youth was being thought of as a distinct category from that of childhood and that youth themselves were seen as having rights and responsibilities that went beyond those of children.[77]

As the world seemed an increasingly changing and unpredictable place in these years of Depression, war, and, later Cold War, camp was expected to provide children with the sense of security that urban life, presumably, could not. Mary Northway paid special attention to fostering children's sense of security at camp. In a 1942 article entitled "Security Pegs for Campers," she explained: "The good ground for security which camping offers ... is the fact that its very centre is life in the out-of-doors. As the child comes to know the law, order and beauty of the physical world ... he discovers a sense of permanency." By the very way in which nature was defined – in contrast to human life, so constant and never-changing – it seemed to promise the stability deemed lacking in the urban environment of impermanence and flux. In the same article, Northway offered that security was fostered by the hard work of camping. Indeed, she claimed, "camp is wrongly called simple":

> It is not nearly so simple to collect wood, bring it in, pile it, light it and make it continue to flame, as it is to turn an electric switch on a city range; it is not nearly so simple to build a shelter to protect one from the rain as it is to unlock one's own front door. But for anyone who has discovered he can satisfy his own basic life needs through the work of his own mind and his own hands, the discovery gives a security that has permanent effect.[78]

Security was deemed no less, and perhaps more, important in postwar years, the desire for it shaping political, economic, and domestic life. At the level of childhood, fostering security now meant more than just the filling of material needs: providing children with positive psychological experiences was also crucial. Under the influence of Freudian thinking, popularized during the postwar years, childhood experiences were understood to have lasting importance. In 1949, a Fresh Air Fund appeal posed the rhetorical question, "How much of later success in life has its roots in childhood!"[79] As if in response, in 1950, a private camp brochure stated unequivocally, "The happiest adults are those who had happy and fruitful childhood experiences."[80] Starting from such premises, camps saw themselves as providing not only happy experiences for young campers but also life-long emotional and psychological stability.

Once at camp, campers of the 1950s were subject to administrators who had increasingly psychological aims. If mental hygiene notions of the importance of personality had been circulating since the 1920s, by the postwar years, as Cohen argues, these ideas had become part of "the common stock of knowledge," reflected widely in the language of child-rearing and educational discourse. Likewise, at camp, language was increasingly psychologized. In 1950, at Ahmek, it was argued that children should use arts and crafts projects "to express their innermost feelings," while a CGIT camp manual of the same year advised using sports – "especially those using balls" – as a way of "releasing hostility."[81] In other postwar camp literature, the canoe trip was lauded for fostering not only "self-reliance" and "initiative" but also a facility with "cooperation" and a sense of "responsibility" for one's fellow camper.[82] Counsellors, too, were encouraged to conceptualize campers and their potential problems using psychological concepts and jargon. Literature from the privately run Camp Winnebagoe declared in 1946, "A thorough knowledge of child psychology is imperative in order to analyse the mental attitude of every camper."[83] At the province's Bark Lake Camp for counsellors-in-training, the eight-hour course entitled "Understanding the Camper" contained all the staples of postwar thinking regarding permissive child-rearing and the "basic needs of the individual," such as the need for "self-respect," "success," "dominance," and "new experiences."[84] Even religiously oriented camps were incorporating the insights of more secular experts. The postwar CGIT counsellor was advised to "read some recommended materials on the psychology of adolescents" and to attempt to discover "what makes her [camper] tick."[85] At the Y's Camp Pine Crest, spiritual goals were likewise refracted through a psychological lens. A 1951 report declared, "Our primary concern ... is for the all round growth and personality development of each individual, in ways consistent with our Christian ideals."[86]

As in earlier decades, in postwar years, campers' parents and homelife came in for criticism. If postwar families put great stock in the value and comforts of home, and if educators continued to regard it as a key influence in a child's life, camp enthusiasts reflected the expert view that the home was not, by itself, enough. As was typical of this era, mother-blaming was common. In Mary Northway's writings, some middle- and upper-class mothers were accused of "protecting [the child] as a little god," while others were accused of "thrust[ing him] brutally at an early age to fend for himself."[87] In Fresh Air Fund appeals, working-class mothers were blamed for creating homes of "constant bickering"[88] and for their tendency "to leave dust unmolested on the floors, to leave beds unmade, dishes unwashed, clothes unhung and children untended."[89] Such criticisms suggested, as did modern psychology and the mental hygiene movement, that other socializing agents were needed not just as a last resort for difficult children but to keep all children on the path of normal child development. In effect, the home was reconceptualized as only one in a constellation of factors that promised to turn out the properly socialized child. As the province's chief director of education claimed in 1947, "It is wholesome ... for boys and girls to get away for a time from their home, no matter how good that home may be."[90] Others agreed that extra-familial institutions had distinctive roles to play. "The family and the camp have different objectives," Director Mary Hamilton stated in 1958: "The family is concerned mainly with the individual interests of the child, while the camp sees the child as a member of a group and seeks her adjustment to it."[91] Clearly, as in the wider society, the mental hygiene point of view now permeated the articulation of camp goals, the planning of camp programming, and the thinking about the camper one hoped to change.

"Like Progressive Schools in the Woods"

From the late 1920s onward, camp life was influenced not only by psychological but also by educational expertise. As early as 1929, *Camping and Character* was proclaiming that efficient camp programming required "the most critical consideration of educational technique."[92] Ten years later, Camp Ahmek's "Talks to Counselors" stated: "The whole life of the camp is the curriculum. The process of living, the interaction of persons within activities of many sorts ... constitute the educative process.[93] By 1936, CGIT literature preached a similar message, that camping was "a necessary part of the modern girl's education."[94] By the postwar period, the influence of educational theory at camp was widespread and accompanying it was a keen sense of the movement's progress. As a brochure from the private Camp Wabikon stated in 1952, "For a long time we thought of camp as a place to send youngsters to get them out of the city for the summer. This is still worthwhile, but camping today is recognized as a unique educational experience."[95] Administrators of private, fresh air, and agency camps agreed that something new was going on, that camping itself represented "one of the most significant educational innovations of the century."[96] Though its relationship to formal education was conceptualized as auxiliary or complementary, by the closing months of the Second World War, it was proudly proclaimed that "the best summer camps are like progressive schools in the outdoors."[97]

As much as camp administrators felt that they were embarking on a unique pedagogical journey, by the 1930s, ideals of progressive education were the much talked-about fashion in educational circles throughout North America. In particular, the ideas of John Dewey, American philosopher and educator, were taken up by numerous others and formed the basis for what became known as "progressive" education. Among the key aspects of Dewey's approach to education was the call to respect each child as an individual, with varying and specific needs. Indeed, Dewey castigated traditional education for its lack of innovation, its reliance on rote-learning, its narrow definition of the curriculum, and its coercive disciplinary practices. By contrast, his new approach promised "education for the whole child" – education that would unfold in an organic and child-centred way. In this respect, the "field trip" – an adventure out into the "real world" – might be more useful than the typical teacher-led lesson. Ultimately, Dewey envisioned that children educated in this manner would not only evince an open and creative attitude towards learning but would also grow into adults appreciative of the aims of a truly democratic society.[98] Education defined in this way clearly fit well with the aims and perspective of the mental hygiene movement.

Camp administrators were influenced by these new trends and regarded their own work as part of the progressive movement in education. At many camps, for instance, much was made of the shift from regimented programming to a free and open system of activities, increasingly to be chosen by campers themselves. Camps self-consciously promoted this notion of their work and of how far it had come since the "old days" of camping. In 1939, after his conversion to a more child-centred program, private camp director Taylor Statten was already looking back on his early approach to camping as "militaristic."[99] This whiggish view of the movement's progress was shared by others. By 1940, Mary Northway was claiming of camps in general that "informality has largely superseded highly scheduled programmes ... No longer does the director ... prepare a curriculum complete for every day of the season."[100] This perspective seemed to hold sway equally at fresh air and agency camps. In 1947, Bolton administrators proudly declared: "There is nothing institutional about Bolton Camp. Every activity is planned for the utmost enjoyment of each individual child ... Every child is treated as a guest and there is no regimenting. Each can do what he likes best."[101] Likewise, in 1942, the YMCA boasted of the "free and easy informality" at Camp Pine Crest.[102]

Along with the new-found antipathy for regimentation, the adoption of a child-centred approach transformed attitudes towards competition and punishment at many camps. In the 1920s, through the awarding of all manner of prizes, badges, and trophies, children had been encouraged to work at their camp skills. Even girls, generally discouraged from competing and from developing an active physicality in school-based physical education programs, were not entirely excluded from competition at camp, even if they were treated more carefully than boys.[103] Female campers competed in end-of-season all-day "colour wars" at Camp Kawagama, for the "Worthy Woodsman" award at Tanamakoon, and sometimes, at their own behest, for setting the record for the fastest canoe-trip time.[104] From the perspective of the progressive educator, however, competition was regarded as an artificial way of encouraging interest and awards, as a behaviourist crutch. Echoing the progressive educator's love of education for its practical application, camps now sought to have children "do things because they wanted to" and not simply in order to achieve recognition or "points." In the 1930s, Ahmek consciously sought to "eliminat[e] competitions as far as possible." The practice of awarding prizes of many kinds was abandoned, and even debates were considered "taboo" "because of the competitive element."[105] At Camp Tanamakoon, the administration looked back somewhat smugly on the years when the awarding of trophies was common: "The old cups at Tanamakoon are safely stored in cupboards as a memento of ancient days,"[106] Director Mary Hamilton stated in 1958. At the Y's Camp Pine Crest, administrators agreed that this was the kind of learning that would "probably stick" since "boys found learning an enjoyable process, which they did because they wanted to; they did not have to learn."[107] Overall, camps were less concerned with skill acquisition than with socialization, now the camp's highest goal. "The experience of campers in social relationships is what influences or educates them," Camp Ahmek's 1939 handbook stated, "not the activities of swimming, canoeing, dramatics ... as such."[108] Under the new system, corporal punishment – still freely resorted to in formal educational settings but increasingly under fire from modern psychology – was officially frowned on, and forms of positive reinforcement were advocated in its place. As Taylor Statten optimistically suggested to counsellors in 1939, "I hope we shall be able to go through the entire season without using the word 'don't.'"[109]

The influence of new pedagogical theories was experienced not just in a negative sense (discouraging regimentation and competition) but also in a positive one (encouraging a hands-on and direct approach to learning). Camps took great pride in the fact that, as they saw it, children learned much more at camp than "within the four walls of any school," as YMCA promotional literature put it.[110] Administrators at Ahmek relished the story of the school teacher who instructed her students, "You'll have to stop picking those flowers now and come in for your botany lesson."[111] The weaknesses of formal education were, in fact, regularly noted. A reviewer of *Camping and Character* stated: "The primary purpose of the authors has been to set forth the camp as an educational agency, succeeding in fulfilling a function wherein the state school, weighed down by authority and tradition, is failing. Education today is a thing disassociated with life, a thing of air-tight compartments with no incentives and no motives, and sadly warped ideals."[112]

In contrast, learning at camp was thought to be purposeful. For instance, participation in much-anticipated canoe out-trips was dependent on one's ability to paddle and swim. According to the same thinking, camp lessons in geography and weather took place at an experiential and not an intellectual level. "Maps are no longer things belonging to blackboards, but tools to help the camper arrive where he wants to go," Mary Northway insisted in 1940. "Clouds are known as indicators of weather, and wind direction becomes an item to watch and consider."[113] Even at fresh air camps, where camping trips often involved no more than an overnight in the woods, it was proudly stated of boy campers in 1950: "Their campcraft is put to work immediately. They learn how to use knives and axes to build themselves bough beds on overnight camp-outs."[114] Likewise at the Y's Tapawingo for girls, a 1951 report claimed that "children learned campcraft by *doing*" and not via formal classes. In each case, as with the much-publicized "project approach" of the new educators, knowledge was not to be broken down into discrete subjects but absorbed unconsciously as an integrated whole. Mary Northway was openly critical of those who resisted this approach, stating: "I have known camps where 25 parts of a sailboat have had to be learned before one can go sailing. Children are not very interested in learning names difficult to spell and to pronounce. They are interested in being in a dinghy on a windy day."[115]

Progressive education at camp also meant the training of a new kind of "teacher" – the counsellor. Of all leaders, it was agreed that the counsellor was most important – as some put it, "the most vital single factor in the camp situation" and "the most important man in camp."[116] Except for a half-holiday per week, counsellors were expected to be on the job every moment of the day, not only getting campers out of bed in the morning, monitoring their bodies and behaviours, and teaching them camp skills but also acting as living, breathing examples of health, fitness, right values, and attitudes. All told, counsellors were expected to show not only the understanding of a psychologist and the loving guidance of a parent but also, as one source put it, "something of the detachment of a doctor."[117]

If no one seriously regarded camp as a replacement for formal schooling, this did not prevent its promoters from designing grand visions of its scope and potential. As early as 1937, the *Star* was sharing the ideas of an American camping authority who called for "large public camps near every city in Canada and the United States." As part of the public system of education, he predicted that government-owned summer camps would be "the next big step forward in education."[118] In the final analysis, camp administrators saw themselves as the most truly progressive educators, those who had grasped the genius of "the natural." This "naturalness" described both its setting (in wilderness and rural contexts) and its structure (child-centred and holistic). By contrast, traditional education was deemed doubly artificial: set in the constructed spaces of urban society and organized in a constructed and artificial manner. As *Camping and Character* stated: "The paramount educational asset of the summer camp ... lies in the naturalness and simplicity of life in the woods in contrast with the complexity and artificiality of civilized city life."[119] Even in their "modernness," then, camp enthusiasts revealed their antimodern tendencies.

Assessing the Impact of Progressive Education at Camp

One of the early conclusions of Canadian historians of progressive education is that, quite simply, it failed to have a significant impact. From this view, problems of understaffed institutions, teachers untrained in progressive pedagogy, and the desire to turn out well-behaved citizens and malleable workers meant that formal education in Canada continued to function much as it always had until at least the 1960s. In Neil Sutherland's view, the 1920s to 1950s saw not a progressive educational breakthrough but, rather, "the triumph of formalism."[120] More recently, Paul Axelrod concludes of the 1950s that results were mixed; that postwar educators were "imperfect problem solvers, neither as villainous nor as saintly as their conflicting popular images implied."[121] My assessment of the camp experiment with progressive education leads to similar conclusions. Camp programs revealed a complex mix of success and failure in the experiment with progressive education.

Admittedly, camps, like schools, did not always live up to educational ideals. For one, the freedom of programming was sometimes exaggerated. Fresh air camps for the poor, with their often large numbers and low staff/camper ratios, were particularly susceptible to ongoing regimentation. While fresh air literature painted a picture of the "free and easy" life of camp, this was clearly an exaggeration.[122] In fact, along with its admiration for freedom, promotional literature revealed an abiding respect for efficiency and order. "At the fresh air camps there is a definite routine," the *Star* noted appreciatively as late as 1949: "Certain activities take place at a certain time.

Meals are served at a definite hour. There is a rest period every day which every child ... must observe."[123] At these camps with large camper populations, a degree of regimentation was no doubt a necessity. For instance, teaching children camping and sporting activities "in shifts of one hundred at a time," as at one fresh air camp on Georgian Bay, clearly did not allow for either individual attention or a free and easy approach.[124]

Even smaller, private camps sometimes displayed a similar attachment to regimentation. In 1946, the Ontario Camping Association had only praise for the "apple pie order" at Camp Tanamakoon, where even staff meetings were infused with a determined efficiency. "Avoid lounging, starting a personal conversation, or making irrelevant remarks" was the camp director's advice: "State your problems and outline what you have to say, clearly and without loss of time."[125] A similar perspective guided organization of camper activities. "Tripping was not a topsy-turvy outing," it was proudly stated of this same camp; rather, "the more efficient the trip, the happier it was."[126] The urge to slip off into the wilderness, to experience the simplicity and grandeur of nature, co-existed somewhat tensely with the ongoing desire for respectability, as advice at Ahmek suggested. "Canoe trip camping means constant warfare against untidy equipment and personal uncleanliness," trippers were informed in 1948: "Don't carry a mirror, but ask someone how you look about the third day out."[127] Departing from camp clearly did not mean departure from decorum or, for counsellors, release from detailed record-keeping. Far from it: counsellors were instructed to keep careful reports of all activities, weather, accidents, and behaviour as well as, generally, to "discourage the hobo attitude."[128] Ultimately, while permissive ideals were touted, the notion that children, by definition, needed to be guided by adult control was not one that would die easily.

Youthful counsellors, as already noted, were not always the wise and willing teachers of the progressive ideal. At times, some acted more like disgruntled workers than like dedicated instructors or mini-psychologists. A 1931 study of Ahmek noted, for instance, that counsellors were not always enthusiastic about the "great amount of clerical work" or record-keeping demanded by the camp.[129] In 1938, a final report from the camp indicated "a certain feeling of tension among staff members," that some felt that "much fun ha[d] departed" from camp life and were ready to "pack [their] trunk[s]."[130] At the Y's Camp Pine Crest, reports likewise complained of counsellors who were "not at all qualified," who lacked "personalized interest," and who weren't overly interested in the details of "campers' routine."[131]

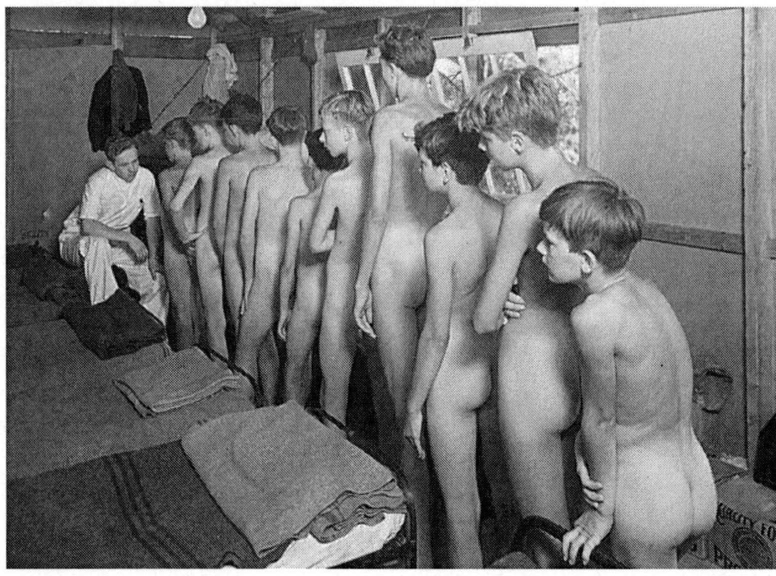

Medical inspection, Bolton Camp, 1936. Influenced by the enthusiasm for progressive pedagogy of the interwar years, camps claimed to eliminate all elements of regimentation and to stress child-centredness. From the looks of this line-up, however, even medical inspections were not private, individual experiences. *Copyright Family Service Association of Toronto.*

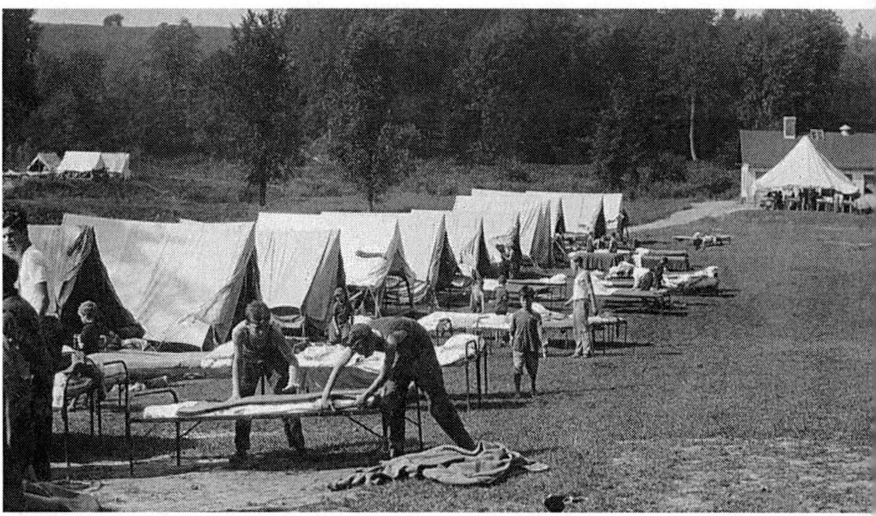

Bolton Camp, c. 1922. In the early years of tenting, the whole affair took on something of a military feel, with boys instructed to keep tents in "two even rows." *Copyright Family Service Association of Toronto.*

From the perspective of campers, relationships with counsellors were sometimes more distant than warm. In part, this distance was built into the structure of camp itself, where counsellors did not always share cabins with campers, an arrangement said to foster independence and cooperation among campers.[132] "When I was in intermediate camp," Shirley Ford remembered of 1930s Glen Bernard, "our counsellor came into the cabin the first day and said 'Hi, I'm so-and-so,' and we didn't see her again for weeks."[133] Bolton fresh air camper Mary Murphy similarly explained that she had few memories of her counsellor, in her view "because they weren't that personal with you."[134] In their defence, one might add that counsellors were often warned to keep their distance from campers due to fears of encouraging "crushes" and, in the worst case scenario, homosexuality. Here, it was thought, camp had some developmental hazards as well as benefits.[135]

In some cases, children themselves could find camp a less than agreeable experience, whatever the belief that learning was to be an organic and enjoyable process. For some, psychological health was more threatened than enhanced by the camping experience. No matter how good the camp, separation from parents and home – for private campers, sometimes as long as two months – could be traumatic. Ahmek reported that each year at its camp saw two or three cases of "hysterical homesickness," campers like fourteen-year-old "Tom" who rarely slept through the night. "I would trade you places any day," he was said to have written home to his brother: "I was sick the other night and it was heckish ... When you see the Pirate Ship in the camp book it looks big but it is small. So is the theatre ... I am in the Intermediate section and it's not much good ... I hope Mom and Dad come home ... so I will be able to go home. I will tell you straight that I will not come back here any more."[136]

Even those campers who generally took to camp life sometimes found homesickness a persistent problem. Ruth-Ellen Soles cried herself to sleep the first night of every camp season. "I did until I was 18," this 1950s Kawagama camper explained: "It became a ritual."[137] According to a 1957 study of homesickness at fifteen camps, this was one of the most common manifestations, as were sleep and digestion problems. In many of these cases, homesickness was accepted as a natural reaction, even a healthy part of growing up. A smaller number, however, led to more intense behaviour problems, suggesting that, as historian Leslie Paris has found at American camps, homesickness could also be an expression of campers' "semi-official and unofficial dissent."[138]

Apart from painful separation from family and friends, camp could disappoint in other ways. As with "Tom" above, camp was sometimes felt to be lacking the excitement promised in glossy brochures. Bad food was another common complaint. At CGIT camps, one postwar manual instructed counsellors to eat camp food "without unfavourable comment in public," while, at Bark Lake, the 1950 administration admitted, "The campers suffered an average *loss of weight*, indicat[ing] that the food quality and quantity were not good."[139] Teenagers, who sometimes spent many summers camping, could face different problems. "The trouble with the seniors is boredom," one postwar source asserted: "If they have come up through the camp, they have done everything there is to do."[140] More traumatic than boredom or bad food was the experience of campers who simply did not fit in. The bed-wetter, the physically uncoordinated or fearful child could all find camp to be a miserable experience. While forced adjustment to the peer group was seen as one of the benefits of camp, administrators were aware that campers also had negative experiences with peers.[141] At Glen Bernard Camp, it was noted in the 1930s that bullies could be "cruel and cutting" and that, generally, "In a community such as this, one or two people actually develop the role of the scapegoats of the group."[142] While scape-goating also occurred at school, at camp there was not even the chance of daily reprieve.

The relative freedom of camp could lead to other uninvited behaviours. Pranks and practical jokes were common at many camps and, as Paris argues, were largely tolerated, if not sanctioned, by camp managements, who saw them as useful in fostering group feeling. Other sorts of camper activities and responses were considered more problematic. Camp Ahmek literature referred disapprovingly to the misuse of equipment, night-time "tent feeds," "dangerous risk-taking," and to lack of cleanliness and punctuality as general problems. A 1947 report on staff training referred to some campers as "complacent," "aggressive," and "unco-operative."[143] Psychologist Mary Northway was open in criticizing the lack of discipline at some camps. "It has become the tradition to have fun by breaking the rules, by rowdyism and lack of discipline," she noted disapprovingly: "At some camps bedtime is set for 9:30, and at eleven, twelve and even two o'clock, campers are found running about disturbing others, raiding tents, waking the maintenance staff – and this is considered having fun."[144]

For their part, staff members did not always choose the most progressive approaches to deal with misbehaving children. Interviews revealed recollections of counsellors hitting children and one camper's being shut up alone in her cabin for "about a day and a half."[145] While Taylor Statten assured the public in 1939 that "the attitude of the camp is that punishment is unnecessary,"[146] clearly, this did not mean that staff at every camp always took a genial, permissive approach.

If camps were not the utopian worlds and controlled laboratories their administrators envisioned, neither did they fail entirely at their educational mission. As with other social institutions, a gap between goals and reality was always apparent, but in terms of the camp setting this did not necessarily entail the "triumph of formalism." In part, this can be read from children's own reactions. For every child who regretted the experience, there were many more for whom camp was a special and long-remembered treat. The Y's Camp Pine Crest was proud to report all the positive experiences at camp in the summer of 1940: "Fifty-two boys extended their Camp periods. Two boys visited the camp and liked it so well they stayed the rest of the summer. Several little boys cried when they had to go home. An eight year old wrote back to the director after he left camp: 'I like Camp very much. I would like to stay next year.'"[147] True enough, many campers showed an excitement, delight, and, sometimes, devotion rarely expressed in connection with institutions of formal education. "Hysterical homesickness" and major behavioural problems appear to have

Camp Tanamakoon counsellors, c. 1940. Uniforms (worn at least some of the time) helped to give the impression of "apple pie order" at Tanamakoon. *Algonquin Park Museum Archives #3155 (George May).*

Tanamakoon guide and Tanamakoon girls, 1946. If camp was meant to be educational, many campers clearly enjoyed this sort of education more than formal schooling. Here, campers at Tanamakoon enjoy a lighter moment with their guide, Sam English. *Algonquin Park Museum Archives #3309 (Don Beauprie).*

been a minority problem, with many children preferring camp life to school. According to Geraldine Sherman, postwar Kawagama camper, "the most eager campers were those who most hated school."[148]

What we know of camp programming and organization further suggests that the summer camp was at least partly successful in its experiment with progressive education. Camps were often more regimented than their literature admitted, but, for many campers, they also offered the most freeing and relaxed atmosphere of any childhood experience. For such campers, it is not the bells and the bugles that are now remembered but, rather, the liberty to experiment with new activities and the general feeling of independence this engendered. Some experienced this particularly in terms of the distance from parental control; others, like Wapomeo camper, Joan Moses, found simply that the pace of camp life was to their liking. "Being a senior girl – from 14 on," she recalled, "we had our own little island across the way from the main girls' island ... The counsellors had their own separate cabins and we had the cabin to ourselves. There were no inspections and if you didn't make your bed the whole summer, that was your problem – and some didn't!"[149] In Moses' experience, camp was very much a world unto itself, where the peer culture of youth dictated the pace as much as the camp administration.

This type of behaviour was not permitted at every camp nor for all ages of campers. For some campers, it was time spent away from camp – canoe tripping – that offered the widest scope for autonomy. Out tripping, one was removed not only from parental control but also from that of most of the camp administration. With only several counsellors – perhaps not much older than themselves – and two or three guides, campers paddled their way through adventure and adversity, with a sense of freedom and independence likely both physical and psychological. Merle Storey looked back on her experience with a bittersweet nostalgia:

> I remember struggling across the portages with the unaccustomed weight of a pack on my back, welcoming the sight of the end of the portage where a canoe was waiting to be loaded, paddling down the silent lakes with only the sound of our own voices echoing across the water and gathering around the campfire at night with the dark forest beyond. It was an unforgettable experience.[150]

While demanding its own kind of discipline, in a sense, tripping eliminated the need for formal regulations. At Keewaydin, where tripping was the very centrepiece of camp life and in-camp programming was virtually non-existent, there was apparently little need for a set of official prohibitions. "Rules didn't exist," claimed 1940s camper, Douglas Creelman: "Thinking about it afterwards, [I realized] we were probably too tired to get into trouble."[151] If administrations were sometimes preoccupied with orderliness and efficiency on trips, this is not what many campers seem to remember.

Even aside from canoe tripping – not a part of every camp's programming – other aspects of activity planning helped to imbue camps with a more child-centred tone than most schools. Indeed, in contrast to the school, with its concern for well-roundedness and facility with every subject, camp programming frequently allowed children to focus on those activities that were of most interest to them. This scenario was less likely to be found at larger camps, where moving large numbers of children from activity to activity did not allow for the same individual freedoms. Even there, however, the structuring of programming – involving hands-on "doing" and active physicality rather than abstract thinking, along with the general novelty of the setting and activities – appears to have made a trip to camp an enjoyable and sought-after privilege for many. More than this, camp provided its own kind of education – about the natural world, about the regions in which children camped and travelled, about physical ability and stamina, and about getting along with others. School educators might well have been envious of this relative success.

As the authors of *Camping and Character* saw it, the application of psychology to the realm of outdoor education heralded the emergence of "the modern summer camp." In this view, to be modern was to grasp the importance of the camp as the tool of social science and education, to understand the parameters and importance of child psychology, and to enthusiastically apply the insights of progressive pedagogy. This striving to "be modern" might seem at odds with the camp's natural ethos and simple life rhetoric. As we've seen, the pull of the modern and the antimodern were both essential aspects of the camp phenomenon. In the eyes of camp promoters and administrators, successful modern living entailed regular trips back to the natural world. When individuals like Mary Northway, accomplished academic and successful camp director, claimed later in life that "there was a time when I felt that I was living kind of a schizophrenic life: one side getting a PhD in psychology, the other, running a camp, and never the two should meet,"[152] she was perhaps alluding to contrasts between the male-dominated world of scholarship and the all-female setting of camp. Certainly, on a broader level, the two did meet, academic psychology deeply affecting the camping movement and the camp, turning out children – in its own eyes at least – of sounder psychological health. As administrators agreed, camp was "a new type of education ... made necessary by modern conditions."[153] Ultimately, whatever the antimodern aspects that inspired its birth, when it came to its vision of childhood and education, the summer camp had its face not backwards towards the past but forward towards a future in which children would be increasingly analyzed, understood, and shaped by the tenets of psychological and educational expertise.

5

Shaping True Natures in Nature: Camping, Gender, and Sexuality

Looking back on his experience as a postwar camp administrator, Gord Wright mused in a 1973 interview, "I don't think that you could make a girls' camp boyish ... [or] a boys' camp girlish."[1] Many others would apparently have agreed. Camp administrators – whether of the private, fresh air, or agency varieties – believed in the naturalness and significance of gender differences, a fact that directly affected their camping programs. In short, camps had high hopes for shaping "the child" but that child was always a gendered subject. Fears that, under modern conditions, children were growing up "too quickly," that many were "missing their childhoods," were often closely linked to worries over proper gender formation. In a sense this was ironic – preindustrial "youth" were ushered into regular work routines and what would later be considered adult responsibilities at much earlier ages than would be typical in the twentieth century. This lament for "lost childhoods," then, was more an assertion of what should be than a declaration of what had been in the past. Still, with ongoing changes in the terms of work, with radical transformations in the organization of space, and with the continual appearance of technological innovations, pinpointing some place of stability seemed attractive. In this world of flux, who knew whether men and women were not also changing? The signs seemed to be there already: those men released from manual labour were thought to be growing "soft" in both mind and body. And what of girls and women? Who knew where expanding opportunities for education, feminist demands for new rights, and increasing prospects for adventure and consumption might lead?

Showing off at Camp Temagami, c. 1930. As with outdoor activities for adult men, camping at private institutions allowed boys to prove their masculinity to their peers. There seemed to be no other reason for achievements like the one pictured here. *Courtesy Upper Canada College Archives.*

Such worries clearly shaped the development of summer camps. For one thing, the vast majority of camps before the postwar period were strictly single-sex. Girls' camps were themselves an interwar innovation, and one that was accepted only cautiously at first. While girls' camping gradually gained acceptance, before the Second World War, only a few adventurous souls dared to experiment with coeducational models. Whether camps were all-girl, all-boy, or coeducational, the setting of camp was key. The notion of camp as "the quiet land where life is ruled by Nature's slow laws"[2] seemed to promise the necessary contrast with fast-paced urban social worlds, which were blamed for causing all manner of gender "abnormalities." The benefit of sending the potential delinquent to camp was, as one juvenile court judge put it in 1948, that "he's more normal and all's right with the world."[3] And, when it came to being "normal," as other historians of childhood and youth have argued, learning how to be the proper boy or girl was key.[4]

Grooming Social Leaders, Taming Social Deviants: Masculinity at Camp

From the start, summer camp was seen as the rightful domain of boys. Since the late nineteenth century, outdoor activities like big-game hunting and strenuous canoe tripping were considered natural tonics for a flagging, increasingly citified adult masculinity.[5] The benefit of camp was that it promised to influence the boy while his gender identity and masculine abilities were still in vulnerable formation. As many saw it, boys and nature were a perfect fit. From this perspective, the essence of boyhood was the struggle against containment, the desire for rough physical activity, and a generally active (rather than passive) approach to the surrounding world. To a certain extent, such notions applied to all boys, regardless of class. While private camp director Taylor Statten asserted that camp life "satisfies that 'lure of the wild' which is strong in every normal boy," fresh air camp promoters argued that "the country provides the only natural setting for a boy to grow," and YMCA camp literature held that camp would make a boy "manly."[6] In short, camps of all types and descriptions agreed that this was the place, if ever there was one, for the "making of men."[7]

While many camps sought to "make men," the ideal man was pictured differently in different settings, confirming, as Tina Loo has argued, that, "masculinities are often defined against other men, at play as well as at work."[8] Modern masculinity took distinctly classed forms, with strong connections to the work one performed. Work itself changed radically over the course of the late nineteenth and early twentieth centuries, with Taylorism rationalizing the labour process along ever more efficient lines. One end result was the assembly line; others included the deskilling of workers and the breeding of a new class of industrial managers. These managers were men who could no longer claim any proficiency at craft work but who constructed their masculinity in terms of their mental rather than their physical prowess, their organization of the labour process, and their control over others.[9] According to historian Anthony Rotundo, the fact that the work of middle-class men was increasingly distanced from physicality only compelled bourgeois men to assert it, and all manner of passions, more vigorously in other realms. Rotundo's model of "passionate manhood" stresses not bourgeois containment and manly restraint (which he regards as older Victorian ideals) but the glorification of man's passionate nature, now regarded as in need of nurture against the inroads of emasculating and repressive overcivilization.[10]

Certainly, this argument helps explain the appeal of competitive athletics and rigorous outdoor activity, which had been increasing from the turn of the twentieth century onwards. As historians on both sides of the border have found, the desire of men like American president Theodore Roosevelt for immersion in "the strenuous life" was typical of many men of his time who battled it out on playing fields, competed with each other on hunting expeditions to "bag" the largest game, and outdid one another at "shooting" dangerous rapids or at traversing long distances on wilderness out-trips.[11] As we shall see at camp, twentieth-century bourgeois masculinity would become a complex mix of both toughness and refinement. Ultimately, finding the proper balance would be what made one a true gentleman and a "good sport."

Not surprisingly, since concern with civilization's "softening" effect was a particularly bourgeois preoccupation, it was at elite private camps that the emphasis on "toughening" and on rugged physical testing was most prominent. At these upscale institutions, a concern with boyish effeminacy was an undercurrent of camp literature, a concern that sought to address fatherly fears.[12] It was regularly promised that the "poorly co-ordinated," the "non-athletic," and the "imaginative and dreamy" boy would all develop a more rugged manhood at camp.[13] Putting it simply, and drawing on prevailing stereotypes, in 1928, Director Taylor Statten offered that camp was particularly beneficial for that boy "inclined to be a sissy."[14]

One of the essential components of the summer camp in this regard was its all-male environment. This emphasis reflected a re-evaluation of Victorian gender ideals, which constructed women as the moral superiors of men and the noble bearers of "civilization."[15] Women were still considered the civilized sex, but antimodernists worried that it was precisely a problem of overcivilization that was afflicting modern men. It wasn't a long way from this notion to asserting that women's influence had perhaps become too strong. In his study of gender and private camps, Kristopher Churchill agrees that the all-male camp setting was largely a reaction against the "feminization of childhood."[16] The fact that all the major actors in the boy's life and those charged most directly with his care – from mother, to teacher, to Sunday school instructor – were women was no longer praised; it was increasingly lamented. In camp literature, this point was sometimes made explicitly: "Fathers are often aware of the desirability of getting the boy away from the female when there is evidently too much 'petticoat' government," *Camping and Character* stated in 1929: "Housekeepers, maids, and governesses in too great an abundance are not the best means for developing the social abilities and attitudes of the boy."[17] This way of thinking persisted and was given new psychological import in the postwar period as the leading child psychologists defined one of the primary tasks of the growing child – always constructed in male terms – as achieving independence from the mother.[18] Summer camp could help bring this about, while, at the same time, like other burgeoning boys' clubs, allowing adult men to have a counter-influence on a boy's life.[19]

As a result of such attitudes, in the everyday life of the boys' private camp, administrators sometimes went to great lengths to ensure that women – and girls – were kept out. In the Ahmek of the early 1920s, for instance, visiting mothers were not permitted to stay overnight at the camp but, rather, were forced to book into local hotels.[20] At some camps, even wives and daughters of staff members were not permitted on site.[21] At the all-American Camp Keewaydin of Temagami – perhaps a more direct inheritor of the "Rooseveltian" tradition of passionate manhood – both hostility to women and dedication to "toughening" were particularly marked. Since its founding in 1903, staff members and their families (wives and children) were housed on opposite ends of this island camp, a good twenty minutes' paddle between them. Staffmen were permitted to visit only during their off-days between canoe trips. By 1925, a new director took an increasingly hard line on staff contact with women, as campers themselves recall and as the camp historian describes:

> [He] resented their presence. They distracted the men from their devotion to the trials and spoiled the Brotherhood's healthy male preserve ... He decided that this had to cease and issued stringent new rules: no staff were permitted to visit their wives after the arrival of the campers ... visits by staff to neighboring islands were forbidden; and women were banned from Keewaydin.[22]

As a result, the camp became something of a "male bastion," a place where, it was recalled, "swimming no longer required a bathing suit" and where "urinat[ing] in the open ... became safe and acceptable."[23]

If the all-male atmosphere was meant to put distance between campers and the civilized world, the canoe trip – a staple at most elite private boys' camps – extended this distance to all possible limits. Indeed, the further one travelled from civilized spaces, the more masculine the terrain apparently became. As Haliburton's Camp Kilcoo for boys was proud to declare, "the ... setting is one of rugged simplicity," with air that was "bracing and acts like a tonic" and a lake "large enough to convey a sense of freedom."[24] "Exploring and penetrating" such "virgin" landscapes was what gave the edge to canoe tripping, as a postwar Temagami brochure insisted. "Nothing could be more fascinating to the adventurous spirit of a boy than a canoe trip into the primitive wilderness," it stated, claiming also that parts of the reserve's landscape still lay "practically unexplored."[25] Here, the typically male prerogative of exploring defined the middle-class man as much with regard to his relationship with nature as with regard to his relationship with the opposite sex. Both "adventures" conveyed a similar sense of manhood – of the excitement of acting in an assertive way on the object of one's desire (whether woman or landscape) and the importance of being the first one there. The physical demands made on trippers were often significant; in 1922, at Camp Temagami, portages could be as long as two and a half miles.[26] As 1940s camper Doug Creelman remembered in 2000, tripping at Keewaydin meant "just two people to a canoe. None of this bunch of people sitting in the middle, waving."[27] Those boys who excelled at these skills and proved their ability on shorter forays were sometimes rewarded by being allowed to participate in more demanding and prestigious trips: at Temagami, a trip to the "private reserve off Eagle Rock, where the fishing was great" and, at Keewaydin, a summer-long trip to James Bay.[28] There were also social benefits to developing one's canoeing prowess. Those with superior tripping skills were treated with admiring respect and, at Keewaydin, were permitted admittance to the "Gigitowin," or camp "brotherhood." "Admission to The Gigitowin is a signal honor [sic] to either a staff member or a camper," the camp newsletter stated in 1915, "for it means that such a one has made good at Keewaydin in every way."[29]

The construction of private camp as the "maker of men" held as much in later postwar years, though gender worries sometimes took new form. With corporate capitalism now firmly established, social science experts of the 1950s obsessed increasingly about the subservient status and "other-directed" tendencies of the middle-class "organization man."[30] Indeed, the authors of *Crestwood Heights* noted in 1956 that "boys appear to be sent to camp more often than girls since the camp experience is seen as particularly important for them, and perhaps somewhat analogous to the toughening under male masters at the traditional boys' private school."[31] Even as the world changed around them and gender roles seemed unstable, camps seemed to offer a world where men would always be "men." A postwar Camp Temagami brochure was still reassuring parents:

> Life at camp cultivates a love of the out-of-doors and of the simple and wholesome pleasures of life ... Under sympathetic guidance, even the most

Boys at Camp Temagami, c. 1930. Boys at private camps were frequently sent by fathers who worried about the possibility of raising "sissies." Honing one's woodcraft skills, as these boys are doing, was meant to guard against such risks. *Courtesy Upper Canada College Archives.*

> diffident boy gains in health, strength and endurance. He acquires powers of initiative, becomes self-reliant and resourceful: and, in general, develops qualities of character and judgement that go to "make a man of him" in every true sense of the word.[32]

Making men remained a constant camp goal throughout this period, but forging rough and tough masculinity was only part of the camp story. Keewaydin was perhaps unique in this respect since evidence from other camps suggests that there was also a refined quality to the masculinity espoused. Not surprisingly, those who saw themselves as grooming future men of prominence – whether in the business, social, or political realm – were reluctant to cultivate a purely "he-man" style masculinity. Many believed that physical grit was meant to accompany, not overwhelm, social grace and political savvy. Directors, for instance, were expected to be not only "virile and red-blooded" but also "gentlemanly," as Taylor Statten put it in 1922.[33] In part, this included exhibiting the more typically "feminine"

Showing off a mahor catch, Camp Temagami, c. 1930. Almost every activity one engaged in at private boys' camps offered the possibility of proving one's manhood. Here boys at Temagami show off a major catch, though it seems unlikely that it was their own. *Courtesy Upper Canada College Archives.*

qualities of "unselfish[ness]" and "abundant patience," but it also required cultivation of good sportsmanship and an understanding of "fair play." A.L. Cochrane, founder of Camp Temagami, was lauded both for his athletic achievements and for the manner in which he approached his game. In fact, this outdoorsman was shrewd in balancing the demands of gender and class: "His camp had been a school of clean living and manly activity," his obituary stated in 1921: "Though he is [sic] no prude, no boy has ever heard anything from him, or seen anything done by him, which was not fair and honourable and above board."[34]

This model of the refined outdoorsman grew more compelling with time. Taylor Statten's experience serves as a telling example, revealing a gradual rethinking concerning the kind of men he wanted campers to become. References to "sissies" gradually disappeared from camp literature; instead, by the 1930s, comments on the early "militaristic" feel of camp, on the disappearance of boxing from the roster of camp activities, and on the general antipathy to competition suggested a distancing from the macho ideal of manhood that historians have linked with men's outdoor adventure. Increasingly psychologized interpretations of the camper's needs may have been one factor in this reassessment. Statten's 1939 comments on the changing treatment of "the timid camper" suggest that, in his eyes, modern men were expected to promote a more "civilized" ideal:

> The he-man tradition tended to label such a camper a "sissy." What he needed was "roughing it" – and the rougher the better. So he frequently became the object of the "snipe hunt," the dumped cot, or the tent pulled down over his head as he slept. In the modern camp the best resources of insight and leadership available are utilized to develop in such an individual a sense of competence and self-confidence in social participation.[35]

Clearly, the lesson for well-to-do campers was to learn to resist softness without developing into brutes, cheats, or uncultured "he-men."

In order to cultivate not only the tough but also the refined side of modern men, private camps offered lessons about the proper and manly relationship to nature. As far as offering models for emulation, it was increasingly men like Tom Thomson and, in some cases, the "Indian" – not a Teddy Roosevelt – who provided the ideal of manhood to which campers aspired. At Camp Ahmek, Thomson was heralded as a solitary, spiritual, non-materialistic figure, better known for communing with nature than for conquering it.[36] The Statten camps held regular ceremonies of homage to this camper-artist who spent much of his later years painting in Algonquin Park before his untimely death on their own Canoe Lake in 1917.[37] Native men were idealized for their superior canoeing and survival skills and for the admirable autonomy this engendered, in contrast with the essential dependence of urban (white) men. If, as Loo argues, middle-class men went "hunting for masculinities" in nature, the camping man was clearly tracking a unique sort of beast. He was a man who, without question, held his own on a wilderness canoe trip but who conceptualized "conquest" as a mastery of skills rather than as the bringing down of big game, who had admiration rather than contempt for Native guides, and who took time to "enjoy the sunset."[38] Without a doubt, nature was still the site in which his gender identity was forged, but the pathway to virility took a slightly different course. Likewise, at agency camps, administrators may have wanted to make boys "manly," but the manliness envisaged was of a well-behaved, good citizen variety. In contrast to boys in the macho environment of, say, Keewaydin, boys at YMCA camps were instructed to: "always wear a bathing suit," "urinate only in toilets," "observe proper table manners," and, generally, to conduct themselves using "gentlemanly language and conduct."[39]

When it came to shaping masculinity, fresh air camps had different priorities. On the one hand, administrators believed that camp should offer a healthy dose of cathartic experience. "A boy needs a place to run," the *Toronto Daily Star* quoted one mother as saying, apparently endorsing her viewpoint: "He is like an animal, a young horse, he cannot be kept tied."[40] The message seemed to be that city living was sapping boys' energy, as other stories also suggested. The *Star*'s 1943 account of city boys challenging the local bully at camp was telling:

> Sandy was a bully. Sandy was tough. Sandy was anti-social. But Sandy was no physical weakling – he kept in trim by beating up other boys ... The first night at camp he started throwing his weight around, and the other kids, still enervated from the city's humid heat, took it. The second night, with a husky supper under their belts and the wine of the country in their veins, they lipped him back. The third night they beat him up.[41]

Of course, the story here was not only about city boys being "fortified," it was also about "Sandy" being "tamed."[42] Fresh Air Fund descriptions of boys like "Pat O'Hara," one of "The Fighting Irish," and "young Butch Jones," survivor of "gang warfare,"[43] similarly suggested that working-class masculinity was in a sorry, though not always "soft," state. The task in these cases was to rein in city boys who, more often than not, were regarded as little toughs, ready to settle disagreements with their fists, hunt down squirrels with sling-shots, and regard dangerous street play as fun. Fund promoters promised, in 1922, that camp would give the working-class boy "the chance to become a real man" and, in 1951, that he could "trade in his sling-shot for a bow and arrow in the archery course" and his street play for all kinds of "manly sports."[44] At least some boys suspected that this taming was in the works, that camp might involve more containment than entertainment. "No camp for me," stated one lad in 1938, "just a place for girls and women."[45] Aware of these views, the Fresh Air Fund worked to dispel the image of fresh air camp as a girlish, feminine space, perhaps a result of its emphasis on mothers and infants. In 1951, when the *Star* was still insisting that "there is a place where [the city boy] will fit in and they're not all sissies either," one can't help but think the battle was not entirely won.[46]

"Taming" was clearly one of the subtexts of the fresh air experience for boys. One way to tame boys at camp was to have them develop useful skills. The working futures of boy campers were clearly a matter of concern, especially given the poor examples so many were thought to have in their unemployed or otherwise shiftless fathers. In contrast to the private camp, however, there was no talk of grooming social leaders here; rather, there were veiled references to skill-training for those expected to be the manual labourers of the future. Throughout the period of this study, fresh air camp programming for boys was meant to do more than entertain: it was meant to provide rudimentary skills that would be useful later in life. Although arts and crafts programs for boys could also include more traditionally "girlish" activities, like basket-weaving, even here it was noted in 1935 that boys were "one step ahead of the girls" since they also "cut their own bases from wood and punch the holes in them."[47] Other crafts – like leather work and small furniture construction – were taught only to boys.[48] When it came to the objective of arts and crafts programming, boys' "crafts" had a very practical aspect. At Bolton, boys learned basic principles of construction using real tools in their craft program. At times, these skills came in handy around the camp. A 1941 report described how "boys with pick and shovel, axes, saws and hammers, cleared a site, levelled the ground and laid a plank foundation for a tent at the Indian Village. Another group constructed a bridge over a ravine ... Another phase was stage equipment for the outdoor theatre."[49] At a fresh air camp run by B'nai B'rith, crafts came under the heading of "vocational guidance" in 1941, as did "classes in model aircraft, woodcraft, ... clay modelling, soap carving, leathercraft, lino-cutting, papier mache, [and] photography."[50] While no doubt staff members anticipated boys' enjoyment of these activities, they also hoped that learning to work with one's hands was a skill these campers could apply in later life.

Boys work on Indian crafts at Bolton Camp, c. 1950. Arts and crafts were designed to interest boys at fresh air camps, but they were also meant to teach them useful skills they could put to use later in life. *Copyright Family Service Association of Toronto.*

When it came to the futures of poor working-class boys, what administrators most feared, however, was not men who were merely unproductive but men who were possibly criminal. Fresh air literature made regular references to the problem of delinquency, depicted most often as a boy problem. These references appeared occasionally in the interwar years, but, as we've seen, they increased during the war and shortly after. During this time, minor occurrences were read as having great symbolic importance. While a stolen bicycle might seem like "nothing much to get terribly excited about," the *Star* insisted in 1941 that it could also be read as a "danger signal," "an indication that possible criminals are in the making."[51] In the case of one youth, enduring a cold, quarrelsome father, it was argued in 1949, "the environment that is shaping this growing boy's personality can prepare him for the hateful underworld of crime."[52] Camp promoters blamed delinquent behaviour on a number of things: the squalid nature of urban environments, "life crises" that afflicted poor children, modern schooling that left children unoccupied a full two months of the year, and, as already noted, mothers' entry into paid labour.[53] Poverty, in itself, was rarely treated as a key causal factor, although it was asserted that it was boys from "poor homes" who most readily displayed the "amazing ... depravity" that brought them to court.[54]

However challenging their task, fresh air camp administrators had faith that camp could address and transform unacceptable boy behaviour, delinquent or otherwise. In contrast to private camps, where peer groups were often transferred directly from city to camp, fresh air institutions saw their work partly as weakening the influence of urban working-class peer groups, frequently referred to as "gangs." In their stead, camp would provide a new set of carefully selected peers and, more important, would plan and survey their interactions. "Summer boredom" would be addressed by detailed program planning that allowed campers a minimum of free time and, presumably, little chance of getting into trouble. More positively, by introducing boys to a new set of wholesome outdoor activities, camps also saw themselves as teaching the camper that, as the *Star* put it in 1940, "boys can be leaders in ... things [other] than mischief." In the case of "one east-end bad boy," it was stated: "he learned that boys have more respect for the captain of a baseball team than for the captain of a robber gang ... and that boys who never play hookey are not necessarily sissies."[55] The issue, then, was not one of suppressing manhood entirely but, rather, of replacing unacceptable working-class expressions with a more refined variant.

In this general hope of influencing the later lives of their campers, of making better men, camps for boys were of one mind. Though each might conceptualize the boy's problems and the necessary solutions differently, they shared the belief that modern conditions threatened the existence of healthy manhood. By removing the boy from city living for even a limited time, camps sought to carefully shape what they unselfconsciously considered a more "natural" masculinity.

Learning to Be Delicate, Learning to Be Daring: Femininity at Camp

On the surface, camp literature seemed strangely silent on the subject of girls. While tales of little boys gone bad littered the pages of the *Star*'s appeals and guarantees as to camp's "manly" qualities filled private camp brochures, little was said in either about the problem of girls. In part, this reflected the fact that girls were relative newcomers on the camping scene. Prior to the interwar period, it was apparently common sense to think that "camps were for boys *not* girls," as one history of camping stated in 1967.[56] Mary Northway agreed that, when she attended Glen Bernard in the early 1920s, it was "considered quite something for girls to go to camp ... [something] quite adventurous."[57] Even as camping for girls was opening up, it seemed many were still unsure as to its suitability for the "weaker sex." This situation didn't change overnight, either. Fewer camps for girls seems to have been the norm right up to the postwar period. As late as 1949, of OCA-affiliated camps, forty-eight were for boys only and a mere twenty for girls only. In terms of single-sex camps, this translated into capacities of almost five thousand boys and only two thousand girls at any one time.[58]

Seen against the backdrop of prevailing gender ideals, confusion over the proper role of girls is hardly surprising. True enough, the interwar years saw certain challenges to conservative definitions of femininity: new political privileges, improved access to education, progressive changes in women's dress, and greater opportunities in athletic and sporting endeavours. However, as Veronica Strong-Boag has shown, the liberating potential of new experiences was reduced by ongoing adherence to a domestic and maternal definition of womanhood.[59] All women may have won the vote and some women may have felt the freedom to smoke and dance with the flappers, but it was still widely understood that a growing girl could take for granted a future centred on marriage and motherhood. Moreover, while freedoms were won in terms of women's participation in public and educational life, women – especially those not white and middle class – continued to suffer the consequences of a gender-biased legal system. Through the law, the sexuality of girls and women was regulated and, sometimes, criminalized, while charges of physical and sexual abuse against them were often discounted.[60] Postwar years saw persistence, if not intensification, of conservative gender roles, with the new push for consumption and the rise of middle-class suburbs representing a new "containment" of women; in effect, encapsulating a modern incarnation of separate spheres of ideology.[61] Still, the 1950s, like earlier eras, were not without their tensions. Whatever the ideals, the truth was that women performed wage work outside the home in ever growing numbers and conservative codes of sexual conduct co-existed with added emphasis on beauty and sex appeal.[62] In short, femininity was increasingly contested terrain in these years, with ideal and reality frequently in conflict with regard to what, exactly, a modern woman was to be.

The physical education of women and girls provides a perfect example of the interplay of these cultural tensions. On the one hand, since the turn of the century, girls' schooling had expanded to include physical education. Outside of school, girls' clubs like the CGIT and the Guides encouraged qualities of independence and athleticism among female youth. At university, young women were introduced to an increasing range of team sports. At the same time, social observers and physical educators alike worried about the potentially damaging effects of too vigorous physical activity on growing girls and women. So central was the girl's future maternal role deemed to be that, since the turn of the century, physical education and athletic activities had largely been organized around the protection of her reproductive capacities. Into the interwar period this tendency persisted so that even as girls and women were introduced to new sports, heated debates over the appropriateness of female competition ensued. As historian Helen Lenskyj explains, modified versions of men's sport also appeared: women's ice hockey was not to include body checking, while girls were sometimes encouraged to play tennis standing still! The overriding concern to "protect," rather than to "develop," women's bodies no doubt inhibited the growth of a strong and confident physicality in many girls and women.[63]

These attitudes also influenced modern thinking about the appropriateness of girls' camping. If there was no question that boys would benefit from their stay in the woods, observers had mixed feelings when it came to girls' participation in outdoor activity. In fact, women had long been associated not with rugged nature but with civilization. As Adele Perry has shown, in earlier generations, this belief spurred the promotion of female immigration to frontier settlements, the assumption being that women would domesticate these "wild" spaces and the men who inhabited them.[64] When it came to sending modern girls out to rough it in the bush, however, twentieth-century observers were now less concerned with the female impact on "the wild" (no longer a thing to be tamed) as they were with nature's influence on femininity (a thing to be protected). Camp literature rarely addressed this issue directly; clearly, camps had an interest in welcoming girls as new consumers of the outdoor experience. Further from public view, however, camping enthusiasts worried about how girls might "fit" in nature. Camp directors themselves questioned the appropriateness of certain sites as the setting for feminine education. Mary Hamilton, founder of Tanamakoon in 1925, admitted that she initially considered Algonquin Park "too wild for a girls' camp."[65] Almost twenty-five years later, those who set up the province's counsellor training camp at Bark Lake in Haliburton had similar concerns regarding the site's "suitability for girls."[66] Towards the end of the Second World War, the federal government articulated the restrictive view under which early camps had been operating, even if this were not entirely the view of their founders. As it considered sponsoring camps in 1944, the state received this advice from the Division of Child and Maternal Hygiene: "In formulating a physical education program for girls, it would be well to keep in mind the fact that the most perfect accomplishment of a woman is the birth of a baby, and she should first be made as fit as possible for this function."[67] Three years later, the minutes of the National Council on Physical Fitness indicated ongoing difficulties in reconciling fitness and femininity:

> There is considerable confusion of opinion and lack of reliable information concerning what should constitute the programme of Physical Activities for girls and women and what the dosage should be for the several types at each developmental level. It is recommended that the council sponsor a research project set up on a sound scientific basis and that the approval of the Canadian Medical Association be obtained before the project is initiated.[68]

In the face of adult worry about camp's harmful effects, promoters of private, agency, and fresh air camps did their best to construct camp as a fitting, even feminine undertaking. As Meg Stanley has noted of women's canoe tripping in these years, notions of appropriate femininity shaped the entire experience, as it did life at camp.[69] As girls were now to be welcomed to camp, both the camp's setting and its purpose were reconceptualized. For instance, a 1931 brochure for the CGIT's all-girl Camp Halcyon emphasized nature's maternal qualities:

> Girls need the growth that comes from outdoor life. Their bodies are in greater need of strengthening and training than their brothers'. Boys take physical freedom for granted, and girls generally have it thrust upon them. Let the girls go. Let them go to the mountains and stretch their bodies and minds. Let them have a glimpse of what it means to get close to the earth and know the "mother" feel of it.[70]

"Bracing" air and "rugged" terrain were not made mention of here; likewise, when it came to girls, fresh air appeals depicted nature as tranquil and calming with "cool, quiet woods" and "lovely lakes."[71] In 1928, at Camp Wapomeo for girls in Algonquin Park, camp was not touted as the place for "toughening"; instead, the site was said to have "the appearance of a

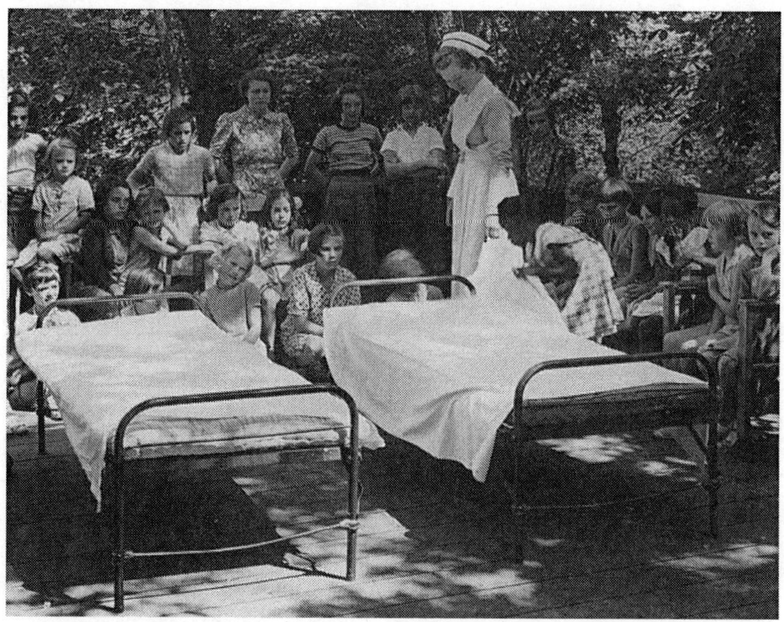

Bed-making instructions for girls, Bolton Camp, c. 1920s. The public health nurse was one of the key symbols of modernity at fresh air camps. Ironically, she also helped to reinforce a traditional vision of domesticity among female campers, seemingly the only ones targeted for lessons in bed making. *Copyright Family Service Association of Toronto*

fairy land," where forests gave off "life-giving fragrance" and winds contained "nothing but purifying influence."[72] As it did with regard to formal education, some camp literature stressed the need to prepare girls for their primarily domestic futures. In some cases, this was a matter of introducing activities aimed solely at girls, like bed-making, sewing, crocheting, and the planning of afternoon tea parties at fresh air camps.[73] In others, it was a matter of how one placed the emphasis. At CGIT camps in 1935, "camp craft" was reinterpreted as domestic education in "outdoor kitchens." Included in the list of the long-term benefits of campcraft were: "tidyness," "ability to use utensils economically and simply," and "experience in cooking out-of-doors[, which] helps in home cooking."[74] While even boys took some part in cooking on canoe trips, at girls' camps, this activity was more than a matter of immediate necessity: it was clearly valued with an eye to its long-term usefulness. "We believe that it is of real value for a group of girls to plan a series of menus," private camp literature explained, "to consider nutritional and enjoyable meals" since, as was noted in 1942, "girls are going to have the job of making meals for their families."[75]

Archery at Bolton Camp. Certain camp activities were thought to be especially suitable for girls. Dancing, dramatic arts, and archery, pictured here, were all thought to develop the feminine attributes of poise and grace. *Copyright Family Service Association of Toronto.*

As at boys' camps, certain aspects of programming were gender-specific. Camps frequently encouraged girls in their artistic development, a field widely regarded as suitably feminine. A history of the Statten camps stated that "dancing and an extended arts and crafts program replaced boxing and wrestling" in the girls' program.[76] Theatre, or "dramatics," was one low-budget activity offered at both girls' and boys' camps, but it was girl campers who were the more direct target. As the Statten camps' newsletter put it in 1931: "Every normal girl likes dramatics. It satisfies a natural urge in her for self expression" – a view that seemed to be shared also by fresh air camp administrators.[77] Musical and craft programming were also invariably gendered: while boys at Bolton were said to sing "with great gusto, sea shanties and other rousing songs," girls were led in "folk songs and other light, pretty songs, with a few noisy, funny ones mixed in";[78] while boys worked on their construction and other "manly" skills, girls spent their time in basketry, knitting, and painting.[79]

Concerns about feminine appearance also shaped camp life. Especially in earlier years, some camps required girls to wear "white dresses" on

Start of a canoe trip from Northway Lodge, 1915. In the early years of camping, even some camp directors worried about the impact of rugged nature on girls' femininity. Perhaps because of this, girls were sometimes saddled with the same restrictive clothing at camp as at home in the city. *Algonquin Park Museum Archives #1306 (William A. Mudge).*

Sundays, "great big heavy bloomers" the rest of the week, and "dark, heavy, woolen swimsuits" consisting of sleeveless tops that "hung down well below the waist over woolen shorts." These are just a few examples of how girls' bodily comportment could be restricted at camp.[80]

More informal dress codes generally prevailed as time went on, but as late as 1940, at least one fresh air camp continued to prohibit "the wearing of slacks, shorts and beach pyjamas."[81] In encouraging girls to have greater concern for their appearance, however, camps were treading a fine line. Especially in postwar years, administrators were critical of girls who cared *too much* about such things and who, it was thought, were easy targets for the marketing of consumer goods.[82] In particular, teenagers' preoccupation with consumer culture was sometimes blamed for their lack of interest in camp. In 1944, the Bolton Camp Committee discussed the fact that "the Camp had to face [many problems] in providing a programme for girls, some of whom were accustomed to getting their entertainment at dance halls, and who would regard an ordinary programme for girls of their age as slow and childish."[83] This, another report explained, referred mainly to "the older camper – [the girl eleven to sixteen] – who, in this day of unnatural living and sophistication, is ill-equipped to meet life's problems."[84] Camp directors argued that even girls from more respectable families were easily tantalized by the fruits of consumer culture. In postwar years at the upscale Winnebagoe, Bert Danson was disgusted to see middle-class girls absorbed in their private world of beauty, fashion, and records:

> You know, we had kids come to our camp and they wouldn't do a flaming thing all day except lie on the dock and sunbathe. I'm really referring to the girls. They just socialized and did their hair and listened to records. This is what they come to camp for ... I had a mother say to me, "You know ... Barbara took five bathing suits to camp. She wore all five ... and not one of them ever got wet."[85]

All of this suggests that, for girls, so the thinking went, modernity posed unique risks. If boys who knew only city living were in danger of becoming "soft," modern girls, it was feared, might become unnaturally "hardened." Bodies could be hardened by excessive exercise and indiscriminate outdoor activity, but attitudes also – especially ones regarding sexuality – could be hardened in a cultural atmosphere of ever-increasing temptation. The belief was widely held that, under the influence of a burgeoning consumer culture, girls were simply growing up "too fast," a charge made especially in connection with working-class youth. The vital concern here was with sexual precocity and potential promiscuity, what in these years could win one the label not only of "immoral" but also of "delinquent."[86] One-time private camper, later counsellor, Shirley Ford, observed of some working-class campers at CGIT camp:

> I remember the girls were more interested in being sophisticated and learning to put on make-up. Camp just wasn't their thing ... They just wanted to learn how to grow up fast ... [I]t wasn't time to teach someone to be a decent paddler ... [U]sually it was make-up and "how can I attract boys?" That was just because that was where they were coming from. The outdoor life just wasn't an important part of their ethos.[87]

Still, in their attempt to hold campers' interest, as in other areas, camps sometimes incorporated the very culture they claimed to be countering. Mirroring the broader cultural preoccupation with female beauty, young campers at Tanamakoon were treated to "hot showers, a manicure, and shampoo" during the "Elizabeth Arden Hour," while at least one CGIT camp arranged a beauty contest for its campers in 1951.[88]

Even as girls participated in typically "campy" activities, concerns of gender were often not far from mind. Girls at the provincially run Bark Lake, who were supposed to be training for their future role as camp counsellors, sometimes found the program less than challenging. As far as woodcraft went, disappointed campers commented in a 1953 survey that this aspect of camp life was "very elementary" and "much easier than expected," in keeping, it seems, with the camp's notion that "you had to be very, very careful with girls."[89] At this camp, canoe tripping was reserved for boys since, even as late as the 1950s, as one administrator recalled, "It was very, very difficult to get them to see that the programs could be similar. [Girls] couldn't do a [canoe-trip] sleep-over. My God, there might be an animal or something."[90]

Even at camps that immersed girls in the rigours of canoe tripping, traditional femininity was reinforced in other ways. Girls' trips were often shorter than those for boys, and they were often protected from some of the hardest work by the presence of male guides. Boys' camps also employed tripping guides, but at girls' camps they appear to have been charged with a larger range of tasks. In a 1941 brochure, parents were assured by Northway Lodge, the American girls' camp that was very proud of its rugged "pioneer" tradition, that "licensed, experienced guides are in charge of canoe trips."[91] In some cases, these guides were responsible for most of the portaging, carrying of extra packs, choosing of sites, pitching of tents, chopping of wood, and lighting of fires, leaving girls, according to one account, with only the tasks of "cooking, cleaning, and packing."[92] In contrast to the pattern at boys' camps, girls were not rewarded in the same way for the skills they did develop. For instance, girls chosen to be honoured with a membership in Northway Lodge's "Senior Forestry" were rewarded more for their altruism than for their expertise in camp skills. In the official camp history, Ann R. Prewitt explained of the club in 1980: "This group is not a popularity sorority or recognition for excellence in sailing, swimming or canoeing. It is ... made up of older girls who quietly and selflessly have a 'seeing eye and a willing hand' [the camp's motto]."[93] Such girls, it was boasted, "unobtrusively" helped initiate in-camp activities in a manner keeping with idealized notions of femininity.

Clearly, girls' camps were products of their time, but it is important to note that they could also, inadvertently, open windows onto another world. Protecting femininity and inculcating domesticity were part, but not the whole story, of girls' summer camping. If, back in the city, the rule was

Director [Mary Hamilton] and handyman of Camp Tanamakoon. Early camp administrators may have had gendered notions as to the relative abilities of boys and girls, but, by their very love of the outdoors and their willingness to explore and enjoy it, they also offered girls unique role models for their time. To the left, George May, the camp's handyman, seems to stand separate from the action, which may have been a statement about gender as well as class. *Algonquin Park Museum Archives #3310 (Don Beauprie).*

that "boys did and girls watched,"[94] this was not the case at camp. Even if camps "took care" with girls, like other girl-centred organizations, they also offered broad scope for female abilities and ambitions, in some cases endorsing more liberal definitions of what a girl – and woman – could be.[95] Especially at all-girl private canoe-tripping camps, girls were frequently challenged to think for themselves and to build up strong bodies and practical skills. Even at some agency camps, like the YWCA's somewhat more pricey Camp Tapawingo, girl campers tasted the excitement and the adventure of tripping. In these settings, female camp directors, who were normally in charge of all-girl camps, played important roles as walking examples of more assertive womanhood. Like a minority of adventurous women since the turn of the century, they indulged their love of outdoor adventure regardless of social convention.[96] Indeed, it is hardly surprising that Mary Northway – single woman with a PhD in psychology and the founder of her own out-tripping camp for girls – praised independence in girl campers. Her own life, like those of other female directors, was marked by significant career and personal achievements.[97] Not coincidentally, most female directors were also upper-middle class, professional, single women, factors that facilitated their life-long commitment to camping. Though male directors sometimes questioned the ability of "maiden ladies" to effectively raise children at camp, others recognized the single-minded devotion that the eschewal of marriage allowed. Of Mary Edgar, founder and early director of Glen Bernard, it was stated: "Her husband, her children, were all in her camp ... She devoted all her loving, interests, and thoughts to that. There weren't the distractions of close family."[98] Such examples clearly offered "lessons" distinct from those of camp cooking and weaving.

At a more concrete level, canoe tripping offered a practical route for girls ready to take on more challenging roles. Even where male guides were deemed necessary, the physical and psychological demands of tripping could sometimes be significant. Paddling for hours each day, cooking, eating and sleeping outdoors, and enduring the vagaries of weather required a fortitude in girls rarely required in other (certainly, other middle-class) settings. And, though girls often took shorter trips than their male counterparts, even in the early years at Wapomeo, some trips for girls were as long as two weeks, which was considered "a very ambitious expedition for girls."[99] Girls were expected to be more than passive passengers on such trips. To be eligible for tripping in 1947, a Wapomeo camper had to prove she could "paddle stern over [a] set course," "paddle canoe alone ... with varying wind," as well as "load, unload, portage ... [and] rescue a dumped canoe." She was also expected to be familiar with the general care of her craft, and this included knowing how to "repair [a] simple leak."[100] Girls at the Y's Tapawingo went on shorter (and fewer) trips than did those at private camps, but the requirements for doing so were similar. When embarking on these trips, girls were told to be "prepared for any emergency." In 1941, mocking fashion and stressing utility, female camp directors instructed girls to bring "real waterproof coats, not the thin, pretty capes glamorous in the movies but worthless in real rain." As they put it plainly, "Good camping is not sissy camping ... Planning with foresight makes possible adventure, travelling with discipline makes possible freedom."[101]

Many girls, apparently, heeded this advice. Their pride in accomplishing challenging and uncommon feats shines through their accounts of canoe-trip journeys. The completion of a challenging trip at Wapomeo in the late 1930s – in record time – instilled a keen sense of achievement in young female campers. "For some reason we decided to go in two days," recalled Elizabeth Shapiro, "and by paddling furiously we reached [the final destination] in that time. We were so elated that we sent a telegram

Glen Bernard girls portaging on a trip to Mattawa, 1927. Programming at girls' camps sometimes reinforced domestic definitions of womanhood; they also sometimes cultivated less traditional forms of femininity, especially on canoe trips as we see here. *Trent University Archives, Ontario Camping Association fonds, 72-007 /1 / 4 -#59.*

to Camp to prove we had done it!"[102] For other campers, it was not the time taken to finish a trip but the difficulties surpassed – hours of paddling, rough portages, unexpected accidents – that elicited pride. As Joan Moses put it of her summers at Wapomeo in the late forties, "I loved a lot of aspects of the canoe trips, like the physicality of it, and the feeling that you kept up with the group ... that you carried your weight."[103] Similarly, Geraldine Sherman felt that postwar tripping at Kawagama represented

"Rangers" at Camp Tanamakoon, c. 1940s. During the Second World War, girls (as well as boys) at several Algonquin camps were asked to take on the duties of absent park rangers. This photo suggests that girls took pride in developing their woodcraft skills, and also that standards of clothing were relaxed to allow them to do so. *Algonquin Park Museum Archives #3141 (George May).*

"our opportunity to grow in frightening ways that our sheltered middle-class families would never have permitted."[104] Likewise, in 1951, YWCA administrators claimed of the girls at Tapawingo that "[they] developed an avid interest in the beautiful Georgian Bay area and took great pride in 'discovering' new routes and places." As at private camps, they claimed, "the more stories of poor weather and mishaps overcome, the greater the pride of the group."[105]

Woodcraft was another area in which girls could develop a set of quite unconventional skills. If limited at some camps, at others, it was not. At Tanamakoon, for example, with no boys around to help out with the chores, girls learned to be handy with the hammer and saw, sometimes at their own behest. "The campers had a yen to build things," Director Mary Hamilton recalled, looking back in 1958: "The hatchet, saw and hammer became creative in their hands."[106] Over the years at this Algonquin camp, girls built furniture, fences, lean-to's, and more. Successful shingling of the outdoor theatre in the interwar years drew admiring respect from one (unnamed) journalist:

> [A] home-made theatre was set up this summer at Camp Tanamakoon ... There are all sorts of snapshots showing campers astride the peak of a roof, industriously shingling, or working away with might and main at other occupations that her grandmother might have stigmatized as not quite ladylike, forgetting that her own pioneer mothers and grandmothers did all these things and more.[107]

At Tanamakoon, older girls' thorough knowledge of woodcraft and ease with outdoor living was what made them eligible to assist in the province's Wartime Rangers program in the 1940s. For effectively shouldering their responsibilities, these campers had "fire ranger badges ... conferred upon them," an honour for which many strove and which made the program so popular that "all campers wanted to volunteer."[108]

Not surprisingly, in such settings, certain girls – commonly referred to as "tomboys" and elsewhere ridiculed for their lack of feminine graces – could find encouragement of their so-called boyish interests and abilities. Take the case of "Jo" at one all-girl camp in 1940: "She was a real little boy," explained psychologist and camp director Mary Northway, but that didn't prevent her from obtaining top marks on the camp's popularity scale or from receiving this positive psychological assessment in 1940:

> Jo is one of the most interesting of the campers. She is always thinking of something different to do and doing it well ... She had been brought up among brothers and liked all the boys' games, slang, and mannerisms. She established herself as an authority on baseball and became a leader in this and other informal activities. She was the centre of mischief, arranging pranks and organizing special activities without advice of counsellors ... Jo was a figure of the limelight; her activities were usually spectacular and her sayings widely quoted.[109]

Even at the postwar co-ed Kawagama, girls felt less pressure to conform than they did in some urban settings. Geraldine Sherman remembers two of her cabinmates from the mid-1950s: Joan K., "already tall and angular, tough in an era when cute and cuddly were at a premium," and Susan M. "a chunky, bespectacled 14-year-old ... wretchedly unhappy at Forest Hill Collegiate, where ... being smart was ... not as important as good hair and cashmere sweaters."[110] Both adored camp life. Even for those not particularly inclined to be "boyish," single-sex camps provided an atmosphere in which female friendships were fostered and female abilities developed to the utmost. Not only the tough girls but everyone at Tanamakoon strove to attain the (interestingly titled) "Worthy Woodsman" award, which, according to Director Mary Hamilton, "[was] the highest and most coveted in camp."[111] All campers, in Hamilton's eyes, also felt a special sense of ownership in the camp since, as she put it, "they felt they had a real stake in its building; they felt they had invested in it something of themselves."[112]

Camps that offered girls the most challenging outdoor experiences were, most often, private, canoe-tripping institutions. As we've seen, agency camps sometimes also included a scaled-down version of the canoe trip, but the Y's Tapawingo, the example explored here, also charged higher than average fees. It was the girl, then, from the relatively well-to-do family who had these opportunities open to her, allowing her to develop a feminine identity that included a degree of resourcefulness, even toughness, that acted as a counterpoint to the lady-like demeanour expected of her in other settings. These opportunities were available to her owing largely to the experiential (as opposed to theoretical) feminism of that group of single, career-minded women nurtured by the more comfortable classes. From their camp settings, these women challenged their campers mentally and physically, working to show them that girls truly could be "at home" in the woods.

Coeducation and the Construction of Heterosexuality

One of the defining features of camp life before the Second World War was its sex-segregated nature. Even where interwar camps offered accommodation for both sexes, they were not always coeducational in any meaningful sense. At the fresh air camp Bolton, which welcomed both boys and girls since its 1922 founding, establishment of distinct girls' and boys' sites allowed administrators to plan completely sex-segregated programming. Contact between boys and girls was almost non-existent. Mary Murphy, 1940s camper, recalls no interaction with boys whatsoever. When asked, her response was direct: "*What* boys? We didn't see the boys. When I was at the camp I used to think they were a lot further away and I realize they weren't – [they were] just down the hill."[113]

Camps, of course, were not unique in this regard; they were part of a world in which children's lives were broadly gender segregated. For students who attended single-sex private schools, the education received at camp was no different from that received during the rest of the year. Even for the majority, who were educated at coeducational public schools,

Drama performance at Bolton Camp, 1940. Before the 1950s, there were few truly co-educational activities at Ontario camps. Here we see one example, and the kinds of lessons in gender it might have been offering. *Copyright Family Service Association of Toronto.*

sex-segregation was more common than it might at first appear. Beyond the obvious example of "domestic science" classes for girls and "manual training" for boys, public school children also encountered separate playgrounds, entrances, even stairways and cloakrooms that regulated student interaction even before children set foot in the classroom. As the realm in which the sexes were deemed to be most different, physical education was sex-segregated from the start. Outside of school, organized leisure generally kept boys and girls apart.[114]

Gender-segregation, then, was to be expected in the realm of summer camping, and those who failed to heed this fact felt the full force of social disapproval, a scenario that mirrored the hostility to coeducation expressed in other settings.[115] When director Taylor Statten proposed establishing a girls' counterpart to his boys' camp in the early 1920s (not even on the same site but on an island on the same lake), his entire board of directors resigned. As the official camp history puts it, "Critics insisted that parents would be scandalized at the thought of boys and girls in such close proximity."[116]

Statten went ahead with his project, founding Camp Wapomeo for girls, but, given the context, it is hardly surprising that he took a generally conservative approach. In the early years, staff members were ordered to pay careful attention to preventing any boy-girl contact not regulated by the camp administration. Far from condoning a free and easy mingling of the sexes, one history of the camps notes: "There was ... a certain amount of tension created by the strictness with which the boys' and girls' camps were kept apart."[117] The geographical layout of the two camps – with girls accommodated on first one, then two islands approximately a mile from the boys' camp – was one Statten always considered fortuitous. It was helpful in avoiding what he called "some of the problems of the coeducational camp," though he chose not to enumerate these publicly. As camp brochures explained, the camps were completely "independent units" but still close enough together to allow for their efficient management.[118] It not being enough that girls were isolated in their island setting, the administration also established a geographic boundary – a floating lifeguard tower in the middle of the lake – to mark the borders of the boys' and girls' territories. According to the official camp history, staffed from 9:00 in the morning until 4:30 at night, this tower "was more an immigration post than a tower to guard lives."[119] Not until the late 1920s were girls and boys offered any regular contact at these camps and then only during Sunday chapel.[120] New provisions also allowed brothers and sisters weekly Sunday visits but only if meeting away from both camps.[121] Early published studies of this camping enterprise – *Camping and Character* prominently among them – made nary a mention of coeducation and barely acknowledged the existence of the girls' camp. When it came to gender, even progressive educationalists were reluctant to challenge tradition too openly.

If coeducational camping seemed to present dangerous possibilities, sex-segregated camping was also known to have its problems. From the perspective of camp administrations, same-sex attachments were one of the long-recognized dangers of camp. In 1928, staff at Camp Ahmek were instructed to be indirect and light-hearted in dealing with campers who might get a little too affectionate with each other. "Never allow two campers to sleep in the same bed," the counsellor handbook warned: "Indicate that this is a silly, uncamperlike thing to do. A real camper would not think of doubling up with another."[122] The 1939 edition had more to say on the matter. The sharing of beds was still strictly prohibited, but now it was also added that "any indications of physical intimacy should be discouraged. Adults who exhibit tendencies in this direction are under suspicion of being homosexually inclined."[123] Fears of homosexuals leading campers astray seemed to have been common, with the result that severe restraints on affection between counsellor and camper were instituted.[124] In 1937, the Margaret Eaton School's course in camp education gave more leeway on the matter but was similarly concerned to balance need for affection against the danger of unhealthy attachments between staff and girl campers:

> We must love those children. Not in a wishy-washy way, because you must watch crushes, but you must make them feel they are liked ... This is a great opportunity for a wise counsellor to step in and give some satisfaction to that desire for affection. We have to be careful here though, because this comes closer than anything else to sex, and we have to watch homosexuality in every camp.[125]

As intimated here, campers themselves sometimes became quite infatuated with female staff. "Crushes" were frequently discussed and were regarded as indicative of a less mature camper. One female camper, who included in the list of things she brought back from camp "a crush on one of the senior girls," was labelled "fundamentally insecure." In the same article, the teenager who resisted such attachments was offered as a prime example of the healthy individual. In her own words, the ex-camper explained in 1937, "Although people are always pointing to summer camps as the breeding places for crushes, I seem to have escaped pretty well."[126] That the camp looked on these affections as serious issues is clear from the comment that, left completely unchecked, seemingly innocent crushes could take on "pathological proportions."[127]

Clearly, conservatism reigned when it came to gender relations at interwar camps, but a few adventurous souls also dared to experiment with coeducational camping. These were a handful of camps that catered to a Jewish clientele. As early as 1933, Sadie Danson set out to start a more truly coeducational camp as a way to market to the well-to-do portion of Ontario's Jewish population. At this and several camps of its kind, girls and boys up to sixteen or seventeen years old were accommodated on the same physical site (if sometimes in different sections), ate in the same dining hall, and generally encountered each other coming and going throughout the day. At Winnebagoe, canoeing, sailing, tennis, and theatre were also coeducational activities.[128] Responses to these gender "experiments" were, perhaps predictably, negative. This time it was Taylor Statten who was said to have remarked: "Mrs. Danson, you can run a girls' camp or you can run a boys' camp, but you can't mix them together. You'll not only have problems, you'll have moral problems ... it will be just one great *kibbitz*."[129] In fact, Statten's comments foreshadowed the anti-Semitic critique of other observers of Winnebagoe's appearance, those who connected the project with what they considered the loose morals of the Jewish community.[130] In 1946, when Irwin Haladner founded Temagami-based Wabikon, he considered that there were still few truly co-ed camps around. At his new institution there was no division of the camp into boys' areas and girls' areas but, instead, every one of the five "units" included two cabins each of boys and girls. Each day, as campers planned their activities, they were left to organize themselves into either single-sex or co-ed groups.[131] According to one interviewee, the camp was frowned upon by campers at the nearby Camp Keewaydin, partly for its predominantly Jewish clientele but also for its inclusion of girl campers.[132]

In the face of general resistance to joint education of the sexes, why did certain camps buck the trend? One of the major factors appears to have been practical in nature. Camps were frequently run not just by individuals but by whole families whose various members helped out during the summer. Being able to accommodate their own children – sons and daughters – for the duration of the summer was certainly an advantage. For Taylor Statten, the hassle of sending his daughter to camps outside of Algonquin Park was what first got him thinking about founding a camp for girls.[133] Directors were also aware that parents of potential campers had similar concerns. The predominance of single-sex camps necessitated not only separate trips to deliver, visit, and retrieve one's sons and daughters but also shopping twice for what was considered a "good" camp. While eliminating these inconveniences, the co-ed camp also promised contact between potentially homesick brothers and sisters. In the end, at both Winnebagoe and Ahmek/Wapomeo, administrators found parents more taken with the convenience of the new situation than "scandalized," and both enterprises prospered as the years went by. Quite simply, coeducation made good business sense.[134]

Pedagogical thinking was initially secondary to these practical considerations, but, by the end of the Second World War, shifting thinking about the relative importance of heterosocial interaction also explains the emergence of coeducational camping. After all, learning to be the proper boy and girl was a relational concept. At co-ed camps, the notion increasingly took hold that controlled contact between the sexes might be better than complete isolation. As campers themselves remember it, gender segregation was fostering nervous and uncomfortable relations between the sexes. More than one recalls the self-conscious and embarrassed way in which girl and boy campers from single-sex camps treated their rare meetings.[135] As sociologist Mary Louise Adams has shown, the postwar period saw the emergence of a broad cultural concern with reinforcing heterosexual identities and orientations among Canadian youth. Under the influence of psychoanalytic development theory, heterosexuality was increasingly identified as a crucial marker of maturity and, in Adams' words, "determined one's ability to make claims on normality, that most important of postwar social classifications."[136] Since at least the interwar years, youth themselves had also been demanding increased contact with the opposite sex. The interwar dance hall "craze" was one example of this desire; more broadly, it was evident in the emergence of a public-centred and consumption-oriented system of dating.[137] Outside the assumed safety of the family home, youth proved their worth in the dating economy and experimented with sexuality beyond the reach of parental supervision. Partly to counter purely peer-controlled leisure, adults turned to offering mixed-sex entertainments: high school dances in the interwar years and postwar "teen canteens" being just two examples.[138]

The world of camping felt the impact of this broad cultural shift in postwar years. The Statten camps now began to preach openly about the merits of coeducational camping. In their postwar brochures, coeducation was not touted as mere business pragmatism but as pedagogical imperative:

> This type of camping is endorsed by leading educators as one filling a real need of vigorous boys and girls for companionship ... The coeducational aspects of the camps have a strong appeal to thoughtful parents who appreciate the value to boys and girls of their playing and working together under the right influences. Children learn to appreciate the finer qualities in one another. Shyness, self-consciousness, and the tendency to make superficial judgements soon disappear.[139]

Other evidence reinforces the impression that inculcation of "normal" and healthy heterosexuality was coeducation's modus vivende. As one prominent educator put it quite explicitly as early as 1940, the purpose of any camp was "to establish heterosexual attitudes."[140] Few camp directors would have relied on such language, but that didn't mean they didn't share this belief. Director Bert Danson informally questioned whether single women could effectively run a camp. In his view, married couples had more to teach children than "maiden ladies" since "you have to have experiences in life" to mould children. Heterosexual marriage was understood to constitute one of the fundamental human experiences, a notion that formed the subtext at coeducational (if not all) camps.

Significantly, the coeducational camp was not only seen as a good place but also as the perfect place to shape sexual attitudes. Hedley S. Dimock, one of the co-authors of the 1929 *Camping and Character*, hardly mentioned the existence of Statten's camp for girls in this educational treatise; however, in 1951, he devoted a whole essay to the subject of coeducational camping. Dimock was now adamant that, as far as boy-girl relationships were concerned, "Camp becomes an ideal educator ... for a successful experience can ... be had more easily at camp than anywhere else."[141] Camp devotees assumed that nature fostered an environment that kept sexual innocence intact. Purity of surroundings and purity of character were assumed to go hand in hand. The urban environment, on the other hand, was criticized for its damaging artificiality, now with regard to girl/boy relations. "Consider the case of an aggressive girl," Dimock suggested. "In the city she goes 'out' quite often but has never been part of a large mixed group. Basically she doesn't feel secure in her group relations with boys. She depends on many of the formal aspects of city dating to keep up her prestige among men."[142] Camp, then, would provide an alternative to modern dating culture, a place where her merely "superficial adjustment" would be replaced with "natural ... spontaneous" group interactions. At the same time, camp was seen as good medicine for those "whose boy-girl experiences ha[d] been very limited or non-existent." Administrators strongly believed that such children would benefit from postwar modifications in their camp programmes. Camps Ahmek and Wapomeo now allowed boy and girl campers to meet on riding trips, sailing and canoe races, and at theatre practice, council ring ceremonies, and campfires. On occasion, campers were even permitted a certain number of "spontaneous activities," such as "a race across the lake in canoes [or] a hike to a nearby fire tower."[143]

Other programming encouraged heterosexual attitudes in more explicit ways. Dances and socials were common fare at early co-ed camps. At Winnebagoe, Arowhon, and Kawagama, these were a matter of regular, though not always pleasant, weekly occurrence.[144] Geraldine Sherman recalls being fourteen in 1955 and the poignant mix of sadness and desire such evenings instilled:

> For many of us, Saturday-night dances at the Hub were torture. We wore dresses, propped up the walls and longed for romance while listening to "Mr. Sandman" and "Love is a Many-Splendored Thing." When the evening

> ended, we crept back to our cabin, eyes down, trying to avoid couples groping beside the path or necking on the basketball court. Staff roamed the woods with flashlights searching for the disobedient.[145]

At Ahmek and Wapomeo, the Statten administration was more cautious with the use of such "city" activities, regarding other aspects of camp life as "more successful."[146] Nonetheless, there too postwar years saw the inauguration of the annual "Starlight Terrace Dance," held at summer's end, as a grand finale to the camping season. Though the camp tennis courts had to suffice as the only available dance floor, every effort was made to create an intriguing and romantic atmosphere. "Lanterns strung across the courts provided ideal illumination," one source indicated, "and a piano, along with the amplifier and hi-fi records, produced enchanting music." Nature, apparently, also helped out, providing "a full moon and a gentle lake breeze" that were said to "accentuat[e] the romantic setting."[147] Though it is none too clear how children plucked from urban homes dancing on tennis courts in the wilderness was less contrived than "city dating," the inconsistencies were, apparently, ignored.[148] In any case, even those campers who, like Jim Buchanan, claims he never knew how to dance, or Sylvia Silbert, whose shyness prevented her from taking an active part, no doubt absorbed the fundamental lessons of such events, which made it clear where one was meant to focus one's longings.[149]

Indirectly, camp life also shaped understandings of sexuality through the vicarious experience of romance that single counsellors modelled for young campers. If administrators liked to think camp life was protecting campers from the preoccupation with sex and romance that mass culture exhibited, the truth was that campers could be quite attuned to young love budding all around them. Indeed, staff romances were a matter of common knowledge among campers and may have gone some way towards instilling the excitement – not to mention emphasizing the normativity – of heterosexuality. Elizabeth Shapiro remembers, while tripping, watching as one besotted staffman flew over their campsite, dropping a message in a bottle for his love object, their counsellor. Significantly, she recalls the responses of her cabin-mates, "We thought this was the most romantic thing we had ever seen!!"[150]

If coeducation was gradually becoming more popular, it was not without its risks, as directors were aware. The choice of the term "brother-sister" camps to describe Statten's postwar project was no doubt a conscious one as construction of a sibling-like relationship between the two was useful in distracting attention away from other interpretations. Even as camps fostered broadly heterosexual orientations, there was concern about encouraging exclusive, one-to-one relationships. Where sexual experimentation resulted, scandal could easily follow. Accordingly, camp literature advised that it was always better to put emphasis on the group – an emphasis campers also recall – rather than on those couples that, it was stated "form quite naturally."[151] Rules preventing overly close contact were also implemented, as at Winnebagoe and Wapomeo, where under no circumstances were boys to enter girls' cabins and vice versa.[152] Clearly, if a camp were to keep its reputation intact, it was a careful and tenuous balance that had to be struck between encouraging a healthy orientation and discouraging sexual experimentation.

This strong belief in the utter normalcy of heterosexuality perhaps explains why attitudes to same-sex attachments, if anything, were more relaxed in postwar years. As in other postwar settings, there is indication that these were treated as part of a normal, albeit temporary, tendency of childhood and youth. Under the influence of Freudian theory, psychosexual dramas were increasingly accepted as the stuff of every normal childhood, and repression of these urges was seen as possibly detrimental.[153] Although still concerned to prevent development of "exclusive relationships," the Tanamakoon Counsellor's Guide also advised: "If a child has a 'crush' the thing is not to repress it ... but to try and understand the camper's need of expressing her affection and admiration and to help her redirect that energy into work and into caring for other campers."[154] Mary Northway similarly stated that crushes could serve as a kind of "temporary security," which could be replaced, in one case, with "conferences and organization work of a constructive nature" as the young woman matured.[155] In part, such differences in approach may have been a function of gender, but they were also a function of time. Indeed, male homosexual tendencies have always sparked the most worries among those in youth and child work, with girls' "crushes" being regarded as largely emotional in nature. Freudian thinking seemed to lie behind the *Crestwood Heights* observers' matter-of-fact observation: "It is at the summer camp that girls are expected to have their crushes on other girls, and boys to go through the homosexual phase of their development." The casual tone, in fact, suggests that these were treated as natural "stages," with feelings that required "working through" before one could dispense with them.[156] A mock wedding of two CGIT campers apparently raised few eyebrows in 1952. On the contrary, the camp newsletter explained that it was "amid much hilarity [that] Skippy (Catherine C.) was wed for better or worser [sic] ... to the Chief Camper (Marguerite L.)" with several campers standing in as "bridesmaids ... and ... Groomsmen" for "the giddy couple."[157] Given that adult homosexuality was so harshly castigated in these years, one should not be too quick to read this more relaxed approach as genuinely permissive. This leniency may have had more to do with the coding of childhood as a time of freedom, when a certain sexual ambiguity was to be permitted. This freedom ended (as did so many others) with the onset of adulthood, when deviance from heterosexual norms, as historians of sexuality have documented, would be far from tolerated.[158]

By the postwar years, constructing both heterosexuality and coeducation as the "natural" choice became increasingly commonplace. In 1946, the Ontario Camping Association praised the Statten administration, generally castigated some twenty years previously, for its "significant co-educational programme."[159] Still, the change was gradual. As late as 1949, of one hundred OCA-affiliated camps, only eighteen of these were co-educational, with only twelve accommodating children past the age of puberty.[160] At the same time, at those camps that did choose the coeducational route, child development was recast in the language of hetero-normativity, as in this postwar camp brochure:

> Wabi-kon is a co-educational camp. Boys and girls participate together in the program if they wish ... They all sit together at meals, and play together. If campers don't want boys and girls together in any or all activities they don't have to. There is no compulsion but usually they like to be together. This is natural. Part of growing up is learning to get along with others of both sexes.[161]

Time had clearly shifted co-education from the outlandish to the mainstream, with those who ignored its usefulness now regarded as neglecting a fundamental aspect of child socialization.

Together or Apart? Responses and Outcomes of Co-Education

What, one may wonder, did campers make of all this? Did they like their single-sex arrangements? Did they welcome coeducation? For one thing, those who grew up at single-sex camps rarely seemed to give them a second thought. "I never thought of Wap[omeo] being for girls only," admitted Elizabeth Shapiro, interwar camper (and later staff member) at Statten's girls' camp: "I had grown up with the two-camp idea, and besides this, I had always gone to an all-girls private school."[162] Looking back, Douglas

Creelman felt much the same about the all-male Camp Keewaydin: "It was the only way to do it. There was no question."[163]

If children accepted single-sex arrangements, they didn't uniformly like them. For athletic boys, camp clearly offered the chance to shine not simply in the constrained hours of physical education or after-school sports practice but almost 100 percent of the time. By the same token, incompetence with camp skills could create awkward, humiliating, and even devastating experiences. For boys not fond of physical activity or simply more interested in other things, the all-male and physically demanding experience of camp may have felt more like an ordeal to be endured than a manly adventure to be anticipated. For the skinny boy who dreaded the drudgery of the canoe trip, the bed-wetter forced to share a cabin with five or six others, or the homesick camper who simply missed the familiarity of family, parts of camp life could be experienced as sheer misery. No doubt campers who recalled long hours of paddling and portages that were "absolutely murder"[164] would have felt some sympathy for the fictional creation of the canoe-trip "dead-weight" described in the pages of Keewaydin's official history:

> He wakes up scared every morning because he knows there will be more portages and lots of paddling. He is always last across the portage and his canoe is always in the rear. [The staffman] never complains. He should. [He] makes him last for everything. Christ, he slows down the whole section. Last week, he even infected them with the illness he had. No one says anything but he knows what they're thinking.[165]

Some now-grown campers believe segregation had more positive effects on girls than it did on boys. Looking back on their youth, they were more likely to regard gender-segregated camping not only as a matter of tradition but also as a positively beneficial arrangement. While some girls at single-sex camps might have preferred an integrated approach, others were content with the status quo. When asked her opinion, Shirley Ford, also a private school student, initially replied, "I didn't know anything else." However, on further reflection, she added: "I felt very free. We could go skinny dipping, run around in our underwear and nobody cared."[166] To the suggestion that she might have preferred a co-ed situation, her answer was simple: "Absolutely not." Jane Hughes agreed, stating matter-of-factly, "There were lots of boys in the city for ten months of the year."[167] In defence of their preference, ex-campers argue that, on their own, girls could avoid the demands of too-early heterosexual conditioning – in some ways, a new twist on the old argument that girls "grow up too fast." "I think at the early teen age," Shirley Ford asserted, "it's helpful for girls to be with girls so that they ... more solidly find out who they are, without being pressed by society to play the boy-girl games." Others, if less articulate, were no less convinced that the arrangement was to the girls' advantage. "It would be different with boys," stated Marjorie Royce. When asked how, she responded: "Well, the sex always comes into it, the competition. I think the girls are better by themselves and vice-versa ... I'd hate to have it mixed up."[168]

Some campers who were part of coeducational experiments disagreed. One Wapomeo camper recalls that, when council ring became co-ed, it was "much more exciting, with all those BOYS!" In summing up her camp experience, she admitted, "I don't know that I would have enjoyed Wap[omeo] so much if there hadn't been a boys' camp so handy."[169] Boy campers could be equally excited about the nearby presence of girls, as Jim Buchanan explains. "I remember [in the late 1950s] ... a kid ... that was totally love sick for this kid at Wapomeo. He was really desperate."[170] Buchanan himself admitted having his own camp crush on a popular Wapomeo camper from Montreal, though he resigned himself to the fact that "my chances of success were limited." Adults were well aware of camper enthusiasm for coeducation; Dimock noted that teenagers had particular "interest."[171] At times it was not fellow campers but counsellors who were the target of this interest and the object of intense crushes. As Silvia Silbert explains with regard to riflery classes at Kawagama in the early postwar years: "I don't know whose idea it was or why they thought it up, but I have a picture of the riflery instructor and I know why we decided to do it. He was gorgeous. We all took sailing for the same reason. He was gorgeous too."[172] James Felstiner confirms that girl campers were not the only ones afflicted by such emotional attachments. "We adored two Wap[omeo] staff," this Ahmek camper explained: "[We] talked about them often, and tried to hang out with them whenever they were at Ahmek."[173]

Certain campers were especially happy at having crushes develop into much-envied camp romances. At 1950s Kawagama, having a camp boyfriend was "a big part of the camp experience" and something of a status symbol, according to one camper, who added that, without one, "we were miserable."[174] From the perspective of the more fortunate, Joan Moses recalls her Winnebagoe experience: "There were socials, which were fun. I always had a boyfriend."[175] Events could also work in reverse, however, and when camp romances went sour, the rest of the experience could be tainted as well. One Wapomeo camper had her "acting debut" (in the camp's production of *Oklahoma*) "overshadowed by a break-up with her camp boyfriend." According to a 1986 *Globe and Mail* article, "She still fumes about what a 'rotten guy' he was."[176] In happier cases, administrators and ex-campers alike claimed that the special circumstances of camp fostered the development of solid, long-term relationships since it allowed adolescents to know each other in a more genuine way than was possible back home. In the words of Barb Gilchrist, 1930s camper and, later, director of Glen Bernard Camp, "Where else can you learn so thoroughly and deeply about another person than on a canoe trip?"[177]

Crushes and innocent romances were accepted, some would say expected, outcomes of coeducational camping, but others were not. In fact, coeducation developed some of its own problems as youth were eager to experiment with (and not just daydream about) heterosexuality and romantic love. The proliferation of rules aimed at keeping male and female campers apart can partly be read as a response to their own concerted efforts to get together. Late-night rendezvous and (usually limited) sexual experimentation appear to have been common. At Ahmek, the floating life tower, meant to demarcate the boundary line between the sexes, became something of a regular meeting spot for adventurous teenagers brave enough to steal off in canoes after dark. "We all knew the few rules," explained Elizabeth Shapiro, "and as a teenager it was daring to try and get around them – for instance, meeting a boy after bedtime. This was not easy to do and was pretty heart-pounding which made it all the more inviting."[178] In fact, this occurred so commonly that the Statten administration instituted a system of boating "night patrols." In the early postwar years, the system was newly invigorated by the purchase of a new boat by the Wapomeo director. "It wasn't very fast," the official camp history states, "but it had a powerful searchlight, capable of ferreting out the young bucks who circled [the girls' camp] each night."[179] Youth at other camps were similarly defiant in breaking the rules. At each of camps Arowhon, Kawagama, and Winnebagoe, there is someone who recalls campers who broke curfew to meet after dark or, worse, who had to be "dragged out of bushes" after Saturday dances.[180]

Camp staff could also push the limits of the acceptable in ways more disturbing to administrators. At Winnebagoe, for instance, one male counsellor was sent home for "fooling around" with a fourteen-year-old female camper, while, at Keewaydin, one staffman was let go when it was discovered he was gay and, reportedly, engaging the interest of one teenage camper.[181] In the absence of more detail, it is difficult to categorize these liaisons as outright abuse or mutual experimentation, though likely both were a part of the summer camp story. It was, however, occasionally acknowledged that counsellors were still youths themselves and often "going through some of the same stages as many of the older campers." In efforts to avoid altogether such problems, camps sometimes favoured the hiring of young husband-and-wife teams. As they put it at Ahmek: "Many camps have found that young married couples make very successful counsellors ... [T]hey are older and have worked out their sex relationships to a greater degree ... [than] the single counselors."[182]

For many youth, camp did more than merely shape their sexual orientations: it frequently provided opportunity for their first sexual experiences. Whatever directors thought of the purifying influence of pine trees and sparkling lakes, the freedom and spaciousness of camp in some cases facilitated, rather than inhibited, sexual experimentation. In this sense, camp was not in contrast with but, rather, of a piece with other newly created spaces of modernity – parks, movie theatres, and drive-in theatres – which offered youth the chance to escape adult supervision.[183] Old-growth forests and nearby islands were more than simply places of natural beauty, they also offered sites in which sexually curious teenagers could evade adult surveillance. Certainly, opportunity was not lacking. Canoe trips at some girls' camps allowed groups of female campers and their counsellors, along with one or two male guides, to slip away into the wilderness for sometimes a week or more. One camper at Wapomeo recalls of her counsellor and their male guide: "She and Steve used to sneak off in the canoe after we were supposed to be settled for the night – lots of giggles!"[184] Even at single-sex camps, the presence of lakes and the tendency of camps to cluster in certain areas could mean a trip to a nearby girls' or boys' camp was only a canoe ride away.[185] Even right back in camp, a group of ex-"Kawagamites" has vivid recollections of the "Teetor Totter Gang" – whose members competed with each other in "endurance kissing contests." Susan Palter – daughter of Kawagama's director – similarly recalls the sexual "IQ test" and the complex list of do's and don'ts that characterized the sexual code of conduct among postwar youth:

> You wanted to score high enough to show that you'd had some experience, but not so much that you were a slut. Have you ever been kissed? Have you ever been kissed on the lips? ... Have you ever petted above the waist? Below the waist? And there were all these taboos, things you were supposed to have done and not done – an elaborate dance that could only have happened in the '50s. It was so pure.[186]

Camp administrators would likely have viewed the issue from a different perspective, but that didn't mean that they could prevent such exploration. Even away from the city and out in the woods, it seems that youth culture was developing largely independently of adult control. Camps may have seen themselves as offering models of "pure" boy- and girlhood in contrast to modern culture, but the shift towards co-ed camping and the inclinations of campers themselves facilitated the same heterosexual experimentation that was an essential part of postwar urban dating culture.

In a world in which children met with the lessons of gender at every turn it is difficult to isolate the camp's precise impact on the development of gender and sexual identity. Indeed, by its very nature, the force of gender normativity is felt precisely because the same messages are broadcast repeatedly from so many quarters. If we cannot say, then, that camp alone "made" men (or women) of its campers, this does not mean that all gender analysis is futile. As this chapter shows, camp administrators clearly viewed themselves as offering a much-needed hand in guiding the gender development of their campers. In doing so, they often served to reinforce the gender socialization that went on elsewhere; but sometimes they also reshaped the direction of that development – an aim that had clear class dimensions. With regard to campers at co-ed institutions, administrators also believed the key to more holistic personal growth lay with the introduction of gender-integrated programming.

Many considered camp the ideal antimodern context for this project, but those who initiated the shift to co-ed camping also saw themselves as riding the crest of a new modernity of gender relations. Time apparently proved them right. If, in 1949, less than one fifth of OCA-affiliated camps were co-ed, by the year 2000, the situation was quite reversed. In that year, over two-thirds of more than two hundred OCA camps declared themselves co-ed.[187] Bert Danson's belief that girls and boys needed to be "brought up together" now seemed to be widely shared. "To me, this is modern camping," he insisted.[188] Many others would now agree. Ultimately, the trick to ensuring that modern boys were not "soft" and modern girls not unduly "hardened" seemed to rest with getting both out of the city, away from consumer culture; however, it also rested on their ability to mingle with each other under the wise supervision of adults who knew the value of shaping "true natures" in the natural world.

6

Totem Poles, Tepees, and Token Traditions: "Playing Indian" at Camp

In 1899, Pauline Johnson, famous "Mohawk princess" and Aboriginal performer, paid a visit to the small northern Ontario town of Sundridge. As Johnson served up her fare of dramatic poems and recitations, one ten-year-old girl was particularly enthralled. Recounting the incident later in life, Mary S. Edgar, the young white girl in question, recalled, "I was fascinated and wished I were related to her," a longing only heightened by Johnson's later visit to the Edgar family home. Later in life, little Mary's wish was, in one sense, granted. The summer of 1922 found thirty-three-year-old Edgar the director of a newly established summer camp for girls. There she presided over the camp's "Indian" council ring, crafted her own "Indian" legends, and entertained campers in her wigwam-style cabin. On a visit to the camp sometime during the interwar years, Chief Mudjeekwis of the Rice Lake Anishnabe extended the hand of friendship and bestowed on her the honour of an "Indian" name. Over the years, in her role as "Ogimaqua," Edgar, the white woman, would imaginatively weave herself and her campers into the family of "Indians."[1]

In her fascination with all things Indian, Edgar was not alone. As least as early as the 1890s, white audiences throughout Canada, the United States, and Britain thronged local halls and auditoriums to see and hear celebrities like Johnson, whose appearances fanned the flames of interest in the performing Indian. In the same period, North Americans crowded their way into the rodeos and Buffalo Bill shows that prominently featured Aboriginal performers. If, as with Edgar, this outsider fascination slipped over into the desire for insider status, what most of these "wannabee"

Campers at Bolton Camp, 1939. "Playing Indian" was a favourite activity of boys at many camps, one in which they were encouraged to indulge by camp administrators. *Copyright Family Service Association of Toronto.*

Indians did with the impulse to "go Native" is not well known. The story of Grey Owl's faux-Indian fame points in one direction, but it is unlikely that many took their enthusiasm to such extremes. For many who were not seeking wholesale changes of identity, playing Indian on a part-time basis sufficed.[2] Summer camp was one site in which this impulse was readily indulged, a place where, it was claimed, children learned to "live like Indians during the camping season."[3]

This chapter attempts to make sense of this curious cultural phenomenon and to place this cultural appropriation within a broad historical context. By exploring camps' Indian programming, representations of Aboriginal people in camp literature, and the dynamics of Aboriginal employment at camp, it takes a critical look at the fascination with playing Indian. What becomes apparent is that the incorporation of so-called Indian traditions was part and parcel of the broader antimodernist impulse in twentieth-century Ontario. Like the summer camp phenomenon as a whole, it reflected middle-class unease with the pace and direction of cultural change, with a world that appeared to be irrevocably industrial, decidedly urban, and increasingly secular. As historian Leslie Paris has concluded in the American context, racial play-acting at summer camp was not a matter of respecting the experiences of racial minorities.[4] In the same way, at Ontario camps, "going Native" had little to do with honouring (or even accurately portraying) Aboriginal tradition but much to do with seeking a balm for the non-Native experience of modernity. Above all, playing Indian at summer camp reflected the modern desire to create a sense of belonging, community, and spiritual experience by modelling antimodern images of Aboriginal life. These impulses point to a racialized expression of twentieth-century antimodernism – ones springing from adult experience but articulating themselves on the landscape of childhood. When playing Indian, children were offered the emotional outlet of intense experience not frequently promoted by modern child-rearing experts and standing in contrast to the camps' simultaneous preoccupation with order and control. This chapter explores the nature of this phenomenon, its multiple meanings, and its commercialization at camp. It also explores its impact on campers and, briefly, some of its possible political implications. Ultimately, this phenomenon underlines what Stallybrass and White argue: what the socially powerful cast as "low-Other" is constantly "both reviled and desired."[5]

In the scholarly world, playing Indian has been understood as a form of cultural appropriation, a practice that has been the source of intense debate among historians, literary critics, journalists, and others. Hartmut Lutz, German literary scholar, provides a useful explanation of the concept: "What is at issue ... is the kind of appropriation which happens within a colonial structure, where one culture is dominant politically and economically over the other, and rules and exploits it ... It is a kind of appropriation that is selective ... and that is ahistorical in that it excludes from its discourse the historical context, especially, here, the history of Native/non-Native relations."[6] This is clear enough from other histories of "playing Indian" – studies by Phillip Deloria and Shari Huhndorf among others – which show that the phenomenon was clearly rooted in desires to fill the personal, social, and national aspirations of settler societies. Deloria effectively situates this phenomenon within the context of social and cultural change that put traditional identities and values in question and intensified the appeal of Native symbols, rituals, and role playing. Other scholars argue that the appeal of playing Indian was heightened as time went on by the marginalization, displacement, even death of real Aboriginal peoples. Ultimately, as Native peoples posed a decreasing threat to white society, negative stereotypes about them could more often give way to positive ones.[7]

Indian programming at camp grew out of this earlier history of playing Indian, but it was also linked to the activities of modern youth organizations, particularly those inspired by the writings of Ernest Thompson Seton. This naturalist, artist, master storyteller, and founder of the League of Woodcraft Indians was, without a doubt, instrumental in fuelling youthful interest in going Native. His critique of modernity was inseparable from a marked romanticization of Aboriginal culture. "Our civilization is a failure," he commented on one occasion, while his writings on Indian lore conversely idealized "Indian life" and encouraged Euro-North Americans – especially children – in its emulation. His instructional manuals, like *The Red Book: Or, How to Play Indian*, no doubt also influenced the nature of Indian programming at many camps. In certain cases, Seton's influence was even more direct. During the early years at Camp Ahmek, Seton was given "free rein" at the camp, and, according to Taylor Statten's biographer, he "constructed an Indian cabin ... He showed the campers how to make sweat lodges, how to perform Indian dances correctly, [and] how to conduct the Council Ring."[8]

The summer camp drew on these earlier traditions, but it also offered a novel setting in which to play Indian. Here was a world, geographically removed from home and city, in which the combination of new surroundings and isolation offered the perfect backdrop for the construction of alternate identities. Indeed, as children first heard of these camps – Temagami, Keewaydin, Ahmek, and so on – the foreign nature of the experience was announced. From the moment children arrived at camp, the experience was designed to make them feel they had been transported from the modern world to the Indian past. As they first passed though entrance gates that served to demarcate the boundary between the two worlds, campers encountered camp names constructed from purportedly "Indian" languages. One camp director's son recalled that "all the popular camps of the day had Indian names."[9] Campers themselves were sometimes "renamed": "Ojibwa," "Algonquin," "Cree," and "Blackfoot" commonly marking their cabins or sections. Gazing about the grounds, children would quickly have noticed that not only names but also the material culture of camp – its tepees, totem poles, and, sometimes, whole "Indian villages" – confirmed the Indian connection. At camps of all sorts, arts and crafts time saw children variously carving, painting, and constructing their own totem poles, tepees, and "Indian heads." As they went about their activities, children were reminded that the very earth on which they walked had once been "Indian land." This point was brought home in a special way to campers who thrilled at the chance to observe, listen, and learn from the Aboriginal staff employed at some camps. Finally, campers would also have discovered the Indian council ring, set off geographically from the rest of camp. In this woodsy, chapel-like setting, "young braves" would "sit in solemn pageant" on their rough-hewn wooden benches, awaiting the words of "the chief" delivered from his sacred "Council rock." Having been duly blanketed and face-painted, and sometimes in "breech clouts," these make-believe Indians would make use of everything from tom-toms and rattles to shields and headdresses.[10] At one level, then, the summer camp experience was understood as a recreation of the Indian way of life. "The Native Canadians ... were campers," educator Mary Northway put it in 1946: "In their small groups they lived a simple, outdoor life, striving against the elements and using natural resources to furnish their existence."[11] To this way of thinking, Indians were campers and campers were Indians. Nothing, it seemed, could be more "Indian" than camping.

Meanings behind the Masks

The inclusion of Indian programming was explained by administrators in straightforward terms: quite simply, it was included for its educational value. For them, building totem poles, painting tepees, and performing Indian rituals were ways to learn about, and express admiration for, the nation's Aboriginal heritage. In 1929, *Camping and Character* boasted that Ahmek's council ring dances and dramas were based on actual "historic ceremonies," affording children "much incidental historical understanding of primitive life and religion."[12] In the 1920s and 1930s at Glen Bernard Camp, it was claimed, Mary Edgar instructed her campers to carefully consult the appropriate "reference books" on North American Indians in choosing their own tribal names, songs, and yells. Some camp names were chosen in a similar manner. In 1925, Director Mary Hamilton conferred with a number of sources, including "the library, Pauline Johnson's family, Ernest Thompson Seton, Indian people and authorities on Indian lore" before settling on the name of Tanamakoon.[13]

Strict attention to historical accuracy, however, was not generally the rule. Ironically, since praise of Indians was premised on the presumably "primitive," even ageless, nature of their practices, so-called Indian culture at camp was sometimes quite literally "made up." A familiar example is the use of simulated Indian names. If certain camps were careful to choose names that had real meanings in indigenous languages, many others were happy enough if the overall effect was an Indian tone. Thus were born institutions like the New Frenda Youth Camp and Camp Wanna-com-bak. Likewise "Indian games" held during council ring – "talk contests," "singing battles," and marshmallow-eating contests[14] – often bore little connection to Aboriginal cultures. Stories, no less than names and games, could also be creative fabrications. Recalling Mary Edgar's love of sharing "Indian legends" with her interwar campers, her successor at Glen Bernard Camp admitted: "How many of them were [from] her own fertile imagination and how many she [had] read about was a little hard to say."[15] At Ahmek, the invitation to invention was made quite explicit. In what appears to be a postwar Indian council ring handbook, the staff was encouraged: "Improv[e] and whenever possible invent an Indian story to give the game more glamour."[16] Suggestions for design of a "medicine man" outfit in the same handbook went no further than to suggest, "He should be dressed in some weird costume with many things trailing." In 1933, fresh air campers at Bolton were described as making tepees out of "discarded, leaky tents" then painting them up "in true Indian style, or," as it was admitted, "what they conceived to be Indian style."[17]

Invention could also take more inadvertent forms, sometimes via the careless blending of one Aboriginal tradition with another. All too often, objects of Native material cultures were presented in utterly jumbled fashion. The desire to create an Indian atmosphere at Bolton in 1937, for instance, meant that the totem pole (a uniquely Northwest Coast tradition) and the tepee (used only by Plains groups) could be displayed unproblematically side by side, with an Omaha "tribal prayer" thrown in for good measure. Likewise, at Ahmek, council ring incorporated everything from the American "Zuni Council Call," the Plains Indians' "Thirst Dance," and the (apparently popular) Omaha tribal prayer. In 1931, Ahmek's "Indian village" showcased not only tepees and birch bark canoes but also, somewhat inexplicably, a number of "weird looking animals," including a six-foot long centipede. In such cases, camps were not penetrating the intricacies of Native history or culture; rather, like a long line of explorers, settlers, and academics before them, their images of Native peoples were based on a fantastical amalgam of Aboriginal traditions projected onto one mythic Indian Other – another version of the white man's Indian.[18]

In all of these cases, the child's experience of this culture – and not its realistic depiction – was clearly the central concern, a point underscored in the following advice:

> If you have no serious objection to a little subterfuge, it is possible to enliven your Indian program ... by "discovering an Indian Burial Ground." It can either just happen or you can make it known that this camp was once the home of such and such a tribe and that arrow heads, bits of pottery and other evidence has [sic] been found ... Please yourself how far you want to go with this kind of thing. Once started, the ball will continue to roll. Bones and all kinds of things will be brought to your attention for there's nothing excites a camper more than discovery.[19]

If discovery excited children, if Indian ceremonies awed them, and if games of scalping allowed them to "let off steam," Indian programming had done its job. In certain circumstances, then, campers were sometimes encouraged to be excitable and to indulge in imaginative and often passionate play.

Clearly, Indian programming was not about honouring Aboriginal traditions, but this needn't imply that it was without purpose or meaning in the life of the camp. Like antimodernists of earlier periods, camp enthusiasts were on the trail of intense experience, something Indian programming offered in abundance. Council ring, for instance, could function not merely as Saturday night entertainment but also as the symbolic centre of camp. It was here that important visitors were introduced, here that opening and closing ceremonies were held, here that directorships sometimes formally changed hands. In effect, council ring offered the ritual, solemnity, and spirit of communalism that such events demanded and that seemed to be lacking in modern life.

Indeed, the feeling that spiritual connection was hard to come by in modern society is a difficult thing to chart and was likely related to a host of factors. Some have argued that the twentieth century was an increasingly secular age.[20] Others have disagreed, showing the deep connections between Christianity and Canadian social and institutional life at least until the 1960s. They acknowledge, however, that the early twentieth century saw a shift away from evangelicalism as the dominant form of Christian expression. By the turn of the century, these historians of religion argue, evangelical Protestantism was increasingly unattractive to those who sought to replace its other-worldly orientation with an emphasis on here-and-now social reform. With their new social gospel orientation, they eschewed the evangelical focus on a heavenly afterlife and, instead, sought to improve the quality of life on earth in the wake of rapid urbanization, increased immigration, and industrial development.[21] Ultimately, whether Canadians were leading more secular lives or were simply not finding their desire for transcendent experience met by modern liberal Protestantism, it is possible that the Indian programming of camp filled a growing, though perhaps largely unarticulated, need.

Certainly we have evidence that the world of camping felt the effects of wider cultural and religious shifts. Without question there were camps with strongly religious, sometimes evangelical, agendas in these years. At camps run by the Canadian Girls in Training and the YMCA, religion was clearly central. Even the CGIT, however, which was adamant that its purpose was "the realization of Christian ideals, attitudes and actions," was critical of "the ordinary revivalistic [sic] service" and churches "cluttered with people who came in on a wave of emotion."[22] Other camp administrators seemed to agree, retaining broadly Christian aims and assumptions but also explicitly distancing themselves from evangelicalism as a potentially divisive force. For instance, while chapel services were held at both Camp Ahmek and Camp Bolton, their literature also suggested that camp was "no place for any high pressure evangelism" and, for instance, that "no camper has been known to change his religious faith at Bolton camp."[23] Ahmek administrators were even more direct, openly criticizing "the meagreness of conventional forms of religion" and their tendency to be "excessively formal" and dependent on "theological concepts and terminology [that are] meaningless to boys."[24] While that most prominent Ontario camping personality, Taylor Statten, was deeply involved in the YMCA before embarking on camp work, he also tellingly remarked before entering the Y: "If anyone tries to talk to me about religion, I'll slug him and get out."[25]

If many camp administrators were distancing their work from evangelical religion, they continued to place value on the spiritual experience and on the power of shared rituals and beliefs. Part of the essential meaning of camp was that it was more than a collection of unconnected individuals: above all, it was a community. A common spiritual striving, broadly defined, was deemed invaluable in nurturing this sense of community even at camps without a primarily religious focus. We see this at Ahmek, where references to "the value of persons," the search for "higher values," and the indescribable "camp spirit" suggested the incorporation of a liberal, humanistic spirituality. Despite its distancing from institutional religion, this camp still ultimately claimed: "To many counsellors and campers, Ahmek has been their one outstanding religious experience." They were careful to add, however, that religion was a concept "as flexible, changing and real as life itself."[26]

From this perspective, the Indian appeared as the perfect adherent of "natural" religion and the ideal model for camper emulation. When

Camping and Character referred to the camps' more "primitive Christianity" and to taking a "genuinely indigenous approach" to spiritual values, such allusions were not coincidental.[27] They pointed to popular readings of the Indian as the most simple and naturally spiritual of men – as Seton put it, "a Christ-like figure," or Longfellow, as having "pure religion without hypocrisy."[28] As these examples suggest, enthusiasm for Aboriginal culture and distaste for organized religion often went hand in hand.

At many summer camps, the council ring ceremony was the central vehicle for channelling an experience of this "pure religion" to urban campers. Through it, campers could immerse themselves in ritual that contained no reference to Christian theology but, rather, offered an air of novel freshness. The ceremony was typically a weekly or bi-weekly event, held after dark, involving the entire camp. "It has been used as a vehicle through which much sound teaching can be given without effusive moralizing," a short history of Bolton Camp explained in 1938.[29] At the Statten camps the ceremonies were treated with equal seriousness. Only those who had actively participated, it was claimed, could "know the deep meaning of such an hour."[30] Discussions of council ring's physical layout also point to its importance. The area itself was treated as a semi-sacred space, and the rituals it facilitated were treated as quasi-religious. "The choice of a site for the Council Ring is important," one handbook advised: "Select an area reasonably remote from any buildings ... A flat space ... surrounded by trees will lend enchantment. Atmosphere is very important ... Find another site for the ordinary camp fires and wiener roasts."[31] Without question, the backdrop of nature was deemed essential in creating the desired atmosphere. At Bolton, this was achieved by situating the ceremonies "in a most appropriate forest setting," while, at Glen Bernard, Mary Edgar rejoiced in her discovery of "the glen, a perfect amphitheatre for a Council Ring."[32] To this way of thinking, trees became markers of the borders of intimacy, rocks became symbolic altars to be used by presiding chiefs, and the wide-open sky suggested the loftiness of the entire enterprise.

The organization of council ring proceedings points to further parallels with religious ritual as well as to that blend of catharsis and control, freedom and order, that characterized the rest of the camp experience. The usual roster of activities included a dramatic fire-lighting ceremony followed by prayers to "the gods," some form of camper recitations or reports (often of nature sightings), "Indian challenges" or contests, and a sombre closing ceremony. All was to be guided by a strict "order of procedure," in keeping with the belief that "everything that is done at the council ring is deliberate," or, as it was put in 1948 at Bark Lake Camp, "everything on the programme is planned ahead."[33] Creating the desired atmosphere also depended on knowing when to keep quiet and when to join in the noise-making. At certain points "absolute silence" was considered something of an iron law, while, at other times, input from the "braves" (like lay participation) was essential. As council ring's central organizing feature, the fire itself cannot be overlooked. Fire, which often holds a sacred place in religious ritual, here held pride of place, providing a circular and, thus, communal ordering to the ritual.

Before gaining entry to this sacred space, campers were expected to undergo transformation at several levels. If, broadly speaking, all of camp

Senior Camp – Indian Council Ring, Glen Bernard Camp, interwar years. Council ring ceremonies where campers dressed up and acted "like Indians" were common at many camps in the interwar period and sometimes beyond. *Trent University Archives, Ontario Camping Association Camp Photos Folder, Box 1 - 72-007 /8 /2 - #457.*

Indian War Council at Kilcoo, 1938. *Trent University Archives, Ontario Camping Association fonds, 72-007 /1 / 6 / - #86.*

life reflected the desire to "go Native," it was at council ring ceremonies that campers were, in essence, "born again" as Indians. The first step in this process was external change. Here nature itself helped with the process, eliciting positive reference to the Indian appearance of sun-browned campers. Suntans were assumed to be one of the healthy by-products of a summer at camp; however, this implied not only physical benefits but also the psycho-spiritual advantages of "going Native," as both Deloria and Paris have shown. In the Ontario context, one mother and her children who returned from fresh air camp in 1927 were described as "mortals from another world. The mother is browned by the kiss of summer winds ... And the children? They look like four little nut-brown papooses – as tough as nails – sparkling and effervescent."[34] To complement their Indian "skins," campers anticipating council ring were expected to take on Indian dress. When postwar campers at Bark Lake Camp "dress[ed] up in blankets, towels, feathers and war paint," they were following long-time camp tradition. Evidence suggests that "dressing up Indian" was the routine long before this time.[35]

Other aspects of the transformative process were less visible, if no less real. Fundamentally, one was to be open to a new way of feeling and of experiencing the self. Sometimes this meant accepting a new Indian name, according to Ahmek literature, "the highest honour that can be conferred upon [a] ... camper."[36] More than anything, however, it required a willingness to be transported metaphorically to another time and place, to enter into a new state of mind, and to open oneself up to mystical experience. Directors were reminded that "convincing leadership" was "key" to creating the right atmosphere to facilitate this change. They were also told this demanded not only "dress[ing] for the part" but also that the chief himself "become enchanted" and open to "the emotional appeal of the Red man."[37] According to a memorial talk delivered after his death, Taylor Statten was one director who took such advice to heart:

> Each week at camp seemed to await the Council Ring ... One gathered a blanket and a flashlight and marched off to the Council Ring as an actor in a well-rehearsed play ... somehow, the austere and [pervasive] presence of the Chief transformed the play into a realistic re-enactment of all Indian ceremonies of all time. The twentieth century slipped away in the darkness and all evidences of modern civilization were ... somehow forgotten ... It was a shock returning from this other world in which we had all been participants ... and the validity of the experience was owing to the magnificent skill of the Chief. He was really THE CHIEF.[38]

In this atmosphere, members of the camp community could find themselves emotionally stirred, personally connected, and perhaps even spiritually moved – experiences one might have expected of the nineteenth-century Methodist camp meeting or evangelical church service. Here, without explicit reference to religion, one could taste the beauty of ritual, embrace feelings of awe, and experience the power of the communal event. In this context, one's own experience was the focal point, while Aboriginal people were far from mind.

The fact that council ring filled spiritual purposes is also suggested by looking at camps that retained strong Christian objectives. This is evident in two different ways. For one, in these settings, less intense focus seems to have been placed on playing Indian. In fact, while CGIT, YMCA, and other religious agency camps also held Indian ceremonies, these camps had clear spiritual agendas that influenced their approach to the council ring ceremony. In short, directors were careful to direct the council ring's spiritual potential to Christian ends. Perhaps fearing the pagan overtones of the ritual, CGIT administrators demanded that girls attend in uniforms (not Indian dress) and saw to it that bugles replaced Indian drums. Campers were instructed that, ultimately, the ritual had Christian meaning, that, for instance, "[the] fire represents the spirit of the camp council, a spirit whose foundation, we hope, will be our loyalty to Jesus Christ."[39] From a second perspective, it is significant that religious camps still chose to make use of council ring ceremonies. Their adoption in this setting underscores the point that the ritual was widely appreciated for its spiritual uses. At the YMCA's Camp Pine Crest, which proudly declared itself "a Christian camp," administrators in 1940 listed "daily chapel talks, weekly church services [and] Indian council ceremonies" as "provid[ing] boys with specific examples and ideas for Christian living." Apparently, administrators of many camps were in agreement that children were most open to discussions of life's higher purposes in the natural, yet solemn, setting of the council ring and, as one YMCA camp manual put it, under the "subtle spell of the fire."[40] This clarifies that, as with the rest of the agenda at the agency camp, the goal was always to strengthen ties to the organization (and often to a denominational church), not just to the camp.

Playing Indian could shape camp experience; it could also inform identity at all manner of camps. As in the world of art and literature, a clearer definition of national identity and a distancing from the unsavoury colonial past was another of the welcome by-products of claiming Indian connections. In fact, proving one's association with Indians was a sure-fire way to found a "Canadian tradition" and to establish one's "Canadian" roots. To achieve this feat at camp, outdoor enthusiasts ignored their immigrant roots and constructed themselves – as those who chose to "live like Indians" – as the figurative "heirs" of Native tradition. This helped to confer a sense of belonging in a country in which their presence was really quite recent, as historian Gillian Poulter has shown in other contexts. The first step in this process involved casting Indians as historical actors in a far distant past. Director Mary Hamilton's 1958 account of Algonquin Park history was typical:

> To the uninitiated the name of Algonquin spells Indian. One thinks of wise men of the forest who knew this country well and trapped and fished here in the days when all the wilderness of forest and stream belonged to them. These associations are true, but Algonquin Park is much more than

> an Indian hunting ground. It is an expanse of twenty-seven hundred square miles of forest ... It is a land that finds a place in history associated with the records of Champlain, it was the happy hunting ground of the Algonquin Indians ... In the days of Tom Thomson it became the gathering place for members of the Group of Seven.[41]

Clearly, there was tension here between giving Aboriginal peoples their due and the construction of a narrative that assumed their eventual irrelevance. The same tone marked Mary Edgar's prompting to past campers in the 1970s: "We need often to remind ourselves that this country which we proudly call 'this land of ours' once belonged to the Indians," that "it was the smoke from their camp-fires which first ascended to the sky."[42] Clearly, camps had much in common with the salvage anthropologist who lamented, but also assumed the inevitability of, the Indian's cultural demise. From this perspective, the Indians emulated were those of strictly precontact innocence. Any cultural change or adaptation on their part was read simply as decay. "Real Indians," so it was understood, were no longer a people who "lived among us" or who had a place in the modern world.[43]

Having rendered contemporary Aboriginal peoples virtually invisible, white campers could now step in to fill the void as their remaining heirs. In doing so, they distinguished themselves – true lovers of nature – from other less enlightened elements of their society. In this respect, the Ahmek camp newsletter drew parallels between campers and early Native peoples in 1931. The author suggested that, like "the redmen" of the past, it was now "the new dwellers of the out-of-doors" who were being "pushed further and further afield." The enemies now were not from the east but, rather, were annoying cottagers from the south who "bring with them their city habits and customs." These philistines were described as "inane bands of jazz-makers [who] violate the silence of the night," as those who brought "hot dog stands and shabby food 'joints'" to the wilderness and, ultimately, as "idolaters in the temple of the Great Spirit."[44] By contrast, camps painted themselves as respectful followers of Indian ways, as inheritors of Native traditions and practices, especially in postwar years. At Bolton, campers who fished, tented, and axe handled were depicted in 1950 as receiving "instruction in skills of the historic past," while, in 1952, CGIT campers were said to be learning to live "as did their Indian brothers and sisters."[45] In speaking of the use of the Aboriginal "tumpline" (a heavy leather strap that was tied around goods, then around the forehead of the hiker) for hiking, the historian of Keewaydin, writing in 1983, considered his camp to be "the custodian of ancient practices and devices long since discarded elsewhere."[46] Ultimately, if campers were the children of these earlier Aboriginal siblings, their role as inhabitants of Indian land – the entire country, of course – could be regarded as only natural. They were legitimate "Canadians," and this was their home.

These retellings, borrowings, and inventions were the base elements of the camps' Indian programming. They suggest that the history of playing Indian is not only one of longing but also one of privilege. Dramatic reinventions of campers as Indians merely served to emphasize the shared whiteness of the actors under the paint, to their freedom in taking "Indianness" on and off at will. Indeed, it was precisely because they felt so deeply assured of their status as "white" that they could play at being, and long to be, Indian. Camp enthusiasts were not seeking a true change of status but a revised, more pleasing image of their own racial character. Via their role as summer campers, lovers of the outdoors claimed an identity that was vaguely counter-cultural but, at the same time, still clearly white. One would be hard pressed to argue, for instance, that playing Indian was a truly progressive form of "transgression" – that it inverted or challenged the social status quo – even if it contained some "carnivalesque" features. As most scholars of American minstrel performances agree, when whites put on other racial faces they were not making attempts at accurate representations of the Other or at honouring the experience of subaltern cultures. On the other hand, their acts should not be read as simple denigration since they also revealed a certain longing on the part of white actors. In short, if being "white" meant acting strictly according to a "civilized" code of conduct, being "Indian" for a time might be a freeing experience.[47]

Playing Indian at camp, like "blacking up," represented a similar white, middle-class, and privileged longing to identify with the socially marginal, the "low-Other" of Canadian society. Like the Setons and the Grey Owls they resembled, camp enthusiasts sought from Aboriginal peoples connection to a time of premodern simplicity, a golden age of social harmony and calm. These idealized figures operated much as did the pre-industrial Folk in modern Nova Scotia, who, in McKay's words, were "less people in their own right and more incarnations of a certain philosophy of history."[48] In the context of the summer camp, Aboriginal peoples were seen as living the enviable simple life, while whites were seen as those impoverished by modernity's flow. Indeed, at camp antimodernist tendencies were frequently expressed in racialized terms, with a simple, if unarticulated, equation undergirding common thinking on the question.

Quite simply, white equalled "modern" and "Indian" equalled "premodern" or "primitive." Rearticulating much older primitivist tendencies in Western culture, twentieth-century camps also fuelled their own unique version of primitivism.[49] From this perspective, the Indian was regarded as the quintessential primitive man, and identification with him was seen as a way of distancing campers from distasteful elements of mainstream society. This perspective persisted in the late twentieth-century historical imagination of the camping community. Note the 1983 description of the Aboriginal worker in the history of Camp Keewaydin: "The guide's values were different from those of a white middle- or upper-class young man," it was explained: "[He] had no schooling but had been educated by Nature and life."[50]

Admiration for this proximity to nature was coupled with romanticization of the Indian's presumed distance from modernity. In 1950, the *Toronto Daily Star*'s reading of the camp project at Bolton explained: "City children ... will learn there were no department stores, super-markets or Saturday matinees for the Indians."[51] Where Aboriginal guides were employed, they were similarly praised for not being implicated in the culture of consumption. Keewaydin's camp historian claimed of their Native workers: "The early guide never owned an automobile. He owned a canoe. With it, he earned his livelihood, hunted ... and engaged in any leisure activity."[52] The Indian was one who did not rely on the comforts of mass culture but, instead, accepted the challenge of real physical work. In effect, the canoe was not regarded as technology at all, nor the Indian as a user of technology – a view that helped confirm his/her status as premodern.[53] If, like most stereotypes, this notion of the Indian as living at a distance from the modern world had some foundation in reality, it also ignored modernity's very real impacts on Aboriginal cultures. Ultimately, this encouraged essentialist thinking that cast certain groups as something other than "real Indians."[54]

Paralleling the camps' praise for the idealized Indian was a mock derision and scorn for "the white Man." In keeping with earlier primitivist tendencies, those who glorified the Indian also offered a social critique of their own society, however limited. In the case of playing Indian, this manifested itself as a semi-serious attack on "whiteness," understood as a symbol for implication in modernity. This critique took both implicit and explicit forms. Beyond the image of the hardy guide lingered the counter-image of the white man, living an alienated, compartmentalized, and ultimately unsatisfying existence. Behind praise for the Indian's "natural" training was criticism of the dry formality of institutional education. In certain cases, whiteness came in for more explicit attack. At Bolton Camp, boys participated in dramatic re-enactments of historic Native/white conflicts, with one 1937 description noting "the treachery of a band of marauding whites."[55] In 1950, use of the derogatory "pale-face" – "pale-faced campers" or white visitors as "chiefs in the pale-faced world" – also revealed attempts to see through Aboriginal eyes and to decentre whiteness as the assumed vantage point.[56] Looking back on the dominant culture from this new perspective, campers could join in the performance of the fire-lighting ceremony, which bid them to declare: "Light we now the council fire, built after the manner of the forest children. Not big like the whiteman's where you must stand away off so front all roast and back all gooseflesh; but small like the Indian's, so we may sit close and feel the warmth of fire and friendship."[57] Here, whiteness was represented as not only synonymous with ostentation but also with a cold, impersonal culture, lacking in true intimacy.

By superficially critiquing whiteness, members of the camping community could distance themselves from the hollowness of modern alienation and excess, essentially allowing them to reconceptualize their relationship to modernity. Via the summer camp experience, white urban Ontarians could think of themselves as existing outside the limits of the dominant culture. Clearly, the critique was a shallow one that lasted only so long as one's stay in the woods. What made "going Native" at camp such an act of privilege was the fact that campers could comfortably "go home" to whiteness once they returned to their urban environments, settings in which the benefits, or "wages of whiteness,"[58] were generally irresistible.

If anxieties about modernity and identity were clearly adult concerns, likely all the children knew was that playing Indian was fun. Still, "fun" could certainly be engineered to have developmental benefits. Not only at the broad spiritual level but also at the level of the child's psycho-social development, the use of purportedly Indian games, Indian villages, and role-playing at camp was regarded as providing a vigorous and healthy play life. On the one hand, Indian programming was praised for fostering more imaginative, self-initiated play, a contrast with ready-made leisure options back home. "Through the Council Ring, campers learn to create their own amusement," *Camping and Character* was proud to state in 1929: "They cannot depend on the elaborate facilities for amusement that the modern city affords. They must utilize benches, brooms, rope, poles and hemp sacks, and they must do the entertaining themselves."[59] At the same time, this educational/recreational wisdom was refracted through the prism of "primitivist" child development theory. In this, camps were influenced by theories of "race capitulation" popularized by G. Stanley Hall. According to Hall, boys in particular needed to indulge their savage tendencies in childhood so that they might, as the human race itself had ostensibly done, progress beyond them to civilized adulthood.[60] Camps, for their part, encouraged boys to indulge their "savage" impulses in games of "scalping," which were promoted as allowing "campers and staff alike to let off steam."[61] Games of "pioneers and Indians" were regarded in a similar light; in one case, a 1935 observer at Bolton happily reported that this included "blood-curdling yells" from "fierce-visaged boys of ten."[62] In this instance then, the camp offered itself not only as a physical escape from the city but also as metaphoric release from the emotional confines of modern childhood.

As these references suggest, the use of Indian programming could have deeply gendered meanings. In many ways, immersion in Native lore was regarded as a particularly masculine project, one useful in fostering a rugged masculinity in city-bred boys. In the early years at Bolton, so-called Indian programs were targeted only at boys. "Indian lore is the great feature at the boys' camp," proclaimed the annual report for 1935: "A hike and a picnic at the Indian village and the privilege of spending rest hour in real Indian wigwams, painted in lurid colours and electrifying designs, satisfy the hearts of seven-year-old boys ... who are far too superior to be content with ... games of 'London Bridge.'"[63] One postwar handbook advised the use of blood brother ceremonies and fictional re-enactments of tests of pain and endurance as part of boys' council ring ceremonies.[64] These were clearly meant to foster male bonding and a sense of manliness that required withstanding great (if imaginary) trials without complaint.

Girl campers, on the other hand, were encouraged to emulate a very different sort of Indian. At their camps the emphasis of Native lore activities was on the development of artistic abilities rather than on primitivist catharsis, with weaving and painting of "Indian themes" being popular. The tone of other Indian programming was also appropriately feminine. For instance, a description of "Indian day" at Camp Tanamakoon had no savage or primitivist overtones: "[The girls] had been in another world," it was recounted, "a world of quiet feet, gliding canoes and spirited dances."[65] On the other hand, girls' camps also made more challenging uses of Indian programming, as they did with other activities. At Tanamakoon and many CGIT camps, the council ring provided girls valuable opportunities for public speaking. The inducement to bravery that sometimes went along with acting "like Indians" may also have subtly encouraged a more active and assertive model of womanhood. One interesting incident at Tanamakoon – involving the director's fear of mice – reveals the symbolic importance attached to a number of racial categories. When Mary Hamilton discovered that girls had heard of her particular phobia, she made future efforts to provide a more courageous example. In her words, "We did not see how we could expect the little braves to be brave when the Big Chief was yellow."[66]

Selling the Experience, Buying Aboriginal Labour

Try as they might to temporarily escape it, camps and their campers were hopelessly enmeshed in modernity. More than this, like other expressions of antimodernist sentiment, the camp phenomenon was a reaction against modern life, but it also reinvigorated the very culture it regularly critiqued. It did this not only by indulging modern concerns with identity but, rather, by becoming, itself, another piece of the culture of consumption. Those in charge of "selling" the camp were quick to discover that "Indianness" provided the ideal marketing tool for its times. In this context, proving one's camp was most truly Indian had valuable cultural cachet, which easily translated into dollars and cents.

Camp owners, whatever antimodern tendencies they exhibited, were also shrewd businesspeople who were well aware of the need to compete with urban attractions. And compete they did, frequently using the Native theme as a focal point of advertising. Promotional events incorporating all things Indian were typical. Taylor Statten, founder-director of Camp Ahmek, was known to conduct council ring ceremonies not only at camp but also back in Toronto during the winter months, events that his biographer describes as "good advertising" for his camps.[67] Indian imagery also proliferated on camp brochures, which – in a world of limited media alternatives – were often the only source of information for those weighing their options from urban arm chairs. In what appears to be an early postwar brochure from Ahmek, director Taylor Statten was showcased in full Indian dress, complete with buckskin jacket, feather headdress, and hand drum. As late as 1960, Camp Sherwood was forced to reverse its decision to replace Indian imagery with medieval imagery. It was conceded quite simply that "the council rings and the feathered garb and war-paint [were] an unbeatable combination for exciting the imagination."[68]

Whatever social, spiritual, or nationalist needs it addressed – or perhaps precisely because of this fact – Indian programming was also part and parcel of the business of camp. When it came to camp budgets, Indian programming could be costly in a number of ways. For Seton's expertise in Indian lore, Camp Ahmek paid the handsome sum of twenty dollars per day in 1922.[69] Creating an Indian atmosphere also influenced the architectural design of many camps. Primitive simplicity may have been the desired aesthetic of camp life, but this didn't rule out substantial expenditures – $600 at Bolton Camp in 1926 – to set up elaborate council ring programs. As for other architectural features – the Indian villages, Edgar's "wig-wam" style cabin, or Ahmek's "totem poles from British Columbia" – one can only guess as to the cost.[70] Finally, according to one postwar source, Indian costuming was considered one of the necessary expenditures of camp. This handbook instructed: "It is not necessary to buy an expensive costume; but if you intend to remain in the camping business over a period of years, an expenditure in this direction would be justified."[71]

In efforts to hold the attention of young campers, securing a few Aboriginal staff or visitors was regarded as well worth the expense. As already noted, certain Ontario camps were marked by an ongoing, if limited, Native presence. One form this took was the appearance of Aboriginal guest performers. At Glen Bernard Camp, Mary Edgar brought guests "Dawendine," of the Ontario Six Nations; Chief Mudjeekwis, of the Rice Lake Anishnabe; and Nanaki, a Blackfoot from the "Western Plains" to participate in council ring ceremonies over the years.[72] Elsewhere, the thrill was to be found in witnessing performances of a different sort, where presumably more "primitive" Native locals interacted with the camping community. Camps in remote areas like Algonquin and Temagami had the edge here, the possibility of encounters with local Aboriginals partly defining, and also providing added attraction to, their "wilderness" settings. In some cases, Aboriginal people, hired initially to guide directors into remote locations, were kept on as regular staff.[73] At camps Ahmek, Keewaydin, Tanamakoon, and Temagami, Aboriginal men were employed as trip guides and as canoeing and woodcraft instructors not, seemingly, in large numbers but nevertheless as indispensable teachers and also as attractions. During the interwar years at Ahmek, administrators boasted of their canoeing instructor: "Bill ... is a full-blooded Ojibway Indian from the Golden Lake Reserve. His father is a chief."[74] At least two camps – Temagami and Keewaydin – employed Chief Jean-Paul Whitebear as woodcraft instructor since; according to the Keewaydin historian, the chief's presence had "considerable promotional value."[75] Less glamorously, Aboriginal women were sometimes hired on as kitchen staff and Aboriginal men as maintenance workers.[76]

The Joe Lake Store near Camp Ahmek. Bill Stoqua (second from left) with other Ahmek staff. Stoqua, an Anishnabe from the Curve Lake Reserve was said to be "the son of a chief" and was idolized by boys at Ahmek for his superb canoeing skills. *Algonquin Park Museum Archives #5081 (Mary Clare).*

From the Aboriginal perspective, camp work had obvious advantages. In all parts of the province, whatever the state of Aboriginal economies, Native bands welcomed the chance to make what must have looked like relatively "easy money" for work at summer camps. In regions like Temagami and Algonquin Park, Anishnabe bands and Métis who spent the fall and winter trapping and hunting, and sometimes logging, were often eager for summer wage work. Throughout the first half of the twentieth century, they found positions as canoe-trip guides at several camps, including the American-owned, all-male Camp Keewaydin. As in earlier periods, this work provided relatively good wages and a high degree of labour control.[77] In the early 1930s, Keewaydin guides were earning between four dollars and five dollars per day, handsome sums when one considers that, in other parts of the province, whole Aboriginal families were surviving on as little as twelve dollars to fifteen dollars per month.[78] Directing canoes full of thirteen-year-old prep school boys no doubt presented its own unique challenges, but it likely compared favourably with the alternatives: the hard physical labour and risks involved in mining or logging.

Boys at Temagami work on their woodcraft skills, c. 1930, as their (possibly Aboriginal or Métis?) instructor looks on. *Courtesy Upper Canada College Archives.*

Camp demand for Aboriginal performers also provided opportunities for bands in more southerly parts of the province. Significantly, this kind of work gave not just men but also certain Aboriginal women – among the most disadvantaged of wage labourers – the option of relatively enjoyable work. During the interwar years, Six Nations member "Dawendine" – otherwise known as Bernice Minton Loft – made appearances across the province, including at the fresh air camp Bolton and the privately run Glen Bernard. At Glen Bernard, she was paid to spend two weeks sharing stories with small groups of campers and also making appearances before the whole camp at council ring ceremonies.[79]

Loft's case is an interesting example. Like Pauline Johnson, who apparently served as one of her inspirations, Loft was born into the Six Nations Reserve at Grand River, Ontario, a group with a long history of contacts (and cooperation) with the dominant white culture.[80] Early on in their history, they adopted Christianity and a settled agricultural lifestyle, while acting as allies to the British during the American Revolution and again in 1812. Loft's parents, for their part, were residential-school educated and ensured that she was educated (and spoke English) from an early age. Well educated for her time, Loft was accepted by the Department of Indian Affairs as a teacher at one of the local reserve schools. At the same time, the Loft family also ensured that young Bernice grew up acquainted with Iroquoan (specifically Cayugan) history, crafts, and medicines. In the 1920s,

Loft's uncle, First World War veteran Frederick O. Loft, founded and led the first pan-Indian political organization, the League of Indians of Canada. By the 1930s, the adult Loft discovered that she too might be suited for a public role, given her knowledge of Aboriginal culture and her comfort in operating within non-Native society. As historian Cecelia Morgan has shown, during that decade, Loft ran something of a lecture circuit of Ontario and western New York, sharing her knowledge of Aboriginal cultures not only at summer camps but also at church groups, service clubs, schools, and universities.[81]

How should one read the appearances of Loft and other Aboriginal performers at camp? Certain scholars argue that, in their lives "on-stage," performers gave yet another example of Aboriginal people "playing Indian," a phenomenon for which there were numerous precedents. Indeed, racial play-acting was not a phenomenon restricted to the white community; Aboriginal people had been on display – in effect, "playing Indian" – almost since the point of contact.[82] Other scholars insist that the question must also be viewed from the Aboriginal perspective. They point out that performers like Loft (and others) had their own reasons for participating in such performances. According to historian H.V. Nelles, Native people who played something of the noble savage in commemorative events in the early twentieth century were also presenting themselves "as peoples with a rich culture." Even if these images were stereotypic, Nelles argues, Indian administrators set on assimilating Native peoples to "civilized" ways sensed the potentially subversive message of such performances. As one who has looked at Loft's experience in particular, Morgan similarly concludes that performance work offered women a rare invitation to enter the social spotlight, a chance to make their own statements about their cultural situations. Deloria, too, has argued that performing Indians could sometimes act as "bridge figures, using antimodern primitivism to defend native cultures against the negative stereotypes left over from colonial conquest." Finally, historian Paige Raibmon's advice that scholars abandon the categories of "authentic" and "traditional" in analyzing these complex responses to colonialism is well taken here.[83]

In the camp setting, too, we should not assume Aboriginal people were simply content to "play Indian" for white audiences or that they themselves were "inauthentic" recreations of "traditional" cultures. Camp performers may well have felt dignity and satisfaction in offering positive (if sometimes essentialist) portrayals of Indian life. At Bolton Camp, observers who witnessed Loft's appearance in 1937 approvingly referred to her as "a lovely cultured woman." At Glen Bernard, Loft was received with great warmth and excitement on the part of girl campers. "Girls were delighted with her attractive Indian costume and all the interesting heirlooms she showed them belonging to her Mohawk ancestors," Director Mary Edgar related to one of Loft's friends in 1935, "but particularly they enjoyed getting acquainted with 'Dawendine' herself." In 1954, Loft was included among the guests at the eighty-fourth birthday celebrations of Camp Temagami's founder, A.L. Cochrane, at Toronto's Royal York Hotel. Referred to in this case as "Princess Dawendine, daughter of a Mohawk chief," Loft was invited to present Cochrane with a symbolic award, in this case an "illuminated scroll" that she herself had drawn.[84]

Aboriginal guides, for their part, also garnered significant respect at camp. No surprise since they played essential and demanding roles on canoe out-trips, their tasks including the planning of routes, the directing of travel, and the making of final decisions about the safety of weather and water conditions. According to one history, in the eyes of Keewaydinites, "a guide was something close to a God, a wilderness God, when it came to his judgement and ability. He was never questioned; it was an unwritten rule." The same history suggests that Keewaydin guides formed close peer-like relationships – even "partnerships" – with the white staffmen on trips.[85]

On the other hand, for Aboriginal staff, limiting stereotypes and economic exploitation were also part of the story of camp. Visiting performers may have done their best to provide more realistic depictions of Aboriginal life, but, like participants in Wild West shows and fairs, they were also constrained by white expectations of the "performing Indian."[86] Appearance was a crucial issue in this regard, with audience preference favouring visitors in traditional dress. True to form, Native guests invariably presented themselves "in the garb of [their] race," as a report from Bolton Camp explained in 1937.[87] Mary Edgar, director of Glen Bernard, recalled: "It was a thrill of surprise for us when Nanaki – a Blackfoot woman who visited camp in the early fifties – descended the steps of the council ring wearing her elaborately beaded white doe skin costume and head band."[88] The preference, as with the historical narratives of camp administrators, was for the ahistorical, timeless Indian. (Who knows, however, whether Nanaki didn't obtain this outfit from Malabar's costume store, as Loft did at the start of her performing career!) As these encounters suggest, Aboriginal people were aware of and played to such tastes, a fact that could take its psychic toll. According to Morgan, Loft, for one, agonized frequently over career and identity issues. She was critical not only of the limits of her own knowledge but also of white perceptions of her. "First and foremost when I go to speak my Indian blood stands out," she once told a close (white) friend, "I am then of necessity a little bit aloof from your people."[89] One can't help but see that these Aboriginal performers were individuals who inhabited "two worlds"[90] and not always with great comfort.

Likely few campers realized that behind their elaborate costuming and "on-stage" personae, Aboriginal entertainers often lived far from glamorous lives. Performance work offered much needed wages to individuals like Loft, but (until her marriage in 1937) it didn't save her from a life of hard work and economic insecurity. In letters to friends, she lamented the state of her garden, her backlog of "darning and patching," the strains of chopping and hauling her own wood, and the pressure of caring for an ailing father. Camp work could be the source of other stresses. Several times Loft referred to the fact that Director Mary Edgar called her always "at the last minute," and to Edgar herself as one of "these women who want to be amused [but] don't want to pay for the monkey." Morgan recounts how, in 1935, Edgar offered to pay Loft ten dollars for a week of camp work, after having first promised to pay twenty dollars. Loft admitted frankly, "I was fairly stunned." Clearly she was also somewhat resentful towards those who took avid interest in her cultural background but so little in her actual life situation. Of Edgar she concluded, "I think she thought she was providing a beautiful holiday for an Indian – but evidently ... did not realize how poor I was."[91]

Camp relationships with Aboriginal guides were similarly shaped by cultural stereotypes and the reality of unequal labour relations. While guides were given due respect for their knowledge and skills, as Patricia Jasen and Tina Loo argue, guide relationships with sports enthusiasts and tourists were clearly hierarchical ones, however white travellers (or campers) liked to think of them.[92] At Keewaydin, for instance, guides may have been called "partners," but they could also be assigned servant-like status; on canoe trips, it was not boy campers but Native guides who served as cooks, filling the same role as replacements for female labour that Chinese men filled in northern resource towns.[93] Once back in camp – and after cleaning the soot from the cook pots! – guides retired to separate living quarters in a space geographically distinct from the rest of the camp. Camper recollection confirms that, while they may have been "in camp," Aboriginal staff were not truly "of" it at Keewaydin. "No, they were apart,"[94] responded one wartime camper when asked if guides shared in the general life of the camp, though this situation may well have been preferable to both parties. The tone of camp literature underlines, again, the cultural distance between guides and their employers. Glowingly positive descriptions could easily slip over into more degrading stereotypes, with guides painted as child-like, primitive, instinctual, and even animal-like. "The guides were conservative with their words," Director Mary Hamilton explained at Camp Tanamakoon, "and often, used a grunt when it would serve better ... But they were not silent either. Laughter came easily and they could find gaicty, a childlike gaiety, in the smallest events."[95] In a smilar manner, guides' expert abilities were sometimes portrayed not as acquired skills but as natural "instincts," impulses akin to the bear's inclination to hibernate or the duck's to fly south. Like animals, guides were often noted for their physicality and their silence, the latter easily interpreted as an indication of aloofness.[96]

As with Aboriginal performers, so with guides: it was not just their race but their class position that kept them at a distance from the camp family. To be sure, guide work paid better than other alternatives, but it was not without its tensions, as relations at Camp Keewaydin suggest. In times of economic hardship, as in the 1930s, the administration did not hesitate to cut guide wages by 20 to 25 percent (as also happened to camp staff in other situations).[97] If guides had few options in the years of the Depression, some twenty years later, they were more assertive in dealing with what they saw as unjust treatment. In 1954, the camp decided to eliminate the tradition of parental "tipping," a practice that nicely supplemented the wages of Métis guides. Indignant with this situation, and unsatisfied with promises of a fifty-dollar bonus and improved accommodation, twelve guides – on the day before all trips were to go out – threatened to withdraw their labour. The director's reaction to this move revealed that tensions were an ongoing part of the guide/administration relationship:

> The [director] fumed. He had already discussed their grievances earlier and settled them in a full meeting of the guides. He was tired of them avoiding work, drinking and even not showing up at the island for work in the spring. He was flooded with the unpleasant thoughts of the two occasions he had to make emergency trips to Mattawa trying to hire guides to replace the no-shows. Why, he had just given them a new cabin and bonuses![98]

The stand-off was short-lived. Refusing to give in to guide demands, the director paid guides their wages for the summer and asked them to leave. In the years that followed, white guides gradually replaced Métis labour at this camp.

As all of this suggests, the camp was another twentieth-century cultural "contact-zone" in which Aboriginals and whites met and interacted – but rarely on equal terms.[99] Still, for Aboriginal guides and performers, camp work offered several things: a supplement to longer-standing economies of trapping and hunting, alternatives to more physically demanding work such as logging and mining, and, for performers, paid work that brought public attention and respect. As Raibmon argues, even if such work involved projecting somewhat stereotypic images of Indians, Native peoples who took it "were not simply resisting change ... [T]hey were asserting their right to find a place for themselves within modernity."[100] From the other side of the question, white camp owners were trying to forge their own modern pathway to community, identity, and connection with nature. More than this, and what points precisely to the camp's inescapable entanglement with modernity, they attached deep value to this form of racial play but, at the same time, were willing to market this pseudo-spiritual experience. Again, as Lears' and McKay's work suggests, if not springing from commercial motivations, antimodernism could have clear market value. For those touched by the antimodernist quest, experience – whether of the mystical, physical, or tourist varieties – was a commodity for which they were willing to pay. In this sense, the camp's emergence was merely symptomatic of an age when ever-expanding realms of social and cultural life would be brought within the ambit of the market economy, when even community and connection could be bought and sold for a price. As much as camp enthusiasts claimed to seek understanding of "the Indian," it can't be ignored that they also sought to buy his labour and, ultimately, to "sell" his image to help them in the larger project of "selling" the camp.

A fascinating footnote to the camp as cultural contact zone is the fact that, on rare occasions, Native children found their way to camp. In 1936, the *Star*'s Fresh Air Fund tried to elicit support for sending Nick – "a pure blood Indian of seven winters" – to camp. In keeping with other camp literature, however, the article lamented the passing of a disappearing race: it did not critically engage with present-day Aboriginal dilemmas. "Just a few generations ago," the author regretfully explained, "Nick's ancestors travelled the streams of Ontario in birchbark canoes, galloped bareback through virgin forests on ponies, slept and lived in the open, hardly knew what sickness ... meant." More regrettable, however, than the "cramped" nature of his living quarters or the unsuitability of his "tinder-covered" backyard playground was Nick's disconnection from his ancestral traditions: the fact that "he ha[d] never been in a canoe, ha[d] never even seen one," that he had never slept "under the stars, out in the open."[101] Ironically, the assumption was that this deprived youth would regain a sense of his "Indian" roots at camp. As late as the 1970s, such ideas still held some currency as, at Glen Bernard, plans were discussed to "bring Indian girls to camp" as a way of helping them "treasure their old legends, customs and traditions."[102] Such "solutions" not only reinforced essentialized notions of what it meant to be Indian but also revealed the highly paternalistic notion that white people could show Aboriginal people how to be "Indian."

Assessing Impact

Children did not run camps, nor did they, alone, make decisions to attend them. With adults as both the founders and the paying clients of summer camps, one might argue the entire enterprise was an exchange between adults, reflecting adult aspirations and needs. This is certainly how Susan Houston, former camper at Tanamakoon and later historian of childhood, sees her own childhood experience, believing that Indian programming was more meaningful to adult administrators than to young campers. True enough, directors and other staff could, themselves, get quite caught up in playing Indian. Up at Camp Ahmek, Taylor Statten was rarely called by name, going almost exclusively by "Chief." Other staff at the camp also had a special opportunity to "play Indian" with the institution of the "Gitchiahmek Order" in 1923, in its early years a "staff-only" club. At other camps, adults could be equally affected by the excitement of going Native. At Bolton, one of the visiting camp board members was said to remark of the council ring in 1937: "That Indian ceremony really gave me creeps in the back."[103]

On the other hand, if Indian programming was clearly planned by adults, it also had its impact on children. That certain families patronized the same camps over several generations suggests that powerful loyalties engendered in childhood sometimes endured into adult years. Many children, it seems, were strongly affected by their stays at camp, and it is likely that lessons learned there – Indian programming included – followed campers into later life. Fitting as it did with the rough and tumble aspects of boy culture sanctioned in other social contexts, Indian programming was particularly popular with boys. At Bolton Camp, one observer remarked that "the Indian Ceremonial has been of never-failing interest to the boys," while participation in one "Indian pageant" of 1938 was said to

Chief Taylor Statten. At Camp Ahmek, Statten was widely known as "Chief," and he rarely let anyone else play the lead role in council ring. *Algonquin Park Museum Archives #2380 (Mervin Dupuis).*

have given its male campers "a thrilling experience, so thrilling indeed that many of them insisted on wearing paint, feathers and tomahawks for the rest of their stay at camp."[104]

Where Native guides were employed at northerly, private camps, boyish fascination with the Indian was intensified. In such cases, Aboriginal workers modelled an alluring masculinity premised on their mastery of wilderness skills. At Camp Ahmek, Ojibwa canoeing instructor Bill Stoqua was described as "a perfectionist." Staff recalled that "he had the style and the physique and the appearance ... [A]ll the campers thought if they could paddle like [him] they would have achieved something important."[105]

When it came to the council ring, boys and girls alike appear to have been moved by the ceremony. Looking back on it, some place the experience "in the realm of the holy."[106] In 1929, *Camping and Character* also claimed that the council ring held camper attention and that, in fact, "no single activity contribute[d] more to the camp sense of unity than the weekly Council Ring," while, over twenty years later, the Y's Camp Pine Crest counted the council ring "among the most attractive all-camp activities."[107] At Camp Ahmek, Taylor Statten's daughter, Adele, recalled the interwar council ring as a very formal affair. It was "always done very precisely, very organised and well planned," she explained later in life: "Some of us were in fear and trembling that somebody would do the wrong thing and spoil the atmosphere."[108] Perhaps more positively, Mary Northway recalls of the council ring at Glen Bernard in the 1920s: "[It] was awe-inspiring. At dusk in blankets the Big Chief (little Miss Edgar [the director]) turned us into Indians of a long ago time."[109] Former campers from later years agree that the council ring was a unique and special aspect of camp. According to Jane Hughes, camper in the 1940s and 1950s at Statten's Wapomeo, "we all behaved as if ... in a church service,"[110] remaining quiet except when called on to sing or recite. In a lighter spirit, Jim Buchanan remembers the council ring in the 1950s at Ahmek as "a fun event and certainly ... one of the highlights of camp." Looking back, he admitted he couldn't help indulging the idea of Taylor Statten as truly Aboriginal, even though he knew otherwise. "In many respects he struck you as stoical [sic]," he explained in our interview of 2000, "that he actually had an Indian background ... which he sure as hell didn't. But he seemed like he did."[111]

Beyond the reaches of campers' childish psyches, playing Indian at camp had other repercussions. As we have seen, stereotypes of "Indians," whether positive or negative, were staples of camp programming. By drawing on these, camps did more than shape attitudes of individuals campers: at a broader level, they contributed to the ongoing rationalization of colonialism. Negative images of violence and savagery rationalized colonialism from the humanitarian perspective, while positive stereotypes, by freezing Aboriginal peoples in time, suggested that such noble, premodern creatures couldn't hope to survive in a modern, civilized society. Either way, the colonial project was naturalized; that is, it was simply the way things had to be. On the other hand, silences and omissions regarding the tragic history of Native/white relations did as much harm as did these more explicit messages. Indeed, perhaps more damaging than what camps had to say about the Indian was what they did not say. Nothing, it seems, was ever said about the fact that, as white campers played at being Indian, contemporary Native children were the target of aggressive campaigns aimed to rid them of their "Indianness." Did campers have any idea, one wonders, that, as directors donned Native headdresses, federal laws attempted to bar Aboriginal peoples from appearing publicly in traditional dress? Were they ever aware that, as they enthusiastically participated in Indian rituals, Native bands in western provinces were prohibited from holding their own sundance and potlatch ceremonies?[112]

White children saw "Indians" at camp, but it seems they saw little of the real conditions facing Aboriginal peoples. Even while scholars conclude that racial categories in general are "shifting and unstable," and even "appallingly empty,"[113] for those racialized Others, the biological "unreality" of race conflicted with its pressing social reality in their day-to-day lives.[114] Take only the example of the Bear Island of Temagami, the band from which Keewaydin sought its first guides. By the 1920s, they faced an unenviable set of social and economic conditions. Due to a long-outstanding land claim – dating back to the 1850s – the band had never been formally assigned reserve land. Despite this fact, they adapted gradually to the fact of white encroachment on their land, surviving on a combination of trapping and guiding, including, as we've seen, employment at the area's summer camps. However, without clear hunting and fishing rights, the Temagami band faced continual harassment by local game wardens. Worse than this, resource development in the area and the infiltration of white trappers in the 1930s put the supply of fur into serious decline, leaving many to survive increasingly on relief funds. Postwar years saw little improvement in these conditions. The province continued to equivocate on the issue of establishing a reserve, and problems of alcohol and family breakdown increased.[115]

During this time, the small but influential recreation-based community of Temagami did little to ameliorate and, in some ways, exacerbated the problems of the Bear Islanders. With their own eyes firmly on preserving the area as wilderness escape and/or tourist mecca, white cottagers and resort operators complained variously about Native health problems, their destruction of the visible shoreline, and abuses of alcohol in the Aboriginal community, calling for increased police and medical surveillance as solutions. Camp Keewaydin's employment of Bear Islanders provides one case of how camp communities fit into this picture. At the camp's founding in the first years of the twentieth century, the administration considered Ojibwa men from Bear Island knowledgeable, experienced, and close at hand; in short, the ideal tripping guides. As primarily trappers, they spent the winter on their lines but were available and often looking for summer work. Over the years, however, Keewaydin's preference shifted away from the Bear Island band so that, by the 1920s, the camp sought primarily Métis guides from the more distant town of Mattawa. Although the camp historian is silent on the issue, it is quite possible that, given the situation noted above, the Bear Islanders were increasingly regarded as the undesirable sort of Indians, hardly the noble self-sustaining survivalists that camp life sought to glorify. As far as other questions were concerned – for instance, the Bear Islanders' outstanding land claim – there is no indication that the white community (camps included) had anything to say on the issue. Reminding children that they walked on what had previously been "Indian land" was portrayed not as a matter of controversy, as the basis for a critique of colonialism or social redress, but, rather, as a mildly interesting (if unchangeable) anthropological fact. This was scarcely surprising since the camps' very geographical existence was premised on Native removal from the land. Were camp administrators aware of, or concerned with, the Bear Islanders' long outstanding land claim? Certainly, by the 1970s and 1980s, some camp enthusiasts also dedicated themselves to this struggle.[116] For this earlier period, however, decades still marked by a broad cultural confidence in the colonial project, nothing could be found to indicate camp concern with the social and economic predicament of their Aboriginal neighbours in Temagami.[117]

In other camp contexts, Indian programming did not disappear, but the first questioning of it emerged in the 1940s and 1950s. Pinpointing the exact origin of changing sensibilities is a difficult process, but, in this case, it was quite possibly linked to the renewed spirit of internationalism and racial tolerance that had been steadily gaining influence since the late 1930s. In fact, at camps run by the CGIT, promoting international sensibilities had always been a key aspect of programming (which is understandable of an organization forged during the war years). In 1930, CGIT girls preparing to be counsellors were organized into "a model League of Nations," with their five Bible study groups "representing the five permanent members of the League." During the same summer, some of the programming suggestions developed at camp included "study of other countries to obtain an understanding of their customs and ideas." By arranging talks by missionaries and foreign nationals, CGIT organizers stated that they hoped that girls would "discover the viewpoint of the people of that country."[118] Other camps showed a similar desire to "break down narrow nationalistic attitudes," as Taylor Statten put it, and to encourage "the spirit of world brotherhood,"[119] especially as the governments of the world seemed to be failing at this same task. When war did break out, and as Britain became a theatre of conflict, British children appeared at a number of Canadian camps as "war guests," further heightening the sense of international connections.[120] CGIT camp reports spoke of "break[ing] down the barriers of prejudice"; private camp reports spoke of encouraging discussions of "international relationships"; and fresh air camp reports spoke of "the importance of knowledge, understanding, tolerance, harmony and good will."[121]

Finally, in the aftermath of the war, and as the Nazi plan for "the final solution" became known around the world, the discourse regarding racial and ethnic tolerance intensified, shaping not only government programs for "new Canadians" and immigrant reception work, as Franca Iacovetta has shown, but also summer camp life.[122] A determined spirit of internationalism permeated camp literature, fostered new elements of camp programming, and renewed interest in attracting campers from foreign countries. Not just CGIT camps but others too developed "United Nations Day," "international nights," and "World Friendship Party Night."[123] This new programming had much the same flavour as that endorsed by the Canadian state; it was broadly folkloric, introducing campers to the foods, "costumes," and games of other countries, with the hope that cultural understanding and respect would be fostered.

This general atmosphere of internationalism and cultural respect, however "moderate" and even "hypocritical" (as Iacovetta has shown), heightened sensitivity to Native issues in Canada as a whole and at postwar camps. The revised Indian Act of 1951 was, as Olive Dickason notes, "hardly revolutionary," but it did offer bands an increased degree of self-control, and, significantly, in terms of issues of cultural expression, it repealed legislation banning the potlatch and Sundance ceremonies.[124] At camp, concerns for cultural "respect" engendered a new unease with some of the old ways of presenting Native culture. As early as 1946, Mary Northway attacked the "distortion" that she observed in camps' Indian programs. "Isn't it too bad," she observed, "that the only conception some of our campers, living in haunts so recently inhabited by Indians, have is that Indians were a people who met on Saturday nights dressed in blankets from ... the Hudson Bay store and engaged in marshmallow eating contests?" Some directors went further, eliminating certain features of their Indian programming. In 1958, Mary Hamilton described the earlier decision to do away with the Indian council ring at Tanamakoon: "The familiar 'How! How!,' the tribal set-up and the Indian names still exist," she explained. "As for the Indian council fire, it was short-lived. We decided not to be Indians any longer and proceeded to be our own natural selves."[125] Perhaps as Aboriginal peoples were permitted to express their cultures openly, the sight of white people attempting to represent them appeared more incongruous.

At other camps, these issues weren't considered until much later, sometimes at the behest of outsiders. At the prestigious Taylor Statten camps, it was an Aboriginal youth who articulated what appears to have been the first critique of the council ring. In the early 1970s, this counsellor-in-training, who was also the daughter of the chief of the Ontarian Curve Lake band, complained to the camp administration: "I was so shock [sic] to go to council ring last night ... having to watch you people make fun of my people." Initially, the camp administration attempted to pacify the youth by removing the "dress-up" element from the ceremony, but when this prompted others to complain that "something was lost," the ritual was reinstated in its original form.[126] By the 1980s and 1990s, some camps – like Bolton – were more self-critical. At that fresh air institution, the council ring was not eliminated but modified; the use of broken English was forbidden and campfires with non-Indian themes were also added to programming. Around the camp, Aboriginal names were dropped from cabin sections and the "Blackfoot totem pole" was taken down in response to at least one visitor's complaint. In the "hot" political context of late twentieth-century Native/white relations, playing Indian was not always seen as harmless child's play. On the other hand, the issue was still contested in the late twentieth century, if silently; these traditions continued in many ways at different camps, with Aboriginal names and practices still in evidence. At least as late as 1994, the Indian council ring was still going strong at Camp Ahmek, with staff carefully following Statten's original order of proceedings and campers continuing to dress up in "blankets, feathers, and paint."[127]

The story of camps' Indian programming tells us something about the shifting nature of Native/white relations, but, ultimately, the history of "playing Indian" is the history of white folks and of white middle-class culture. One aspect of this was a recurring antimodernist sentiment that manifested itself, in part, in a fascination with the spiritual potential and the transformative possibilities of playing Indian. This racialized form of antimodernism ultimately served conservative political ends; as with the "folkifying" of Nova Scotian identity, it venerated certain elements of the province's past, at the same time ignoring some of its less palatable, colonial elements. Nevertheless, from the Aboriginal perspective, ironically, it also translated into relatively well-paid camp work, another way for

Aboriginal people to deal with the economic experience of twentieth-century modernity.

As far as modern childhood goes, "playing Indian" represented a contrast with the rigid and controlled approaches advised by child-rearing advice manuals in the interwar years. Tellingly, the diminishing importance of Indian programming coincided not only with a changing climate of racial politics but also with the rise of more permissive, emotional approaches to child rearing in postwar years. Perhaps as children were treated less as machines and were encouraged to be "their own natural selves" on a more regular basis, the catharsis of playing Indian was deemed a more dispensable frill. The postwar decline in the use of Indian programming should not be overestimated, however, as many camps persisted with their Indian play-acting until late into the twentieth century. The fact that the camp administrators were not above marketing this experience was also indicative of the times. Born of antimodernism, the summer camp was a modern animal. Playing Indian in this setting was just one more way of allowing for the simultaneous expression of these competing cultural impulses.

Conclusion: All Antimodern Melts into Modern?

It has become something of a truism of our day that, as modern people, we are out of touch with nature. While storms, floods, and earthquakes routinely disrupt the lives of the most unlucky of us, and while even most Canadians battle the vagaries of cold winters and hot, humid summers, one commonly hears that we live lives alienated from the natural world. And we are not the first to feel this way. Whatever the reality of the situation, to be modern in the twentieth century was to perceive oneself as divorced from nature, to lament this fact, and to look longingly, if only occasionally and half-heartedly, for a bridge back. Summer camp was one product of this way of thinking. As such, it contributed to the construction of nature as an entity existing apart from the machinations of the human world, a distinct and separate space, a place one could visit, indeed should visit, to reconnect with what it meant to be truly human. If previous generations had also felt themselves to be distinct from nature, in their eyes, this was as it should be. In fact, their ability to master nature, to increase their distance from it, was considered to be precisely what made them human. With regard to moderns, however, the further they were able to insulate themselves from the forces of nature, the more they longed to be in touch with them; the more advanced their scientific mastery of the natural world, the more pronounced the popular desire to "protect" it. In this regard, William Cronon's portrait of contemporary attitudes towards wilderness also provides an apt description of these earlier views of nature:

> Wilderness stands as the last remaining place where civilization, that all too human disease, has not fully infected the earth. It is an island in the polluted sea of urban-industrial modernity, the one place we can turn for escape from our own too-muchness. Seen in this way, wilderness presents itself as the best antidote to our human selves, a refuge we must somehow recover.[1]

Not all camps, to be sure, defined their spaces as "wilderness," but they certainly considered them to be fundamentally more "natural" (read: uncontaminated, healthy, even therapeutic) than the urban spaces their campers more regularly inhabited.

This opposing of nature and culture, however reductionist, was more than delusional escapism. On the contrary, it was the result of very real social and economic change. By the interwar and certainly postwar years, city and country were, indeed, experienced by many as very separate entities. For the majority of Ontario's citizens, the city was the physical site of the most significant stresses of modern culture. Primary among these – as in our own day – was work. In short, city space was work space. It also encompassed the spaces in which social obligation and all manner of power relations found concrete expression. By contrast, so-called "natural" space was increasingly holiday space. More and more, when twentieth-century Ontarians found themselves in nature, they found themselves free from work, free from social obligation, in short, free of the most trying pressures of modern life. That did not mean that work and obligation had no place in these settings, as those who laboured in agriculture and resource extraction, at northern resorts, or even in domestic labour at family cottages knew all too well. Perspective, however, was everything. The contrasts with familiar urban geographies, isolation from telephones, the likelihood of freedom from unexpected visitors, and the general liberation from routine all made "natural space" truly relaxing for many, as it still does today.

Summer camp was an off-shoot of this way of thinking, a project envisioned from the start as recreational good fun. For many campers, this was also its outcome. Far from frivolous, however, such a vision of camp life was rooted in, and helped promote, a modern notion of childhood, the very serious work of psychologists and educators. Providing children with fun was to offer one of the building blocks of childhood and to set the emotional foundation of stable adulthood. This treatment of leisure as a realm of vast import was another of the hallmarks of twentieth-century modernity. That choices in this area – the pool hall or the Scout club, the cinema or the summer camp – could "make or break" healthy children was a notion with which social scientists and educators would wrestle for decades to come. Some of the issues that would plague these experts – the rise, for instance, of an increasingly independent child and youth peer culture – were partly of their own making as they continually divided children from each other and from adults in age-segregated groupings. In this respect, some of the problems of the summer camp – with social misfits, unruly "ring-leaders," or sexual adventurers – were merely a reflection of broader trends.

The camp tells us not only about childhood as theory but also about child-rearing practice as it played out in practical contexts. Indeed, this study expands our knowledge of the history of child rearing, a subject focused almost exclusively on psychological advice literature. My findings suggest that progressive and "scientific" approaches co-existed in these years; there was no simple replacement of one with the other. Whether children should be tightly controlled or encouraged to "run free" were matters of contention in these years, and this debate expressed itself, if implicitly, at camp. At a broad level, summer camps were meant to symbolize a return to times of simplicity and freedom. Paradoxically, the camp movement also took flight in precisely those years in which advice literature advocated rigid and controlled approaches to child rearing. On the other hand, the very notion that children were also precious human material – which only increased over the course of these years – fostered regimes of control and regimentation to ensure their physical and emotional development as well as their safety. Ultimately, advice literature may have preached distinct messages in inter- and postwar years; on the ground, parents and educators of both periods dealt with flesh-and-blood children by applying those approaches that they deemed to "work." A little freedom here, a little control there: both marked the history of child rearing at camp.

Approaches to child rearing at camp – and indeed, childhood experience – were also clearly shaped by class and by gender. If the offering of camp holidays implied a more indulgent view of childhood for all classes, the details of camp life point to the persistence of class differences. Indeed, if the summer camp contributed to the spread of what Tina Loo calls "commodity environmentalism,"[2] it was different types of "commodities" that were marketed and sold to campers of different class backgrounds. More than this, camp not only reflected class differences but also, at times, its culture helped to shape class identities. In the twentieth century, how one viewed nature, wilderness, and "roughing it" – in short, the extent of one's antimodernist leanings – came to form one aspect of modern class identities. The latter were further complicated by gender. Indeed, this method of categorizing experience did not "wither away" under modern conditions; rather, as Keith Walden argues, "gender was one of the fundamental constructs imposed on the ... urban industrial environment to make it comprehensible."[3] In the twentieth century these constructs also shaped experiences of escape from those same urban industrial environments, one example being the summer camp. In the final analysis, both axes of identity – class and gender – were central to shaping childhood experience at camp.

One point upon which administrators were agreed was that – regardless of gender or class – children needed to play. In this sense, as a successful cultural institution, the camp and its history also point to leisure as a sphere of growing twentieth-century significance. Leisure was fast becoming the site of educational innovation, the transmission of gender and sexual stereotypes, as well as a key interface between children and youth, on the one hand, and the forces of capitalist consumer culture, on the other. Leisure also became one of the sites of crucial intergenerational conflict and youthful identity formation, issues that would only garner increasing cultural concern as the century progressed.

Connecting these diverse aspects of camp life was the unique form of antimodernist sentiment that originally inspired camp foundings. Like the cultural forms explored by Jackson Lears and Ian McKay, the summer camp emerged as a reaction to urban, industrial culture and represented yet another manifestation of bourgeois longing for authentic experience and nostalgia for simpler times. Further, it revealed the ways in which antimodernism expressed itself powerfully in connection with children and the institution of childhood. The fact that camps did not disappear but, indeed, proliferated in the 1950s and beyond is just one indication that antimodernism remained a strong, if subcultural, tendency throughout this period. Granted, infatuation with modernity in many forms was everywhere to be seen, but antimodernism also percolated beneath the surface, raising questions and dampening the cultural optimism of the day.

If, however, camp enthusiasts can be called antimodernists of any type, they were not the sort, like those of Jackson Lears' Victorian study, who retained much of "an eloquent edge of protest" or "some kind of meaning outside the self" via their camp involvements. Camp enthusiasts did not generally suffer "immobilizing depression" or the "turmoil of [the] divided self" but, rather, were active optimists animated by the promise of therapeutic recreation.[4] For parents, part of that "therapy" was simply achieving temporary escape from the duties of parenting or enjoying the comfort of knowing that youngsters were receiving a good dose of socialization and exposure to "tough" living. Taken as a whole, the camping movement represented not reaction against the ethic of self-fulfilment but, rather, a search for the clearest path to that end. In this, however, it was not unique. In fact, campers shared in a much broader trend, which cast the search for "self" and "identity" as, increasingly, the only meanings worth decoding. The summer camp came of age during what some have called the "century of the child" – a time others have called "the century of psychology."[5] Both are fitting depictions of an era that saw human behaviour classified in increasingly individual terms and social problems met with individualistic solutions. For many twentieth-century Canadians, not just those who frequented camps, the quest for self-knowledge and fulfilment would be limited to the realm of recreation and leisure, the one area in which it was believed, however misguidedly, that individuals wielded full control. No one could rightly expect recreational activity to challenge the terms by which modern society was ordered, nor was it ever designed to do so. Leisure, by its nature, was the modern reward for unsatisfying work. It was of compensatory, not revolutionary, dimensions.

What sort of antimodernism, then, was this? It was both different from, but also of a piece with, other sorts that scholars have explored. Certainly it bears some resemblance to what Ian McKay has found in the case of Nova Scotia. There, he argues, the idea of the Folk represented a "commercial antimodernism," one that both "imitat[ed] an international fashion" and "respond[ed] creatively to ... local conditions and sociopolitical interests."[6] Beyond this, it was an increasingly typical, barely counter-cultural aspect of the popular mentality. Not just an elite group of literati or intellectuals but also educators, social workers, physical and recreation instructors, and the parents of many campers themselves, by their actions, revealed a knee-jerk antiurbanism, a belief in the healing power of nature, in the romanticization of "wilderness," and the simple, even "primitive" longing for a stable sense of identity and community. Indeed, these were fast becoming common reactions to the contradictions of modern culture. They were generally expressed with an air of resigned nostalgia, the sort of feeling one might expect to inspire plans for a nature holiday, not a sustained social critique. More broadly, this widespread, almost unconscious and largely unarticulated antimodernism represented the ambivalence that increasingly marked modern mentalities, the divided consciousness that, even today, sees us avidly consuming the products of technological change, while also frequently lamenting the consequences.

The common thread, then, connecting this and other North American incarnations of antimodernism was its ultimate social impact, what Lears saw as the "reinvigoration of modern therapeutic culture" and McKay as "modernizing antimodernism." Via the camp, modern ways of thinking and feeling about numerous aspects of society, the self, and racial others were reinforced. Preoccupation with intense experience and with identity, and the belief that both were to be sought on the terrain of leisure were all typical of the modern condition. Even in its very "antimodernness," the summer camp further points up the progress of modernity. As Dean MacCannell argues, "The best indication of the final victory of modernity over other sociocultual arrangements is not the disappearance of the non-modern world, but its artificial preservation and reconstruction in modern society."[7] By this measure, camps are part of what MacCannell sees as "the separation of non-modern culture traits from their original contexts and their distribution as modern playthings."[8] Given the tenor of modern society, the search for geographical escape, mental liberation, and physical relaxation, however genuine, was nevertheless commodified through the camp experience.

Camp may well have been part plaything, part tourism, and part modern commodity, but that does not negate the fact that it was the site in which very specific emotional, perhaps even spiritual, needs were met. For those who came to treasure it, camp was part of what gave their modern lives meaning. The point is, in doing so, it was part of, not antithetical to, that modern existence. Indeed, in many ways, the camp experience was part of living fully in the modern world. As their founders saw it, camp holidays frequently put rejuvenating distance between children and their urban homes, improved health, taught social skills (and sometimes social graces), and offered a firmer sense of identity to shield children against the anonymity and disconnection of contemporary society. This book should help draw further attention to how searches for meaning, identity, and fulfillment, though abstract and slippery notions, are a very real (and so far neglected) part of the social, cultural, and perhaps even emotional history of the twentieth century.

The findings here, in the main, corroborate those of American scholars of the summer camp. Most important, this books shares the perspective that the summer camp, though shaped at numerous turns by antimodern sentiment and simple-life nostalgia, was inextricably linked to the urban industrial world from which campers thought themselves to be escaping. Camp administrators north and south of the border saw their work as taking children "back to nature," but in doing so they also segregated children by class and planned programs specific to boys and to girls, respectively. North and south of the border, they borrowed from modern educational philosophy, while also drawing on nostalgic images of the simple life of the past. North and south of the border they invoked notions of tradition – whether Aboriginal or pioneer – to draw closer connections between themselves, their history, and the land. Ultimately, our similar conclusions concerning the camp's implication in the project of modernity and its ambivalence regarding questions of escape, isolation, wilderness, and roughing it, suggest that, whatever the nationalist rhetoric that frequently infused camp literature, the North American culture of consumption, urbanization, and industrialization and its resultant glorification of nature and the simple life were more important than were national cultures in shaping the culture, goals, and experience of the summer camp.

In Ontario, as in the United States, the history of camp life is the history of the pull of competing cultural tendencies. On the one hand, camp reflected the nostalgic lure of the antimodern and, on the other, the fascination with all things modern. Unlike the modernist intellectuals Marshall Berman describes, who generally adopted polarized positions – for instance, the futurist's unqualified view of modernity as "good" or Max Weber's utter contempt for modernity as "bad" – camp enthusiasts adopted more ambivalent positions.[9] Indeed, the history of camping suggests that, if intellectuals had difficulty recognizing the mix that was modernity, so-called "ordinary people" did not. Their own lives reveal a constant engagement with both perspectives. In the end, if campers were not vocal about (or perhaps even conscious of) the contradictions of modernity, they lived them nonetheless. When urban dwellers packed off children for a stay at summer camp, to some extent they offered their implicit critique of modernity. They also, as we have clearly seen, presented their inescapable entanglement with it. Ultimately, the persistence of the summer camp phenomenon into the postwar period revealed that the retreat into nature had become a much-marketed commodity. The limitations of its vision, however, confirmed that true escape from "the modern" was unavailable at any price.

Notes

Introduction

1 CTV, coverage of funeral of Pierre Elliott Trudeau, 3 October 2000.
2 Trudeau's biographers note briefly his years at the upscale Camp Ahmek, Algonquin Park, in the 1930s. Stephen Clarkson and Christina McCall, *Trudeau and Our Times*, vol. 1: *The Magnificent Obsession* (Toronto: McClelland and Stewart, 1990), 37.
3 Pierre Trudeau, "Exhaustion and Fulfilment: The Ascetic in a Canoe," in *Wilderness Canada*, ed. Borden Spears (Toronto/Vancouver: Clarke, Irwin, 1970), 4. First publication in *Jeunesse Etudiante Catholique* (1944).
4 Ibid., 3.
5 Ibid., 4.
6 The seminal work on antimodernism is T.J. Jackson Lears, *No Place of Grace: Antimodernism and the Transformation of American Culture, 1880-1920* (Chicago: University of Chicago Press, 1981). For analysis of Canadian antimodernism, see Donald A. Wright, "W.D. Lighthall and David Ross McCord: Antimodernism and English-Canadian Imperialism, 1880s-1918," *Journal of Canadian Studies* 32, 2 (1997): 134-53; Lynda Jessup, "Prospectors, Bushwhackers, Painters: Antimodernism and the Group of Seven," *International Journal of Canadian Studies* 17 (1998): 193-214; Ross D. Cameron, "Tom Thomson, Antimodernism, and the Ideal of Manhood," *Journal of the Canadian Historical Association* 10 (1998): 185-208; Tina Loo, "Making a Modern Wilderness: Conserving Wildlife in Twentieth-Century Canada," *Canadian Historical Review* 82, 1 (2001): 92-121; Tina Loo, "Of Moose and Men: Hunting for Masculinities in British Columbia, 1880-1939," *Western Historical Quarterly* 32, 3 (2001): 296-319; Michael Dawson, "'That nice red coat goes to my head like champagne': Gender, Antimodernism and the Mountie Image, 1880-1960," *Journal of Canadian Studies* 32, 3 (1997): 119-39; Ian McKay, *Quest of the Folk: Antimodernism and Cultural Selection in Twentieth-century Nova Scotia* (Montreal/Kingston: McGill-Queen's University Press, 1994). McKay argues that the creation of the Folk myth

effectively erased from public memory the real and often tragic history of industrialization and underdevelopment in that province.

7 Allen Smith, "Farms, Forests, and Cities: The Image of the Land and the Rise of the Metropolis in Ontario, 1860-1914," in *Old Ontario: Essays in Honour of J.M.S. Careless*, ed. David Keane and Colin Read, 71-94 (Toronto: Dundurn Press, 1990).

8 Paul Rutherford, "Tomorrow's Metropolis: The Urban Reform Movement in Canada," *Canadian Historical Review* (Historical Papers) 1 (1971): 203. The Garden City Movement, which also influenced thinking in Europe, Britain, and the United States, inspired some quite radical suggestions in the Canadian context, such as Adam Shortt's 1912 proposal for a plan of urban depopulation, where city workers would be shuttled back to country homes. See Rutherford, "Tomorrow's Metropolis," 209. Other studies that deal with the negative impacts of, and negative reaction to, the growth of Canadian cities, include Judith Fingard, *The Dark Side of Life in Victorian Halifax* (Porter's Lake: Pottersfield Press, 1989); Mariana Valverde, *The Age of Light, Soap, and Water: Moral Reform in English Canada, 1885-1925* (Toronto: McClelland and Stewart, 1991); Carolyn Strange, *Toronto's Girl Problem* (Toronto: University of Toronto Press, 1995); Carolyn Strange, "From Modern Babylon to a City upon a Hill: The Toronto Social Survey Commission of 1915 and the Search for Sexual Order in the City," in *Patterns of the Past: Interpreting Ontario's History*, ed. Roger Hall, William Westfall, and Laurel Sefton MacDowell, 255-77 (Toronto: Dundurn Press, 1988).

9 Strange, "From Modern Babylon to a City upon a Hill," and *Toronto's Girl Problem.*

10 This worry, which in Victorian times received the label of neurasthenia, has not received extensive historical treatment in the Canadian context. Studies that touch on it as a prelude to discussions of the back-to-nature craze include: George Altmeyer, "Three Ideas of Nature in Canada, 1893-1914," *Journal of Canadian Studies* 11, 3 (1976): 21-36; Douglas Cole, "Artists, Patrons and Public: An Enquiry into the Success of the Group of Seven," *Journal of Canadian Studies* 13, 2 (1978): 69-78; and Patricia Jasen, *Wild Things: Nature, Culture and Tourism in Ontario, 1790-1914* (Toronto: University of Toronto Press, 1995).

11 Rutherford, "Tomorrow's Metropolis"; Paul Rutherford, ed., *Saving the Canadian City: The First Phase, 1880-1920* (Toronto: University of Toronto Press, 1974); Walter Van Nus, "The Plan-Makers and the City: Architects, Engineers, Surveyors and Urban Planning in Canada, 1890-1939" (PhD diss., University of Toronto, 1977).

12 William Cronon, "The Trouble with Wilderness; or, Getting Back to the Wrong Nature," *Environmental History* 1, 1 (1996): 9.

13 Quoted in Jamie Benidickson, *Idleness, Water, and a Canoe: Reflections on Paddling for Pleasure* (Toronto: University of Toronto Press, 1997), 35. In fact, Allen Smith details the same negative attitudes to forests, trees, and nature in general among Ontario settlers into the late nineteenth century. See Smith, "Farms, Forests, and Cities: The Image of the Land and the Rise of the Metropolis in Ontario, 1860-1914," in *Old Ontario: Essays in Honour of J.M.S. Careless,* ed. David Keane and Colin Read, 71-94 (Toronto: Dundurn Press, 1990).

14 Raymond Williams, *The Country and the City* (London: Chatto and Windus, 1973).

15 Elizabeth McKinsey, *Niagara Falls: Icon of the American Sublime* (Cambridge: Cambridge University Press, 1985); Patricia Jasen, *Wild Things: Nature, Culture, and Tourism in Ontario, 1790-1914* (Toronto: University of Toronto Press, 1995); Karen Dubinsky, *The Second Greatest Disappointment: Honeymooning and Tourism at Niagara Falls* (Toronto: Between the Lines Press, 1999).

16 On these changing views of nature, see Roderick Nash, *Wilderness and the American Mind* (New Haven: Yale University Press, 1973). Historical discussions of Western views of nature are also included in William Cronon, ed., *Uncommon Ground: Toward Reinventing Nature* (New York: W.W. Norton and Company, 1995); Max Oelschlaeger, *The Idea of Wilderness: From Prehistory to the Age of Ecology* (New Haven: Yale University Press, 1991); Peter Schmidtt, *Back to Nature: The Arcadian Myth in Urban America* (Baltimore: Johns Hopkins University Press, 1990). For earlier periods, see Keith Thomas, *Man and the Natural World: Changing Attitudes in England, 1500-1800* (London: Allen Lane, 1983); Carolyn Merchant, *The Death of Nature: Women, Ecology, and the Scientific Revolution* (San Francisco: Harper and Row, 1979).

17 Roy I. Wolfe, "The Summer Resorts of Ontario in the Nineteenth Century," *Ontario History* 54, 3 (1962): 149-61; George Altmeyer, "Three Ideas of Nature in Canada, 1893-1914," *Journal of Canadian Studies* 11, 3 (1976): 21-36; Cole, "Artists, Patrons and Public," 69-78; G. Wall and J. Marsh, eds. *Recreational Land Use: Perspectives on its Evolution in Canada* (Ottawa: Carleton University Press, 1982); Bruce W. Hodgins and Margaret Hobbs, eds., *Nastawgan: The Canadian North by Canoe and Snowshoe* (Weston: Betelgeuse Books, 1985); Bruce W. Hodgins and Jamie Benidickson, *The Temagami Experience: Recreation, Resources, and Aboriginal Rights in the Northern Ontario Wilderness* (Toronto: University of Toronto Press, 1989); Jasen, *Wild Things*; Benidickson, *Idleness, Water, and a Canoe*; Loo, "Of Moose and Men." On the creation of provincial parks during this same period, see K. Morrison, "The Evolution of the Ontario Provincial Park System," in Wall and Marsh, *Recreational Land Use*, 102-19; Gerald Killan, *Protected Places: A History of Ontario's Provincial Parks System* (Toronto: Dundurn Press, 1993).

18 Walter Van Nus, "The Fate of City Beautiful Thought in Canada, 1893-1930," in Canadian Historical Association, *Historical Papers* (1975): 191-210; Rutherford, "Tomorrow's Metropolis: The Urban Reform Movement in Canada, 1880-1920," Canadian Historical Association, *Historical Papers* (1971): 208-9; Smith, "Farms, Forests, and Cities," 83-85. Little has been written on the establishment of urban parks in Canada. For treatment in the Vancouver context, see Robert A.J. McDonald, "'Holy retreat' or 'practical breathing spot'? Class Perceptions of Vancouver's Stanley Park, 1910-1913," *Canadian Historical Review* 65, 2 (1984): 127-53. On an American history of playgrounds, see Dominick Cavallo, *Muscles and Morals: Organized Playgrounds and Urban Reform, 1880-1920* (Philadelphia: University of Pennsylvania Press, 1981).

19 Canadian studies of prohibitive and regulatory approaches to the leisure time of the young have focused more on youth than on children per se. See Cynthia Comacchio, "Dancing to Perdition: Adolescence and Leisure in Interwar English Canada," *Journal of Canadian Studies* 32, 3 (1997): 5-35; Mary Louise Adams, *The Trouble with Normal: Post-war Youth and the Making of Heterosexuality* (Toronto: University of Toronto Press, 1997), 142-50; Strange, *Toronto's Girl Problem*, 118-27.

20 On the playground movement, see Cavallo, *Muscles and Morals*. A full history of the YMCA in Canada has yet to be written. For an older history, see Murray G. Ross, *The YMCA in Canada: The Chronicle of a Century* (Toronto: Ryerson Press, 1951). See also David MacLeod, "A Live Vaccine: The YMCA and Male Adolescence in the United States and Canada, 1870-1920," *Histoire Sociale/Social History* 11, 2 (1978): 5-25. On religious programming for youth, see M. Lucille Marr, "Church Teen Clubs, Feminized Organizations? Tuxis Boys, Trail Rangers, and Canadian Girls in Training, 1919-1939," *Historical Studies in Education*,

3, 2 (1991): 249-67; Patricia Dirks, "'Getting a grip on Harry': Canada's Methodists Respond to the 'Big Boy' Problem," *Canadian Methodist Historical Society Papers* 7 (1990): 67-82. On Seton and the Woodcraft Indians, see Brian Morris, "Ernest Thompson Seton and the Origins of the Woodcraft Movement," *Journal of Contemporary History* 5, 2 (1970): 183-94; John Henry Wadland, *Ernest Thompson Seton: Man in Nature and the Progressive Era, 1880-1915* (New York: Arno Press, 1978); Allen H. Anderson, "Ernest Thompson Seton and the Woodcraft Indians," *Journal of American Culture* 8, 1 (1985): 43-50; Allen H. Anderson, *The Chief: Ernest Thompson Seton and the Changing West* (College Station: Texas A&M University Press, 1986). On the Boy Scouts, see David MacLeod, *Building Character in the American Boy: The Boy Scouts, YMCA, and Their Forerunners, 1870-1920* (Madison: University of Wisconsin Press, 1983); Robert H. MacDonald, *Sons of the Empire: The Frontier and the Boy Scouts Movement, 1890-1918* (Toronto: University of Toronto Press, 1993).

21 On the YWCA in Canada, see Wendy Mitchinson, "The YWCA and Reform in the Nineteenth Century," *Histoire Sociale / Social History* 12, 24 (1979): 368-84; Diana Pederson, "'Keeping our good girls good': The YWCA and the 'Girl Problem,' 1870-1930," *Canadian Women Studies* 7, 4 (1986): 20-24; Diana Pederson, "'Building today for the womanhood of tomorrow': Businessmen, Boosters, and the YWCA, 1890-1930," *Urban History Review* 15, 3 (1987): 225-42. Guiding in Canada has not yet received much attention, but this is starting to be addressed in doctoral work by Kristine Alexander. See Kristine Alexander, "Le mouvement Guide au Canada." *Toujours Prête ou toujours prêt? Le guidisme comme lieu d'éducation unisexe et coéduqué* (Louvain-le-Neuve: Academia bruylant, forthcoming); Kristine Alexander, "Motherhood, Citizenship, Continuity, and Change: The Girl Guides, Gender and Imperialism in Interwar English Canada," Proceedings of the Fifth Annual Graduate Symposium in Women's and Gender History at the University of Illinois at Urbana-Champaign, available at http://www.history.uiuc.edu/hist%20grad%20orgs/WGHS/proceedings.htm. On the CGIT, see Margaret Prang, "The Girl God Would Have Me Be: The Canadian Girls in Training, 1915-1939," *Canadian Historical Review* 66, 2 (1985): 154-83; Marr, "Church Teen Clubs."

22 Camping was central to the programs of both Scouts and Guides, though these groups were more likely to organize short one- or two-week treks into the bush or on rented sites rather than what we would think of as residential summer camping. Many of the first organized residential summer camps were outgrowths of YMCA work, while the CGIT developed its own camps in the interwar years. Some mention of the history of summer camps is included in broader studies of these institutions and back-to-nature studies. See MacLeod, *Building Character*, 233-47; Prang, "Girl God Would Have Me Be," 160; Schmidtt, *Back to Nature*, 96-105.

23 On open-air schools, see Geert Thyssen, "Visualizing Discipline of the Body in a German Open-air School (1923-1939): Retrospection and Introspection," *History of Education* 36, 2 (2007): 247-64; David Hughes, "Just a Breath of Fresh Air in an Industrial Landscape? The Preston Open Air School in 1926: A School Medical Service Insight," *Social History of Medicine* 17, 3 (2004): 443-61; Frances Wilmot, "In Search of Birmingham's Open-air Schools," *Local Historian* 29, 2 (1999): 102-13; Marjorie Cruickshank, "The Open-air School Movement in English Education," *Paedagogica Historica* 17, 1 (1977): 62-74; David Turner, "The Open Air School Movement in Sheffield," *History of Education* 1, 1 (1972): 58-80; Grant Rodwell, "Australian Open-air School Architecture," *History of Education Review* 24, 2 (1995): 21-41. New Zealand is one country that experimented with summer

camps along the lines of other subsidized, fresh air institutions for the poor. On these "health camps" in New Zealand, see Tennant, "Children's Health Camps." See also Stafano de Martino and Alex Wall, *Cities of Childhood: Italian Colonie of the 1930s* (London: Architectural Association, 1988) on the architecture of children's summer camps in Italy.

24 McLeod, *Building Character*, 235. On Gunn's role in camping history, see Leslie Paris, "Children's Nature: Summer Camps in New York State, 1919-1941" (PhD diss., University of Michigan, 2000), 34; W. Barksdale Maynard, "'An ideal life in the woods for boys': Architecture and Culture in the Earliest Summer Camps," *Winterthur Portfolio*, 34, 1 (1991): 3-29. On Gunn and also the history of the Keewaydin camps, see Brian Back, *The Keewaydin Way: A Portrait, 1893-1983* (Temagami: Keewaydin Camp Ltd., 1983); Bruce W. Hodgins and Seana Irvine, "Temagami Youth Camping," in *Using Wilderness: Essays on the Evolution of Youth Camping in Ontario,* ed. Bruce W. Hodgins and Bernadine Dodge, 143-56 (Peterborough: Frost Centre for Canadian Heritage and Development Studies, 1992); Bruce W. Hodgins and Jamie Benidickson, *The Temagami Experience: Recreation, Resources, and Aboriginal Rights in the Northern Ontario Wilderness* (Toronto: University of Toronto Press, 1989), 112-15, 178-84, 192-96, 258-60. On early private camps and Camp Chocorua, see Paris, "Children's Nature," 34-40; Maynard, "'Ideal life.'"

25 Schmidtt, *Back to Nature,* 97. On the general development of fresh air camps, see Paris, "Children's Nature," 50-61; Schmidtt, *Back to Nature*, 96-105.

26 McLeod, *Building Character*, 237. The information on organizational/agency camps is taken, again, from Paris, "Children's Nature," 41-50.

27 Alan Gordon, "Heritage and Authenticity: The Case of Ontario's Sainte-Marie-Among-the-Hurons," *Canadian Historical Review* 85, 3 (2004): 507-31.

28 Camp Temagami's claim to this title rests with the efforts of founder A.L. Cochrane, who, beginning in 1900, organized camp-outs of students from Upper Canada College, where he taught. By 1903, a recognizable "camp" was established at Temagami. While one history of Keewaydin claims that that camp began operating in Temagami in 1902, historian Bruce Hodgins states that a permanent site was not established until the following year. On the establishment of early camps, see Trent University Archives [hereafter TUA], Camp Directories, Ontario Camping Association [hereafter OCA], *Directory of Member Camps*, 1949 and 1955; TUA, OCA Papers, 98-019/13/6, series E, Adele Ebbs Papers, Mary L. Northway, "Canadian Camping: Its Foundation and Its Future," address given to the Manitoba Camping Association Annual Meeting, May 1946; Donald Burry, "The Early Pioneers of the Camping Movement," in Hodgins and Dodge, *Using Wilderness*, 78; Liz Lundell and Beverley Bailey, *Summer Camp: Great Camps of Algonquin Park* (Toronto: Stoddart Publishing, 1994). On the founding specifically of Keewaydin and Temagami, see Back, *The Keewaydin Way*; Bruce W. Hodgins and Seana Irvine, "Temagami Youth Camping," in Hodgins and Dodge, *Using Wilderness*, 143-56. Note that, in 1908, Camp On-da-da-waks was relocated to Golden Lake in North Renfrew County. See TUA, OCA, *Directory*, 1949.

29 TUA, OCA Papers, 78-006/25/40, Charlie F. Plewman, "The Days Leading up to the Formation of the Ontario Camping Association," part of poster "Today: Tomorrow's Yesterday," c. 1967.

30 TUA, OCA Papers, 98-019/13/6, Adele Ebbs, "The Days Leading up to the Formation of the Ontario Camping Association," n.d., 1.

31 Looking back in the 1960s, the OCA estimated only six or seven private camps existed during this period; however, according to their own 1949 and 1955 directories, at least thirty-three camps showed founding dates prior to the Second World War. Data from

other sources increases this number to forty-one. See "Days Leading Up," 1; *OCA Directory of Member Camps*, 1949, 1955; Lundell and Bailey, *Summer Camp*; West, *Summer Camps in Canada*; Brian Back, "Canada's Oldest Camps," available at www.ottertooth.com/Camps/camps-can.htm.

32 Stanley explains that OCA members were worried about scaring off agency camps if minimum standards were enforced. See Meg Stanley, "The Not So Lazy Days of Summer: The Ontario Camping Association and Accreditation," in Hodgins and Dodge, *Using Wilderness*, 41.

33 Northway "Canadian Camping."

34 TUA, OCA Papers, 98-019/13/6, Adele Ebbs, "Carrying the Torch for Camping," address given at the OCA Annual Dinner, 6 April 1976; Ebbs, "The Days Leading Up."

35 TUA, OCA Papers, 78-006/1/1, minutes, OCA Board of Directors, 25 October 1939; TUA, OCA Papers, 78-006/1/1, minutes, OCA Board Meeting, 6 March 1946; Meg Stanley, "The Not So Lazy Days of Summer," in Hodgins and Dodge, *Using Wilderness*, 41. TUA, Camp Directories, OCA, *Directory of Member Camps*, 1949, 1955. These data were also partially supplemented with information from Ann West, *Summer Camps in Canada: A Complete Guide to the Best Summer Camps for Kids and Teens* (Vancouver: Polestar Press, 1995).

36 In 1947, the Department of Education's deputy minister, Dr. J.G. Althouse, estimated that there were "between 500 and 600 organizational and private camps in Ontario at the present time," while 1948 records indicate 469 camp licences had been granted that year. It seems likely that these numbers included statistics on day camps, which are not the focus of discussion here. See OCLC files in possession of Dorothy Walter, Toronto, Copy of Address over CKEY Broadcast, Dr. J.G. Althouse, 25 April 1947, 3; Province of Ontario, "Report of the Minister of Education," in *Education Report*, 1948, 63.

37 OCA, *Ontario Camp Bulletin*, Edition 2, 1946.

38 Ibid.

39 Hedley S. Dimock, *Administration of the Modern Camp* (New York: Association Press, 1948), 21.

40 Nancy Cleaver, "An Old Canadian Custom – Sending the Kids to Camp," *Saturday Night*, 19 April 1952, 16; Peter Newman, "Junior's $10 Million Adventure in the Pines," *Financial Post*, 5 June 1954.

41 Newman, "Junior's $10 Million Adventure."

42 This has, not surprisingly, been the focus of those who have, themselves, been involved in the camping movement in Ontario. See Ontario Camping Association, *Blue Lake and Rocky Shore: A History of Children's Camping in Ontario* (Toronto: Natural Heritage/Natural History, 1984); Back, *Keewaydin Way*; Donald Burry, "A History of the Taylor Statten Camps" (MSc thesis, University of Saskatchewan, 1985). See also Donald Burry, "The Early Pioneers of the Camping Movement," and Bruce W. Hodgins and Seana Irvine, "Temagami Youth Camping," both in Hodgins and Dodge, *Using Wilderness*, 69-87, and 143-56, respectively; Eleanor Eells, *History of Organized Camping: The First 100 Years* (Martinsville: American Camping Association, 1986); David Hurwitz, "How Lucky We Were," *American Jewish History* 87, 1 (1999): 29-59.

43 Abigail Van Slyck, *A Manufactured Wilderness: Summer Camps and the Shaping of American Youth, 1890-1960* (Minneapolis: University of Minnesota Press, 2006); Leslie Paris, *Children's Nature: The Rise of the American Summer Camp* (New York: NYU Press, forthcoming); Leslie Paris, "'Please let me come home': Homesickness and Family Ties at Early Twentieth-Century Summer Camps," in *The American Child: A Cultural Studies Reader*, ed. Caroline

Levander and Carol Singley, 246-61 (New Brunswick, NJ: Rutgers University Press, 2003); Michael B. Smith, "'And they say we'll have some fun when it stops raining': A History of Summer Camp in the United States" (PhD diss., Indiana University, 2002); and Michael Smith, "The Ego Ideal of the 'Good Camper' and the Nature of Summer Camp," *Environmental History* (January 2006), available at http://www.historycooperative.org/journals/eh/11.1/smith.html. See also David Churchill, "Organized Wilderness: The Algonquin Camps and the Creation of the Modern Wilderness," in Hodgins and Dodge, *Using Wilderness*, 105-23; Margaret Johnston and David Churchill, "A Safe Land for Children's Adventures," in Hodgins and Dodge, *Using Wilderness*, 125-42. Some history of Canadian camps, nature, and wilderness is also included in Hodgins and Benidickson, *Temagami Experience*, 112-15, 178-84, 192-96, 258-60; Benidickson, *Idleness, Water and a Canoe*, 48-77. On camping as an educational enterprise, see especially Smith, "And they say we'll have some fun," and Anna H. Lathrop, "'Strap an axe to your belt': Camp Counselor Training and the Socialization of Women at the Margaret Eaton School (1925-1941)," *Sport History Review* 32, 2 (2001): 110-25.

44 Paul C. Mishler, *Raising Reds: The Young Pioneers, Radical Summer Camps and Communist Political Culture in the United States* (New York: Columbia University Press, 1999); Nancy Mykoff, "A Jewish Season: Ethnic American Culture at Children's Summer Camp, 1918-1941" (PhD diss., New York University, 2002); Leslie Paris, "A Home away from Home: Brooklyn Jews and Interwar Children's Summer Camps," in *The Jews of Brooklyn*, ed. Ilana Abramovitch and Seán Galvin, 242-49 (Hanover: University Press of New England, 2002). On girls' camps and femininity, see Susan A. Miller, "Girls in Nature/The Nature of Girls: Transforming Female Adolescence at Summer Camp, 1900-1939" (PhD diss., University of Pennsylvania, 2001); Leslie Paris, "The Adventures of Peanut and Bo: Summer Camps and Early-Twentieth-Century American Girlhood," *Journal of Women's History* 12, 4 (2001): 47-76. On girls' camps in Ontario, see Lathrop, "'Strap an axe to your belt'"; Susan L. Forbes, "'Nothing but a rag between you and the sky': Northway Lodge Girls' Camp and the Wilderness Experience," paper presented to the Canadian Historical Association Conference, Edmonton, 24 May 2000. On masculinity and boys' camping, see Maynard, "'Ideal life,'" esp. pp. 17-22; Kristopher Churchill, "Learning about Manhood: Gender Ideals and 'Manly Camping,'" in Hodgins and Dodge, *Using Wilderness*, 5-27.

45 Mary L. Northway, "Tools for the Job," *Parent Education Bulletin* 13 (1941): 6.

46 TUA, Ronald H. Perry Fonds, 82-016/2/8, "The Summer Camp: Recreation or Education," *Canoe Lake Camp Echoes* 4, 2 (1931): 13.

47 McKay, *Quest of the Folk*.

48 Howard P. Chudacoff, *How Old Are You? Age Consciousness in American Culture* (Princeton: Princeton University Press, 1989). For several other examples of monographs that treat age as a category of historical analysis, see Doug Owram, *Born at the Right Time: A History of the Baby Boom Generation* (Toronto: University of Toronto Press, 1996); Holly Brewer, *By Birth or Consent: Children, Law, and the Anglo-American Revolution in Authority* (Chapel Hill: University of North Carolina for the Omohundro Institute of Early American History and Culture, 2005); Duane Alwin, Ronald L. Cohen, and Theodore M. Newcomb, *Political Attitudes over the Life Span: The Bennington Women after Fifty Years* (Madison: University of Wisconsin Press, 1991). The growing literature on childhood, referenced throughout this book, offers numerous other examples.

49 Northway, "Canadian Camping," 6, 7.

50 Ibid., 6.

51 TUA, OCA Papers, 84-019/1/1, Newsclippings Scrapbook, "Canada's Summer Indians Hit the Trail," *Star Weekly Magazine*, 11 June 1960.

52 According to historian and archivist Bernadine Dodge, "while summer camps exist in all provinces of Canada, the overwhelming majority, and most of the private camps, are situated in Ontario." In her view, the rest of the country has housed mainly agency camps, suggesting that camping as a wider movement (i.e., as a movement that touched children of all economic backgrounds) was unique to Ontario (but also, perhaps, that private camps were central to the Ontario movement). See Bernadine Dodge, Address to the Friends of the Bata Library, Trent University, Peterborough, February 1992.

53 Ross Cameron makes this point in his work on the antimodernism of Tom Thomson. See Cameron, "Tom Thomson," 193.

54 Though the CSET approach was meant to be multifaceted – using the old fourfold approach of the YMCA – observers noted that Statten seemed to favour the physical side above others. This fits with what we know of Statten's view of religion and work with children. For more on this, see Chapter 6, page 224. This "muscular," or "male," approach was what kept the programs from real success, according to historian Lucille Marr, who claims that the less competitive CGIT program for girls was much more successful. See Marr, "Church Teen Clubs."

55 Statten's dedication to, and success at, camp work was recognized internationally in 1941, when he was elected president of the American Camping Association, the only Canadian ever to have been so recognized. For further biographical information on Statten, as well as his role in developing the CSET, see C.A.M. Edwards, *Taylor Statten* (Toronto: Ryerson Press, 1960); Marr, "Church Teen Clubs."

56 TUA, OCA Sound/Tape Collection, 83-002/7/1, Nora Cochrane and Billie (Aileen) Nesbit, interview by Keith Rumble, 22 February 1974.

57 For more on the life of Cochrane, see Upper Canada College Archives, Ann Hall, "Arthur Lewis Cochrane: A Biographical Sketch," unpublished paper, Queen's University, Kingston, 1964. Quotations from 36, 37.

58 According to the camp biographer, Clarke was able to acquire "a magnificent stone house" and to "settle into a style befitting a successful entrepreneur." For more biographical information on A.S. Clarke and the history of the Keewaydin Camp, see Back, *Keewaydin Way*.

59 For biographical information on Edgar, see TUA, Northway Family Fonds – Additions, 90-016/1/34, Mary Northway, "Mary S. Edgar, 1889-1973," *Canadian Camping Magazine* (Summer 1973); TUA, OCA Sound/Tape Collection, 83-002/5/8, Barbara Gilchrist, interview by Jack Pierce, 6 November 1986.

60 On Mary Hamilton and the History of Camp Tanamakoon, see Mary G. Hamilton, *The Call of Algonquin: Biography of a Summer Camp* (Toronto: Ryerson Press, 1958), 16. Anna H. Lathrop, "'Strap a compass and knife and an axe to your belt': The Role of Camp Counselor Training in the Socialization of Women at The Margaret Eaton School (1925-1941)," paper given to the Canadian Historical Association Conference, Edmonton, 24-29 May 2000; John Byl, "Mary G. Hamilton: Committed, Dedicated Pioneer Made a Difference," website of the Canadian Association for the Advancement of Women and Sport and Physical Activity, available at http://www.caaws.ca/e/milestones/women_history/mary_hamilton.cfm.

61 For biographical information on Mary Northway, see TUA, Northway Family Fonds, 90-016/1/1, "Fonds Level Description – Northway Family," curriculum vitae, Mary

Northway, 1979. Raymond also mentions Northway as a significant part of Blatz's work at the institute and, indeed, as integral to the publication of Blatz's final study, *Human Security*. See Raymond, *Nursery World*, 144, 210-16, 220. Northway's dissertation was not only published but also translated into six other languages.

62 The YMCA was probably the most significant player in terms of the agency camp. Not only was the Y among the first to establish Ontario camps, but of the camps associated with the OCA in 1949 (the earliest year for which full OCA statistics are available), the YM/YWCA ran eighteen of the twenty-eight agency camps (or 64 percent). Thousands of other middle-class children went camping with organizations such as the Girl Guides and Boy Scouts in these years, but, as mentioned, these groups did not establish permanent camps. See TUA, Camp Directories, OCA, *Directory of Member Camps, 1949*.

63 These do not represent a truly random sample. Interviewees were located using newspaper advertisements, organizational contacts, e-mail, and conventional mail.

64 David Thelan, ed., *Memory and American History* (Bloomington and Indianapolis: Indiana University Press, 1990); Paul Thompson, *The Voice of the Past: Oral History* (Oxford: Oxford University Press, 1978); John J. Fox, "First Readers: Five Introductions to Oral History," *Oral History Review* 25, 1-2 (1998): 119-28. On the use of oral history to retrieve childhood memories, see Neil Sutherland, "Listening to the Winds of Childhood," in Jean Barman, *Growing Up British in British Columbia: Boys in Private School* (Vancouver: UBC Press, 1984), 3-23; Jean Barman, "'Oh no! It would not be proper to discuss that with you': Reflections on Gender and the Experience of Childhood," *Curriculum Inquiry* 24 (1994): 53-67; Michael H. Frisch, "The Memory of History," *Radical History Review* 25 (1981): 9-23. For one of the most instructive articles on using oral history to understand the "scripts" of people's lives, see Joan Sangster, "Telling Our Stories: Feminist Debates and the Use of Oral History," *Women's History Review* 3, 1 (1994): 5-28.

Chapter 1: Back to Nature

1 On the broad transformation of space in the Victorian city and beyond, see Keith Walden, *Becoming Modern in Toronto: The Industrial Exhibition and the Shaping of Late Victorian Culture* (Toronto: University of Toronto Press, 1997), 224-32; Robert A.J. McDonald, *Making Vancouver: Class, Status, and Social Boundaries, 1863-1913* (Vancouver: UBC Press, 1996); Gunter Gad and Deryck W. Holdsworth, "Streetscape and Society: The Changing Built Environment of King Street, Toronto," in *Patterns of the Past: Interpreting Ontario's History*, ed. Roger Hall, William Westfall, and Laurel Sefton MacDowell, 174-205 (Toronto and Oxford: Oxford University Press, 1988); Barbara Sanford, "The Political Economy of Land Development in Nineteenth-century Toronto," *Urban History Review* 16, 1 (1987): 17-33; Stephen Davies, "'Reckless walking must be discouraged': The Automobile Revolution and the Shaping of Modern Urban Canada to 1930," *Urban History Review* 18, 2 (1989): 123-38; Valerie J. Korinek, *Roughing It in the Suburbs: Reading* Chatelaine Magazine *in the Fifties and Sixties* (Toronto: University of Toronto Press, 2000); Veronica Strong-Boag, "Home Dreams: Women and the Suburban Experiment in Canada, 1945-1960," *Canadian Historical Review* 72, 4 (1991): 471-504; Suzanne Morton, *Ideal Surroundings: Domestic Life in a Working-class Suburb in the 1920s* (Toronto: University of Toronto Press, 1995); Richard Harris and Matt Sendbuehler, "The Making of a Working-class

Suburb in Hamilton's East End, 1900-1945," *Journal of Urban History* 20, 4 (1994): 486-511; Richard Harris, "A Working-class Suburb for Immigrants, Toronto, 1909-1913," *Geographical Review* 81, 3 (1991): 318-32; Kenneth T. Jackson, *Crabgrass Frontier: The Suburbanization of the United States* (New York and Oxford: Oxford University Press, 1985); Robert Fishman, *Bourgeois Utopias: The Rise and Fall of Suburbia* (New York: Basic Books, 1987); Roy Rosenzweig, *Eight Hours for What We Will: Workers and Leisure in an Industrial City, 1870-1920* (Cambridge: Cambridge University Press, 1983); Roy Rosenzweig and Elizabeth Blackmar, *The Park and the People: A History of Central Park* (Ithaca: Cornell University Press, 1992).

2 Walden, *Becoming Modern*, 245. On the erosion of the preindustrial walking city in the United States, see Jackson, *Crabgrass Frontier*.

3 "Urbanization," *The Canadian Encyclopedia* (Edmonton: Hurtig Press, 1988), 2,235.

4 Table 9, "Population of Incorporated Cities, Town and Villages, 1901-1951," Dominion Bureau of Statistics, *Ninth Census of Canada, 1951*, vol. 1 (Ottawa: Minster of Trade and Commerce, 1951).

5 "Worn Out by Sickness, Future Is a Dreary One," *Toronto Daily Star* [hereafter *TDS*], 25 June 1924, 1.

6 Trent University Archives [hereafter TUA], Ronald H. Perry Fonds, 82-016/2/8, "The Summer Camp: Recreation or Education," *Canoe Lake Camp Echoes* 4, 2 (1931): 13.

7 "City Is Concentration Camp to Child Prisoners of Heat," *TDS*, 26 June 1941, 9.

8 "Gladden Young Hearts by Your Donation Now," *TDS*, 26 June 1946, 17.

9 On children's deaths caused by traffic accidents and the general dangers of increased traffic, see "Country Holiday Is Dream for Many – But Can Be True," *TDS*, 18 June 1946, 7; "City Traffic's Shadow Takes Toll of Youth Destined for Holiday," *TDS*, 13 August 1948, 1; "Playing on City Street Six Children Lost Lives, 201 Injured by Traffic," *TDS*, 19 June 1950, 17.

10 *TDS*, 5 July 1924, 1; *TDS*, 9 August 1945, 3.

11 "Needs Holiday, Not Medicine, Doctor Tells Sick Mother," *TDS*, 8 June 1935, 1.

12 "Holiday Chances for Needy Slim Unless Gifts Increase," *TDS*, 10 July 1935, 1.

13 Perry Fonds, "The Summer Camp," 13.

14 TUA, unaccessioned holdings, Taylor Statten, *Talks to Counsellors* (Taylor Statten Camps, 1928), 19.

15 United Church Archives/Victoria University Archives [hereafter UCA/VUA], 85.095C, box 14, file 6, Canadian Girls in Training [hereafter CGIT] Camps, National Girls Work Board, "Morning Watch," 1940.

16 Marjorie Trotter, "A Girls' Religion," *The Torch* 9, 2 (1933): 38.

17 Mary L. Northway, "Tools for the Job," *Parent Education Bulletin* 13 (1941): 6.

18 Hedley S. Dimock and Taylor Statten, *Talks to Counselors* (New York: Association Press, 1939), 17.

19 AO, RG-2-73, box 6, file – "National Council on Physical Fitness, 1949," Doris W. Plewes, "Physical Fitness," transcript of radio address, CKCO, Ottawa, 5:15 PM, 6 February 1949.

20 Camps run by socialists were also part of the Ontario landscape and, had they been studied here, would no doubt have contained more radical rhetoric and solutions. For an exploration of Camp Naivelt near Brampton, run by socialist-Jewish leftists, see Esther Reiter "Secular Yiddishkait: Left Politics, Culture, and Community," *Labour* 49 (2002): 121-46.

21 Tillotson, *Public at Play*, 11
22 Dimock and Statten, *Talks to Counselors*, 17.
23 Plewes, "Physical Fitness" (emphasis in original). That everyone shared in a bounty of recreational time seemed to be an unquestioned assumption of such literature, in which commentaries on social change were framed in generally classless terms. In 1939, Camp Ahmek's *Talks to Counselors* prefaced its practical advice with the observation that "there has been a great shift in the centre of gravity of life from one of labor to one of potential leisure" (Dimock and Statten, *Talks to Counselors*, 16). State-generated literature revealed similar attitudes and assumptions. In 1948, it was noted: "We all face increasing leisure. What shall we do with it? One of the tragedies of our times is the variety and beauty of things around us and the silly and sometimes sordid use we make of them." See Dr. Lindsey Kimball, quoted in *Community Courier*, 15 November 1948, back cover.
24 In one such text, presumably for study in politics and citizenship, the writer was critical of commercial amusements on the grounds that they required "only a minimum amount of physical and mental exertion." See J.A. Corry, *Democratic Government and Politics* (Toronto: University of Toronto Press, 1946), 418-20. Quoted in Tillotson, *Public at Play*, 22.
25 Dimock and Statten, *Talks to Counselors*, 17.
26 Perry Fonds, "The Summer Camp," 13.
27 Quoted in Liz Lundell, *Fires of Friendship: Eighty Years of the Taylor Statten Camps* (Toronto: Fires of Friendship Books, 2000), 12.
28 "Come On! Kick in and Smile! Give Kids the Break You Got," *TDS*, 28 August 1930, 25.
29 "Is Real Pleasure to Help Those Who Help Themselves," *TDS*, 7 June 1924, 1.
30 *TDS*, 24 June 1920, 5; "Reminiscent Army Man Defines Joys of Childhood," *TDS*, 2 July 1943, 18.
31 Abbie Graham, quoted in Dimock and Statten, *Talks to Counselors*, 18.
32 TUA, Camping Literature Collection, Ontario Boys' Work Board – W.A. Milks, ed., "The Camp Director's Manual," n.d., 5.
33 UCA/VUA, 85.095C, box 30, file 3, "Report of the Third Ontario Camp Council", 1929, 2, 4.
34 UCA/VUA, 85.095C, box 42, file 49, Ryde Lake Camp newsletter, 1955. On growing concerns about the failure of modern churches to hold the interest of children and youth, see M. Lucille Marr, "Church Teen Clubs, Feminized Organizations?: Tuxis Boys, Trail Rangers, and Canadian Girls in Training, 1919-1939," *Historical Studies in Education* 3, 2 (1991): 249-67; Patricia Dirks, "'Getting a grip on Harry': Canada's Methodists Respond to the 'Big Boy' Problem," *Canadian Methodist Historical Society Papers* 7 (1990): 67-82; David MacLeod, "A Live Vaccine: The YMCA and Male Adolescence in the United States and Canada, 1870-1920," *Histoire Sociale/Social History* 11, 2 (1978): 5-25; Margaret Prang, "The Girl God Would Have Me Be: The Canadian Girls in Training, 1915-1939," *Canadian Historical Review* 66, 2 (1985): 154-83. George Altmeyer proposes that the metaphor of regarding "nature as temple" was one of the newly emerging, more positive views of the natural world in late nineteenth-century Canada. See George Altmeyer, "Three Ideas of Nature in Canada, 1893-1914." *Journal of Canadian Studies* 11, 3 (1976): 21, 36.
35 W. Barksdale Maynard, "'An ideal life in the woods for boys': Architecture and Culture in the Earliest Summer Camps," *Winterthur Portfolio*, 34, 1 (1991): 9.
36 David E. Shi, *The Simple Life: Plain Living and High Thinking in American Culture* (New York, Oxford: Oxford University Press, 1985). Shi explores the simple life in groups as contrasting as seventeenth-century Puritans, Emerson-style transcendentalists, twentieth-

century conservationists, and modern-day Boy Scouts. In the context of twentieth-century Nova Scotia, McKay stresses the importance of local contexts in shaping visions of the simple life. For instance, he reveals how, in Nova Scotia, the development of a "folk" identity helped connect middle-class Nova Scotians with a golden past before the intensification of class conflict in the industrial era. See Ian McKay, *Quest of the Folk: Antimodernism and Cultural Selection in Twentieth-century Nova Scotia* (Montreal/Kingston: McGill-Queen's University Press, 1994).

37 UCA/VUA, CGIT Collection, 85.095C, box 31, file 1, "CGIT Camps, 1944," brochure; UCA/VUA, CGIT Collection, 85.095C, box 31, file 1, "CGIT Camps, 1942," brochure; Family Service Association of Toronto Archival Collection [hereafter FSATA], Neighbourhood Workers' Association [hereafter NWA], "Log of Bolton Camp, 1941."

38 TUA, Ronald H. Perry Fonds, *Canoe Lake Camp Echoes* 4, 1 (1931): 40; TUA, Ronald H. Perry Fonds, "The War Whoop," *Canoe Lake Camp Echoes* 4, 3 (1931): 38-42, 53-55. Of the "hotel," one parent observed: "I was astonished at the size and the remarkably good management of the place. Even the bell ringing system was organized." TUA, Ronald H. Perry Fonds, "The War Whoop," *Canoe Lake Camp Echoes* 4, 3 (1931): 55.

39 TUA, OCA Sound/Tape Collection, 83-002/2/5, Mary Northway, interview by Cathy Stuart and Warren Anderson, 21 January 1975.

40 OCA, *Ontario Camp Bulletin* 2, 1946.

41 Lundell, *Fires of Friendship*, 22.

42 Diane Balmori, "Architecture, Landscape, and the Intermediate Structure: Eighteenth-Century Experiments in Mediation," *Journal of the Society of Architectural Historians* 50, 1 (1991): 38-56.

43 Craig Kilbourn, *Adirondack Furniture and the Rustic Tradition* (New York: Harry N. Abrams, 1987). Summer camp buildings could also be said to be following in the tradition of the "intermediate structure," again a British innovation of the eighteenth century that rejected the symmetry and order of classical architecture in an attempt to lessen the divide between architecture and landscape. See Balmori, "Architecture, Landscape and the Intermediate Structure."

44 Maynard, "'Ideal life,'" 23.

45 Lundell, *Fires of Friendship*, 21.

46 UCA/VUA, 85.095C, box 14, file 1, "CGIT Camp Manual," 1950, 57-58. On outdoor theatres, see FSATA, NWA minutes, Bolton Camp Committee, 13 June 1934; Lundell, *Fires of Friendship*, 44. At Ahmek, the imposing log theatre, constructed in 1927, was built across a small stream that emptied into Lake Canoe. With the stage facing outwards towards the lake, audiences were forced not only outdoors but into canoes in order to view the performance. See Lundell, *Fires of Friendship*, 44. On other outdoor chapels, see Hedley S. Dimock and Charles E. Hendry, *Camping and Character: A Camp Experiment in Character Education* (New York: Association Press, 1929), 137-38; Shirley Ford, interview by author, 20 June 2000; TUA, Camp Pine Crest Fonds, 78-009/2/4, Camp Pine Crest, Brochure, "Health and Fun at Pinecrest, 1950."

47 Mary G. Hamilton, *The Call of Algonquin: Biography of a Summer Camp* (Toronto: Ryerson Press, 1958), 16.

48 FSATA, NWA, "Log of Bolton Camp, 1941."

49 At Bolton Camp, even though campers never left the two-hundred-acre property, overnight hikes were still arranged at the camp's "Indian village" or "Hilltop Lodge." See FSATA, NWA, "A Lilt and a Song to Life: Bolton Camp in 1934," 11.

50 Hamilton, *Call of Algonquin*, 117.

51 Since true appreciation of nature was thought to be impossible without the ability to identify, at Bolton, campers took part in "identification tests" pertaining to sixty species of trees and flowers. See FSATA, NWA, "New Interests at Bolton Camp in 1935," 11.

52 OCLC files in possession of Dorothy Walter, Toronto, Ontario, Dr. J.G. Althouse, transcript of CKEY Broadcast, 25 April 1947, 1.

53 Quoted in Jamie Benidickson, *Idleness, Water, and a Canoe: Reflections on Paddling for Pleasure* (Toronto: University of Toronto Press, 1997), 190.

54 James W. Buchanan, interview by author, 22 July 2000, Toronto.

55 TUA, OCA Sound/Tape Collection, 83-002/005/024, Mary Northway, interview by Jocelyn Palm, 17 November 1981.

56 TUA, OCA Sound/Tape Collection, 83-002/5/27, Harry Ebbs, interview by Bert Danson, Toronto, January 1982.

57 Lundell, *Fires of Friendship*, 67; TUA, Ronald H. Perry Fonds, 82-016/3/1, "Important Information for Parents of Ahmek and Wapomeo Campers," 1950. Bark Lake – site of the provincial government camp – at only 130 miles from Toronto, just southeast of Minden, was a shorter trip but one made more difficult by a three-mile walk in from the main road on "a very rough trail," where flies and mosquitoes could sometimes be fierce. Conditions were such that even local contractors were reluctant to take up the job of improving the road. See TUA, OCA Sound/Tape Collection, 83-002/8/10, Jack Passmore, taped memories of Bark Lake Camp, 8 May 1982.

58 Getting to Temagami required fifteen hours from Detroit and Buffalo, twenty-four from New York or Chicago. See Bruce W. Hodgins and Jamie Benidickson, *The Temagami Experience: Recreation, Resources, and Aboriginal Rights in the Northern Ontario Wilderness* (Toronto: University of Toronto Press, 1989), 110.

59 TUA, OCA Sound/Tape Collection, 83-002/5/24, Mary Northway, interview by Jocelyn Palm, 17 November 1981.

60 Quoted in Lundell, *Fires of Friendship*, 12. Campers expressed similar sentiments, especially those at Algonquin and Temagami locations. A Keewaydin ex-camper stated, "Yes, it's fair to say that Keewaydin, even today, is in a wilderness. There is no highway access. It is on an island 25 miles by boat from the lake's single town, highway and railroad station." Robert Foster to Sharon Wall, 8 September 2000. Other campers agreed. "I definitely thought of the camp area as wilderness," recalled one Ahmek camper in later life. "I had never been in the deep woods before. I do remember thinking the first day I arrived ... and got into [a] canoe ... that my parents would never be able to find me there." James Felstiner, e-mail interview by author, April 2001.

61 TUA, OCA Sound/Tape Collection, 83-002/5/24, Mary Northway, interview by Jocelyn Palm, 17 November 1981.

62 Ralph Barford, interview by author, 23 August 2000, Toronto.

63 Douglas Creelman, interview by author, 23 June 2000.

64 OCLC files in possession of Dorothy Walter, Toronto, Ontario, Marjorie Booth, unpublished paper, "History of the Development of OCLC, Bark Lake," 1973, 17.

65 "Camp Timagami [sic]," *College Times*, Easter 1924, 43; TUA, OCA Papers, 72-007/2/5, brochure, "Camp Temagami (Cochrane Camp)," c. 1950; "A Canoe Trip in Timagami [sic]," *College Times*, Summer 1922, 33. For a fuller discussion of the treatment of Native peoples and cultures within the camp setting, see Chapter 6. This discussion is indebted to Jonathan Bordo's "Jack Pine: Wilderness Sublime or Erasure of the Aboriginal Presence from the Landscape," *Journal of Canadian Studies* 27, 4 (1992-93): 98-128.

66 For the argument of historians and cultural geographers on this point, see D.A. West, "Re-searching the North in Canada: An Introduction to the Canadian Northern Discourse," *Journal of Canadian Studies* 26, 2 (1991): 108-19; Rob Shields, *Places on the Margin: Alternative Geographies of Modernity* (London: Routledge, 1991); Barry Lopez, *Arctic Dreams: Imagination and Desire in a Northern Landscape* (New York: Scribner, 1986); Daniel Francis, "Great White Hope: Myth of the North," in *National Dreams: Myth, Memory, and Canadian History*, 152-71 (Vancouver: Arsenal Pulp Press, 1997); Sherrill E. Grace, *Canada and the Idea of North* (Toronto: University of Toronto Press, 2002).

67 On the north as myth symbol for Canadian nationalists, see Carl Berger, "The True North Strong and Free," in *Nationalism in Canada*, ed. Peter Russell, 4-14 (Toronto: McGraw-Hill, 1966); S.D. Grant, "Myths of the North in the Canadian Ethos," *Northern Review* 3/4 (1989): 15-41; Bruce W. Hodgins and Margaret Hobbs, eds., *Nastawgan: The Canadian North by Canoe and Snowshoe* (Weston: Betelgeuse Books, 1985); Francis, "Great White Hope."

68 Derek Gregory, *Geographical Imaginations* (Cambridge: Blackwell, 1994); Peter A. Jackson, *Maps of Meaning: An Introduction to Cultural Geography* (London, Winchester: Academic Division, Unwin Hyman, 1989). See also John Berger, *Ways of Seeing: A Book Made by John Berger (and others)* (New York: Viking Press, 1972).

69 Francis, "Great White Hope," 163.

70 TUA, Ronald H. Perry Fonds, 82-016/2/8, "A White Sheet and a Windy Lake," *Canoe Lake Camp Echoes* 3, 1 (1930): 29.

71 TUA, OCA Sound/Tape Collection, 83-002/2/5, Mary Northway, interview by Cathy Stuart and Warren Anderson, 21 January 1975.

72 AO, Legislative Press Clippings, MS-755, reel 86, "Drew Outlines Plans for Children's Camps," *Globe and Mail*, 12 July 1944.

73 Karen Dubinsky, *Improper Advances: Rape and Heterosexual Conflict in Ontario, 1880-1929* (Chicago: University of Chicago Press, 1993), 143-62.

74 In 1944, a member of the National Council on Physical Fitness, commenting on the lack of fitness among service-aged men, argued that this showed "that the cultural and recreational life of many of our citizens is by no means adequate." AO, RG-2-75, box 1, minutes of National Council on Physical Fitness, 29-30 August 1944. For scholarly discussions of recreation, youth, and the public good, see Shirley Tillotson *The Public at Play: Gender and the Politics of Recreation in Post-war Ontario* (Toronto: University of Toronto Press, 2000); Gail Pogue and Bryce Taylor, "History of Provincial Government Services of the Youth and Recreation Branch, Part 1: 1940-1950," *Recreation Review* 7 (November 1972): Supplement no. 1.

75 Among the commission's various publications concerning its final observations and recommendations is Canadian Youth Commission, *Youth and Recreation: New Plans for New Times* (Toronto: Ryerson, 1944). For historical discussion of the commission, see Linda Ambrose, "The Canadian Youth Commission: Planning for Youth and Social Welfare in the Postwar Era" (PhD diss., University of Waterloo, 1992); Linda Ambrose, "Cartoons and Commissions: Advice to Junior Farmers in Postwar Ontario," *Ontario History* 93, 1 (2001): 57-79.

76 Report to the Honourable Brooke Claxton, Minister of National Health and Welfare, quoted in Pogue and Taylor, "History of Provincial Government Services."

77 In 1945, the state awarded grants to sixty-seven camps. Five years later, the number had risen to close to two hundred, with a total of $25,000 awarded; by 1955, over $40,000 had

been awarded to more than 350 camps. Province of Ontario, *Report of the Minister of Education*, 1945, 90; 1950, 33; 1955, 13.

78 W. Ross Thatcher (MP from Moose Jaw), in Dominion of Canada, *Debates, House of Commons*, 24 April 1952, 1570; Paul Martin (Minister of National Health and Welfare), in Dominion of Canada, *Debates, House of Commons*, 9 June 1954, 5687. In fact, one of the ongoing problems was the Ontario government's reluctance to accept federal monies and (presumably) "interference" in the realm of recreation. Indeed, to the chagrin of recreational institutions and personnel, Ontario did not accept coverage under the act until 1949, five years after its initial enactment. See Gail Pogue and Bryce Taylor, "History of Provincial Government Services of the Youth and Recreation Branch, Part 2: 1950-1960," *Recreation Review* 7 (March 1973): Supplement no. 2, vi.

79 Tillotson, *Public at Play*. Meg Stanley points out that the Canadian Youth Commission displayed the same ambivalence. See Stanley, "Not So Lazy Days," 34-46.

80 Northway, "Canadian Camping," 12; See also Stanley, "Not So Lazy Days." The results were almost embarrassing for the Drew government. When pushed in 1949 to defend Drew's promise to create "a whole network of summer camps" (presumably run by the government itself), even the minister of education admitted, "No, there is no such thing as a network of anything, that I know of. Networks, nonsense." AO, Legislative Press Clippings, MS-755, reel 86, "Drew Outlines Plans for Children's Camps," *Globe and Mail*, 12 July 1944; Mr. Dana Porter in Province of Ontario, *Legislature of Ontario Debates*, 29 March 1949, 1573-4. In other national contexts, the state could be more supportive of summer camps. Margaret Tennant has found that a very tight relationship developed between state and voluntary interests in the context of fresh air camps in New Zealand. She concluded that this partnership allowed the movement "to gain ... substantial state endorsement and funding while retaining the appearance of a community enterprise." See Margaret Tennant, "Children's Health Camps in New Zealand: The Making of a Movement, 1919-1940," *Social History of Medicine* 9, 1 (1996): 69-87, esp. 70.

81 OCA, *Ontario Camp Bulletin* 1, 1946.

82 Especially for camps in the early years of establishment, those dependent on public funds, or those managing budgets during times of economic hardship, creating a "simple" lifestyle could be easier on camp budgets. At CGIT camps, as late as 1955, girls were required to bring their own mattress covers, "to be filled with fresh straw at camp." While this may have helped to create a "campy" feel, one wonders whether it was also a matter of financial necessity. It also seems more a matter of necessity than choice that the private Camp Wapomeo for girls – an island camp – had no electricity right into the 1950s, while its "brother" camp, Ahmek, was completely "hooked up" just after the Second World War. UCA/VUA, CGIT Collection, 85.095C, box 42, file 45, "CGIT Camp at Ryde Lake," brochure, 1955. On Wapomeo, see Lundell, *Fires of Friendship*, 86; Elizabeth Shapiro, e-mail interview by author, 18 February 2001.

83 Roderick Nash, *Wilderness and the American Mind* (New Haven: Yale University Press, 1973), 60. Nash further points out that preservationists – like present-day environmentalists – typically hailed from "refined urban situations." Ibid., 201.

84 This history is still largely unwritten. For studies that touch on tourism, cottaging, and resorts in these areas, see Patricia Jasen, *Wild Things: Nature, Culture and Tourism in Ontario, 1790-1914* (Toronto: University of Toronto Press, 1995), chaps. 5 and 6; Hodgins and Benidickson, *Temagami Experience*; G. Wall, "Recreational Land Use in Muskoka," in *Recreational Land Use: Perspectives on Its Evolution in Canada*, ed. G. Wall and J. Marsh,

47-174 (Ottawa: Carleton University Press, 1982); Roy I. Wolfe, "The Summer Resorts of Ontario in the Nineteenth Century," *Ontario History* 54, 3 (1962): 149-61; and Gerald Killan, *Protected Places: A History of Ontario's Provincial Parks System* (Toronto: Dundurn Press, 1993), 48-52.

85 Lundell, *Fires of Friendship*, 11.

86 TUA, OCA Sound/Tape Collection, 83-002/5/1, Ron Perry, interview by Bruce Harris, 2 December 1981.

87 TUA, OCA Fonds, 72-007/2/7, Camp Winnebagoe, 1946 brochure.

88 "About Dirt Street and Fair Cashmere," *TDS*, 5 August 1920, 8.

89 "Mother Toils Unsparingly for Fatherless Children," *TDS*, 25 June 1929, 19.

90 FSATA, "The Story of Bolton Camp," in booklet entitled *After Twenty Years: A Short History of the Neighborhood Workers Association* (Toronto: The Association, 1938), 44; Mary Murphy, interview by author, 7 June 2000.

91 "Street Is Named after Children's Emancipator," *TDS*, 24 August 1938, 1, 8.

92 "Kiddies Anxiously Awaiting Their Trip to the Country," 15 June 1920, 1; "Remember the Poor Children Who Appeal to Their Friends," 14 June 1920, 1; "Sunshine and Fresh Air Will Give Health to Child," *TDS*, 12 June 1930, 23.

93 *TDS*, 10 August 1923, 1.

94 *TDS*, 24 June 1929, 17; *TDS*, 25 June 1937, 1.

95 "Country Vague Dream to Little Prisoners of Hot City Streets," *TDS*, 5 July 1935, 1. On the numbers accommodated at Bolton and elite private camps see, respectively, FSATA, "The Story of Bolton Camp," 44; TUA, OCA, "1949 Directory of Member Camps."

96 UCA/VUA, CGIT Collection, 85.095C, box 26, file 3, minutes of the meeting of the Camp, Conference, and Convention Committee of the Ontario Girls' Work Board, 18 December 1924. On the location of other agency camps, see OCA, "1949 Directory."

97 R. Seeley, R. Alexander Sim, and Elizabeth W. Loosley, *Crestwood Heights: A Study of the Culture of Suburban Life* (Toronto: University of Toronto Press, 1956), 310.

98 Shields, *Places on the Margin*.

99 William Cronon, "Introduction: In Search of Nature," in *Uncommon Ground: Toward Reinventing Nature*, ed. William Cronon (New York: W.W. Norton and Company, 1995), 25.

100 Alexander Wilson, *The Culture of Nature: North American Landscape from Disney to the Exxon Valdez* (Toronto: Between the Lines, 1991).

101 I.S. McLaren has shown that human suppression of forest fires in the Athabasca River Valley of Alberta, for instance, led to the development of a monocultural forest of pines where a much more diverse range of vegetation once grew. See I.S. MacLaren, "Cultured Wilderness in Banff National Park," *Journal of Canadian Studies* 34, 3 (1999): 7-58. Tina Loo's work on Canadian wildlife conservation reveals that gaming laws to "protect" wildlife supply introduced a host of species foreign to particular regions. See Tina Loo, "Making a Modern Wilderness: Conserving Wildlife in Twentieth-Century Canada," *Canadian Historical Review* 82, 1 (2001): 92-121.

102 Anne Whiston Spirn, "Constructing Nature: The Legacy of Frederic Law Olmsted," in Cronon, *Uncommon Ground*, 111.

103 As historian A.R.M. Lower put it, the area was already getting "thinned out." Quoted in Wolfe, "Summer Resorts," 155.

104 Wall, "Recreational Land Use," 146, 148.

105 Ibid.; Wolfe, "Summer Resorts." For more on the local history of the Muskoka region, see Florence B. Murray, ed., *Muskoka and Haliburton, 1615-1875: A Collection of Documents*

(Toronto: University of Toronto Press, 1963); Niall MacKay, *By Steam Boat and Steam Train: The Story of the Huntsville and Lake of Bays Railway and Navigation Companies* (Erin: Boston Mills Press, 1982).

106 For discussion of the economic history of resource development in northern Ontario, see Ian M. Drummond, *Progress without Planning: The Economic History of Ontario from Confederation to the Second World War* (Toronto: University of Toronto Press, 1987), chaps. 4 and 5; K.J. Rea, chap. 8, *The Prosperous Years: The Economic History of Ontario, 1939-1975* (Toronto: University of Toronto Press, 1985), chap. 8. On the relationship between resource development and provincial government policy in Ontario, see H.V. Nelles, *The Politics of Development: Forests, Mines and Hydro-Electric Power in Ontario, 1849-1941* (Toronto: Macmillan, 1974).

107 This is Gerald Killan's reading of the management of Ontario's provincial parks during the first half of the twentieth century – one that seems to fit equally well in the case of Temagami. See Killan, *Protected Places,* 36-73.

108 In Algonquin, clear-cutting along the shorelines of lakes and rivers was the source of public outcry as early as 1910. Likewise in Temagami, in the early years of the century, the damming of waterways to provide power to local mining, pulp and paper, and hydroelectric industries was viewed critically when it raised water levels and caused shoreline flooding and threatened recreational fishing. At the same time, water "stained brown by the logs" of lumber companies offended the aesthetic sensibilities of recreational canoeists, who complained in 1905 that "this somewhat spoils the effect." See "Down the Sturgeon River," *Rod and Gun* 6 (March 1905): 550. Quoted in Hodgins and Benidickson, *Temagami Experience,* 124.

109 On the development of Temagami and ensuing conflicts with recreationalists and Native bands, see Hodgins and Benidickson, *Temagami Experience*; Matt Bray and Ashley Thomson, eds., *Temagami: A Debate on Wilderness* (Toronto: Dundurn Press, 1990). One source on more recent history would be Ontario Ministry of Natural Resources, *Lake Temagami Plan for Land Use and Recreation Development* (Toronto: MNR, 1973); On Algonquin, see Killan, *Protected Places,* 36-73; K. Morrison, "The Evolution of the Ontario Provincial Park System," in Wall and Marsh, *Recreational Land Use,* 102-21. Local histories of Algonquin Park also include Bernard S. Shaw, *Canoe Lake, Algonquin Park: Tom Thomson and Other Mysteries* (Burnstown: General Store, 1996); Dan Strickland, Russ Rutter, and Heather Lang-Runtz, eds., *The Best of* The Raven*: 150 Essays from Algonquin Park's Popular Newsletter – A Centennial Collection* (Whitney: Friends of Algonquin Park, 1993); Ottelyn Addison, *Early Days in Algonquin Park* (Toronto: McGraw-Hill Ryerson, 1974); Algonquin Park Leaseholders Association/Ontario Department of Lands and Resources, *Algonquin Park: A Park for People* (Ontario: Algonquin Park Leaseholders Association, 1969); Audrey Saunders, *Algonquin Story* (Toronto: Ontario Department of Lands and Forests, 1963).

110 Lundell, *Fires of Friendship,* 11.

111 Killan, *Protected Places,* 38.

112 Lundell, *Fires of Friendship,* 11.

113 Milks, "Camp Director's Manual," 12.

114 TUA, Camp Pine Crest Fonds, 78-009/2/1, Camp Pine Crest, "Waterfront Recommendations," 1951.

115 Milks, "Camp Director's Manual," 13.

116 TUA, OCA Sound/Tape Collection, 83-002/5/24, Mary Northway, interview by Jocelyn Palm, 17 November 1981.

117 Michele Lacombe, "'Songs of the open road': Bon Echo, Urban Utopians and the Cult of Nature," *Journal of Canadian Studies* 33, 2 (1998): 152-67.
118 TUA, OCA Papers, 98-019/13/6, series E, Adele Ebbs Papers, Mary L. Northway, "Canadian Camping: Its Foundation and Its Future," address given to the Manitoba Camping Association Annual Meeting, May 1946, 5.
119 Spirn, "Constructing Nature," 91.
120 TUA, Adele and Harry Ebbs Papers, 80-014/1/4, "Christmas Letter from Chief and Tonakela," 1956. Interestingly, during "clean-up campaigns" at Ahmek, some recall that Statten took on the bearing of something of a sergeant-major organizing a work detail, which stood in contrast to the wilderness lover who encouraged campers to "enjoy the sunset." See TUA, Ronald H. Perry Fonds, 82-016/2/8, *Canoe Lake Camp Echoes* 4, 3 (1931): 31; Lundell, *Fires of Friendship*, 19.
121 TUA, Ronald H. Perry Fonds, 82-016/2/8, *Canoe Lake Camp Echoes* 4, 3 (1931): 31. In the same year, a channel was blasted through a dangerous area of the waterfront, thus eliminating the need "to paddle away around the point or maneuver [one's] canoe through the treacherous channel." Ibid.
122 TUA, Northway Family Fonds – additions, 90-016/1/34, Mary Northway, recollection of Glen Bernard Camp, 16 May 1982; FSATA, NWA, "Fresh Air Report – Season of 1933," 9.
123 FSATA, NWA, "Log of Bolton Camp," 1941; NWA, pamphlet, "Theatre Night in Support of Bolton Camp," 15 January 1924.
124 FSATA, Dale Callendar, unpublished paper, "History of Bolton Camp," 1997, 1; Minutes, Bolton Camp Committee, 22 November 1923; Minutes, Bolton Camp Committee, 7 October 1924; Minutes, Bolton Camp Committee, 1 December 1925.
125 FSATA, "The Story of Bolton Camp," in NWA, "After Twenty Years: A Short History of the Neighborhood Workers Association" (Toronto: The Association), 1938, 45.
126 FSATA, NWA, Bolton Camp Publicity Scrapbook, "Bolton Fresh Air Camp 'Wonderful,' Says Teacher,'" *TDS*, 19 August 1937.
127 FSATA, Bolton Camp Publicity Scrapbook, "Bolton District Popular for Holiday Seekers," *Bolton Enterprise*, 19 November 1938. Indeed, existing photos of the camp reveal a level of domestication that few of us today would deem anything approaching "natural." See FSATA, Bolton photo albums, 1920-1950s.
128 OCA, *Ontario Camp Bulletin* 1, 1946.
129 TUA, OCA Fonds, 72-007/2/7, Camp Winnebagoe, brochure, 1946.
130 Danson quote from TUA, OCA Papers, 78-004, box 2, file 31, J. Budge, transcript of interview with Bert Danson, 15 February 1973, 4.
131 Statten, "Talks to Counsellors," 22; "Camp Wapomeo: A Woodcraft Camp for Girls," brochure, c. 1938.
132 TUA, OCA Papers, 72-007/2/5, brochure, "Camp Temagami (Cochrane Camp)," c. 1950 (emphasis added); TUA, OCA Fonds, 72-007/5/5, National Council of YMCAs of Canada, Camp Standards Clinic, 1947, M. McIntyre Hood, "What the Camp Study Revealed," 4.
133 For the literature on postwar child-rearing, see Chapter 4, note 13.
134 Hodgins and Benidickson, *Temagami Experience*, 177.
135 TUA, Ronald H. Perry Fonds, 82-016/2/8, "The Algonquin Park Road," *Canoe Lake Camp Echoes* 4, 1 (1931): 26.
136 TUA, Ronald H. Perry Fonds, 82-016/2/8, "More about the Park Road," *Canoe Lake Camp Echoes* 4, 2 (1931): 18.
137 FSATA, "Bolton Camp: Report of Operation, 1937," 10; NWA, Bolton Camp Publicity Scrapbook, "The Happy Community," unnamed newspaper/periodical, August 1943.

138 TUA, OCA Fonds, 72-007/2/7, Camp Winnebagoe, brochure, 1946; Susan A. Miller, "Girls in Nature/The Nature of Girls: Transforming Female Adolescence at Summer Camp, 1900-1939" (PhD diss., University of Pennsylvania, 2001), 102.

139 On comic books at camp, see Seeley et al., *Crestwood Heights*, 312; Dimock and Hendry, *Camping and Character*, 325. On the modern urban dance culture and youth, see Cynthia Comacchio, "Dancing to Perdition: Adolescence and Leisure in Interwar English Canada," *Journal of Canadian Studies* 32, 3 (1997): 5-35; Kathy Peiss, *Cheap Amusements: Working Women and Leisure in Turn-of-the-Century New York* (Philadelphia: Temple University Press, 1986). On dances at camp, see Bert Danson, interview by author, 12 June 2000; TUA, Adele and Harry Ebbs Papers, 80-014/1/4, "Christmas Letter from Chief and Ton-akela [Taylor and Ethel Statten]," 1956. For just one example of films on camp life, see TUA, OCA Fonds, 82-009/1/1, movie, Camp Onawaw, 1938. As early as 1923 and again in the 1940s, members of the Bolton Camp Committee suggested that "moving pictures be made of the camp to be used in future publicity." Minutes, Bolton Camp Campaign Committee, 8 May 1923, 3; 27 September 1945. For movies as useful tools to ensure that "the memories of camp are kept alive," see Dimock and Hendry, *Camping and Character*, 325. For Paris's exploration of movie-making and showing (of even box office Hollywood hits) at camp, see her chapter entitled "Great Old Times in the Woods: Popular Culture at Interwar Summer Camps," in Paris, "Children's Nature," 297-338.

140 TUA, OCA Papers, 98-019/13/6, series E, Adele Ebbs Papers, Mary L. Northway, "Canadian Camping: Its Foundation and Its Future," address given to the Manitoba Camping Association Annual Meeting, May 1946, 5.

141 TUA, OCA Sound/Tape Collection, 83-002/8/10, Jack Passmore, memories of Bark Lake Camp, Bark Lake, 8 May 1982. It should be noted that, at Bark Lake, tents were not as "rustic" as we might think, being complete with wooden platforms, five-foot-high side walls, and space to accommodate six or seven campers on cots. See OCLC files in possession of Dorothy Walter, Toronto, Ontario, Marjorie Booth, unpublished paper, "History of the Development of OCLC, Bark Lake," 1973, 23, 39. On the persistent use of tents at other camps, see TUA, OCA Papers, 82-009/2/2, "Northway Lodge: A Pioneer Camp for Girls," brochure, c. 1941; Back, *Keewaydin Way*.

142 All Temagami references from TUA, OCA Papers, 72-007/2/5, brochure, "Camp Temagami (Cochrane Camp)," c. 1950. This view evidently lived on in historical memory. Almost twenty-five years later, Cochrane's daughters remembered his camp in much the same terms. "The key features were the real camping life away from the island," they explained, "canoeing, portaging, making all their meals over fires, erecting tents ... [and] meeting very few people." See TUA, OCA Sound/Tape Collection, 83-002/7/1, Nora Cochrane and Billie (Aileen) Nesbit, interview by Keith Rumble, 22 February 1974.

143 TUA, OCA Papers, 86-018/6/39, Dr. [Harry] Ebbs, "Tripping Fitness Program," 1962.

144 Shirley Ford, interview by author, 20 June 2000, Toronto.

145 Kathryn Wirsig, e-mail interview by author, 30 January 2001.

146 David Bawden, e-mail interview by author, 31 January 2001.

147 OCLC files in possession of Dorothy Walter, Toronto, Ontario, Marjorie Booth, unpublished paper, "History of the Development of OCLC, Bark Lake," 1973, 45.

148 Gord Wright, interview by Marjorie Booth, 26 November 1973, Alliston, Ontario. Due to sentiments such as these, at some camps, resistance to technological amenities continues up to the present day. Robert Foster, now a successful journalist, recalls the rugged lifestyle fostered at Keewaydin during his stay in the late 1930s and 1940s, but he also adds that

some of these conditions still prevailed in the year 2000. "Keewaydin did not have running water until 1947 and it still has no electric power," he states. "Lighting is by oil lamps and candles. Cooking is done on a huge wood stove. Refrigeration is accomplished in an ice house." Robert Foster to Sharon Wall, 8 September 2000.

149 Giddens argues that, under conditions of modernity, it is typical for nature to be seen as "constituted independently of human social activity," thus ignoring the reality of our increasing control of nature and the extent to which the latter becomes a "created environment." See Anthony Giddens, *Modernity and Self-identity: Self and Society in the Late Modern Age* (Stanford: Stanford University Press, 1991), 144-80.

150 Shirley Ford, interview by author, 20 June 2000, Toronto.

Chapter 2: Socialism for the Rich

1 Hedley S. Dimock and Taylor Statten, *Talks to Counselors* (New York: Association Press, 1939), 36.

2 Taylor Statten, *Talks to Counsellors* (Taylor Statten Camps, 1928), 5.

3 While serving a broadly middle-class clientele, agency camps may have seen the most extensive class mixing. At these camps, the option of sending a child for one, two, or three weeks meant that campers not only from middle-class but also perhaps from the upper-middle class and the lower-middle class may have been present. The addition of subsidized stays for children from social service agencies in the 1950s likely meant a smaller number of working-class children also attended these camps.

4 For trends in the writing of Canadian working-class history, see Craig Heron, "Towards a Synthesis in Canadian Working-Class History: Reflections on Bryan Palmer's Rethinking," *Left History* 1993 1, 1: 109-21; Bryan D. Palmer, *Rethinking the History of Canadian Labour, 1800-1991* (Toronto: McClelland and Stewart, 1992); Greg Kealey, "Writing about Labour," in *Writing about Canada: A Handbook for Modern Canadian History,* ed. John Schultz, 145-74 (Scarborough: Prentice Hall, 1990); Bettina Bradbury, "Women's History and Working-class History," *Labour* 19 (1987): 23-43; David Bercuson, "Through the Looking Glass of Culture: An Essay on the New Labour History and Working-Class Culture in Recent Canadian Historical Writing," *Labour* 7 (1981): 95-112. For one of the few studies that focuses more directly on the Canadian middle class, see Andy Holman, *A Sense of Their Duty: Middle-class Formation in Victorian Ontario Towns* (Montreal/Kingston: McGill-Queen's University Press, 2000).

5 Peter Newman, *The Canadian Establishment*, vol. 1 (Toronto: McClelland and Stewart-Bantam, 1979), 347. John Porter, *The Vertical Mosaic: An Analysis of Social Class and Power in Canada* (Toronto: University of Toronto Press, 1965); Wallace Clement, *The Canadian Corporate Elite: An Analysis of Economic Power* (Toronto: McClelland and Stewart, 1975).

6 Jean Barman, *Growing Up British in British Columbia: Boys in Private School* (Vancouver: UBC Press, 1984). Quotations on character taken from page 45. For more information on the history of private schooling in Canada, see Carolyn Gossage, *A Question of Privilege: Canada's Independent Schools* (Toronto: Peter Martin Associates Ltd., 1977); Richard B. Howard, *Upper Canada College, 1829-1979: Colborne's Legacy* (Toronto: Macmillan, 1979); A.H. Humble with J.D. Burns, *The School on the Hill: Trinity College School, 1865-1965* (Port Hope: Trinity College School, 1965); John Anthony Cheyne Ketchum, "'The most

perfect system': Official Policy in the First Century of Ontario's Government Secondary Schools and Its Impact on Students between 1871 and 1910" (EdD diss. University of Toronto, 1979).

7 Porter states: "The acquisition of social skills and the opportunities to make the right contacts can be important reasons for the higher middle classes to send their children to private schools. Along with the private schools go the private summer camps, in which much of the same socializing process continues." See Porter, *Vertical Mosaic*, 285.

8 *College Times*, Christmas 1923, Summer 1925, Christmas 1934. For more on the life of Cochrane, see Upper Canada College Archives, Ann Hall, "Arthur Lewis Cochrane: A Biographical Sketch," unpublished paper, Queen's University, Kingston, 1964.

9 TUA, OCA Papers, 72-007/2/5, "Camp Temagami (Cochrane Camp)," brochure, c. 1950.

10 On teachers as camp staff, see Brian Back, *The Keewaydin Way: A Portrait, 1893-1983* (Temagami: Keewaydin Camp Ltd., 1983); TUA, OCA Papers, 82-009/2/2, "Northway Lodge: A Pioneer Camp for Girls," brochure, 1941; TUA, OCA Papers, 72-007/2/5, Camp Tamakwa, brochure, c. 1950

11 Jane Hughes, interview by author, 26 June 2000.

12 Gordon Deeks and Richard B. Howard, "Temagami Magic," *Old Times* (Summer 1995), 34.

13 On the recruitment of private school students, see TUA, OCA Papers, 72-007/2/5, "Camp Temagami (Cochrane Camp)," brochure c. 1950; TUA, OCA Sound/Tape Collection, 83-002/5/8, Barbara Gilchrist, interview by Jack Pierce, 6 November 1986; Marjorie Royce, interview by author, 24 August 2000. For Danson quote, see TUA, OCA Papers, 78-004/2/31, Bert Danson, transcript of interview by J. Budge, 15 February 1973.

14 At fresh air camps, fees were not completely abolished: parents were asked to pay on a sliding scale, according to income. Still, in 1949, a year for which a broad range of camp fees is available, of eight fresh air camps known to be operating, only two charged as much as seven dollars per week. Statistical information from TUA, OCA Fonds, 72-007/5/5, National Council of YMCAs of Canada, Camp Standards Clinic, 1947, M. McIntyre Hood, "What the Camp Study Revealed," 5; TUA, OCA "1949 Directory of Member Camps."

15 In the 1920s, tuition (including room and board) at Upper Canada College was $750 (or seventy-five dollars per month). Some private schools in British Columbia charged even less, ranging from $500 to $825 per year. See Howard, *Upper Canada College*, 197; Barman, *Growing Up British*, 46.

16 This average is based on a sample of thirty-six boys' and girls' private camps. See TUA, OCA, "1949 Directory of Member Camps."

17 Douglas Creelman, interview by author, 23 June 2000, Toronto.

18 Ibid. For the average skilled worker, making $2,067 in 1949, such expenses would have amounted to two or more months' wages. See Series E41-48, "Annual Earnings in Manufacturing Industries, Production and Other Workers, by Sex, Canada, 1905, 1910 and 1917 to 1975," in *Historical Statistics of Canada*, 2nd ed., ed. F.H. Leacy (Ottawa: Statistics Canada, 1983). For individual camp fees, see Bruce W. Hodgins and Jamie Benidickson, *The Temagami Experience: Recreation, Resources, and Aboriginal Rights in the Northern Ontario Wilderness* (Toronto: University of Toronto Press, 1989), 113; Liz Lundell, *Fires of Friendship: Eighty Years of the Taylor Statten Camps* (Toronto: Fires of Friendship Books, 2000), 53. True enough, some camps, like schools, established "bursaries" to help assist certain campers.

At at least one camp, however, these were admitted only based on some kind of outstanding musical or athletic achievement rather than strictly on a "needs" basis. Mary Williamson, conversation with author, 25 November 2002.

19 TUA, OCA Papers, 72-007/2/3, "Camp Tanamakoon," brochure, 1950; TUA, OCA Papers, 72-007/2/5, "Camp Temagami (Cochrane Camp)," brochure, c. 1950; Peter Newman, "Junior's $10 Million Adventure in the Pines," *Financial Post,* 5 June 1954.

20 TUA, OCA Papers, 88-006/3/1, Taylor Statten Camps form letter, 19 May 1922.

21 TUA, OCA Papers, 72-007/2/5, "Camp Temagami (Cochrane Camp)," brochure, c. 1950.

22 Leslie Paris, "Children's Nature: Summer Camps in New York State, 1919-1941" (PhD diss. University of Michigan, 2000), 121. In Paris's view, this was also true of ethnic/religious groups – Jews for example – who reinforced their particular cultural commitments by sending children to a wide variety of "kosher or non-kosher, Orthodox, Conservative, or Reform; Yiddish-speaking, Zionist, or socialist, exclusively Jewish or religiously mixed" camps. Ibid., 105.

23 TUA, Ronald H. Perry Fonds, 82-016/2/8, "Friendship," *Canoe Lake Camp Echoes* 4, 1 (1931): 7.

24 Mary L. Northway, *Appraisal of the Social Development of Children at a Summer Camp* (Toronto: University of Toronto Press, 1940), 12.

25 Elizabeth Shapiro, e-mail interview by author, 17 February 2001; Douglas Creelman, interview by author, 23 June 2000, Toronto

26 Elizabeth Shapiro, e-mail interview by author, 17 February 2001.

27 On the history of American tourists in Canada, see Tina Loo, "Making a Modern Wilderness: Conserving Wildlife in Twentieth-Century Canada," *Canadian Historical Review* 82, 1 (2001): 106; Hodgins and Benidickson, *Temagami Experience*, 117-18, 187, 208; Roy I. Wolfe, "The Summer Resorts of Ontario in the Nineteenth Century," *Ontario History* 54, 3 (1962): 149-61; Wall, "Recreational Land Use in Muskoka." For "American" camps in Ontario, see OCA, "1949 Directory." Back, *Keewaydin Way*; Brian Back to Sharon Wall, e-mail, 23 September 2002; Liz Lundell and Beverley Bailey, *Summer Camp: Great Camps of Algonquin Park* (Toronto: Stoddart Publishing, 1994). For the influence of Americans at "Canadian" camps, see Ralph Barford, interview by author, 23 August 2000; Bert Danson, interview by author, 12 June 2000; David Bawden, e-mail interview by author, 31 January 2001. Camps fees and location from TUA, OCA, "1949 Directory of Member Camps."

28 The preference for university students was openly stated in the literature of Winnebagoe, Tamakwa, Tanamakoon, Temagami, Wabikon, and the Statten camps. See TUA, OCA Papers, 72-007/2/7, Camp Winnebagoe, brochure, 1946; TUA, OCA Papers, 72-007/2/5, Camp Tamakwa, brochure, c. 1950; Mary G. Hamilton, *The Call of Algonquin: Biography of a Summer Camp* (Toronto: Ryerson Press, 1958), 85; TUA, OCA Papers, 72-007/2/5, "Camp Temagami (Cochrane Camp)," brochure, c. 1950; TUA, Ronald H. Perry Fonds, 82-016/2/8, *Canoe Lake Camp Echoes* 4, 2 (1931): 7; TUA, OCA Papers, 72-007/2/9, Camp Wabi-kon, "General Qualifications of Counselor Staff members," c. 1952; Hedley S. Dimock and Charles E. Hendry, *Camping and Character: A Camp Experiment in Character Education* (New York: Association Press, 1929), 11. On American counsellors, see TUA, Ronald H. Perry Fonds, 82-016/2/8, "Training Staff, 1931," *Canoe Lake Camp Echoes* 4, 3 (1931): 46; TUA, OCA Fonds, 78-006/12/14, Bert Danson to Ontario Camping Association, 12 April 1954.

29 TUA, Ronald H. Perry Fonds, 82-016/2/8, *Canoe Lake Camp Echoes* 4, 2 (1931): 7.

30 Back, *Keewaydin Way*, 115. TUA, OCA Papers, 78-004/2/31, Bert Danson, transcript of interview by J. Budge, 15 February 1973, 14; TUA, OCA Sound/Tape Collection, 83-002/6/5, Eugene Kates, interview by Adele and Harry Ebbs, 13 August 1985, Toronto; TUA, OCA Sound/Tape Collection, 83-002/2/5, Mary Northway, interview by Cathy Stuart and Warren Anderson, 21 January 1975; TUA, Sound/Tape Collection, 83-002/5/1, Ron Perry, interview by Bruce Harris, 2 December 1981; TUA, Ronald H. Perry Fonds, 82-016/2/8, *Canoe Lake Camp Echoes* 3, 1 (1930): 37.

31 Statten, *Talks to Counsellors*, 1.

32 "Camp," *College Times*, Christmas 1920, 45.

33 TUA, Ronald H. Perry Fonds, 82-016/2/8, "Friendship," *Canoe Lake Camp Echoes* 4, 1 (1931): 7.

34 On the importance of the canoe trip, see TUA, Camp Pine Crest Fonds, 78-009/2/1, "Report on Camp Pine Crest – 1953"; TUA, OCA Papers, 72-007/2/5, Toronto YWCA, "Camp Tapawingo," 1951; TUA, OCA Papers, 72-007/5/13, YMCA, 1953 Camp Charts.

35 TUA, Camp Pine Crest Fonds, 78-009/2/1, Camp Pine Crest, "Director's Report," 1950; Ibid., "Report on Camp Pine Crest – 1953"; Ibid., Camp Pine Crest, "Out-trip Report for First Period, 1955"; TUA, OCA Papers, 72-007/2/5, Toronto YWCA, "Camp Tapawingo," 1951.

36 Robert Foster to Sharon Wall, 8 September 2000.

37 Hodgins and Benidickson, *Temagami Experience*, 114; Algonquin Park Museum Archives (APMA), Camp Files – Pathfinder, "Pathfinder: A Woodcraft Camp," brochure, 1927; APMA, Camp Files, Waubuno, "Camp Waubuno," brochure, 1926; TUA, Ronald H. Perry Fonds, 82-016/2/8, *Canoe Lake Camp Echoes* 4, 1 (1931): 24; TUA, Brochure Files, "K," "Camp Kawagama," brochure, c. late 1940s; TUA, Adele and Harry Ebbs Papers, 80-014/1/8, "The Taylor Statten Camps," brochure, c. 1950; TUA, Camp Pine Crest Fonds, 78-009/2/4, Camp Pine Crest, brochure, 1950; Ibid., 78-009/2/1, Camp Pine Crest, "Director's Report," 1951.

38 TUA, Ronald H. Perry Fonds, 82-016/2/8, "Training Staff, 1931," *Canoe Lake Camp Echoes* 4, 3 (1931): 46.

39 TUA, OCA Papers, 72-007/2/7, Camp Winnebagoe, 1946 brochure.

40 Lundell, *Fires of Friendship*, 28.

41 Elizabeth Shapiro, quoted in Lundell, *Fires of Friendship*, 31.

42 Anonymous Arowhon camper, e-mail interview by author, 27 July 2000.

43 Statten, *Talks to Counsellors*, 22.

44 Ibid., 18. Emphasis in original.

45 TUA, Ronald H. Perry Fonds, 82-016/2/8, "Summer Music," *Canoe Lake Camp Echoes* 4, 3 (1931): 47.

46 TUA, OCA Papers, 72-007/2/7, Camp Winnebagoe, brochure, 1946.

47 Ibid.; Hamilton, *Call of Algonquin*, 126; TUA, Ronald H. Perry Fonds, 82-016/2/8, "A Brass Band," *Canoe Lake Camp Echoes* 3, 1 (1930): 42. At Ahmek, band membership cost ten dollars in 1930, with instrument rental costing another ten.

48 TUA, OCA Papers, 72-007/2/5, "Camp Temagami (Cochrane Camp)," brochure, c. 1950; 72-007/2/7, Camp Winnebagoe, brochure, 1946; 88-006/3/1, Taylor Statten form letter, 19 May 1922; OCA Sound/Tape Collection, 83-002/2/5, Mary Northway, interview by Cathy Stuart and Warren Anderson, 21 January 1975; Hamilton, *Call of Algonquin*, 20; Gordon Deeks and Richard B. Howard, "Temagami Magic," *Old Times*, Summer 1995, 34-38; Lundell, *Fires of Friendship*, 110, 118.

49 TUA, Ronald H. Perry Fonds, 82-016/2/8, "A White Sheet and a Windy Lake," *Canoe Lake Camp Echoes* 3, 1 (1930): 29-30.
50 Northway, *Social Development*, 38; Hamilton, *Call of Algonquin*, 27.
51 TUA, OCA Papers, 72-007/2/7, Camp Winnebagoe, brochure, 1946.
52 Hamilton, *Call of Algonquin*, 147.
53 Dimock and Statten, *Talks to Counselors*, 20.
54 At Ahmek, this included matters of health, safety, sanitation, visitors, property, and equipment. See Dimock and Hendry, *Camping and Character*, 106-7. At Tanamakoon, the duties of each "little chief" included: "to act as representative of the tribe, to make the necessary announcements in assembly, to take leadership at camper meetings, and take charge of opening proceedings at the Council Fire." See Hamilton, *Call of Algonquin*, 55; TUA, OCA Sound/Tape collection, 83-002/5/8, Barbara Gilchrist, interview by Jack Pierce, 6 November 1986; Camp Winnebagoe, brochure, 1948.
55 TUA, OCA Sound/Tape collection, 83-002/5/8, Barbara and John Gilchrist, interview by Jack Pierce, 6 November 1986.
56 The democratic theme was, in fact, popular at other camps, particularly, in my findings, at those run by the CGIT. There, at regularly run camp councils, girls were encouraged to develop their confidence, speaking talents, and critical skills.
57 Given that consensus and not democracy was the more common political tool of Native bands, it appears that little thought was given to the accuracy of such metaphors, a common tendency in the appropriation of Native culture at camp.
58 What descriptions of this democratic system explained in passing, but never emphasized, was that (non-elected) adult administrators outnumbered campers in this cabinet 2:1, thus ensuring campers got a taste of democracy without giving them any power to change things without administrative approval. See Dimock and Hendry, *Camping and Character*, 106-7.
59 Dimock and Hendry, *Camping and Character*, 125-26.
60 Statten, *Talks to Counsellors*, 11.
61 TUA, OCA Sound/Tape Collection, 83-002/5/3, Helen Stewart, interview by Bruno Morawetz, 12 January 1983.
62 Statten, *Talks to Counsellors*, 15.
63 Dimock and Statten, *Talks to Counselors*, 27.
64 Hamilton, *Call of Algonquin*, 144.
65 In the 1920s, at Tanamakoon, uniforms consisted of khaki middies and bloomers, hats, long stockings, and green ties. In later years, middies and bloomers were discarded for "shorts and shirts." See Hamilton, *Call of Algonquin*, 19-20. On the other hand, in 1930 counsellors at Wapomeo themselves suggested that a camp uniform – of "green shorts, blazer, and grey broadcloth shirts" – would "add greatly to the general smartness of the camp." See TUA, Ronald H. Perry Fonds, 82-016/2/8, *Canoe Lake Camp Echoes* 3, 1 (1930): 52; See also TUA, OCA Papers, 82-009/2/2, "Northway Lodge: A Pioneer Camp for Girls," brochure, c. 1941.
66 Dimock and Statten, *Talks to Counselors*, 27.
67 The urge to transport urban comforts and technology to settings idealized as wilderness has been noted by others who have explored the upper- and middle-class enthusiasm for nature-based recreation. See Tina Loo, "Of Moose and Men: Hunting for Masculinities in British Columbia, 1880-1939," *Western Historical Quarterly* 32, 3 (2001): 310-11; Hodgins and Benidickson, *Temagami Experience*, 194-206; and Douglas W. McCombs, "Therapeutic

Rusticity: Antimodernism, Health and the Wilderness Vacation, 1870-1915," *New York History* 76, 4 (1995): 409-28. On comforts at American summer camps, see Maynard, "An ideal life in the woods," 20-22, and Paris, "Children's Nature," 209-16, for a discussion of the debates surrounding the shift from tents to cabins at early American camps.

68 TUA, OCA Papers, 88-006/3/1, Taylor Statten form letter, 19 May 1922; TUA, Ronald H. Perry Fonds, 82-016/2/8, "Warm Water in the Wilderness," *Canoe Lake Camp Echoes* 4, 3 (1931): 36. Staff-camper ratios from TUA, OCA "1949 Directory of Member Camps"; TUA, OCA Papers, 82-009/2/2, "Northway Lodge: A Pioneer Camp for Girls," brochure, 1941. On "smoothing it," see TUA, OCA Sound/Tape Collection, 83,002/10/9, Adele Ebbs, interview by Jack Pearse, 22 May 1986.

69 TUA, Camping Literature Collection, Ontario Boys' Work Board, W.A. Milks, ed., "The Camp Director's Manual," n.d., 36-37.

70 On steamer ride at Pine Crest, TUA, Camp Pine Crest Fonds, 78-009/2/1, Camp Pine Crest, "Pre-Camp Information," 1949. On staff-camper ratios, see Hood, "What the Camp Study Revealed"; TUA, OCA "1949 Directory of Member Camps." Conditions did vary. In 1951 Camp Tapawingo, with higher than average camp fees, boasted an unusual one staff member for every three campers. See TUA, OCA Papers, 72-007/2/5, Toronto YWCA, "Camp Tapawingo," 1951.

71 TUA, Ronald H. Perry Fonds, 82-016/2/8, "Friendship," *Canoe Lake Camp Echoes* 4, 1 (1931): 7.

72 Mary Hamilton referred to "a firm bond of friendship" between her own Tanamakoon and Ahmek, Wapomeo, Glen Bernard, Temagami, and two other camps not studied here (Oconto and Ouareau). She also mentioned an exchange of counsellors-in-training between Tanamakoon, Wapomeo, and Glen Bernard. "The campers became staunch friends," she explained, "as were already the directors." See Hamilton, *Call of Algonquin*, 42, 54-55. Seven of twelve founding members of the OCA were directors of camps studied here, including Ahmek, Wapomeo, Temagami, Glen Bernard, Tanamakoon, and Winnebagoe. During the period of this study, it was a matter of ongoing effort to get organizational or agency camps more involved, suggesting that it was, in fact, dominated by private camp interests. See TUA, OCA Papers, 78-006/25/40, Charlie F. Plewman, "The Days Leading up to the Formation of the Ontario Camping Association," part of poster entitled "Today: Tomorrow's Yesterday," c. 1967; TUA, OCA Papers, 78-006/1/1, minutes, OCA, 1941; TUA, OCA Papers, 78-006/1/1, minutes, OCA Board Meeting, 6 November 1946. For the official history of the OCA, from the perspective of those involved, see Ontario Camping Association, *Blue Lake and Rocky Shore: A History of Children's Camping in Ontario* (Toronto: Natural Heritage/Natural History, 1984).

73 Peter Stallybrass and Allon White, *The Politics and Poetics of Transgression* (Ithaca: Cornell University Press, 1986).

74 Back, *Keewaydin Way*, 55. Ultimately, of course, Clarke's brashness paid off when, in 1906, the islands were officially removed from the reserve and leasing was permitted. In the case of Camp Temagami, A.L. Cochrane and a small party of boys canoed into the area, looked around, and simply set up camp when they found "a lon[g] island with a beautiful sandy beach." See Hall, "Arthur Lewis Cochrane," 15-16.

75 Donald Burry, "A History of the Taylor Statten Camps" (MSc thesis, University of Saskatchewan, 1985), 23.

76 Lundell, *Fires of Friendship*, 107. In 1973, a minority report from members of a state-appointed advisory committee – including representation from the president of the OCA

and other local lease-holders – argued that, "if the camps have benefited from their Park location ... the converse is true that the Park has benefited from them ... in the large measure of public respect and support for the Park that had its beginning among the alumni of these camps" (17). In the end, the camps were permitted to stay in the Park, where they remain to this day. See "Algonquin Provincial Park: Advisory Committee Report," Government Policy, 16 July 1973.

77 TUA, OCA Sound/Tape Collection, 83-002/6/5, Adele and Harry Ebbs, interview of Eugene Kates, 13 August 1985.

78 As late as 1941, the OCA still spoke of the need to "reach out" to fresh air and agency camps, confirming the latter's lack of integration with that organization. See TUA, OCA Papers, 78-006/1/1, minutes, OCA Board and Executive Committee, 5 May 1941.

79 Douglas Creelman, interview by author, 23 June 2000.

80 For studies that confirm the persistence of anti-Semitism in this period, see David Rome, *Clouds in the Thirties: On Antisemitism in Canada, 1929-1939 – A Chapter on Canadian Jewish History* (Montreal: Canadian Jewish Congress, 1977); Irving Abella and Harold Troper, *None Is Too Many: Canada and the Jews of Europe, 1933-1948* (Toronto: Lester and Orpen Dennys, 1982); Gerald J. Tulchinsky, *Taking Root: The Origins of the Canadian Jewish Community* (Toronto: Lester Publishing, 1992).

81 Joan Moses, interview by author, 19 July 2000. At home in Toronto, Moses recalls signs on city beaches reading "No Dogs, No Jews" and being called "dirty Jew" at school. Other interviewees recall similar experiences of anti-Semitism in this period. Anonymous Arowhon ex-camper, e-mail interview by author, 27 July 2000.

82 For Jewish camping in the American camp context, see Nancy Aleen Mykoff, "A Jewish Season: Ethnic-American Culture at Children's Summer Camp, 1918-1941" (PhD diss., New York University, 2002); Leslie Paris, "'A home away from home': Brooklyn Jews and Interwar Children's Summer Camps," in *Jews of Brooklyn*, ed. Ilana Abramovitch and Séan Galvin, 242-49 (Boston: University Press of New England/Brandeis University Press, 2001). Paris, "Children's Nature," 61.

83 TUA, OCA Papers, 72-007/2/7, Camp Winnebagoe, brochure, 1946. Bert Danson was an invaluable resource regarding the history of both Winnebagoe and other Jewish camps in Ontario. See Bert Danson, "A History of Residential Summer Camps for Jewish Children in Ontario," unpublished paper shared with author, June 2000; Bert Danson, interview by author, 12 June 2000; TUA, OCA Papers, 78-004/2/31, Bert Danson, transcript of interview by J. Budge, 15 February 1973. On other Jewish camps in the Canadian context, see Ester Reiter, "Secular Yiddishkait: Left Politics, Culture, and Community," *Labour* 49 (2002): 121-46. For Jewish camps in the American context, see David Hurwitz, "How Lucky We Were," *American Jewish History* 87, 1 (1999): 29-59; Paris, "A home away from home," 242-49; Mykoff, "A Jewish Season."

84 On camps founded during the 1930s, see *OCA Directory of Member Camps*, 1949, 1955; Lundell and Bailey, *Summer Camp*; West, *Summer Camps in Canada*; Brian Back, "Canada's Oldest Camps," available at www.ottertooth.com/Camps/camps-can.htm. On falling enrolments and the availability of staff at private camps, see Back, *Keewaydin Way*; Donald Burry, "A History of the Taylor Statten Camps" (MSc thesis, University of Saskatchewan, 1985), 38-39, 39-40.

85 Dan Gibson to Donald Burry, 20 December 1984, quoted in Burry, "A History of the Taylor Statten Camps," 40.

86 TUA, OCA Papers, 78-006/1/1, minutes, OCA Open Meeting, January 25, 1943.

87 On high school-aged counsellors, see TUA, OCA Papers, 78-004/2/31, Bert Danson, transcript of interview by J. Budge, 15 February 1973; TUA, OCA Papers, 72-007/2/5, "Camp Temagami (Cochrane Camp)," brochure, c. 1950.

88 Barbara Hays, quoted in Lundell, *Fires of Friendship*, 94. TUA, Adele and Harry Ebbs Papers, 80-014/1/8, Virginia T. Cobb to Mr. and Mrs. Taylor Statten, 16 February 1942, and response from Adele Ebbs, n.d.

89 On the Wartime Rangers Programs at various camps, see Judith Ridout, "The Beginnings of Tanamakoon," transcript of address given at Camp Tanamakoon Reunion, Toronto, July 2000; Upper Canada College Archives [hereafter UCCA], Biography Files – A.L. Cochrane, Parkyn Ian Murray re: A.L. Cochrane, 1940.

90 TUA, OCA Papers, 72-007/2/5, Camp Tamakwa, brochure, c. 1950. For other food references, see TUA, OCA Papers, 72,007/2/7 Camp Winnebagoe, brochure, 1946; TUA, Adele and Harry Ebbs Papers, 80,014/1/8, "The Taylor Statten Camps," brochure, c. 1950.

91 Lundell, *Fires of Friendship*, 52. As Loo puts it, "Eating moose meat or venison regularly meant one was poor or rural or both." Clearly, the Ahmek community wanted to present itself as neither. See Loo, "Creating a Modern Wilderness," 112. For references to "waiters" and so on, see TUA, OCA Sound/Tape Collection, 83-002/7/1, Nora Cochrane and Billie (Aileen) Nesbit, interview by Keith Rumble, 22 February 1974; TUA, OCA Papers, 78-004/2/31, Bert Danson, transcript of interview by J. Budge, 15 February 1973; Hamilton, *Call of Algonquin*, 16; TUA, OCA Papers, 72-007/2/9, Camp Kawagama, "Counselor-Waiter Contract," 1952.

92 At Winnebagoe, it was claimed that "conditions at [the] camp are equivalent to the very best: ... modern plumbing, flush toilets, hot and cold showers, and complete drainage." See TUA, OCA Fonds, 72-007/002/007, Camp Winnebagoe, brochure, 1946. On hot showers elsewhere, see TUA, Brochure Files-"K," "Camp Kawagama," c. 1950.

93 TUA, OCA Fonds, 72-007/2/7, Camp Winnebagoe, brochure, 1946. Horses were no doubt a costly part of camp programs. At Camp Wabikon in Temagami, horses purchased just outside Toronto were driven north two hundred miles then hauled seventeen miles by boat into camp. See TUA, Sound/Tape Collection, 83-002/5/5, Irwin Haladner, interview by Adele Ebbs, 4 May 1982. On Tamakwa's amenities, see TUA, OCA Papers, 72-007/2/5, Camp Tamakwa, brochure, c. 1950.

94 For just a few examples: Temagami was promoted (and remembered) as the "the *premier* camp in Ontario," Glen Bernard as the *oldest* girls' camp, Tanamakoon as "one of the *best* private girls' camps," and Winnebagoe as the "first *co-ed* camp in Canada." Ralph Barford, interview by author, 23 August 2000; Marjorie Royce, interview by author, 24 August 2000; Nancy Cleaver, "An Old Canadian Custom: Sending the Kids to Camp," *Saturday Night*, 19 April 1952, 17; Bert Danson, interview by author, 12 June 2000. Emphases added.

95 Sherman, "Girls of Summer," 104. Sherman, however, puts a different interpretation on this phenomenon, stating that the parallel could be made because: "Our first taste of freedom, our first flirtation with adulthood, came at camp, not on campus."

96 Clement, *Canadian Corporate Elite*, 247. Ahmek reference from TUA, Ronald H. Perry Fonds, 82-016/2/8, *Canoe Lake Camp Echoes* 4, 3 (1931): 11.

97 Sherman, "Girls of Summer," 102. On Americans at "Canadian" camps, see Ralph Barford, interview by author, 23 August 2000; Bert Danson, interview by author, 12 June 2000; David Bawden, e-mail interview by author, 31 January 2001.

98 TUA, OCA Papers, 72-007/2/5, Camp Tamakwa, brochure, c. 195[?].
99 TUA, Adele and Harry Ebbs Papers, 80-014/1/8, "The Taylor Statten Camps," brochure, c. 1950.
100 Newman, "Junior's $10 Million Adventure."
101 TUA, OCA Papers, 72-007/2/5, Camp Tamakwa, brochure, c. 195[?].
102 Franca Iacovetta, *Gatekeepers: Reshaping Immigrant Lives in Cold War Canada* (Toronto: Between the Lines Press, 2006).
103 James Felstiner, e-mail interview by author, April 2001. Peter Newman looks back on his years at Upper Canada College in much the same way. There, as one of the few Jews and – worse, in his view – as a new (Czech) immigrant to Canada, he recalls that the boys "made me feel like an outsider," picking on him regularly for his accent. Still, if never quite at home, Newman views the school as forcing him to learn to speak English without an accent, thus helping him to "integrate" easily into Canadian society. No doubt the social training, contacts, and education helped too. See James FitzGerald, *Old Boys: The Powerful Legacy of Upper Canada College* (Toronto: Macfarlane, Walter and Ross, 1994), 82.
104 Ibid.
105 Joan Moses, interview by author, 19 July 2000.
106 TUA, OCA Papers, 88-006/3/7, Adele Ebbs, transcript of interview, 1986, 15.
107 TUA, OCA Papers, 88-006/3/7, transcript of interview with Adele Ebbs, 1986, 20; James Felstiner, e-mail interview by author, April 2001.
108 Joan Moses, interview by author, 19 July 2000.
109 TUA, OCA Papers, 86-018/6/39, "A Handbook for Canoe Tripping: Common Practices in Canoe Tripping at Camp Wapomeo," 1963, 10.
110 TUA, OCA Papers, 78-004/2/31, Bert Danson, transcript of interview by J. Budge, 15 February 1973, 3.
111 Marjorie Royce, interview by author, 24 August 2000. Jane Hughes, another ex-camper and staff member at Glen Bernard, also saw the two camps as contrasting: "There was never the same opportunities to keep in touch with people" (Jane Hughes, interview by author, 26 June 2000).
112 TUA, Ronald H. Perry Fonds, 82-016/3/1, Taylor Statten to Parents of Ahmek and Wapomeo Campers, 28 November 1949. As for the length of camp stays, in the postwar period at a number of camps, the trend appears to have been towards the option of shorter stays (of one month). See TUA, OCA Papers, 78-004/2/31, Bert Danson, transcript of interview by J. Budge, 15 February 1973; OCA Sound/Tape Collection, 83-002/5/8, Barbara Gilchrist, interview by Jack Pierce, 6 November 1986; Douglas Creelman, interview by author, 23 June 2000; Jane Hughes, interview by author, 26 June 2000.
113 TUA, Camp Pine Crest Fonds, 78-009/2/1, Ted Yard to Keith Cleverdon, 2 March 1954.
114 Pinecrest records from 1953 show in more detail the range of choices that parents made. In 1953, 10 percent of Pine Crest campers stayed for only one week; approximately 25 percent stayed two weeks; just over 50 percent stayed three weeks; and only about 12 percent stayed four weeks or more. The YWCA's Camp Tapawingo suggested a similar pattern. In 1951, after experimenting with various options, the administration concluded that offering three three-week periods would be optimal. I suggest, again, that these two camps appear to have been among the "higher class" of agency camps, with higher fees, higher staff/camper ratios, and more extensive amenities. In this case, they may have been better placed to attract a slightly wealthier clientele than the typical agency camp and,

therefore, parents who might opt for longer stays for their children. For evidence on length of stays at agency camps, see TUA, OCA Directory, 1949; TUA, Camp Pine Crest Fonds, 78-009/2/1, Camp Pine Crest, "Director's Report," 1949; 1950; 1951; TUA, Camp Pine Crest Fonds, 78-009/2/1, "Report on Camp Pine Crest – 1953"; TUA, OCA Papers, 72-007/2/5, Toronto YWCA, "Camp Tapawingo," 1951.

115 On time spent at camp, see Statten, *Talks to Counsellors*, 16; "Camp Timagami [sic]," *College Times*, Easter 1924, 43. On return campers at other camps, see Dimock and Hendry, *Camping and Character*, 322; Douglas Creelman, interview by author, 23 June 2000; TUA, OCA Papers, 72-007/2/7, "Camp Winnebagoe," brochure, 1946.

116 TUA, OCA Papers, 78-004/2/31, Bert Danson, transcript of interview by J. Budge, 15 February 1973.

117 TUA, OCA Sound/Tape Collection, 83-002/2/5, Mary Northway, interview by Cathy Stuart and Warren Anderson, 21 January 1975.

118 TUA, Northway Family Fonds – Additions, 90-016/1/34, Mary Northway, "Recollection of Glen Bernard Camp," 16 May 1982.

119 Shirley Ford, interview by author, 20 June 2000.

120 TUA, OCA Sound/Tape Collection, 83-002/2/5, Mary Northway, interview by Cathy Stuart and Warren Anderson, 21 January 1975.

121 TUA, Ronald H. Perry Fonds, 82-016/2/8, *Canoe Lake Camp Echoes* 4, 2 (1931): 22.

122 Dimock and Hendry, *Camping and Character*, 325; Hamilton, *Call of Algonquin*, 43-44; Marjorie Royce, interview by author, 24 August 2000.

123 Elizabeth Shapiro, e-mail interview by author, 17 February 2001.

124 Shirley Ford, interview by author, 20 June 2000.

125 Dimock and Hendry, *Camping and Character*, 322.

126 Hamilton, *Call of Algonquin*, 85.

127 James Felstiner, e-mail interview by author, April 2001.

128 Bert Danson, interview by author, 12 June 2000. Directors' children seemed particularly adept at finding life partners. Both of Taylor Statten's offspring, who spent all of their childhood summers at camp, found spouses there, while even at the all-girl Glen Bernard, camper Barb Gilchrist met and eventually married the director's nephew, who had been "around the camp" since the age of ten onwards. See TUA, Adele and Harry Ebbs Papers, 80-014/1/6, "Taylor Statten Campers Gathering for Reunion," *Toronto Star*, 14 November 1972; TUA, OCA Sound/Tape Collection, 83-002/5/8, Barbara Gilchrist, interview by Jack Pearse, 6 November 1986. On the phenomenon of camp marriages more generally, see TUA, Adele and Harry Ebbs Papers, 80-014/1/6, "Taylor Statten Campers Gathering for Reunion," *Toronto Star*, 14 November 1972; Deborah Wilson, "Upper Crust Recalls Summer Camp: 65-Year History Honoured," *Globe and Mail*, 20 October 1986; Sylvia Silbert, interview by author, 16 June 2000; Anonymous Arowhon ex-camper, e-mail interview by author, 27 July 2000; David Bawden, e-mail interview by author, 31 January 2001.

129 Bert Danson, interview by author, 12 June 2000.

130 TUA, OCA Papers, 78-004/2/31, Bert Danson, transcript of interview by J. Budge, 15 February 1973, 15. For more on these relationships at Winnebagoe, see Joan Moses, interview by author, 26 July 2000; Bert Danson, interview by author, 12 June 2000.

131 TUA, OCA Sound/Tape Collection, 83-002/7/1, Nora Cochrane and Billie (Aileen) Nesbit, interview by Keith Rumble, 22 February 1974. As Karen Dubinsky has shown, honey-

mooning was a ritual that included the wider community even up to the late nineteenth century, but, by the 1950s, for most couples, it had become a thoroughly private affair. See Karen Dubinsky, *The Second Greatest Disappointment: Honeymooning and Tourism at Niagara Falls* (Toronto: Between the Lines, 1999).

132 TUA, OCA Papers, 78-004/002/031, Bert Danson, transcript of interview by J. Budge, 15 February 1973; "Camp Timagami [sic]," *College Times*, Easter 1923, 17.

133 In fact, in 1931, this came to a grand total of six hundred "paid-up subscribers," and during this year, two thousand copies were printed. See TUA, Ronald H. Perry Fonds, 82-016/2/8, "The Echo's Reception," *Canoe Lake Camp Echoes* 4, 1 (1931): 7.

134 Anonymous Arowhon ex-camper, e-mail interview by author, 27 July 2000.

135 James Felstiner, e-mail interview by author, April 2001.

136 TUA, Ronald H. Perry Fonds, 82-016/2/8, "The September Adult Camp," *Canoe Lake Camp Echoes* 3, 1 (1930): 49.

137 Nancy Shore, quoted in Sherman, "Girls of Summer," 106. On September adult camp at Ahmek, see TUA, Ronald H. Perry Fonds, 82-016/2/8, "The September Adult Camp," *Canoe Lake Camp Echoes* 3, 1 (1930): 49; TUA, Ronald H. Perry Fonds, 82-016/2/8, "The September Camp," *Canoe Lake Camp Echoes* 4, 1 (1931): 28.

138 Ralph Barford, interview by author, 23 August 2000.

139 Joan Moses, interview by author, 26 July 2000.

140 Hamilton, *Call of Algonquin*, 159-60.

141 "Taylor Statten Campers Gathering for Reunion," *Toronto Star*, 14 November 1972; Ralph Barford, interview by author, 23 August 2000.

142 Stephen Clarkson and Christina McCall, *Trudeau and Our Times*, vol. 1: *The Magnificent Obsession* (Toronto: McClelland and Stewart, 1990), 37. A *Toronto Star* article also stated that improving his English was another objective of Trudeau's stay. See "Taylor Statten Campers Gathering for Reunion," *Toronto Star*, 14 November 1972.

143 Deborah Wilson, "Upper Crust Recalls Summer Camp: 65-Year History Honoured," *Globe and Mail*, 20 October 1986.

144 Bert Danson, interview with author, 12 June 2000.

145 Ian Murray, "64-Year Link between UCC and Temagami," *College Times*, Winter 1958, 93.

146 Elizabeth Shapiro, e-mail interview by author, 17 February 2001.

147 Marguerite (Clark) Davis, quoted in Lundell, *Fires of Friendship*, 31.

148 Susan Morgan, quoted in Sherman, "Girls of Summer," 103.

149 J.F. Conway, "Why Can't Summer Camp Just Be, Well, Summer Camp?" *Hamilton Spectator*, 3 September 1987.

Chapter 3: "All they need is air"

1 "Sorry to Leave Fresh Air Camp Says Young Lad," *Toronto Daily Star* [hereafter *TDS*], 23 July 1925, 1.

2 Ross Harkness, *J.E. Atkinson of the* Star (Toronto: University of Toronto Press, 1963), 31.

3 Neil Sutherland, *Children in English-Canadian Society, 1880-1920: Framing the Twentieth-century Consensus* (Toronto: University of Toronto Press, 1976), 39 (reissued by Wilfrid Laurier University Press in 2000). Aside from fighting the spread of contagious disease – diphtheria and tuberculosis, in particular – inspections exposed a variety of ailments that

school-aged children typically faced: extensive tooth decay, enlarged tonsils, defective eyesight and hearing, and head lice. Mona Gleason takes a less sanguine view of inspections, arguing that their implementation was shaped by clearly middle-class assumptions concerning race, class, and gender. See Mona Gleason, "Race, Class, and Health: School Medical Inspection and 'Healthy' Children in British Columbia, 1890-1930," *Canadian Bulletin of Medical Health* 19 (2002): 95-112. For more on the Canadian public health movement, see Heather McDougall, *Activists and Advocates: Toronto's Health Department, 1883-1983* (Toronto: Dundurn Press, 1990); Nora Lewis, "Physical Perfection for Spiritual Welfare: Health Care for the Urban Child, 1900-1939," in *Studies in Childhood History: A Canadian Perspective*, ed. Patricia T. Rooke and R.L. Schnell, 135-66 (Calgary: Detselig, 1982); Sutherland, *Children in English-Canadian Society*; Kari Dehli, "'Health Scouts' for the State?: School and Public Health Nurses in Early Twentieth-century Toronto," *Historical Studies in Education* 2, 2 (1990): 247-64; Paul Adolphus Bator, "'The struggle to raise the lower classes': Public Health Reform and the Problem of Poverty in Toronto, 1910 to 1921," *Journal of Canadian Studies* 14, 1 (1979): 43-49. On the National Council on Child Welfare, see P.T. Rooke and R.L. Schnell, *Discarding the Asylum: From Child Rescue to the Welfare State in English Canada, 1800-1950* (Llanham: University Press of America, 1983), 347-86; Sutherland, *Children in English-Canadian Society*, 85-86.

4 R.A. Hobday, "Sunlight Therapy and Solar Architecture," *Medical History* 41, 4 (1997): 455-72; Grace Goldin, "Building a Hospital of Air: The Victorian Pavilions of St. Thomas' Hospital, London," *Bulletin of the History of Medicine* 49, 4 (1975): 512-35; Andrew Sackett, "Inhaling the Salubrious Air: Health and Development in St. Andrews, NB, 1880-1910," *Acadiensis* 25, 1 (1995): 54-81; Marjorie Cruickshank, "The Open-air School Movement in English Education," *Paedagogica Historica* 17, 1 (1977): 62-74; David Turner, "The Open Air School Movement in Sheffield," *History of Education* 1, 1 (1972): 58-80; Grant Rodwell, "Australian Open-air School Architecture," *History of Education Review* 24, 2 (1995): 21-41.

5 Though some claim the decline of the schools was owing to their own "success" and improvements in public health in the postwar period, Rodwell argues that hostile public reaction to the schools – commonly known in Tasmania as "the freezing works," helped to bring about their demise. See Rodwell, "Australian Open-air School Architecture." Aside from the challenges of inclement weather – also noted in other settings – Rodwell notes problems with teacher apathy and with unwelcome local guests (sometimes even animals) taking refuge in the schools at night.

6 On the history of the Ontario CAS and its fresh air experiments, see Leonard Rutman, *In the Children's Aid: J.J. Kelso and Child Welfare in Ontario* (Toronto: University of Toronto Press, 1981), 31-34; John Bullen, "J.J. Kelso and the 'New' Child-Savers: The Genesis of the Children's Aid Movement in Ontario," *Ontario History* 82, 2 (1990): 107-28.

7 On the scope of early fresh air work, see "Fresh Air Work Develops from Humble 1902 Start to Magnificent Proportions," *TDS*, 3 June 1927, 19; "*Star* Fresh Air Fund Opens, Large Sums Needed at Once" *TDS*, 11 June 1920, 1; "Don't Let Little Ones Bear Pangs of Disappointment," *TDS*, 19 June 1922, 1.; "A Soaring Monument of Love Built of Children's Smiles," *TDS*, 1 June 1923, 1; "*Daily Star* Fresh Air Fund Opens Today Its 24th Season," *TDS*, 5 June 1925, 1. On later years, see "Has Known Life's Rigors, Boy Must Have Vacation," *TDS*, 6 July 1929, 17; "Toronto Children Pining for Holidays in Country," *TDS*, 1 June 1930, 1; "*Star* Fresh Air Fund Opens for 31st Year," *TDS*, 1 June 1932, 2; "*Star* Fresh

Air Fund Opens, 10,000 Children Need Help," *TDS*, 3 June 1935, 1; "11,300 Children, Mothers, Aided by Fresh Air Fund," *TDS*, 31 August 1936, 1; "Army of 500,000 Gone On, New Children Need Camp," *TDS*, 1 June 1939, 1. "Anonymous $500 Contribution Seen Symbolic of Fund's Needs," *TDS*, 15 June 1940, 1; "Fund Again to Give Holiday to City's Underprivileged," *TDS*, 7 June 1943. On the capacities of various fresh air camps, see Trent University Archives [hereafter TUA], Ontario Camping Association [hereafter OCA]), "Directory of Member Camps," 1949.

8 In 1937, the *Star* referred to the city's providing $20,000 for "clinics and summer camps." See "Funds Provided for Clinics and Camps," *TDS*, 2 June 1937, 2; "Little Children of the Slums Plead for Their Birthright," *TDS*, 21 July 1922, 1. On Bolton, see "*Star*'s Fresh Air Work Will Have Wider Scope if Funds Are Provided," TDS, 12 June 1928, 21; "Largest Fresh Air Camp in Ontario Now Open," *TDS*, 23 June 1928, 17.

9 Mariana Valverde, *The Age of Light, Soap and Water: Moral Reform in English Canada, 1885-1925* (Toronto: McClelland and Stewart, 1991), esp. conclusion. For more on the shift towards scientific philanthropy and its relationship to social work, see also James Pitsula, "The Emergence of Social Work in Toronto," *Journal of Canadian Studies* 14, 1 (1979): 35-42; James Struthers, "'Lord give us men': Women and Social Work in English Canada, 1918 to 1953," in Canadian Historical Association, *Historical Papers* (1983): 96-112; Patricia T. Rooke and R.L. Schnell, "Child Welfare in English Canada, 1920-1948," *Social Service Review* 55, 3 (September 1981): 484-506; Rooke and Schnell, *Discarding the Asylum*, 337-86. On the rise of social work in the United States, see John Ehrenreich, *The Altruistic Imagination: A History of Social Work and Social Policy in the United States* (Ithaca: Cornell University Press, 1985); Ruth Hutchison Crocker, *Social Work and Social Order: The Settlement Movement in Two Industrial Cities* (Chicago: University of Chicago Press, 1992).

10 Mirroring the provincial system of Mothers' Allowance, hierarchies were established to help determine "what constitute[d] a 'needy' person." In 1934, one "prominent social service worker" offered her assessment: "In category number one is what is known as 'the single-room family,' then comes 'the top attic family,' then 'widows and their children,' 'deserted mothers with children on their hands,' and 'the wives of men who have had their spirits crushed' by chronic unemployment." See "Heat-baked Single Rooms House Neediest Families," *TDS*, 6 June 1934, 1.

11 "Struggle against Great Odds Carried on in Heart of City," *TDS*, 11 August 1920, 1.

12 The Exchange reportedly served other functions as well, providing information on and referring children to the appropriate camps, arranging medical examinations and transportation of all potential campers; but yearly reports boasting the number of "duplications prevented" in the years after its establishment, suggests that this aspect took priority. See Family Service Association of Toronto Archival Collection [hereafter FSATA], Neighbourhood Workers' Association [hereafter NWA], "A Dream That Came True: Fresh Air Report, 1922"; FSATA, NWA, "Bolton Camp: Fresh Air Report, 1923," 14; FSATA, NWA, "Bolton Camp – 1924," 5.

13 "Fresh Air Homes Will Ring with Laughter of Poor Kids," *TDS* 12 June 1920, 1.

14 "Ask Only Room to Run and Play," *TDS*, 8 August 1940, 21. A 1946 article elaborated: "The men and women who investigate the cases for the [fund] are careful people. Sometimes they would like to say more, but their profession demands they just set down the facts." See "Packed in City Tenements, Pine for Holiday in Camp," *TDS*, 5 July 1946, 3. See also Pitsula, "Emergence of Social Work," 39. Quite fittingly, the standing biography

of Charlotte Whitton, quintessential Canadian social and child welfare worker of this period, is entitled *No Bleeding Heart.* See P.T. Rooke and R.L. Schnell, *No Bleeding Heart: Charlotte Whitton, a Feminist on the Right* (Vancouver: UBC Press, 1987).

15 "Poor Boy Faces Operation, Who Will Be Good Fairy?" *TDS*, 2 August 1924, 1.

16 "Crash Orphans Five Tots Aunt Offers Them Shelter," *TDS*, 19 July 1934, 1. This point is further confirmed by studies of the administration of relief during the 1930s and the struggle for unemployment insurance of this same period. See James Struthers, "'*No fault of their own*': *Unemployment and the Canadian Welfare State, 1914-1941* (Toronto: University of Toronto Press, 1983); James Struthers, "A Profession in Crisis: Charlotte Whitton and Canadian Social Work in the 1930s," *Canadian Historical Review* 62, 2 (1981): 169-85; Carmela Patrias, *Relief Strike: Immigrant Workers and the Great Depression in Crowland, Ontario, 1930-1935* (Toronto: New Hogtown Press, 1990), 20-26.

17 Gale Wills does not dispute that social work was partly rooted in a socially conservative and individualistic approach. At the same time, she insists that it also had roots in more progressive ideology that sought (and still seeks) change on a structural level. See Gale Wills, *A Marriage of Convenience: Business and Social Work in Toronto, 1918-1957* (Toronto: University of Toronto Press, 1995). In 1921, for instance, when demand for the fund's services was increasing, the condition at the root of the problem was stated without reserve. "The reason for the greater need," it was explained, "may be stated in one word: 'unemployment.'" See "Little Children in the Shadows Face Hard Times," *TDS*, 4 June 1921, 1. For other examples, see "Children Pine for Country Air and Cooling Breezes," *TDS*, 8 June 1922, 1; "Herded in Upstairs Rooms, No Place for Them to Play," *TDS*, 21 June 1922, 1; "Disappointment Hovers over Fresh Air Workers," *TDS*, 14 July 1922, 1.

18 All references in this paragraph from FSATA, Family Service Association of Toronto, "Family Service Association: Historic Background," 5 April 1972.

19 FSATA, NWA, "The Gateway to Health and Happiness: Bolton Camp Speaks Again, 1933," 15.

20 "Gave Up Little Home to Live in One Room," *TDS*, 18 June 1924, 1.

21 "Children Are Not to Blame for Impoverished Condition," *TDS*, 21 June 1930, 19.

22 "Family Fights Starvation, Father's Nerves Are Shattered," *TDS*, 28 June 1929, 19; "Without Food, Need Clothes, Face Eviction," *TDS*, 20 July 1929, 17. For other articles on fathers, see "All Days Are Blue Days Where This Family Works," *TDS*, 2 August 1930, 17; "The Family's Father," *TDS*, 2 June 1923, 1. On alcohol, see "Case Histories Show How Your Aid Needed to Give Camp Holiday," *TDS*, 8 July 1949, 4; "First Holiday Camp Starts at Bolton," *TDS*, 8 June 1931, 2; "Summer Draws to End but Many Still Vainly Crave Rest from Heat," *TDS*, 18 August 1949, 12. On critiques of deserting fathers, see "Five Must Live on $11 a Week," *TDS*, 7 August 1920; "When Baby Comes to Home Which Father Has Deserted," *TDS*, 18 June 1923, 1; "Mother and Children Live in Single Room," *TDS*, 17 June 1924, 1; "Coward Left Family to Shift for Itself," *TDS*, 19 August 1924, 1; "Deserted Wife and Children Need Tonic of the Country," *TDS*, 25 June 1926, 19; "Happiness Comes to Many through Star Summer Fund," *TDS*, 9 June 1930, 21; "Children Who Need Comfort Must See Picnic Paradise," *TDS*, 8 July, 1931, 1.

23 James Struthers, "'In the interests of the children': Mothers' Allowance and the Origins of Income Security in Ontario 1917-30," in *The Limits of Affluence: Welfare in Ontario, 1920-1970*, 19-49 (Toronto: Ontario Historical Studies Series, 1994); Veronica Strong-Boag, "'Wages for housework': Mothers' Allowance and the Beginnings of Social Security in

Canada," *Journal of Canadian Studies* 14, 1 (1979): 24-34; Linda Little, *No Car, No Radio, No Liquor Permit: The Moral Regulation of Single Mothers in Ontario, 1920-1997* (Toronto: Oxford University Press, 1998); Cynthia Comacchio, *Nations Are Built of Babies: Saving Ontario's Mothers and Children* (Montreal/Kingston: McGill-Queen's University Press, 1993); Katherine Arnup, *Education for Motherhood: Advice for Mothers in Twentieth-century Canada* (Toronto: University of Toronto Press, 1994); Wills, *A Marriage of Convenience*, 57-76. In the American context, see Molly Ladd-Taylor, *Mother-work: Women, Child Welfare, and the State, 1890-1930* (Urbana: University of Illinois Press, 1994); Theda Skocpol, *Protecting Soldiers and Mothers: The Political Origins of Social Policy in the United States* (Cambridge, MA: Belknap Press of Harvard University Press, 1992).

24 "Toronto's City-Sick Kiddies Cry, 'Can we go to camp?'" *TDS*, 2 June 1931, 21. On innocence, see "Innocent Children Suffer Wrongs of Drunken Father," *TDS*, 10 August 1929, 1; "Innocent Child Is Most Often Victim," *TDS*, 2 August 1928, 23; "Innocent Little Children Fear They Are Forgotten," *TDS*, 21 August 1928, 19.

25 FSATA, NWA, "New Interests at Bolton Camp in 1935," 5.

26 TUA, 72-007/2/9, Irwin Haladner to staff members, "Letter #7," 6 June 1952 (emphasis in original); TUA, Camp Pine Crest Fonds, 78-009/2/1, Camp Pine Crest, "Annual Report," 1940.

27 "Seven Weak, Puny Children in Dire Need of a Holiday," *TDS*, 25 August 1920, 1; FSATA, NWA, Bolton Camp Publicity Scrapbook, "2000 Children Seek Bolton Camp Holiday," *TDS*, 18 June 1935. On a municipal level, a 1937 estimate stated, "7000 Undernourished in City [of Toronto]," *TDS*, 29 June 1937, 1.

28 "Frail Bodies Are Rebuilt by Powers of Fresh Air," *TDS*, 12 July 1930, 21.

29 On tuberculosis, see "T-B Afflicts Parents Menaces Children, Too. Here's Where You Aid," *TDS*, 29 July 1940, 17; "Fresh Air Fund Bulwark in Anti-tuberculosis Fight," *TDS*, 18 August 1941, 32; "Making Fight against TB Fresh Air Camp to Help," *TDS*, 27 June 1947, 11. For recent historical treatment of tuberculosis in Canada, see Katherine McCuaig, *The Weariness, the Fever, and the Fret: The Campaign against Tuberculosis in Canada, 1900-1950* (Montreal/Kingston: McGill-Queen's University Press, 1999); Wayne Norton, "*A whole little city by itself*": *Tranquille and Tuberculosis* (Kamloops: Plateau, 1999); Pat Sandiford Grygier, *A Long Way from Home: The Tuberculosis Epidemic among the Inuit* (Montreal/Kingston: McGill-Queen's University Press, 1994); Stuart C. Houston, *R.G. Ferguson: Crusader against Tuberculosis* (Toronto/Oxford: Hannah Inst./Dundurn Press, 1991); Carolyn Heald, "Documenting Disease: Ontario's Bureaucracy Battles Tuberculosis," *Archivaria* 41 (1996): 88-107. On deaths at camp, see FSATA, NWA, "Fresh Air Report – Season of 1933," 9.

30 "Take a Peep at This Picture of Some Slum Homes in City," *TDS*, 30 July 1920, 24.

31 "Fresh Air Camps Increase Weight and Boost Health of Countless Poor Children," *TDS*, 31 August 1927, 14.

32 "Florrie, Pale and Underweight, Stifles in Room with Three Others," *TDS*, 20 August 1920, 1.

33 "Sir Adam Beck Helps the Fresh Air Fund," *TDS*, 31 July 1920, 1-2. Ironically, the bias that favoured rural space as providing fresh air allowed Bolton to continue operating even in years when there were complaints that the air was less than fresh. In contrast to *Star* descriptions of clover-scented air, in 1931, the Bolton Camp Committee wondered what to do about the "serious fly and smell nuisance" emanating from an adjacent pig farm. See FSATA, NWA minutes, Bolton Camp Committee, 30 January 1931.

34 "Send Poor Boy to Fresh Air Camp, Take Him Away from Dusty Lane," *TDS*, 6 July 1922, 1. On rickets, see "Skyshine Stops Rickets Toronto MOH Declares," *TDS*, 13 June 1932, 1; "Fresh Air Camps Called Best Preventative I Know," *TDS*, 11 June 1936, 1; "Sun, Fresh Air, Food, Would Help Cut Toll of Children in Slums," *TDS*, 3 July 1948, 17. On camp menus, see "Babies Wax Fat with Rich Fare at *Star* Camps," *TDS*, 15 June 1928, 21.

35 For my discussion of the category of "whiteness" and racial politics at camps, see Chapter 6.

36 *TDS*, "Babies Wax Fat"; FSATA, NWA, Bolton Camp, "1943 Report: In the Fourth Year of the War."

37 "Children in Summer's Heat Droop like Wilted Flowers," *TDS*, 18 June 1932, 1.

38 FSATA, NWA, "Bolton Camp: Fresh Air Report, 1923," 7.

39 "Fatherless Lad Sad Victim of Poverty," *TDS*, 3 June 1936, 2.

40 "Fresh Milk and Vegetables Unknown to Poor Children," *TDS*, 16 June 1927, 1.

41 FSATA, NWA, "New Interests at Bolton Camp in 1935," 16.

42 Ibid.

43 Margaret Tennant, "Children's Health Camps in New Zealand: The Making of a Movement, 1919-1940," *Social History of Medicine*, 9, 11 (1996): 70. See also Margaret Tennant, "'Fattening human stock': Dr. Elizabeth Gunn and the Establishment of Children's Health Camps in New Zealand," *Historical News* 63 (1991): 8-11; Margaret Tennant, "Complicating Childhood: Gender, Ethnicity, and 'Disadvantage' within the New Zealand Children's Health Camps Movement," *Canadian Bulletin of Medical History* 19, 1 (2002): 179-99. Gleason takes a similar view of school medical inspection, arguing that it "pathologized" children and families who did not fit prescribed health norms. For his part, Rodwell shows that open-air schools – sometimes as much as 60 percent cheaper than conventional buildings – were advocated as much in the name of cost-cutting as for their contribution to health. See Gleason, "Race, Class, and Health"; Rodwell, "Australian Open-air School Architecture."

44 "Canada's First 'Work Camp' Builds Gull Lake Cottage," *TDS*, 25 June 1940, 5.

45 FSATA, NWA, "Some Advances in Camp Programme, Bolton Camp Report, 1939."

46 Interestingly, as Jean Barman has noted, in the interwar years, baseball was seen as a particularly working-class (and American) sport. In her study of boys' private schools in British Columbia, she quotes one former pupil who explained that the sport was forbidden at his school as it was "fit only for public school brats." Quoted in Jean Barman, *Growing Up British in British Columbia: Boys in Private School* (Vancouver: UBC Press, 1984), 75.

47 In 1928, the *Star* stated that "Milk, butter, eggs, fruit, vegetables, constitute a large part of the menu." See *TDS*, "Babies Wax Fat." Another article made reference to the benefits of "milk and eggs." See "Earnest Letters Tell Benefits Camp Gives," *TDS*, 28 August 1935, 7; "Prosperity for Some but Kiddies Deprived of Milk, Butter, Eggs," *TDS*, 14 June 1948, 19. Cooking classes for mothers were similarly restricted to "proper instructions for cooking vegetables and fruit." See FSATA, NWA, "Camp as an Educational Opportunity: The Story of Bolton Camp for 1936," 11. In 1950, the first references to "meat and fish," "hamburgers," "meatballs," "weiner roasts" and "balony" appear. See "Child Taken on Trip for Night under Stars," *TDS*, 12 June 1950, 21; "Pale-faced City Tikes Taught Indian Lore by Expert Woodsmen," *TDS*, 7 June 1950, 25. For Ross's thoughts on British working-class diets, see Ellen Ross, *Love and Toil: Motherhood in Outcast London, 1870-1918* (New York/Oxford: Oxford University Press, 1993), 32.

48 TUA, OCA, Sound/Tape Collection, 83-002/4/9, Blackie Blackstock, interview by Harry Ebbs, n.d.

49 "Ill-health Casts Spell of Adversity over Family," *TDS*, 10 June 1930, 21. Other appeals stated, "There were no conveniences in the house," and, in another case, "The house is old and lacks all the modern conveniences." In 1927, one family was even without a stove. See "You May Carry Smiles to City's Grim Corners," *TDS*, 3 August 1921, 1; "Three Brothers Watch Fund with Eager, Hopeful Hearts," *TDS*, 6 August 1924, 1; "In Candle-lighted Home, Scant Clothing, No Stove, Veteran's Babes Need Aid," *TDS*, 22 August 1927, 17.

50 "Money Left in 1853 Will Helps Children to Holiday," *TDS*, 10 July 1940, 18.

51 "Happy Caravan Will Start for 2 Weeks in Fresh Air," *TDS*, 4 July 1940, 19.

52 "Camp Never Too Crowded to 'Squeeze' in Extra Cot," *TDS*, 10 August 1940, 35. This is especially ironic in light of observers' constant worries over overcrowding in working-class homes.

53 FSATA, NWA, "New Interests at Bolton Camp in 1935," 7.

54 This reading is supported by the evidence from a B'nai B'rith fresh air camp, where, included in discussion of "vocational guidance" for boys, were references to such crafts as "model aircraft, woodcraft ... clay modeling, soap carving, leathercrafts, [and] lino-cutting' among others." See "Lads You Send to Camp Cannot Help but Benefit," *TDS*, 20 June 1940, 4.

55 FSATA, NWA, "Bolton Camp: Report of Operation, 1937," 2.

56 FSATA, NWA, "Camp as an Educational Opportunity: The Story of Bolton Camp for 1936," 7.

57 FSATA, NWA, "Bolton Camp, 1924," 3, 1.

58 FSATA, NWA, "New Interests at Bolton Camp in 1935," 5; FSATA, NWA, Bolton Camp Publicity Scrapbook, "I Spend a Day with Happiness," *TDS*, 9 July 1944, 1 (emphasis added). One bit of anecdotal evidence from 1941 also, somewhat humorously, pointed to the cultural gap between counsellor and camper: "One of the workers was conducting a sports quiz," the annual Report explained. "Not knowing that tennis was an unknown game to the boys [the worker] posed this question: 'If we say "love all" what game are we thinking of?' There was quite a silence, then little Squibby ... looked up and said, 'Christianity.'" See FSATA, NWA, "Log of Bolton Camp, 1941."

59 FSATA, NWA, "New Interests at Bolton Camp in 1935," 16.

60 "Road Strewn with Rocks Has Paradise at Its End," *TDS*, 28 July 1930, 17.

61 "Invest in Toronto's Future, Officials Urge Fund Aid," *TDS*, 17 July 1943, 4.

62 "Ease a Father's Woe, Give Kiddies Holiday," *TDS*, 16 July 1931, 2.

63 In the 1938 booklet summarizing the camp's history to date, it was estimated that thirty mothers were sent for every one hundred children each year, which was 23 percent of the camp population. See FSATA, NWA, "The Story of Bolton Camp," in booklet entitled "After Twenty Years: A Short History of the Neighbourhood Workers' Association" (Toronto: The Association, 1938), 39; Minutes, Bolton Camp Committee, 19 September 1939, 18 September 1941, 24 September 1942, 23 September 1943. Fresh Air Fund statistics for two years – 1922 and 1936 – show that mothers made up 16 percent and 20 percent of the camp population, respectively. See "24,000 Is Urgently Needed, Buy Fresh Air for Children," *TDS*, 13 July 1923, 1; "11,300 Children, Mothers, Aided by Fresh Air Fund," *TDS*, 31 August 1936, 1.

64 See note 24 in this chapter for the literature on mothers' allowances, maternal education campaigns, and social work initiatives with mothers.

65 "Mother Wasted by Illness, Can't Care for Her 3 Tots," *TDS*, 21 July 1933, 1.

66 "'Send Ma to camp and we'll stay home' Plead Buck and Pals," *TDS*, 4 August 1939, 1. The tendency of poor working-class women to deny themselves food in an attempt to care for the nutritional needs of the rest of the family is documented by Ellen Ross for turn-of-the-century Britain. Ross mentions that this family survival strategy was "diagnosed" by at least one (uninformed) doctor as "auto-starvation," which might help to explain the appearance of "anorexia nervosa" on the Fresh Air Fund's list of working-class maladies (above). See Ross, *Love and Toil*, 54-55.
67 "Sickness and Sorrow Visit Many of the Poorest Homes," *TDS*, 15 July 1920.
68 "Their Transportation," *TDS*, 16 June 1923, 1. On criticism of mothers, see "A Neighbourhood News Item: Another Baby Is Announced," *TDS*, 3 August 1923, 1; "Dwellers in Streets of Shattered Hopes Pine in Summer Heat," *TDS*, 28 August 1933, 1; "Think Sad-eyed Children Stunted by Hard Life," *TDS*, 26 June 1934, 1; "First Holiday Camp Starts at Bolton," *TDS*, 8 June 1931, 2. For more on social workers and the bias against married women's wage work right up to the postwar period, see Struthers, "Lord Give Us Men," 101; Franca Iacovetta, "Making 'New Canadians': Social Workers, Women and the Reshaping of Immigrant Families," in *Gender Conflicts: New Essays in Women's History*, ed. Franca Iacovetta and Mariana Valverde, 261-302 (Toronto: University of Toronto Press, 1992).
69 "War or Peace – They Need Help," *TDS*, 23 July 1940, 17. On postwar child-rearing, see Chapter 4, note 13.
70 On Bolton's programming for mothers, see FSATA, NWA, "Bolton Camp: Fresh Air Report, 1923," 12; FSATA, NWA, "Some Advances in Camp Programme, Bolton Camp Report, 1939," 3; FSATA, NWA, "Camp as an Educational Opportunity: The Story of Bolton Camp for 1936," 11; FSATA, NWA, "Bolton Camp: Report of Operation, 1937," 9; FSATA, NWA, "Some Advances in Camp Programme, Bolton Camp Report, 1939," 3; FSATA, NWA, "The Story of Bolton Camp," 1938, 53; FSATA, NWA, "Reich Camp Still in Mind, Trio Need Fresh Air Here," *TDS*, 21 June 1950, 8. On state-run cooking classes for new immigrants in the postwar period, see Franca Iacovetta, *Gatekeepers: Reshaping Immigrant Lives in Cold War Canada* (Toronto: Between the Lines Press, 2006), chap. 6.
71 As already noted, this is the title of Katherine Arnup's study of the twentieth-century educational campaigns aimed at mothers. See Arnup, *Education for Motherhood*.
72 "Mothers Learn Child Care through Fresh Air Camps," *TDS*, 18 June 1934, 1.
73 FSATA, NWA, "Camp as an Educational Opportunity: The Story of Bolton Camp for 1936," 10. On child discipline, see FSATA, NWA, "Bolton Camp – 1924," 3.
74 "City Mission Carries on Fresh Air Work 46 Years," *TDS*, 16 July 1940.
75 FSATA, NWA, "Some Advances in Camp Programme, Bolton Camp Report, 1939," 3; FSATA, NWA, "Fresh Air Report – Season of 1933," 6-7.
76 *TDS*, "'Send Ma to camp.'"
77 "Mothers Still Knit, Camping at Bolton," *TDS*, 29 July 1940, 2.
78 "Fresh Air Work Develops from Humble 1902 Start to Magnificent Proportions," *TDS*, 3 June 1927, 19. Nineteen hundred and twenty-one seems to have been a record year; in the 1930s and 1940s, donations were never quite as high, what with the impact of the Depression and with competition from wartime charities in the 1940s.
79 FSATA, NWA, "The Story of Bolton Camp," in booklet entitled "After Twenty Years: A Short History of the Neighbourhood Workers' Association," 1938, 41.
80 "Children Undernourished, Four in a Miserable Home," *TDS*, 1 June 1922, 1.
81 "Father Sick, Son Cut Down: Family Faces Hard Struggle," *TDS*, 15 July 1924, 1. On poverty's impact on working-class families in the early twentieth century, see Michael J.

Piva, *The Condition of the Working Class in Toronto, 1900-21* (Ottawa: University of Ottawa Press, 1979); Terry Copp, *The Anatomy of Poverty: The Condition of the Working Class in Montreal, 1897-1929* (Toronto: McClelland and Stewart, 1974). See also Craig Heron, *The Canadian Labour Movement: A Short History* (Toronto: Lorimer, 1996), 58-84; Bryan D. Palmer, *Rethinking the History of Canadian Labour, 1800-1991* (Toronto: McClelland and Stewart, 1992), 214-40. For the impact of the Depression on working-class families, see Denyse Baillargeon, "'If you had no money, you had no trouble, did you?': Montreal Working-Class Housewives during the Great Depression," *Women's History Review* 1, 2 (1992): 217-37; Lara Campbell, "Respectable Citizens of Canada: Gender, Family, and Unemployment in the Great Depression, Ontario" (PhD. diss., Queen's University, 2002).

82 FSATA, NWA, "Fresh Air Report – Season of 1933," 9. On the pressure on fresh air camps, see "Star Fresh Air Fund Faces Certain Deficit Unless Cash Donated," *TDS*, 27 August 1931, 23; "Fresh Air Treasurer Needs $3000 badly," *TDS*, 31 August 1931, 16; FSATA, NWA, "New Interests at Bolton Camp in 1935," 1; FSATA, NWA, minutes, Bolton Camp Committee, 20 March 1930. On camp closings, see "Many Camps Must Close if Funds Not Forthcoming," *TDS*, 4 July 1932, 1. On funds raised by the Fresh Air Fund in the 1930s, see "Star Fresh Air Fund Opens for 31st Year," *TDS*, 1 June 1932, 2; "Pleas Already Piling up for Chance to Go to Camp," *TDS*, 1 June 1933, 1; "Open Star Fresh Air Fund for Children and Mothers," *TDS*, 1 June 1934, 1; "Star Fresh Air Fund Opens, 10,000 Children Need Help," *TDS*, 3 June 1935, 1; "11,300 Children, Mothers, Aided by Fresh Air Fund," *TDS*, 31 August 1936, 1; "Girl Who Can't Speak Radiant with Smiles at Thought of Camp," *TDS*, 20 July 1938, 1; "Army of 500,000 Gone on New Children Need Camp," *TDS*, 1 June 1939, 1. On Bolton's upbeat attitude, see FSATA, NWA, "Fresh Air Report – Season of 1932," 1; FSATA, NWA, minutes, Bolton Camp Committee, 13 June 1934.

83 On experiments with back-to-the-land schemes as a solution to the problem of unemployed workers in Canada, the United States, and Australia during the Great Depression, see T.J.D. Powell, "Northern Settlement, 1929-1935," *Saskatchewan History* 30, 3 (1977): 81-98; S.W. Dyer, "Back to the Land: Settlement Schemes for Adelaide's Unemployed, 1930-35," *Labour History* 1976 (31): 30-37; Joseph D. Conwill, "Back to the Land: Pennsylvania's New Deal Era Communities," *Pennsylvania Heritage* 10, 3 (1984): 12-17.

84 In her study of child-saving organizations in Boston, Gordon demonstrates that working-class women were able to push agencies to take action on the issue of wife-beating, a realm that agencies themselves did not regard as their proper sphere. See Linda Gordon, *Heroes of Their Own Lives: The Politics and History of Family Violence* (New York: Penguin Books, 1988).

85 "Veteran of Empire's Wars Now in Rags and Poverty," *TDS*, 11 August 1932, 1; "Five Dollar Bill Helps Family out of Trouble," *TDS*, 15 June 1931, 1, 11; "Jobless for Months, Children Need Help," *TDS*, 17 June 1931, 2; "Life Loses Hope for Needy When Mother, Children Ail," *TDS*, 18 August 1931, 1, 4. On hospital bed and burial site requests, see "Could Not Allow Young Lad to Die," *TDS*, 11 June 1932, 2; "Burial in Country Is Coveted for City Child Who Never Knew Joy of Fragrant Open Spaces," *TDS*, 17 July 1937. 1.

86 "Leather Bench Kept Busy as Any Confessional Box," *TDS*, 17 August 1932, 1.

87 "Pawns Wife's Ring, Last Thing to Go," *TDS*, 31 July 1931, 5.

88 On fathers at Bolton, see FSATA, NWA, "Camp as an Educational Opportunity: The Story of Bolton Camp for 1936," 13. For the *Star*'s response to unusual requests, see "Do Something by Saturday, and Saturday Has Arrived," *TDS*, 16 August 1930, 19; *TDS*, "Burial in Country Is Coveted"; *TDS*, "Five Dollar Bill Helps."

89 "Some Women Are Whipped, Their Courage Has Failed," *TDS*, 17 June 1933, 1.

90 "Dull Faces Become Happy as Mothers Get Camp Air," *TDS*, 7 June 1934, 1; FSATA, NWA, "Bolton Camp: Report, 1938," 7.

91 "Poverty, Ill-health, Strife Follow Winter out of Work," *TDS*, 6 June 1930, 19.

92 "Poor Forlorn Individuals Pay for City's Greatness," *TDS*, 16 August 1932, 1.

93 "Wife of Lifer Is Broken by Fate of Her Husband, Lives Only for Daughter," *TDS*, 29 August 1927, 19.

94 "Pallid Children of Slums Call to City's Mother Heart," *TDS*, 4 June 1930, 21.

95 "Fund Again to Give Holiday to City's Underprivileged," *TDS*, 7 June 1943; "First Holiday in 15 Years, Mother 'Happy as a Lark,'" *TDS*, 31 August 1944.

96 On rationing at Bolton, see FSATA, NWA, minutes, Bolton Camp Committee, 28 May 1942, 28 September 1944. On dealing with labour shortages at Bolton, see FSATA, NWA, minutes, Bolton Camp Committee, 30 May 1944.

97 FSATA, NWA, "Some Advances in Camp Programme, Bolton Camp Report, 1939," 1.

98 "War or Peace – They Need Help," *TDS*, 23 July 1940, 17. On wartime fund-raising for the camps, see "Your Help Meant Happiness to Thousands," *TDS*, 31 August 1940, 1; "July Carnival Helps Star Fresh Air Fund," *TDS*, 25 June 1941, 36. On cadets and officers at Bolton Camp, see FSATA, NWA, minutes, Bolton Camp Committee, 28 May 1942, 23 September 1943, 30 May 1944.

99 "Just Two Weeks at Camp May Keep Boys out of Jail," *TDS*, 8 August 1941, 16. For discussions of the panic over wartime delinquency, see Jeffrey Keshen, "Wartime Jitters over Juveniles: Canada's Delinquency Scare and Its Consequences, 1939-1945," in *Age of Contention: Readings in Canadian Social History, 1900-1945*, ed. Jeffrey Keshen, 364-86 (Toronto: Harcourt Brace, 1997). For discussions of working mothers and impacts on children, see FSATA, NWA, Bolton Camp Publicity Scrapbook, "Give Holiday to 1000 War Workers' Kiddies," *TDS*, June 2, 1942; FSATA, NWA, minutes, Bolton Camp Committee, 22 April 1943. On juvenile delinquency in early Fresh Air Fund appeals, see "Frank Gets Chance to Become a Real Man," *TDS*, 16 July 1924, 1; "Denied Life's Comforts, Children Deserve Holiday," *TDS*, 10 June 1929, 19. For 1940s references, see "The Need Is Great, Time Short," TDS, 20 July 1940, 19; "21 Cramped up in 11 Small Rooms, 17 Children Need New Scene," *TDS*, 13 June 1940, 21; "Once East End Bad Boy Peter Got Camp Help Now Pays Way, 2 More," *TDS*, 9 July 1940, 17; "Let There Be No Broken Hearts," *TDS*, 7 August 1940, 17; "Only 2C from Each of Us Would Give 15,000 Holiday," *TDS*, 30 June 1947, 18.

100 "Camp Fire, Fresh Air, 'God's Gift to Boys' Judge Sees Big Need," *TDS*, 19 August 1948, 1. On the Family Service's reference to "family problems,' see FSATA, NWA, Family Service Association of Toronto, "Family Service Association: Historic Background," 5 April 1972; FSATA, NWA, minutes, Bolton Camp Committee, 22 April 1943. On sending soldiers' families and children of war workers to camp, see FSATA, NWA, Bolton Camp Publicity Scrapbook, "Give Holiday to 1000 War Workers' Kiddies," *TDS*, 2 June 1942; FSATA, NWA, minutes, Bolton Camp Committee, 18 September 1941, 24 September 1942. On how the camp combated delinquency, see *TDS*, "The Need Is Great"; *TDS*, "21 Cramped Up"; *TDS*, "Just Two Weeks."

101 FSATA, NWA, "Bolton Summer Camp, 1944."

102 "You Can Work Miracles, Aid Star Fresh Air Fund," *TDS*, 2 June 1947, 35.

103 FSATA, NWA, Bolton Camp Publicity Scrapbook, "Hundreds Still Need Help Ere Summer Ends, Let Fund Act for You," *TDS*, 4 August 1949.

104 As far as Fresh Air Fund allocations went, in 1947, eighteen camps (other than Bolton) shared the remainder of the funds, no one of them receiving more than $1,500. See FSATA, NWA, Bolton Camp Publicity Scrapbook, "14,180 Children and Mothers Helped to Happiness by Star Fresh Air Fund," *TDS*, 4 December 1948. Regarding the number of campers fresh air camps could accommodate, the average of 115 was calculated based on fifteen fresh air camps (excluding Bolton) affiliated with the OCA in 1949. See TUA, OCA handbook, 1949.

105 FSATA, NWA, Family Service Association of Toronto, "Family Service Association: Historic Background," 5 April 1972, 5.

106 Postwar articles that forefronted health as a primary concern include: "Girl Prays for *Star* Camp, Every Horse Is Her 'Daisy,'" *TDS*, 8 June 1945, 23; "Visit at Fresh Air Camp New Lease on Life to Child," *TDS*, 13 June 1945, 16; "Fresh Air, Camp Rest Guard Child's Health," *TDS*, 14 August 1946, 13; "Fresh Air Fund Dollars Aid in Fight for Health," *TDS*, 5 June 1947, 5.

107 According to Iacovetta, food had significant symbolic importance in the early postwar period. The image of Canada as a land of plenty portrayed against the backdrop of a "Europe in ruins" was, she argues, a recurring subtext of the Federal Citizenship Branch's cooking classes for new immigrants. See Franca Iacovetta, *Gatekeepers: Reshaping Immigrant Lives in Cold War Canada* (Toronto: Between the Lines Press, 2006), chap. 6.

108 "Every Donation Means Happiness for Child," *TDS*, 6 August 1946, 13. Mothers' petitions pointed in the same direction. "My three boys are terribly underweight and sickly, and I can't seem to do anything for them," was how one mother appealed to the *Star*. See "Visit at Fresh Air Camp, New Lease on Life to Child," *TDS*, 13 June 1945, 16.

109 "Sun, Fresh Air, Food, Would Help Cut Toll of Children in Slums," *TDS*, 3 July 1948, 17.

110 On polio, see "Gifts for Camp Fund Urgent if All Needy to Be Given Holiday," *TDS*, 4 July 1951, 21; Christopher J. Rutty, "The Middle-class Plague: Epidemic Polio and the Canadian State, 1936-37," *Canadian Bulletin of Medical History* 13, 2 (1996): 277-314; Christopher Rutty, "'Do something! ... Do anything!' Poliomyelitis in Canada, 1927-1967" (PhD diss., University of Toronto, 1996).

111 "Hope Camp Will Show Tenement Child New Life beyond His Home," *TDS*, 12 July 1949, 3.

112 Tennant, "Children's Health Camps," 78.

113 "Slums to Bolton, Brave Children Need Reprieve," *TDS*, 12 June 1925, 1.

114 "Earnest Letters Tell Benefits Camp Gives," *TDS*, 28 August 1935, 10; FSATA, NWA, "The Story of Bolton Camp," 51. On weighing-in, see "Boy! Look at Them Go to Camp with Law's Sirens," *TDS*, 25 June 1940.

115 By 1940, the tone at one camp was much less congratulatory, with advice that campers not put on more than three and a half pounds while at camp. See "Puny Mites of Slums Race to New Health with Fresh Air 'Cure,'" *TDS*, 12 July 1940, 17.

116 FSATA, NWA, "A General Report of Work at Bolton Camp, 1922."

117 "Skyshine Stops Rickets Toronto MOH Declares," *TDS*, 13 June 1932, 1.

118 This is one of the conclusions of Arnup's study, which attributes mothers' openness to educational campaigns to the fact that urban women were increasingly removed from networks of relatives, by whom new mothers had traditionally been taught. Smaller family sizes also meant that fewer girls had experience with child care before the birth of their own babies. See Arnup, *Education for Motherhood*, 117-36. It also supports a more complex

reading of the role of nurses, as does Kari Dehli's work, in which she argues that nurses "often found themselves in a contradictory relationship to the people they visited, their supervisors, and to the emerging health and welfare bureaucracy." See Dehli, "'Health Scouts' for the State?" 248.

119 FSATA, NWA, "To the Friends of Bolton Camp," 1 September 1926, 2.
120 FSATA, NWA, "Bolton Camp: Fresh Air Report, 1923," 12.
121 FSATA, NWA, "Bolton Camp – 1924," 3; "Fresh Milk and Vegetables Unknown to Poor Children," *TDS*, 16 June 1927, 1.
122 One mother stated in 1926 that she feared for the mental health of her husband, an apparently shell-shocked war veteran, if he were to be left alone for two weeks. See FSATA, NWA, "To the Friends of Bolton Camp," 1 September 1926, 2.
123 On the importance of child labour to working-class family economies well into the twentieth century, see Rebecca Coulter, "The Working Young of Edmonton, 1921-31," in *Childhood and Family in Canadian History*, ed. Joy Parr, 143-59 (Toronto: McClelland and Stewart, 1982); Dominique Jean, "Le recul de travail des enfant au Quebec entre 1940 et 1960: Une explication des conflits entre les familles pauvres et l'etat profidence," *Labour/Le Travail* 24 (Fall 1989): 91-129; Neil Sutherland, "'We always had things to do': The Paid and Unpaid Work of Anglophone Children between the 1920s and the 1960s," *Labour/Le Travail* 25 (Spring 1990): 105-41; Craig Heron, "The High School and the Household Economy in Working-class Hamilton, 1890-1940," *Historical Studies in Education* 7, 2 (1995): 217-59.
124 FSATA, NWA, "A Dream That Came True."
125 "Gives Up Her Chance of Holiday Fearing Others May Need It," *TDS*, 20 August 1938, 1, 2.
126 "Mother Giving Thanks for Great Work of Fund," *TDS*, 30 August 1945, 4; "Strove Hard That Children Might Be Allowed Vacation," *TDS*, 19 July 1929, 19.
127 Administrators were also careful to add that "no one at camp knows anything about the financial arrangements which are made back in the city." See FSATA, NWA, Bolton Camp Publicity Scrapbook, "Restful Holiday for Tired Mothers at Bolton Camp," *North Toronto Herald*, July 1946.
128 Leila Warnock, interview by author, 2 June 2000.
129 "Uncle Bob's Big Job, Will You Help Him?" *TDS*, 3 August 1920, 7; *TDS*, "Gives Up Her Chance."
130 FSATA, NWA, minutes, Bolton Camp Committee, 9 September 1939.
131 "Fresh Milk and Vegetables Unknown to Poor Children," *TDS*, 25 June 1923, 1.
132 "Reich Camp Still in Mind, Trio Need Fresh Air Here," *TDS*, 21 June 1950, 8.
133 In fact, if many of the staff were recruits from private camps, it was not surprising that they, like the campers, regarded Bolton as a charity – to which two week's work was their contribution – with true camp loyalty reserved for their own camps. See FSATA, NWA, "New Interests at Bolton Camp in 1935," 5; FSATA, NWA, "Bolton Camp: Report, 1938," 8; FSATA, NWA, minutes, Bolton Camp Committee, 19 September 1939.
134 Scott argues that the way oppressed groups typically conduct themselves in the presence of society's "power holders" – their "public transcript" – is necessarily constrained, protecting their "hidden transcript" or true opinions and beliefs from scrutiny. See James C. Scott, *Domination and the Arts of Resistance: Hidden Transcripts* (New Haven: Yale University Press, 1990).
135 Mary Murphy, interview by author, 7 June 2000.
136 Leila Warnock, interview by author, 2 June 2000.

137 FSATA, NWA, "Bolton Camp, 1924," 1.
138 On the gratitude of grown campers, see "Remembers an Act of Kindness, Helps," *TDS*, 16 August 1929, 2; "Hardened in Grim Struggle, Wants Chance for Children," *TDS*, 16 August 1935, 1, 15; "Shared Fresh Air Vacation, Now Help Others to Share," *TDS*, 9 August 1941, 20; "Boys Now Overseas Write of *Star*'s Fresh Air Camp," *TDS*, 11 August 1943, 17; FSATA, NWA, Bolton Camp Publicity Scrapbook, "He Was at Camp Once Now Saves to Send Others," *TDS*, n.d. On children's appeals, see "Widow Brings Six Children Longing for Green Fields," *TDS*, 11 July 1928, 1; "My Children's Eyes Shone as I Spoke of Holidays," *TDS*, 21 June 1945; "Kiddies' Pathetic Appeal Wins Them Brief Holiday," *TDS*, 8 August 1930, 17. On waiting lists, see FSATA, NWA, Bolton Camp Publicity Scrapbook, "Bolton Camp Opens Today for Summer," *Globe and Mail*, 22 June 1935.
139 "Three Little Girls and Four Boys, All in Need of Fresh Air Outing," *TDS*, 24 June 1921, 1; "Mother Would Love to Go if Only for Baby's Sake," *TDS*, 10 June 1922, 1; "Mother Should Be in Bed But Has to Keep at Work," *TDS*, 8 August 1922, 1; "Widow Brings Six Children"; "Simple Letter Asking for Help Gives Glimpse of Tragedy," *TDS*, 7 August 1930, 21; "Visit at Fresh Air Camp New Lease on Life to Child," *TDS*, 13 June 1945, 16.
140 "Fresh Air Camp Seemed Like Heaven, Mother Says," *TDS*, 19 June 1935, 1.
141 *TDS*, "Mother Should Be in Bed."
142 FSATA, NWA, "Fresh Air Report – Season of 1932," 1.
143 FSATA, NWA, "Some Advances in Camp Programme, Bolton Camp Report, 1939," 2; FSATA, NWA, "New Interests at Bolton Camp in 1935," 15.
144 FSATA, NWA, Bolton Camp Publicity Scrapbook, "He Was at Camp Once."
145 Asked about her most vivid memory of Bolton, her first response was "the breakfast." Judging from her memories, ice-cream was, apparently, another valued treat in the postwar years at Bolton, serving as dessert, competition prize, and the excuse for group trips into town. Mary Murphy, interview by author, 7 June 2000.
146 FSATA, NWA, "Bolton Camp: Report of Operation, 1937," 5; FSATA, NWA, "Some Advances in Camp Programme, Bolton Camp Report, 1939," 4. In 1935, however, administrators still felt the need to justify such luxuries in terms of their contribution to general social education. The public was assured that such activities had a "deeper purpose": "In them we hope to overcome the backwardness and awkwardness of some of our mothers, to teach them to dance for the joy of dancing and to laugh because they are really happy." See FSATA, NWA, "New Interests at Bolton Camp in 1935," 13.
147 "City Mission Carries on Fresh Air Work 46 Years," *TDS*, 16 July 1940; "Costs Up – More Needy – Record Sum Is Asked for Fresh Air Fund," *TDS*, 4 June 1950, 3.
148 See Shirley Tillotson's *The Public at Play: Gender and the Politics of Recreation in Post-war Ontario* (Toronto: University of Toronto Press, 2000), 21-34 on shifting views of recreation and leisure in the postwar context.
149 FSATA, NWA, "Bolton Summer Camp, 1944."
150 FSATA, NWA, "Bolton Camp, 1943 Report: In the Fourth Year of the War."
151 "Outing Helped His Children, Father Would Help Others," *TDS*, 18 August 1933, 1.
152 FSATA, NWA, "Camp as an Educational Opportunity: The Story of Bolton Camp for 1936," 13.
153 FSATA, NWA, Bolton Camp Publicity Scrapbook, "Bolton Camp Underway for 1935 Season," *The Mail*, 26 June 1935; FSATA, "The Story of Bolton Camp," in booklet entitled "After Twenty Years: A Short History of the Neighborhood Workers Association," 1938, 44, 48.
154 "Labor Calls Criticism of *Star* Funds Despicable," *TDS*, 2 August 1951, 1, 3.

155 Ibid.

156 FSATA, NWA, "A Dream That Came True."

Chapter 4: Making Modern Childhood the Natural Way

1 Ontario Camp Leadership Centre files in possession of Dorothy Walter, Toronto, Ontario, Dr. J.G. Althouse, transcript of CKEY Broadcast, 25 April 1947, 1.

2 Anthony Giddens, *Modernity and Self-identity: Self and Society in the Late Modern Age* (Stanford: Stanford University Press, 1991), 144-80. For a general discussion on modernity and the rise of the social sciences, see Peter Hamilton, "The Enlightenment and the Birth of Social Science," in *Modernity: An Introduction to Modern Societies,* ed. Stuart Hall, David Held, Don Hubert, and Kenneth Thompson, 19-54 (London: The Open University, 1996). Reprinted by Basil-Blackwell in 1997.

3 Giddens, *Modernity and Self-identity*, 18.

4 In Rooke and Schnell's view, Victorian childhood was defined by four essential factors: segregation from, and also protection by, adult society as well as social and economic dependence. See Patricia T. Rooke and R.L. Schnell, "Childhood as Ideology," *British Journal of Educational Studies* 27 (February 1979): 7-28. On the fight to end child labour, see Lorna Hurl, "Restricting Child Factory Labour in Late Nineteenth-century Ontario," *Labour/Le Travail* 21 (Spring 1988): 87-121; Dominique Jean, "Le recul de travail des enfant au Quebec entre 1940 et 1960: Une explication des conflits entre les familles pauvres et l'etat profidence," *Labour/Le Travail* 24 (Fall 1989): 91-129; John Bullen, "Hidden Workers: Child Labour and the Family Economy in Late Nineteenth-century Urban Ontario," *Labour/Le Travail* 18 (Fall 1986): 163-87. In the American context, see Viviana A. Zelizer, *Pricing the Priceless Child: The Changing Social Value of Children* (Princeton, NJ: Princeton University Press, 1994).

5 On psychology and child development theories, see Steven Schlossman, "Philanthropy and the Gospel of Child Development," *History of Education Quarterly* 21, 3 (1981): 275-99. See also literature in note 8 of this chapter.

6 Sol Cohen, "The Mental Hygiene Movement, the Development of Personality and the School: The Medicalization of American Education," *History of Education Quarterly* 23 (Summer 1983): 123-49.

7 Mona Gleason, *Normalizing the Ideal: Psychology, Schooling, and the Family in Postwar Canada* (Toronto: University of Toronto Press, 1999), 19.

8 A department of psychology also emerged at McGill University in the 1920s. Mona Gleason provides one of the most informative accounts of the rise of academic psychology in this country. See Gleason, *Normalizing the Ideal,* 19-36. On the mental hygiene movement, see Schlossman, "Philanthropy and the Gospel of Child Development"; Cohen, "Mental Hygiene Movement"; Theresa R. Richardson, *The Century of the Child: The Mental Hygiene Movement and Social Policy in the United States and Canada* (Albany: State University of New York Press, 1989), 112-27; Hans Pols, "Between the Laboratory and Life: Child Development Research in Toronto, 1919-1956," *History of Psychology* 5, 2 (2002): 135-62; Brian J. Low, "The New Generation: Mental Hygiene and the Portrayals of Children by the National Film Board of Canada, 1946-1967," *History of Education Quarterly* 43, 4 (2003): 540-70; Brian J. Low, "The Hand That Rocked the Cradle: A Critical Analysis of Rockefeller Philanthropic Funding, 1920-1960," *Historical Studies in Education*

16, 1 (2004): 33-62; Neil Sutherland, *Children in English-Canadian Society, 1880-1920: Framing the Twentieth-century Consensus* (Toronto: University of Toronto Press, 1976), chap. 1 (reissued by Wilfrid Laurier University Press in 2000). On forced sterilization of the "feeble-minded," see Angus McLaren, "The Creation of a Haven for 'Human Thoroughbreds': The Sterilization of the Feeble-minded and the Mentally Ill in British Columbia," *Canadian Historical Review* 67, 2 (1986): 127-50; and also his monograph, *Our Own Master Race: Eugenics in Canada, 1885-1945* (Toronto: McClelland and Stewart, 1990).

9 Low, "Hand That Rocked the Cradle," 36. Social "improvement" was, of course, a matter of perspective. By analyzing another major Rockefeller-funded project on mass communications and the shaping of public opinion, Low concludes that Rockefeller funding of child psychology research, and specifically that which took a permissive view of child-rearing, was meant to reduce the influence of parents and teachers on children, while leaving them wide open to the influence of the mass media and their peers. Others agree that funding agencies – Rockefeller and others – shaped the research agenda of this period. See Richardson, *Century of the Child*, 109-27; Sol Cohen, *Challenging Orthodoxies: Towards a New Cultural History of Education* (New York: Peter Lang Publishing, 1999), chap 8.

10 Cohen, "Mental Hygiene Movement"; Pols, "Between the Laboratory and Life," 135. For the triumph of the mental hygiene viewpoint in postwar NFB films, see Low, "The New Generation."

11 In what would become known as one of Watson's seminal statements, he summed up his perspective on the limitless malleability of the child: "Give me a dozen healthy infants," he promised, " ... and my own specified world to bring them up in and I will guarantee to take one at random and train him to become any type of specialist I might select – doctor, lawyer, artist ... yes, even beggarman and thief, regardless of his talents." See John B. Watson, quoted in Peter J. Miller, "Psychology and the Child: Homer Lane and J.B. Watson," in *Studies in Childhood History: A Canadian Perspective*, ed. Patricia T. Rooke and R.L. Schnell (Calgary: Detselig, 1982), 73. For more on Watson, see also Ann Hulbert, *Raising America: Experts, Parents and a Century of Advice about Children* (New York: Alfred A. Knopf, 2003).

12 On scientific child-rearing, see Miller, "Psychology and the Child," 57-80; John Cleverley and D.C. Phillips, *Visions of Childhood: Influential Models from Locke to Spock* (New York: Teachers College Press, 1986), 114-24. On the Canadian setting, see Veronica Strong-Boag, "Intruders in the Nursery: Childcare Professionals Reshape the Years One to Five, 1920-1940," in *Childhood and Family in Canadian History*, ed. Joy Parr, 160-78 (Toronto: McClelland and Stewart, 1982); Nora Lewis, "Creating the Little Machine: Child-rearing in British Columbia, 1919-1939," *BC Studies* 56 (Winter 1982/83): 44-60; Katherine Arnup, "Raising the Dionne Quintuplets: Lessons for Modern Mothers," 65-84, and other articles in the special issue of *Journal of Canadian Studies* 29, 4 (1994-95); Katherine Arnup, *Education for Motherhood: Advice for Mothers in Twentieth-century Canada* (Toronto: University of Toronto Press, 1994): 84-116; Cynthia Comacchio, *Nations Are Built of Babies: Saving Ontario's Mothers and Children* (Montreal/Kingston: McGill-Queen's University Press, 1993).

13 On prescriptions for postwar child-rearing, see Arnup, *Education for Motherhood*, 84-116; Doug Owram, *Born at the Right Time: A History of the Baby Boom Generation* (Toronto: University of Toronto Press, 1996): 31-53; Nancy Pottishman Weiss, "Mother, the Invention of Necessity: Dr. Benjamin Spock's Baby and Child Care," in *Growing Up in America: Children in Historical Perspective*, ed. N. Ray Hiner and Joseph M. Hawes, 283-303 (Urbana

and Chicago: University of Illinois Press, 1985); Cleverly and Phillips, *Visions of Childhood*, 54-79; Michael Sulman, "Humanization of the American Child: Benjamin Spock as a Popularizer of Psychoanalytic Thought," *Journal of the History of the Behavioral Sciences* 9 (1983): 258-65; Charles E. Strickland and Andrew M. Ambrose, "The Baby Boom, Prosperity, and the Changing Worlds of Children, 1945-1963," in *American Childhood: A Research Guide and Historical Handbook*, ed. Joseph M. Hawes and N. Ray Hiner, 533-66 (Westport: Greenwood Press, 1985).

14 Jocelyn Motyer Raymond, *The Nursery World of Dr. Blatz* (Toronto: University of Toronto Press, 1991), 42.

15 In addition to his work as founder and first director of the University of Toronto's Institute for Child Study in 1925, Blatz also served as consultant to the Toronto Juvenile Court, as on-site psychologist at several Toronto schools, and as personal psychologist of the Dionne quintuplets, the role that brought him the most public attention. For studies of Blatz, see Raymond, *Nursery World of Dr. Blatz*; Richardson, *Century of the Child*, 112-27; Gleason, *Normalizing the Ideal*, 27-51; Strong-Boag, "Intruders in the Nursery." Several of these scholars agree that, while adopting various elements of behaviourism, Blatz is more properly defined as a "functionalist" psychologist, who stressed that children repeat patterns that "work" for them rather than adopt habits in an automaton-like fashion (as the behaviourists saw it). See Raymond, *Nursery World of Dr. Blatz*, 103; Richardson, *Century of the Child*, 121-22. Mona Gleason points out that the theoretical underpinnings of Blatzian psychology are still a matter of debate. See Gleason, *Normalizing the Ideal*, 43-44.

16 For biographical information on Blatz, see two preceeding notes. For Blatz's camping involvement, see Dimock and Hendry, *Camping and Character*, 159; Trent University Archives [hereafter TUA], Ontario Camping Association [hereafter OCA] Papers, 78-006/1/1, "Second Annual Report of the Committee on Education and Research of the Ontario Section of the American Camping Association," 13 April 1942.

17 TUA, OCA Papers, 72-007/2/9, Irwin Haladner to staff members, "Letter #1," May 1952. See also TUA, OCA Papers, 78-006/25/40, Charlie F. Plewman, "The Days Leading up to the Formation of the Ontario Camping Association" part of poster entitled "Today: Tomorrow's Yesterday," c. 1967.

18 Cohen, "Mental Hygiene Movement," 129.

19 "Have Alley as Playground, No Trees or Grass in Sight," *Toronto Daily Star* [hereafter *TDS*], 5 July 1924, 1.

20 "2 Weeks Camp May Alter Girl's Whole View of Life," *TDS*, 12 August 1942, 10.

21 Dimock and Hendry, *Camping and Character*, 145.

22 Ibid., 146.

23 Mary L. Northway, *Appraisal of the Social Development of Children at a Summer Camp* (Toronto: University of Toronto Press, 1940), 12.

24 Dimock and Hendry, *Camping and Character*, 145.

25 Family Service Association of Toronto Archival Collection [hereafter FSATA], Neighbourhood Workers' Association [hereafter NWA], "The Gateway to Health and Happiness: Bolton Camp Speaks Again, 1933," 15.

26 Dimock and Statten, *Talks to Counselors*, 19. For Blatz's notion of security, see Raymond, *Nursery World*, 145-46.

27 Taylor Statten, *Talks to Counsellors* (Taylor Statten Camps, 1928), 20; TUA, Ronald H. Perry Papers, 82-016/2/8; Dimock, "Camping and Character Growth," 12.

28 Dimock and Statten, *Talks to Counselors*, 20; "You're Tanned and Peppy, What about Poor Kiddies," *TDS*, 21 July 1948, 7; "Fresh Air Fund Needs $417 Daily to Help 5,000 Children

Left," *TDS*, 31 August 1950, 8; "Fund Helps Kiddies Escape Mental, Physical Collapse," *TDS*, 7 July 1947, 4. In 1937, the Project on Shy Children was initiated by University of Toronto psychologists. These scholars now regarded shyness as a pathological condition that foreshadowed all manner of personality problems in later life (while the rambunctious school child was seen as essentially healthy). On the Shy Children Project, see Pols, "Between the Laboratory and Life," 148-50. On shyness as presented in postwar NFB films, see Low, "The New Generation." On the school's new approach to shy students, see Cohen, "Mental Hygiene Movement," 131.

29 TUA, Northway Family Fonds – Additions, copy of Mary Northway, "Socialization," *Camping Magazine* 11, 8 (1939): 4.

30 In 1958, Mary Hamilton reiterated Northway's sentiments, stating: "The camp is a child's world and it is very important that the child should feel at home with her own age group. The fact that she gets along at home, does not necessarily mean she can get along with her own contemporaries." See Mary G. Hamilton, *The Call of Algonquin: Biography of a Summer Camp* (Toronto: Ryerson Press, 1958), 101. On Howard Chudacoff's notion of age consciousness, see his *How Old Are You?: Age Consciousness in American Culture* (Princeton: Princeton University Press, 1989).

31 FSATA, NWA, "The Story of Bolton Camp," in booklet entitled "After Twenty Years: A Short History of the Neighbourhood Workers' Association," 1938, 49.

32 FSATA, NWA, "Some Advances in Camp Programme, Bolton Camp Report, 1939." The YMCA's Camp Pine Crest also divided campers into four different sections according to age. See TUA, Camp Pine Crest Fonds, 78-009/2/4, Camp Pine Crest, brochure, 1945; TUA, Camp Pine Crest Fonds, 78-009/2/4, Camp Pine Crest, brochure, 1946. Ahmek also made provision for "Inkies" and "Chippies" (the youngest campers), "seniors," and others in between. See TUA, Adele and Harry Ebbs Papers, 80-014/1/8, "The Taylor Statten Camps," brochure, c. 1950s; Joan Moses, interview by author, 26 July 2000.

33 On staff-camper ratios, see TUA, OCA, "1949 Directory of Member Camps"; TUA, OCA Papers, 82-009/2/2, "Northway Lodge: A Pioneer Camp for Girls," brochure, 1941.

34 Statten, *Talks to Counsellors*, 11; TUA, Ronald H. Perry Papers, 82-016/2/8; Dimock, "Camping and Character Growth," 10.

35 TUA, OCA Papers, 78-004/2/31, Bert Danson, transcript of interview by J. Budge, 15 February 1973; TUA, OCA Sound/Tape Collection, 83-002/2/5, Mary Northway, interview by Cathy Stuart and Warren Anderson, 21 January 1975; TUA, Northway Family Fonds – Additions, 90-016/1/34, Mary Northway, "Recollection of Glen Bernard Camp," 16 May 1982; Shirley Ford, interview by author, 20 June 2000.

36 Northway, "Socialization," 3.

37 Northway is also mentioned by Raymond as a significant part of Blatz's work at the institute and, indeed, as integral to the publication of Blatz's final study, *Human Security*. See Raymond, *Nursery World*, 144, 210-16, 220. Northway's dissertation was not only published but also translated into six languages. On Elsie Palter's role at Camp Kawagama, see Geraldine Sherman, "The Girls of Summer," *Toronto Life*, September 2001, 100. Adult camp alumni from Kawagama have claimed that whenever one of her campers attained a degree of fame or notoriety – of good or bad variety – Palter returned to her original box of index cards, "well into old age," to verify the accuracy of her original impressions.

38 Everett Rogers lists five categories of response to the presentation of new ideas: the innovators, the early adoptors, the early majority, the late majority, and the laggards. See Everett M. Rogers, *Communication of Innovations: A Cross-cultural Approach* (New York: The Free Press, 1971), referenced in Cohen, "Mental Hygiene Movement," 138.

39 Dimock and Hendry, *Camping and Character*, 256-57, 277.
40 According to Cohen, interwar parent education programs, another offshoot of the mental hygiene movement, sought to change parents' "pre-scientific" views and educate them as to the importance of personality development. Involving parents in studies and questionnaires was one way of drawing them into the mental hygiene perspective. See Cohen, "Mental Hygiene Movement," 129.
41 Dimock and Statten, *Talks to Counselors*, 86-87.
42 TUA, Ronald H. Perry Fonds, 82-016/2/8, *Canoe Lake Camp Echoes* 4, 3 (1931): 42; TUA, Ronald H. Perry Fonds, 82-016/2/8, *Canoe Lake Camp Echoes* 4, 1 (February 1931): 40. On the host of methods for information gathering at Ahmek, see Dimock and Hendry, *Camping and Character,* 256-57, 263-88; Dimock and Statten, *Talks to Counselors,* 24-26.
43 TUA, Ronald H. Perry Papers, 82-016/2/8; Dimock, "Camping and Character Growth," 10-12. These laws received further elaboration in later editions of *Camping and Character.*
44 Dimock and Hendry, *Camping and Character*, 183. For discussion of other cases, see pages 165-201.
45 The project was one of the many carried out by University of Toronto scholars, this one being an attempt to explore the mental health of an entire neighbourhood, pseudonymously named "Crestwood Heights," but understood to refer to Toronto's exclusive Forest Hill neighbourhood. (Incidentally, Taylor Statten would have been quite familiar with this area as he himself was a resident, as, no doubt, were many of his clientele.) The study concluded that children from wealthy backgrounds were no better off, in fact perhaps were worse off, in terms of mental health than were other children, with their families in general in a "perennial state of anxiety" regarding status, achievement, and consumption. On the Crestwood Heights project, see Pols, "Between the Laboratory and Life," 150-52; Low, "Hand That Rocked the Cradle," 50-53.
46 Dimock and Hendry, *Camping and Character*, 160.
47 Mary Northway, "What Are the Camps Achieving," *Camping Magazine* 9, 8 (1937).
48 Hamilton, *Call of Algonquin*, 168.
49 For discussions of parents, see Dimock and Hendry, *Camping and Character*, 167, 183-4, 189. For the evolution of fatherly roles in these years, see Cynthia Comacchio, "'A postscript for father': Defining a New Fatherhood in Interwar Canada," *Canadian Historical Review* 78, 3 (1997): 386-408; and Robert Rutherdale, "Fatherhood and Masculine Domesticity during the Baby Boom: Consumption and Leisure in Advertising and Life Stories," in *Family Matters: Papers in Post-Confederation Canadian Family History*, ed. Edward-Andre Montigny and Anne Lorene Chambers, 309-30 (Toronto: Canadian Scholar's Press, 1988); Chris Dummitt, "Finding a Place for Father: Selling the Barbecue in Postwar Canada," *Journal of the Canadian Historical Association* 9 (1998): 209-23.
50 Ibid., 169.
51 Donald Burry, "A History of the Taylor Statten Camps" (MSc thesis, University of Saskatchewan, 1985), 23.
52 Northway, *Appraisal of Social Development*, 18.
53 At least some difficult campers – who the camp claimed went on to be "first-class counsellors" – didn't seem to bear their camps any lasting animosity. See Dimock and Hendry, *Camping and Character*, 200. Even while still a camper, one boy found the professional presence comforting, recalling warmly his sessions with the camp psychologist and other staff when left behind on a canoe trip in the 1950s. Jim Buchanan, interview by author, 21 July 2000.

54 TUA, Camp Pine Crest Fonds, 78-009/2/1, Camp Pine Crest, "Annual Report," 1940.
55 TUA, OCA Papers, 72-007/2/5, Toronto YWCA, "Camp Tapawingo," 1951.
56 TUA, OCA Papers, 78-006/25/29, "The Early Days of Camp On-Da-Da-Waks," 1950.
57 TUA, Camp Pine Crest Fonds, 78-009/2/1, Camp Pine Crest, "Report on Lumberman Section, June 30-August 25, 1949."
58 TUA, Camp Pine Crest Fonds, 78-009/2/1, Rix Rogers, Camp Pine Crest, "Out-Trip Department – 1951 Report," emphasis in original; TUA, Camp Pine Crest Fonds, 78-009/2/1, Camp Pine Crest, "Annual Report," 1940.
59 "Mother Fights for Health, Her Children Get Holiday," *TDS*, 5 August 1931, 2.
60 FSATA, NWA, minutes, Bolton Camp Committee, 28 September 1944.
61 "Worn Out by Sickness, Future Is a Dreary One," *TDS*, 25 June 1924, 1.
62 In the four or five decades since academics had first considered the social value of play, they built up a significant literature on the subject, not to mention a network of professionally supervised playgrounds that dotted the urban landscape of North American cities. On the history of play, see Bernard Mergen, "The Discovery of Children's Play," *American Quarterly* 27, 4 (1975): 399-420; Morris Mott, "Confronting 'Modern' Problems through Play: The Beginning of Physical Education in Manitoba's Public Schools, 1900-1915," in *Schools in the West: Essays in Canadian Educational History*, ed. Nancy M. Sheehan, J. Donald Wilson, and David C. Jones, 57-71 (Calgary: Detselig, 1986).
63 *TDS*, 21 July 1920, 1; 23 July 1920, 1; 17 August 1927, 17.
64 "11-Year-Old Girl Is Mother, Looks after a Family of Six," *TDS*, 15 August 1923, 1.
65 *TDS*, 6 July 1940, 17. These complaints over the persistence of child labour fit entirely with what historians of childhood and the family have discovered for these years. See Dominique Jean, "Le recul de travail des enfant au Quebec entre 1940 et 1960: Une explication des conflits entre les familles pauvres et l'etat profidence," *Labour/Le Travail* 24 (Fall 1989): 91-129; Neil Sutherland, "'We always had things to do': The Paid and Unpaid Work of Anglophone Children between the 1920s and the 1960s," *Labour/Le Travail* 25 (Spring 1990): 105-41.
66 "Help to Free Pale Wee Girl from Hot Down Town Streets," *TDS*, 24 June 1922, 1.
67 "Need Ten Thousand Dollars to Send Children to Camps," *TDS*, 1 August 1922, 1.
68 Northway, "Socialization," 3. TUA, OCA Sound/Tape Collection, 83-002/5/8, Barb Gilchrist, interview by Jack Pearse, 6 November 1986.
69 Early in the twentieth century, the work of G. Stanley Hall was seminal in putting forth the idea of adolescence as a distinct stage of the human life cycle. Frequently referred to as the "father of American psychology," Hall could also aptly be called the father of adolescence. His 1904 opus, *Adolescence: Its Psychology and Its Relations to Physiology, Anthropology, Sociology, Sex, Crime, Religion, and Education*. 2 vols. (New York, Appleton, 1904), set the tone – if not in all its particulars certainly in its general notion of adolescent "storm and stress" – for academic and popular understandings of youth for years to come. Literature on the twentieth-century history of Canadian youth includes David MacLeod, "A Live Vaccine: The YMCA and Male Adolescence in the United States and Canada, 1870-1920," *Histoire Sociale/Social History* 11, 2 (1978): 5-25; Jane Synge, "Growing Up Working Class in Hamilton in the Early Twentieth Century," in *Childhood and Adolescence in Canada*, ed. K. Ishwaran, 249-69 (Toronto: McGraw-Hill Ryerson, 1979); Rebecca Coulter, "The Working Young of Edmonton, 1921-31," in *Childhood and Family in Canadian History*, ed. Joy Parr, 143-59 (Toronto: McClelland and Stewart, 1982); Margaret Prang, "The Girl God Would Have Me Be: The Canadian Girls in Training, 1915-1939," *Canadian*

Historical Review 66, 2 (1985): 154-83; Craig Heron, "The High School and the Household Economy in Working-class Hamilton, 1890-1940," *Historical Studies in Education* 7, 2 (1995): 217-59; Cynthia Comacchio, "Inventing the Extracurriculum: High School Culture in Interwar Ontario," *Ontario History* 93, 1 (2001): 33-56; Cynthia Comacchio, "Dancing to Perdition: Adolescence and Leisure in Interwar English Canada," *Journal of Canadian Studies* 32, 3 (1997): 5-35; Steven Maynard, "'Horrible Temptations': Sex, Men, and Working-class Male Youth in Urban Ontario, 1890-1935," *Canadian Historical Review* 78, 2 (1997): 191-235; Tamara Myers, *Caught: Montreal's Modern Girls and the Law, 1869-1945* (Toronto: University of Toronto Press, 2006). On postwar youth, see Mariana Valverde, "Building Anti-delinquent Communities: Morality, Gender, and Generation in the City," in *A Diversity of Women: Ontario, 1945-1980*, ed. Joy Parr, 19-45 (Toronto: University of Toronto Press, 1995); Mary Louise Adams, *The Trouble with Normal: Post-war Youth and the Making of Heterosexuality* (Toronto: University of Toronto Press, 1997); Linda Ambrose, "Cartoons and Commissions: Advice to Junior Farmers in Postwar Ontario," *Ontario History* 93, 1 (2001): 57-79; Franca Iacovetta, "Gossip, Contest, and Power in the Making of Suburban Bad Girls: Toronto, 1945-60," *Canadian Historical Review* 80, 4 (1999): 585-623.

70 TUA, Camp Pine Crest Fonds, 78-009/2/4, Camp Pine Crest, brochure, 1948. On "senior island" at Wapomeo, see Joan Moses, interview by author, 26 July 2000.

71 TUA, Adele and Harry Ebbs Papers, 80-014/1/1, Hedley G. Dimock, "Coeducational Camping in Brother-Sister Camps," February 1951, 2-3.

72 John R. Seeley, R. Alexander Sim, and Elizabeth W. Loosley, *Crestwood Heights: A Study of the Culture of Suburban Life* (Toronto: University of Toronto Press, 1956), 314. On secret rendezvous, see Anonymous Arowhon camper, e-mail interview by author, 27 July 2000; Sherman, "Girls of Summer," 102; Joan Moses, interview by author, 26 July 2000.

73 FSATA, NWA, "The Gateway to Health and Happiness: Bolton Camp Speaks Again, 1933," 15.

74 TUA, Adele and Harry Ebbs Papers, 80-014/1/8, Virginia T. Cobb to Mr. and Mrs. Taylor Statten, 16 February 1942, and response from Adele Ebbs, n.d.

75 Shirley Ford, interview by author, 20 June 2000.

76 In a 1946 devotional pamphlet, CGIT girls were told, "There are many unpleasant things about this world – things like wrangling and suspicion on the part of nations, unemployment, poverty, race discrimination ... Perhaps you had an uncle who was shell-shocked in the first Great War or a ... brother who was shot down in a night flight over Germany in World War II ... Perhaps you live in a community that has not taken a very kind attitude toward Japanese Canadians. These are some of the things that help us to see how much we need a better world." See United Church Archives/Victorian University Archives [hereafter UCA/VUA], 85.095C, box 14, file 6, CGIT Camps, National Girls Work Board, "Morning Watch," 1946, 7. The mistreatment of Japanese Canadians had already been discussed in an earlier, wartime devotional pamphlet. See UCA/VUA, 85.095C, box 14, file 6, CGIT Camps, National Girls Work Board, "Morning Watch," 1941. For more on the founding and early years of the CGIT, see Prang, "Girl God Would Have Me Be."

77 On Ebbs' views, see TUA, Adele and Harry Ebbs Papers, 80-014/1/8, Virginia T. Cobb to Mr. and Mrs. Taylor Statten, 16 February 1942 and response, n.d. On the wartime situation at Northway Lodge, see TUA, OCA Papers, 78-006/25/26, Fannie L. Case, "The Story of Northway Lodge, 1906-1942," 9-10.

78 Mary Northway, "Security Pegs for Campers," *Camping Magazine* 14, 4 (1942): 3-7.

79 FSATA, NWA, "Bolton Summer Camp: Tomorrow Belongs to the Children," brochure, 1949.

80 TUA, Adele and Harry Ebbs Papers, 80-014/1/8, "The Taylor Statten Camps," brochure, c. 1950.
81 TUA, Adele and Harry Ebbs Papers, 80-014/1/8, "The Taylor Statten Camps," brochure, c. 1950; UCA/VUA, Canadian Girls in Training Collection, 85.095C, box 14, file 1, CGIT Camp Manual, 1950, 44-45.
82 TUA, Ontario Camp Leadership Centre, Bark Lake Fonds, 98-012/1/1, "Bark Lake Canoeing Programme," 1948; "Report on Canoe Trips," 1949.
83 TUA, OCA Fonds, 72-007/2/7, Camp Winnebagoe, 1946 brochure.
84 TUA, Ontario Camp Leadership Centre, Bark Lake Fonds, 98-012/1/1, "Counselling Course," c. 1948.
85 UCA/VUA, CGIT Collection, 85.095C, box 42, file 39, CGIT Camp Leaders' Manual, c. 1950s.
86 TUA, Camp Pine Crest Fonds, 78-009/2/1, Camp Pine Crest, "Director's Report," 1951.
87 Northway, "Socialization," 3-5, 30.
88 "War or Peace – They Need Help," *TDS*, 23 July 1940, 17.
89 "Little Missionary Marnie, Example of What Fresh Air Camp Does," *TDS*, 9 August 1947, 15.
90 OCLC files in possession of Dorothy Walter, Toronto, Ontario, copy of address over CKEY broadcast, by Dr. J.G. Althouse, 25 April 1947, 3
91 Hamilton, *Call of Algonquin*, 100.
92 Dimock and Hendry, *Camping and Character*, 5.
93 Dimock and Statten, *Talks to Counselors*, 33.
94 Margaret Rieder Paisley, "A Chat about Camps," *The Torch* 12, 2 (1936): 32.
95 TUA, OCA Papers, 72-007/2/6, brochure, "Wabi-kon: A Summer Camp for Boys and Girls," c. 1950.
96 TUA, OCA Papers, 78-006/25/40, Mary Northway to Barry Lowes, 9 March 1964.
97 Archives of Ontario [hereafter AO], Legislative Press Clippings, MS-755, reel 86, "For Children's Welfare," *Globe and Mail*, 14 July 1944.
98 Dewey's thoughts on education are summed up in *The School and Society* (1900) and *Democracy and Education* (1916). For discussions of experimentation with progressive education in Canadian schools, see Gleason, "Psychology in Postwar Schools, *Normalizing the Ideal*, chap. 6; R.S. Patterson, "The Canadian Experience with Progressive Education," and Eamonn Callan, "John Dewey and the Two Faces of Progressive Education," both in *Canadian Education: Historical Themes and Contemporary Issues*, ed. E. Brian Titley, 95-110; 84-95 (Calgary: Detselig, 1990); Neil Sutherland, "The Triumph of 'Formalism': Elementary Schooling in Vancouver from the 1920s to the 1960s," *BC Studies* 69-70 (Spring/Summer 1986): 175-210; Robert Stamp, "Education for Democratic Citizenship," in *The Schools of Ontario, 1876-1976*, ed. Robert Stamp, 164-82 (Toronto: University of Toronto Press, 1982); Jean Mann, "G.M. Weir and H.B. King: Progressive Education or Education for the Progressive State?" in *Schooling and Society in Twentieth-Century British Columbia*, ed. J. Donald Wilson and David C. Jones (Calgary: Detselig, 1980), 91-11; George S. Tomkins, *A Common Countenance: Stability and Change in the Canadian Curriculum* (Toronto: Prentice-Hall, 1986), chap. 10. See also Sutherland, *Children in English-Canadian Society*, chaps. 10-13. For discussion of progressive education in the American context, see Cohen, *Challenging Orthodoxies*, chap. 5.
99 TUA, OCA Papers, 98-019/13/10, Taylor Statten, "Developing the Program on a Group Basis," address to the Conference of the Pacific Camping Association, 16-19 March 1939.

100 TUA, Northway Family Fonds – Additions, 90-016/1/35, copy of Mary Northway, "Camping in Canada," *Canadian Geographical Journal* 20, 6 (1940): 333.
101 FSATA, NWA, "Bolton Summer Camp," first appeal brochure, 1947.
102 TUA, Camp Pine Crest Fonds, 78-009/2/1, Camp Pine Crest, brochure template, c. 1942.
103 On the physical education of girls, the opening up of new programs and debates over competition, see Veronica Strong-Boag, *The New Day Recalled: Lives of Girls and Women in English Canada, 1919-1939* (Toronto: Copp Clark Pittman, 1988), 31-32; Helen Lenskyj, "Femininity First: Sport and Physical Education for Ontario Girls, 1890-1930," *Canadian Journal of History of Sport* 13, 2 (1982): 4-17; Helen Lenskyj, "Training for 'True Womanhood': Physical Education for Girls in Ontario Schools, 1890-1920," *Historical Studies in Education* 1, 2 (1990): 205-23; M. Ann Hall, "Rarely Have We Asked Why: Reflections on Canadian Women's Experience in Sport," *Atlantis* 6, 1 (1980): 51-60. As shown in Chapter 5, camp programs for girls and boys were never identical. Girls were always treated more carefully at camp, although, especially at canoe-tripping camps, they were also exposed to numerous challenges and were given the chance to hone their less traditionally "feminine" skills. See Chapter 5 of this book. See also Lathrop, "Strap an axe to your belt"; Susan L. Forbes, "'Nothing but a rag between you and the sky': Northway Lodge Girls' Camp and the Wilderness Experience," paper presented to the Canadian Historical Association Conference, Edmonton, 24 May 2000. For the treatment of girls at American camps, see Leslie Paris, "Children's Nature: Summer Camps in New York State, 1919-1941" (PhD diss., University of Michigan, 2000); Susan A. Miller, "Girls in Nature/The Nature of Girls: Transforming Female Adolescence at Summer Camp, 1900-1939" (PhD diss., University of Pennsylvania, 2001).
104 Susan Morgan recalls being chosen "by secret ballot" as a "Colour War" captain at the end of camp season as "the ultimate affirming experience ... I'm sure people who get elected to Parliament don't feel better than I [did]." Susan Morgan, quoted in Sherman, "Girls of Summer," 103. On the "Worthy Woodsman" and the "Pine Tree" awards, see Hamilton, *Call of Algonquin*, 117, 144. On making record-time canoe trips, see Elizabeth Shapiro, e-mail interview by author, 17 February 2001. Similarly remembering "a rough, rough, trip" along the Mattawa and Ottawa rivers in the 1920s, Mary Northway explained, "We were always known as the girls who had gone to Mattawa and back." See TUA, OCA Sound/Tape Collection, 83-002/2/5, Mary Northway, interview by Cathy Stuart and Warren Anderson, 21 January 1975.
105 Statten, "Developing the Program on a Group Basis."
106 Hamilton, *Call of Algonquin*, 20.
107 TUA, Camp Pine Crest Fonds, 78-009/2/1, Camp Pine Crest, "Annual Report," 1940.
108 Dimock and Statten, *Talks to Counselors*, 39. Similar statements were made at other camps. "Swimming instruction," according to a Bolton report, "involved a great deal more than the skill of swimming. The qualities of courage, perseverance and self-confidence are all part of the learning process." See FSATA, NWA, "Bolton Camp: Report of Operation, 1937," 3.
109 Statten, *Talks to Counsellors*, 8.
110 TUA, Camp Pine Crest Fonds, 78-009/2/1, "Interim Report to the Camp Pine Crest Committee," 22 September 1952.
111 Dimock and Statten, *Talks to Counselors*, 52.
112 TUA, Ronald H. Perry Fonds, 82-016/2/8, "Camping and Character," *Canoe Lake Camp Echoes* 3, 1 (1930): 17.

113 Northway, "Camping in Canada," 330.
114 "Pale-Faced City Tikes Taught Indian Lore by Expert Woodsmen," *TDS*, Wednesday, 7 June 1950, 25.
115 TUA, Northway Family Fonds – Additions, 90-016/1/25, Mary Northway, "Sustaining Interests," *Camping Magazine* 11, 9 (1939).
116 Hamilton, *Call of Algonquin*, 57.
117 Dimock and Statten, *Talks to Counselors*, 27, for counsellor duties, see 27-34. To help ensure a supply of staff with this level of skills, efforts were made towards establishing a standardized system of "teacher training." In 1925, the Margaret Eaton School of Physical Education in Toronto offered one of the first institution-based courses in counsellor training. In 1941, it merged with the University of Toronto's school to form the School of Physical and Health Education. See Hamilton, *Call of Algonquin*, 169-70. Underscoring its own belief in the educational value of camping, in 1949, the provincial government set up its own counsellor-training camp at Bark Lake in Haliburton. See OCA, *Ontario Camp Bulletin*, edition 2, 1946; TUA, Adele and Harry Ebbs Papers, 80-014/1/5, "Season of 1947 – Programme of Staff Training," 1947; OCA Papers, 72-007/2/8, Camp Responses to Ontario Camping Association, "Confidential Camp Counsellor Survey," 1952; Hamilton, *Call of Algonquin*, 86, 89.
118 FSATA, NWA, Bolton Camp Publicity Scrapbook, "US Visitor Outlines Vast Camp Scheme," *TDS*, 12 April 1937.
119 Dimock and Hendry, *Camping and Character*, 4.
120 Sutherland, "Triumph of 'Formalism.'" For other accounts of the failure of progressive education, see Stamp, "Education for Democratic Citizenship"; Mann, "G.M. Weir and H.B. King"; Patterson, "Canadian Experience with Progressive Education"; Callan, "John Dewey"; Gleason, *Normalizing the Ideal*, 119-39.
121 Paul Axelrod, "Beyond the Progressive Education Debate: A Profile of Toronto Schooling in the 1950s," *Historical Studies in Education* 17, 2 (2005): 227-41.
122 "City Mission Carries on Fresh Air Work 46 Years," *TDS*, 16 July 1940; "Every $7.50 You Send in Sends a Poor Child Away," *TDS*, 29 July 1925, 1; "Fresh Air Fund Donations Buy Shares in Happiness," *TDS*, 5 June 1926, 17.
123 "Children Get New Outlook by Miracle of Fresh Air," *TDS*, 6 June 1949, 5.
124 "Lions Party at Beausoleil Camp Closes Spot Where Lads Had Fun," *TDS*, 20 August 1940, 9.
125 Hamilton, *Call of Algonquin*, 87.
126 Ibid., 135.
127 TUA, Ronald H. Perry Fonds, 82-016/3/5, *Weekly Canoes Paper*, 5 August 1948, 1.
128 TUA, Ronald H. Perry Fonds, 82-016/3/3, "Taylor Statten Camps, Campcraft and Out Trips," June 1948; "Taylor Statten Camps – Canoe Trip Report," n.d.
129 Dimock and Hendry, *Camping and Character*, 156, 279-80.
130 TUA, Ronald H. Perry Papers, 82-016/3/2, "1938 Final Report – Canoeing."
131 TUA, Camp Pine Crest Fonds, 78-009/2/1, Camp Pine Crest, "Report on Lumberman Section, June 30-August 25, 1949"; TUA, Camp Pine Crest Fonds, 78-009/2/1, Camp Pine Crest, "Director's Report," 1949.
132 Liz Lundell, *Fires of Friendship: Eighty Years of the Taylor Statten Camps* (Toronto: Fires of Friendship Books, 2000), 29. This was also the practice at Glen Bernard and, more than likely, other camps as well. See Shirley Ford, interview by author, 20 June 2000.
133 Shirley Ford, interview by author, 20 June 2000.
134 Mary Murphy, interview by author, 7 June 2000.

135 On the danger and frequency of "crushes" and same-sex affection at camp, see Statten, *Talks to Counsellors*, 2; Dimock and Statten, *Talks to Counselors*, 31; TUA, OCA Papers, 98-019/13/10, "Notes from the Course in Camp Education, Margaret Eaton School," 10 February-17 March 1937, 2; TUA, Northway Family Fonds – Additions, 90-016/1/25, Mary Northway, "What Are the Camps Achieving," *Camping Magazine* 9, 8 (1937).
136 Dimock and Hendry, *Camping and Character*, 180.
137 Ruth-Ellen Soles, quoted in Sherman, "Girls of Summer," 102.
138 Paris, "Children's Nature," 164. See also Paris, "'Please let me come home': Homesickness and Family Ties at Early Twentieth-century Summer Camps," in *The American Child: A Cultural Studies Reader*, ed. Caroline Levander and Carol Singley, 246-61 (New Brunswick, NJ: Rutgers University Press, 2003). The 1957 study was carried out by Dr. Taylor Statten, psychiatrist and son of the well-known Taylor Statten who founded Camp Ahmek. See TUA, OCA Fonds, 72-007/5/16, Dr. Taylor Statten, "Homesickness," April and June 1957.
139 TUA, Ontario Camp Leadership Centre, Bark Lake Fonds, 98-012/1/2, "Report of the Camp Director, 1950." UCA/VUA, 85.095C, box 42, file 39, CGIT Camp Leaders' Manual, c. 1950s.
140 Seeley et al., *Crestwood Heights*, 315.
141 As Sutherland notes in the context of formal education, by its nature, the peer group ran according to childish – and not adult – dictates. See Neil Sutherland, *Growing Up: Childhood in English Canada from the Great War to the Age of Television* (Toronto: University of Toronto Press, 1997): 220-53.
142 Northway, *Appraisal of Social Development*, 55.
143 TUA, Adele and Harry Ebbs Papers, 80-014/1/5, "Season of 1947 – Programme of Staff Training," 1947.
144 Northway, "Security Pegs."
145 Shirley Ford, interview by author, 20 June 2000; Bert Danson, interview by author, 12 June 2000.
146 Statten, "Developing the Program on a Group Basis." For Paris's thoughts on camp pranks, see Paris, "Children's Nature," 169-71.
147 TUA, Camp Pine Crest Fonds, 78-009/2/1, Camp Pine Crest, "Annual Report," 1940.
148 Sherman, "Girls of Summer," 101.
149 Joan Moses, interview by author, 26 July 2000.
150 Merle S. Storey, quoted in Lundell, *Fires of Friendship*, 37.
151 Douglas Creelman, interview by author, 23 June 2000, Toronto.
152 TUA, OCA Sound/Tape Collection, 83-002/5/24, Mary Northway, interview by Jocelyn Palm, 17 November 1981.
153 Snedden, quoted in Dimock and Hendry, *Camping and Character*, 328.

Chapter 5: Shaping True Natures in Nature

1 Gord Wright, interview by Marjorie Booth, 26 November 1973, Alliston, Ontario.
2 "Healthful Fresh Air Safeguards Children's Heritage of Innocence," *Toronto Daily Star* [hereafter *TDS*], 10 August 1938, 1, 3.
3 "Camp Fire, Fresh Air, God's Gift to Boys, Judge Sees Big Need," *TDS*, 19 August 1948, 1.
4 As already noted, both Adams and Gleason have focused on the creation of categories of "normalcy" during childhood and youth and their intimate connection with prevailing

gender and sexual roles. See Mary Louise Adams, *The Trouble with Normal: Postwar Youth and the Making of Heterosexuality* (Toronto: University of Toronto Press, 1997); Mona Gleason, *Normalizing the Ideal: Psychology, Schooling, and the Family in Postwar Canada* (Toronto: University of Toronto Press, 1999).

5 On big-game hunting, see Tina Loo, "Of Moose and Men: Hunting for Masculinities in British Columbia, 1880-1939," *Western Historical Quarterly* 32 (Autumn 2001): 296-319. On canoe tripping, see Jamie Benidickson, *Idleness, Water, and a Canoe: Reflections on Paddling for Pleasure* (Toronto: University of Toronto Press, 1997).

6 Trent University Archives [hereafter TUA], Ontario Camping Association [hereafter OCA] Papers, 88-006/3/1, Taylor Statten form letter, 19 May 1922; "Being a Barefoot Boy on Hot City Pavement Not so Good," *TDS*, 21 July 1941, 5; W.A. Milks, ed. *The Camp Director's Manual* (Ontario Boys' Work Board, n.d.), 44.

7 In 1927, a camp hymn was created for Ahmek. Its lyrics reveal how central the theme of masculinity was to the camp project. In part, they read:

> Deep in the wildwood, set like a gem,
> Hail to old Ahmek, the maker of men ...
> Pledge we our hearts to thy spirit again:
> Spirit of Ahmek, the maker of men.

TUA, OCA Papers – Additions, 89-015/1/40, quoted in Taylor Statten Camps, brochure, 1988.

8 Loo, "Of Moose and Men," 319.

9 Stuart Blumin, *The Emergence of the Middle Class: Social Experience of the American City, 1760-1900* (New York, Cambridge: Cambridge University Press, 1989); Joy Parr, *The Gender of Breadwinners: Women, Men, and Change in Two Industrial Towns, 1880-1950* (Toronto: University of Toronto Press, 1990), 140-64.

10 E. Anthony Rotundo discusses this new model in *American Manhood: Transformations in Masculinity from the Revolution to the Modern Era* (New York: BasicBooks, 1993), chaps. 10-11. Gail Bederman makes a similar argument for a shift from the ideal of restrained Victorian masculinity to a more violent and competitive form of turn-of-the-century masculinity. See Gail Bederman, *Manliness and Civilization: A Cultural History of Gender and Race in the United States, 1880-1917* (Chicago and London: University of Chicago Press, 1999).

11 For a discussion of Roosevelt in the context of outdoor pastimes, masculinity, and race, see Bederman, *Manliness and Civilization*, chap. 5. On the popularity and increasing organization of competitive sport before the First World War, see Allan Metcalfe, *Canada Learns to Play: The Emergence of Organized Sport, 1807-1914* (Toronto: McClelland and Stewart, 1987). On outdoor recreation, masculine competitiveness, and identity, see Loo, "Of Moose and Men"; Benidickson, *Idleness, Water, and a Canoe*, 172-87. Even Parr notes, if only in passing, that these same men were likely to turn to sport in their off-hours to prove their manliness in physical terms.

12 TUA, OCA Papers, 78-004/2/31, Bert Danson, transcript of interview by J. Budge, 15 February 1973; Hedley S. Dimock and Taylor Statten, *Talks to Counselors* (New York: Association Press, 1939), 22-23.

13 Keewaydin Camp Brochure, 1921, quoted in Brian Back, *The Keewaydin Way: A Portrait, 1893-1983* (Temagami: Keewaydin Camp Ltd., 1983), 142; TUA, OCA Sound/Tape Collection, 83-002/5/25, Blackie Blackstock, interview by OCA, 1 November 1978.

14 TUA, unaccessioned holdings, Taylor Statten, *Talks to Counsellors* (Taylor Statten Camps, 1928), 16.
15 Rotundo, *American Manhood*, 251-54.
16 Kristopher Churchill, "Learning about Manhood: Gender Ideals and 'Manly Camping,'" in *Using Wilderness: Essays on the Evolution of Youth Camping in Ontario*, ed. Bruce W. Hogdins and Bernadine Dodge (Peterborough: Frost Centre for Canadian Heritage and Development Studies, 1992), 9-10.
17 Hedley S. Dimock and Charles E. Hendry, *Camping and Character: A Camp Experiment in Character Education* (New York: Association Press, 1929), 21-22.
18 Lack of reference to fathers highlights assumptions concerning the already fundamental separation from their offspring that industrialization and the ensuing separation of home and (paid) work had substantially accomplished.
19 Rotundo argues that increasing male influence over boyhood was one of the central objectives of clubs like the YMCA and the Boy Scouts. See Rotundo, *American Manhood*, 258.
20 Liz Lundell, *Fires of Friendship: Eighty Years of the Taylor Statten Camps* (Toronto: Fires of Friendship Books, 2001).
21 A staff member at one (unnamed) camp recounts the story of a fellow staff member forced to house his family at a nearby tourist lodge: "He has three girls and he doesn't think they would fit into camp life. His oldest girl is thirteen and the fellows would want to be dating her and then there would be trouble." Quoted in R. Seeley, R. Alexander Sim, and Elizabeth W. Loosley, *Crestwood Heights: A Study of the Culture of Suburban Life* (Toronto: University of Toronto Press, 1956), 316.
22 Back, *Keewaydin Way*, 116. An ex-camper similarly recalls: "He believed that the presence of women was disturbing to the macho flavour of camp life." See Robert Foster to Sharon Wall, 8 September 2000, in possession of Sharon Wall.
23 Back, *Keewaydin Way*, 116.
24 TUA, Brochure Collection – "K," "Kilcoo Camp," brochure, 1933.
25 TUA, OCA Papers, 72-007/2/5, brochure, "Camp Temagami (Cochrane Camp)," c. 1950.
26 Upper Canada College Archives [hereafter UCCA], "A Canoe Trip in Timagami [sic]," *College Times*, Summer 1922, 35.
27 Douglas Creelman, interview by author, 23 June 2000.
28 "Camp Timagami," *College Times*, Easter 1924, 43; Back, *Keewaydin Way.*
29 *The Keewaydin Kicker*, 1915. Quoted on Keewaydin website, http://www: ottertooth.com/keewaydin. Back, *Keewaydin Way*, 30, 35; Doug Creelman, interview by author, 23 June 2000. Until 2002, the Gigitowin remained an all-male club (although two women – both on staff – were offered membership after 1978. Interestingly, both declined).
30 For a discussion of the gender dimensions of 1950s social science and its focus on the "plight" of the white middle-class male, see Wini Breines, *Young, White and Miserable: Growing Up Female in the Fifties* (Boston: Beacon Press, 1992), chap. 1.
31 John R. Seeley, R. Alexander Sim, and Elizabeth W. Loosley, *Crestwood Heights: A Study of the Culture of Suburban Life* (Toronto: University of Toronto Press, 1956), 315.
32 TUA, OCA Papers, 72-007/2/5, brochure, "Camp Temagami (Cochrane Camp)," c. 1950.
33 TUA, OCA Papers, 88-006/3/1, Taylor Statten form letter, 19 May 1922.
34 "The Departure of a Friend," *College Times*, Summer 1921, 40-41.

35 Dimock and Statten, *Talks to Counselors*, 11.

36 Ross D. Cameron's study of Tom Thomson as a model of antimodern masculinity reveals that this "manly" hero was also depicted (whatever the reality) as a solitary character who was "stoic, quiet, reserved and modest," a sharp contrast with the braggadocios big-game hunters Loo describes. See Ross D. Cameron, "Tom Thomson, Antimodernism, and the Ideal of Manhood," *Journal of the Canadian Historical Association* 10 (1999): 185-208.

37 TUA, OCA Papers, 88-006/3/7, Adele Ebbs, transcript of interview, 1986, 22.

38 The admiration of Aboriginal men should not be overplayed since, as we see in Chapter 6, it was often mixed with older, more negative views of "the Indian."

39 TUA, Camping Literature Collection, Ontario Boys' Work Board – W.A. Milks, ed., "The Camp Director's Manual," n.d., 43, 44.

40 "Boy Like Frisky Colt, Holiday Can Help Him Run in Right Direction," *TDS*, 7 August 1948, 1-2.

41 "Sandy Was Physically Fit, Camp Built Him Morally," *TDS*, 3 July 1947, 17.

42 Paul Bennett uses the image of "taming" working-class boys in connection with turn-of-the-century industrial schools for delinquents. See Paul W. Bennet, "Taming 'Bad Boys' of the 'Dangerous Class': Child Rescue and Restraint at the Victorian Industrial School," *Histoire Sociale/Social History* 21, 42 (1988): 71-96.

43 Family Service Association of Toronto Archival Collection [hereafter FSATA], Neighbourhood Workers' Association [hereafter NWA], Bolton Camp, 1943 Report: "In the Fourth Year of the War"; "Butch Problem Child Needs Remodelling Job Only Camp Can Supply," *TDS*, 2 July 1949, 1.

44 "Frank Gets Chance to Become a Real Man," *TDS*, 16 July 1924, 1; "Lane His Only World, Holiday in Camp Will Give Boy New Outlook," *TDS*, 21 June 1951, 29.

45 "Nature Working Miracles among Children in Camps," *TDS*, 23 June 1938, 25.

46 *TDS*, "Lane His Only World."

47 FSATA, NWA, "New Interests at Bolton Camp in 1935," 7.

48 "Two Camps on Lake Scugog Havens for Needy Families," *TDS*, 11 July 1940, 22; "Pavement Is Their Beach, Boys, Girls Eye Country," *TDS*, 3 June 1949, 13; "Lads You Send to Camp Cannot Help but Benefit," *TDS*, 20 June 1940, 4.

49 FSATA, NWA, "Log of Bolton Camp, 1941."

50 *TDS*, "Lads You Send to Camp."

51 "Just Two Weeks at Camp May Keep Boys out of Jail," *TDS*, 8 August 1941, 16.

52 FSATA, NWA, Bolton Camp Publicity Scrapbook, "Hundreds Still Need Help Ere Summer Ends," *TDS*, 4 August 1949.

53 *TDS*, "Frank Gets Chance"; "Denied Life's Comforts, Children Deserve Holiday," *TDS*, 10 June 1929, 19; "Fresh Air, Sunshine, Gifts Children Need," *TDS*, 17 July 1951, 15; *TDS*, "Just Two Weeks"; FSATA, NWA, Bolton Camp Publicity Scrapbook, "Give Holiday to 1000 War Workers' Kiddies," *TDS*, 2 June 1942.

54 *TDS*, "Denied Life's Comforts." Despite the inflammatory rhetoric, the list of their "crimes" often included little more than the use of "unseemly" language, playing hooky, swimming nude at public beaches, stealing fruit and, sometimes, bicycles, and – in one boy's case – squirting the neighbours' washing with red ink from his water gun. See "Once East-End Bad Boy, Peter Got Camp Help Now Pays Way, 2 More," *TDS*, 9 July 1940, 17; "Only 2c from Each of Us Would Give 15,000 Holiday," *TDS*, 30 June 1947, 18; "Frank Gets Chance," 1; *TDS*, "Just Two Weeks"; *TDS*, "Butch, Problem Child."

55 *TDS*, "Once East End Bad Boy." A similar story of a boy who was "11 but looks 13" explained how "he left the old gang whose influence had brought him to juvenile court." See "Let There Be No Broken Hearts," *TDS*, 7 August 1940, 17.

56 TUA, OCA Papers, 78-006/25/40, Charlie F. Plewman, "The Days Leading Up to the Formation of the Ontario Camping Association," part of poster entitled "Today: Tomorrow's Yesterday," c. 1967.

57 TUA, OCA Sound/Tape Collection, 83-002/2/5, Mary Northway, interview by Cathy Stuart and Warren Anderson, 21 January 1975.

58 Thirteen fresh air camps that served both boys and girls were not included in this sample. All stats from TUA, OCA, "1949 Directory of Member Camps." While the Girl Guides had an OCA entry that indicated 5,400 girls came to their "camps," these were not generally residential camps as they are being spoken of here. Consequently, this number was not included in the sample.

59 Veronica Strong-Boag, *The New Day Recalled: Lives of Girls and Women in English Canada, 1919-1939* (Toronto: Copp Clark Pittman, 1988).

60 Joan Sangster, *Regulating Girls and Women: Sexuality, Family, and the Law in Ontario, 1920-1960* (Don Mills: Oxford University Press, 2001).

61 See Ruth Roach Pierson, *"They're still women after all": The Second World War and Canadian Womanhood* (Toronto: McClelland and Stewart, 1986). The study that set the tone of discussion is Elaine Tyler May, *Homeward Bound: American Families in the Cold War Era* (New York: Basic Books, 1988).

62 Veronica Strong-Boag made more concerted efforts to see women's reasons for gravitating to suburban life. See her "Home-Dreams: Women and the Suburban Experience in Canada, 1945-60," *Canadian Historical Review* 72, 4 (1991): 471-504; and also "'Their side of the story': Women's Voices from Ontario's Suburbs, 1945-1960," in *A Diversity of Women: Ontario, 1945-80*, ed. Joy Parr, 46-74 (Toronto: University of Toronto Press, 1995). On women's wage work, see Joan Sangster, "Doing Two Jobs: The Wage-Earning Mother, 1945-70," in Parr, *A Diversity of Women*, 98-134. Other studies of postwar femininity include Franca Iacovetta, "Gossip, Contest, and Power in the Making of Suburban Bad Girls: Toronto, 1945-60," *Canadian Historical Review* 80, 4 (1999): 585-623; Winnie Breines, *Young, White and Miserable: Growing Up Female in the Fifties* (Boston: Beacon Press, 1992); Stephanie Coontz, *The Way We Never Were: American Families and the Nostalgia Trap* (New York: Basic Books, 1992); Joanne Meyerowitz, *Not June Cleaver: Women and Gender in Postwar America, 1945-1960* (Philadelphia: Temple University Press, 1994).

63 On the expanding opportunities for women in sport and athletics, as well as conservative critiques of the same, see Strong-Boag, *New Day Recalled*, 31-32; Helen Lenskyj, "Femininity First: Sport and Physical Education for Ontario Girls, 1890-1930," *Canadian Journal of History of Sport* 13, 2 (1982): 4-17; M. Ann Hall, "Rarely Have We Asked Why: Reflections on Canadian Women's Experience in Sport," *Atlantis* 6, 1 (1980): 51-60; Helen Lenskyj, "Training for 'True Womanhood': Physical Education for Girls in Ontario Schools, 1890-1920," *Historical Studies in Education* 1, 2 (1990): 205-23.

64 Adele Perry, *On the Edge of Empire: Race, Gender, and the Making of British Columbia* (Toronto: University of Toronto Press, 2001). Marilyn Lake makes a similar argument about the Australian frontier. See Marilyn Lake, *Getting Equal: The History of Australian Feminism* (St Leonard's: Allen and Unwin, 1999). To some extent, such thinking continued to shape thinking in the twentieth century. For instance, all-male mining communities in Ontario were still considered to be wild, untamed spaces due to the lack of female presence.

See Nancy Forestell, "Bachelors, Boarding-houses, and Blind Pigs: Gender Construction in a Multi-ethnic Mining Camp, 1909-1920," in *A Nation of Immigrants: Women, Workers, and Communities in Canadian History, 1840s-1960s*, ed. Franca Iacovetta, Paul Draper, and Robert A. Ventresca, 251-90 (Toronto: University of Toronto Press, 1998).

65 Mary G. Hamilton, *The Call of Algonquin: Biography of a Summer Camp* (Toronto: Ryerson Press, 1958), 7.

66 Ontario Camp Leadership Centre [hereafter OCLC], files in possession of Dorothy Walter, Toronto, Ontario, Marjorie Booth, unpublished paper, "History of the Development of OCLC, Bark Lake," 1973, 17.

67 AO, RG-2-75, box 1, minutes of the National Council on Physical Fitness, 1944.

68 Ibid., 18-21 February 1947.

69 Meg Stanley, "More Than Just a Spare Rib, but Not Quite a Whole Canoe: Some Aspects of Women's Canoe Tripping Experiences, 1900-1940," in *Using Wilderness: Essays on the Evolution of Youth Camping in Ontario,* ed. Bruce W. Hodgins and Bernadine Dodge (Peterborough: Frost Centre for Canadian Heritage and Development Studies, 1992), 55.

70 United Church Archives/Victoria University Archives [hereafter UCA/VUA], CGIT Collection, 85.095C, box 39, file 1, "Camp Halcyon," brochure, 1931.

71 "Once There Was a Princess ... Oh Well ..." *TDS*, 15 August 1941, 10.

72 "Camp Wapomeo," brochure, c. 1928.

73 FSATA, NWA, "Some Advances in Camp Programme, Bolton Camp Report, 1939"; Minutes, Bolton Camp Committee, 17 April 1941.

74 UCA/VUA, CGIT Collection, 85.095C, box 30, file 3, "Report of Ninth Camp Council, 1935," 16-17.

75 The feminine art of presentation was also stressed by the authors, who suggested that, even on the trail, "a few marshmallows [sic] and raisins can turn a pudding into a festive dish." See Mary L. Northway and Flora Morrison, "Adventuring by Canoe in 1941: Part 2," *Camping Magazine* 14, 2 (1942): 2-3.

76 Lundell, *Fires of Friendship*, 28.

77 TUA, Ronald H. Perry Fonds, 82-016/2/8, "Dramatics at Senior Wapomeo," *Canoe Lake Camp Echoes* 4, 2 (1931): 22. Similarly, at Bolton, though the outdoor theatre was meant to accommodate both boys and girls, the 1934 report stated that "naturally" it was used more by the girls' camp. See FSATA, NWA, "A Lilt and a Song to Life: Bolton Camp in 1934," 11.

78 FSATA, NWA, "New Interests at Bolton Camp in 1935," 13.

79 "Two Camps on Lake Scugog Havens for Needy Families," *TDS*, 11 July 1940, 22; "Pavement Is Their Beach, Boys, Girls Eye Country," *TDS*, 3 June 1949, 13; "Lads You Send to Camp Cannot Help but Benefit," *TDS*, 20 June 1940, 4; Lundell, *Fires of Friendship*, 28; TUA, Ronald H. Perry Fonds, 82-016/2/8, "Archery and the Craft Shop," *Canoe Lake Camp Echoes* 3, 1 (1930): 20. Even where the content of activities did not differ, gender could shape their form. For instance, at Bolton, efforts to rid programming of its competitive elements were never applied as fully in the case of boys as they were in the case of girls. The upshot was the naturalization of the view that, especially, older boys – but not girls – "demand a rugged type of individual competition." See FSATA, NWA, "New Interests at Bolton Camp in 1935," 15.

80 TUA, OCA Sound/Tape Collection, 83-002/2/5, Mary Northway, interview by Cathy Stuart and Warren Anderson, 21 January 1975; Sue Ebbs, quoted in Lundell, *Fires of Friendship*, 39.

81 "Give Kiddies Chance Nature Intended," *TDS*, 16 August 1940, 17. The 1920s were apparently most restrictive. For evidence of the early use of uniforms, see TUA, Ronald H. Perry Fonds, 82-016/2/8, *Canoe Lake Camp Echoes* 3, 1 (1930): 52; Hamilton, *Call of Algonquin*, 19-20. At CGIT camps, by at least 1934, the clothing checklist included shorts and, by at least 1946, "slacks" as well. See UCA/VUA, CGIT Collection, 89.095C, box 30, file 1, "Camp Council for Ontario," 1934, 1946. At Wapomeo, in a song written by the campers themselves, one line had girls proudly declaring, "We don't care what we wear." See TUA, Ronald H. Perry Fonds, 82-016/2/8, quoted in *Canoe Lake Camp Echoes* 3, 1 (1930): 58.

82 Cynthia Wright makes the same argument for an earlier period. See her "'Feminine trifles of vast importance': Writing Gender into the History of Consumption," in *Gender Conflicts: New Essays in Women's History*, ed. Franca Iacovetta and Mariana Valverde, 229-69 (Toronto: University of Toronto Press, 1992).

83 FSATA, NWA, minutes, Bolton Camp Committee, 28 September 1944.

84 FSATA, NWA, "Bolton Summer Camp, 1944."

85 TUA, OCA Papers, 78-004/002/031, Bert Danson, transcript of interview by J. Budge, 15 February 1973, 19.

86 Throughout the first half of the twentieth century, female delinquency – largely identified as a working-class problem – was almost solely defined in terms of aberrant sexual behaviour. See Sangster, *Regulating Girls and Women*, chap. 5; Mariana Valverde, "Building Anti-delinquent Communities: Morality, Gender, and Generation in the City," in Iacovetta and Valverde, *Gender Conflicts*, 19-45; Adams, *Trouble with Normal*, chap. 4.; Tamara Myers, "The Voluntary Delinquent: Parents, Daughters, and the Montreal Juvenile Delinquents' Court in 1918," *Canadian Historical Review* 80, 2 (1999): 242-68; Iacovetta, "Gossip, Contest, and Power."

87 Shirley Ford, interview by author, 20 June 2000.

88 Hamilton, *Call of Algonquin*, 146; UCA/VUA, CGIT Collection, 85.095C, box 39, file 4, "Calling All Campers," newsletter, 10 August 1951. For more on the culture of beauty, see Mona Gleason, "Embodied Negotiations: Children's Bodies and Historical Change in Canada, 1930-1960," *Journal of Canadian Studies* 34, 1 (1998): 112-38; Strong-Boag, *New Day Recalled*, 85-86. And, in the American context, see Breines, *Young, White and Miserable*, 95-110; Joan Jacobs Brumberg, *The Body Project: An Intimate History of American Girls* (New York: Vintage Books, 1997); Kathy Peiss, *Hope in a Jar: The Making of America's Beauty Culture* (New York: Metropolitan Books, 1998).

89 OCLC files in possession of Dorothy Walter, Toronto, Ontario, OCLC Survey, c. 1953; Gord Wright, interview by Marjorie Booth, 26 November 1973, Alliston, Ontario. Others seemed to agree that the same activities were not always suitable for girls and for boys. For instance, "work parties" at the Statten camps in the 1950s involved boys assisting in the building of new log cabins, while girls "help[ed] ... to clear the brush and prepare ... meals." See TUA, Adele and Harry Ebbs Papers, 80-014/1/8, "The Taylor Statten Camps," brochure, c. 1950.

90 Gord Wright, Interview by Marjorie Booth, 26 November 1973, Alliston, Ontario.

91 TUA, OCA Papers, 82-009/2/2, Northway Lodge: "A Pioneer Camp for Girls," brochure, c. 1941.

92 TUA, OCA Papers, 72-007/2/9, "Wapomeo Staff Chart," 1952; Doreen Dowler, Hank Laurier, and Hedley G. "Bill" Dimock, all quoted in Lundell, *Fires of Friendship*, 32, 87; Hamilton, *Call of Algonquin*, 132.

93 TUA, OCA Papers, 82-009/2/2, Ann R. Prewitt, "The Lasting Aspect of a Seventy-five-year-old Camp," 1980.
94 This was the view of one 1950s era interviewee quoted in Neil Sutherland, *Growing Up: Childhood in English Canada from the Great War to the Age of Television* (Toronto: University of Toronto Press, 1997), 65.
95 Strong-Boag notes that girls' groups like the Guides, the CGIT, and the Junior Red Cross all encouraged girls to accept "new responsibilities of modern citizenship." See Strong-Boag, *New Day Recalled*, 30. Making a similar case, Margaret Prang takes an in-depth look at the CGIT in "The Girl God Would Have Me Be: The Canadian Girls in Training, 1915-1939," *Canadian Historical Review* 66, 2 (1978): 154-93. What little work has been done on girls' summer camps also suggests they offered a venue in which to explore less traditional notions of girlhood, even if they also sometimes reinforced them. See Anna H. Lathrop, "'Strap a compass and knife and an axe to your belt': The Role of Camp Counselor Training in the Socialization of Women at the Margaret Eaton School (1925-1941)," and Susan L. Forbes, "'Nothing but a rag between you and the sky': Northway Lodge Girls' Camp and the Wilderness Experience," papers given to the Canadian Historical Association Conference, Edmonton, 24-29 May 2000. Historians of girls' camping in the United States have come to similar conclusions. See Leslie Paris, "The Adventures of Peanut and Bo: Summer Camps and Early-twentieth-century American Girlhood," *Journal of Women's History* 12, 4 (2001): 47-76; Miller, "Girls in Nature."
96 Studies of women who took up interests in nature activities are still very limited. See Karen Routledge, "Being a Girl without Being a Girl: Gender and Mountaineering on Mount Waddington, 1926-36," *BC Studies* 141 (2004): 31-58; Pearl Ann Reichwein and Karen Fox, "Margaret Fleming and the Alpine Club of Canada: A Woman's Place in Mountain Leisure and Literature, 1932-1952," *Journal of Canadian Studies* 36, 3 (2001): 35-60; Anna H. Lathrop, "Strap an axe to your belt," 110-25. Stanley," "More Than a Spare Rib"; Michele Lacombe, "'Songs of the open road': Bon Echo, Urban Utopians and the Cult of Nature," *Journal of Canadian Studies* 33, 2 (1998): 152-67; Betty Spears, "Mary, Mary, Quite Contrary, Why Do Women Play?" *Canadian Journal of History of Sport* 18, 1 (1987): 67-75.
97 Mary Northway's life-long career in academic psychology and her connection to renowned psychologist William Blatz are noted in the Introduction, note 61.
98 TUA, OCA Sound/Tape Collection, 83-002/005/008, Barb Gilchrist, interview by Jack Pearse, 6 November 1986.
99 Lundell, *Fires of Friendship*, 28.
100 TUA, OCA Papers, 86-018/6/39, "Camp Wapomeo, Canoe Trip Requirements," 1947.
101 Northway and Morrison, "Adventuring by Canoe," 8. Before being sent out on trips, Tapawingo's campers were expected to prove swimming, diving, and paddling abilities as well as knowing how to save a dumped canoe and to swim it to shore. Tapawingo references from TUA, OCA Papers, 72-007/2/5, Toronto YWCA, "Camp Tapawingo," 1951. The Northway Lodge administration, which had girls living in tents (and not cabins) throughout this period, claimed quite simply that "it never rains at Northway." In later years this was explained as being not a literal truth but, rather, an expression of the camp's refusal to "recognize rain as an impediment." See Prewitt, "The Lasting Aspect."
102 Elizabeth Shapiro, e-mail interview by author, 17 February 2001. Similarly remembering "a rough, rough, trip" along the Mattawa and Ottawa rivers in the 1920s, Mary Northway explained, "We were always known as the girls who had gone to Mattawa and back." See TUA, OCA Sound/Tape Collection, 83-002/2/5, Mary Northway, interview by Cathy Stuart and Warren Anderson, 21 January 1975.

103 Joan Moses, interview by author, 26 July 2000.
104 Geraldine Sherman, "The Girls of Summer," *Toronto Life* (September 2001), 103.
105 TUA, OCA Papers, 72-007/2/5, Toronto YWCA, "Camp Tapawingo," 1951.
106 Hamilton, *Call of Algonquin*, 35.
107 Quoted in Hamilton, *Call of Algonquin*, 37.
108 Judith Ridout, "The Beginnings of Tanamakoon," transcript of address given at Camp Tanamakoon Reunion, Toronto, July 2000. For Rangers' programs at other camps, see UCCA, Biography Files – A.L. Cochrane, Parkyn Ian Murray re: A.L. Cochrane, 1940; TUA, Adele and Harry Ebbs Papers, 80-014/1/8, Virginia T. Cobb to Mr. and Mrs. Taylor Statten, 16 February 1942, and response from Adele Ebbs, n.d.
109 Mary L. Northway, *Appraisal of the Social Development of Children at a Summer Camp* (Toronto: University of Toronto Press, 1940), 54-55.
110 Sherman, "Girls of Summer," 101.
111 Hamilton, *Call of Algonquin*, 117.
112 Ibid., 38.
113 Mary Murphy, interview by author, 7 June 2000.
114 Marta Danylewycz, "Domestic Science Education in Ontario, 1900-1940," in *Gender and Education in Ontario: An Historical Reader*, ed. Ruby Heap and Alison Prentice, 129-47 (Toronto: Canadian Scholar's Press, 1991); Robert M. Stamp, "Teaching Girls Their 'God-given Place in Life': The Introduction to Home Economics in the Schools," *Atlantis* 2, 2, pt. 1 (1977): 18-34; Robert M. Stamp, "Canadian High Schools in the 1920s and 1930s: The Social Challenge to the Academic Tradition," Canadian Historical Association, *Historical Papers* (1978): 76-93; Strong-Boag, *New Day Recalled*, 18, 22; Sutherland, *Growing Up*, 214-15; Lenskyj, "Femininity First," and "Training for 'True Womanhood'"; Adams, *Trouble with Normal*, 80.
115 For reactions to coeducation in other environments, see Sara Z. Burke, "'Being unlike man': Challenges to Co-education at the University of Toronto, 1884-1909," *Ontario History* 93, 1 (2001): 11-31; Carol Dyhouse, *No Distinction of Sex? Women in British Universities, 1870-1939* (London: UCL Press, 1995); Sally Schwager, "Educating Women in America," *Signs: Journal of Women in Culture and Society* 12, 2 (1987): 362-65; Charlotte Williams Conable, *Women at Cornell: The Myth of Equal Education* (Ithaca: Cornell University Press, 1977).
116 Lundell, *Fires of Friendship*, 27.
117 Donald Burry, "A History of the Taylor Statten Camps" (MSc thesis, University of Saskatchewan, 1985), 32.
118 TUA, Adele and Harry Ebbs Papers, 80-014/1/8, "The Taylor Statten Camps," brochure, c. 1950.
119 Lundell, *Fires of Friendship*, 95. Bolton Camp established a similar boundary marker at their camp for boys and girls. Even during periods of free time, the possibility of chance meetings between the sexes was strictly ruled out by the establishment of "the rock" – a large boulder that marked the boundary between the girls' and boys' camps. Campers from both sides were prohibited from travelling beyond it, as Eugene Cashia remembers. See Eugene Cashia, interview by author, 22 August 2000.
120 As ex-camper and academic Don Burry points out, after chapel "it was straight to the canoes and back to Wapomeo." See Donald Burry, "A History of the Taylor Statten Camps," 32.
121 Ibid., 33.
122 Taylor Statten, *Talks to Counsellors*, 1928, 2.

123 Dimock and Statten, *Talks to Counselors*, 31.
124 Staff members were cautioned against "putting their arms around campers" or any other display of "physical familiarity." See Taylor Statten Camps, *Talks to Counsellors*, 1928, 2.
125 TUA, OCA Papers, 98-019/13/10, "Notes from the Course in Camp Education, Margaret Eaton School," 10 February-17 March 1937, 2.
126 TUA, Northway Family Fonds – Additions, 90-016/1/25, Mary Northway, "What Are the Camps Achieving," *Camping Magazine* 9, 8 (1937).
127 TUA, OCA Papers, 98-019/13/10, "Notes from the Course in Camp Education, 2.
128 Bert Danson, interview by author, 12 June 2000. On the other hand, just because they shared the same craft class did not mean that boys and girls worked on the same projects or, when it came to baseball or basketball, that they competed together. On the contrary, the wishes of male campers, who, apparently, "didn't want any part of the girls," prevailed. Ibid.
129 TUA, OCA Papers, 78-004/2/31, Bert Danson, transcript of interview by J. Budge, 15 February 1973, 7-8.
130 Ibid., 43.
131 TUA, Sound/Tape Collection, 83-002/5/5, Irwin Haladner, interview by Adele Ebbs, 4 May 1982.
132 Douglas Creelman, interview by author, 23 June 2000.
133 Lundell, *Fires of Friendship*, 27; Bert Danson also cited the need to accommodate directors' children as instigating thought about co-ed camps. See Danson, interview by author, 12 June 2000.
134 Lundell, *Fires of Friendship*, 27; Danson claims the coeducational option appeared so attractive that other Jewish camps in the province were forced to follow suit merely to remain competitive. See TUA, OCA Papers, 78-004/2/31, Bert Danson, transcript of interview with J. Budge, 15 February 1973, 43. Understanding why camps that took the coeducational imperative most seriously all catered to a mainly Jewish clientele is an interesting question, not fully answerable here. Bert Danson's belief that this was simply a matter of each camp's following suit to stay competitive with Winnebagoe raises the question of why coeducation had such marked appeal in the Jewish community. He himself was well aware that there were other interpretations of this phenomenon, relating, as he put it, to "the Jewish family concept." In fact, it doesn't seem unlikely that, in a time of still widely accepted anti-Semitism, many parents who were contemplating their children's future would consider marriage within the ethnic-religious group as a natural prerequisite for happiness – as, indeed, it was so deemed in Anglo-Protestants and Anglo-Catholic communities as well. Especially for children outside large urban centres, camp provided a chance to connect with a broader Jewish community and to meet possible future mates – as we have seen, a not insignificant objective of the overall project. Finally, considered by others as already beyond the cultural mainstream, Jewish camp administrators may have felt freer to experiment with new ideas.
135 One Glen Bernard camper from the 1940s recalls encountering a group of boy campers while both were out canoe tripping one summer. "It was giggle, giggle, giggle," remembers Shirley Ford, "and then the boys might offer to carry our canoes, and we might have a snack at the end of the portage. And it was giggle, giggle, giggle, but that was about it." See Shirley Ford, interview by author, 20 June 2000. Bert Danson had much the same impression of his own stay at an all-boys camp in Maine when a group of girls came to visit. See Bert Danson, interview by author, 12 June 2000.

136 Adams, *Trouble with Normal*, 10-11; On the "ubiquity" of public expressions of heterosexuality in the postwar period, see Karen Dubinsky, *The Second Greatest Disappointment: Honeymooning and Tourism at Niagara Falls* (Toronto: Between the Lines, 1999), chap. 8.

137 On dance halls, see Cynthia Comacchio, "Dancing to Perdition: Adolescence and Leisure in Interwar English Canada," *Journal of Canadian Studies* 32, 3 (1997): 5-35; Adams, *Trouble with Normal*, 79-80; Katyl Peiss, *Cheap Amusements: Working Women and Leisure in Turn-of-the-Century New York* (Philadelphia: Temple University Press, 1986). For the rise of the new dating culture, which replaced the older nineteenth-century tradition of "calling," see Beth L. Bailey, *From Front Porch to Back Seat: Courtship in Twentieth-century America* (Baltimore: Johns Hopkins University Press, 1988.)

138 Stamp, "Canadian High Schools"; Adams, *Trouble with Normal*, 77.

139 TUA, Adele and Harry Ebbs Papers, 80-014/1/8, "The Taylor Statten Camps," brochure, c. 1950.

140 J.D. Ketchum quoted in Lathrop, "Strap a compass," 13.

141 Ibid., 6.

142 TUA, Adele and Harry Ebbs Papers, 80-014/1/1, Hedley G. Dimock, "Coeducational Camping in Brother-Sister Camps," February 1951.

143 Dimock, "Coeducational Camping," 4.

144 TUA, OCA Fonds, 72-007/2/7, Camp Winnebagoe, brochure, 1946; Bert Danson, interview by author, 12 June 2000; Anonymous Arawhon camper, e-mail interview by author, 27 July 2000; Sylvia Silbert, interview by author, 16 June 2000.

145 Sherman, "Girls of Summer," 102.

146 Dimock, "Coeducational Camping," 3.

147 TUA, Adele and Harry Ebbs Papers, 80-014/1/4, "Christmas Letter from Chief and Tonakela [Taylor and Ethel Statten]," 1956.

148 Certainly, though no sociologist would regard dating as a "natural" phenomenon, at least it was initiated by youth themselves, away from the controlling eye of adults.

149 Sylvia Silbert, interview by author, 16 June 2000; Jim Buchanan, interview by author, 21 July 2000.

150 Elizabeth Shapiro, e-mail interview by author, 17 February 2001.

151 Dimock, "Coeducational Camping," 7-8. Geraldine Sherman recalls of Kawagama that the administration "encouraged relations between boys and girls in groups – though never in pairs," while an ex-Arowhon camper agreed that, despite the organizing of dances and socials, "there was not a great stress on socializing as individuals." See Sherman, "Girls of Summer," 102; Anonymous Arowhon camper, e-mail interview by author, 27 July 2000.

152 Bert Danson, interview by author, 12 June 2000; TUA, Adele and Harry Ebbs Papers, 80-014/1/7, "Wapomeo – Camp Routines," 1958.

153 Adams concludes that, "in typical models of heterosexual development, there existed a secure place for same-sex attractions or crushes," a phenomenon that opened up a degree of cultural space for the expression of youthful homoerotic desire. See Adams, *Trouble with Normal*, 93.

154 Quoted in Hamilton, *Call of Algonquin*, 90.

155 Mary Northway, "Security Pegs for Campers," *Camping Magazine* 14, 4 (1942): 3-7.

156 Under Freudian influence, observers seem also to have become somewhat preoccupied with interpreting behaviour in sexual terms, as the *Crestwood Heights* example also suggests. Note the authors' further observations: "In one mixed camp (which included age groups

from five to eleven), several instances of homosexual crushes between both boys and boys, and girls and girls were noted, and also a few cases of heterosexual attachments, the friendship between a five-year-old girl and a five-and-a-half year-old boy being the most exceptional" (Seeley et al., *Crestwood Heights*, 324, 325).

157 UCA/VUA, CGIT Collection, 85.095C, box 39, file 4, "Calling All Campers," 1952 newsletter. Similarly, an all-girl square dance at a CGIT camp in 1955 and some all-girl theatre at Wapomeo meant that some girls, on occasion, stood in as temporary boys, allowing them to experiment with distinctly non-feminine roles and certainly not repressing any tomboyish tendencies. See UCA/VUA, CGIT Collection, 85.095C, box 42, file 49, Ryde Lake CGIT camp newsletter, 1955; Lundell, *Fires of Friendship*, photo, 72.

158 See John d'Emilio, "The Homosexual Menace: the Politics of Sexuality in Cold War America," in *Passion and Power: Sexuality in History*, ed. Kathy Peiss and Robert A. Padgug, 226-40 (Philadelphia: Temple University Press, 1989). And, in the Canadian context, Daniel J. Robinson and David Kimmel, "The Queer Career of Homosexual Security Vetting in Cold War Canada," *Canadian Historical Review* 75 (1994): 319-45; Gary Kinsmen, "Character Weakness and 'Fruit Machines': Towards an Analysis of the Anti-homosexual Security Campaign in the Canadian Civil Service," *Labour/Le Travail* 35 (1995): 133-61. For studies that see not only the oppression of gays and lesbians in this period but also a certain tolerance of homoerotic tendencies and the "vibrancy" of gay culture, see Adams, *Trouble with Normal*, 91-8; Eric Setliff, "Sex Fiends or Swish Kids? Gay Men in Hush Free Press, 1946-1956," in *Gendered Pasts: Historical Essays in Femininity and Masculinity in Canada*, ed. Kathryn McPherson, Cecilia Morgan, and Nancy Forestell, 158-78 (Toronto: Oxford University Press, 1999).

159 OCA, *Ontario Camp Bulletin*, edition 1, 1946.

160 TUA, OCA, "Directory of Member Camps," 1949.

161 TUA, OCA Papers, 72-007/2/6, "Wabi-kon: A Summer Camp for Boys and Girls," brochure, c. 1950.

162 Elizabeth Shapiro, e-mail interview by author, 25 February 2001. Another ex-camper admits she doesn't recall hearing about even the existence of co-ed camps during her childhood and youth. See Jane Hughes, interview by author, 26 June 2000.

163 Douglas Creelman, interview by author, 23 June 2000.

164 James W. Buchanan, interview by author, 22 July 2000, Toronto.

165 Back, *Keewaydin Way*, 162.

166 Shirley Ford, interview by author, 20 June 2000.

167 Jane Hughes, interview by author, 26 June 2000.

168 Marjorie Royce, interview by author, 24 August 2000.

169 Elizabeth Shapiro, e-mail interview by author, 25 February 2001.

170 Jim Buchanan, interview by author, 21 July 2000.

171 Dimock, "Coeducational Camping," 2-3.

172 Sylvia Silbert, interview by author, 16 June 2000.

173 James Felstiner, e-mail interview by author, April 2001.

174 Sherman, "Girls of Summer," 103.

175 Joan Moses, interview by author, 26 July 2000.

176 Deborah Wilson, "Upper Crust Recalls Summer Camp: 65-Year History Honoured," *Globe and Mail*, 20 October 1986.

177 TUA, OCA Sound/Tape Collection, 83-002/5/8, Barbara Gilchrist, interview by Jack Pearse, 6 November 1986.

178 Elizabeth Shapiro, e-mail interview by author, 25 February 2001. Other campers – even some not directly involved – confirm the popularity of the tower as an after-dark meeting spot. See H. Laurier to Donald Burry, 8 February 1985, quoted in Burry, "A History of the Taylor Statten Camps," 33; Jim Buchanan, interview by author, 21 July 2000.

179 Lundell, *Fires of Friendship*, 86.

180 Anonymous Arowhon camper, e-mail interview by author, 27 July 2000; Sherman, "Girls of Summer," 102; Joan Moses, interview by author, 26 July 2000.

181 Bert Danson, Interview by author, 12 June 2000; Douglas Creelman, interview by author, 23 June 2000. Taylor Statten was also aware of the dangers in this area, stating: "Many a boy has worried himself sick through morbid introspection aroused by some act of physical intimacy on the part of a man of homosexual desires." See Statten, *Talks to Counsellors*, 2

182 Dimock, "Coeducational Camping," 5, 6.

183 On the drive-in theatre, see Doug Owram, *Born at the Right Time: A History of the Baby Boom Generation* (Toronto: University of Toronto Press, 1996), 151-52. On the possibilities for teenage sexual experimentation in school yards and public parks, see Mary Louise Adams, "Almost Anything Can Happen: A Search for Sexual Discourse in the Urban Spaces of 1940s Toronto," *Canadian Journal of Sociology* 19, 2 (1994): 217-32. Indeed, Keith Walden points out that, even by the latter decades of the nineteenth century, youth had been taking advantage of (and observers had been worried about) the possibilities for privacy at Centre Island's Hanlan's Point. See Keith Walden, *Becoming Modern in Toronto: The Industrial Exhibition and the Shaping of Late Victorian Culture* (Toronto: University of Toronto Press, 1997), 255-56. Again, Bailey's study makes the point, more generally, that modern dating culture became an increasingly private act carried out in public spaces, outside parental view and control. See Bailey, *Front Porch to Back Seat.*

184 Doreen Dowler, quoted in Lundell, *Fires of Friendship*, 32. As a young counsellor-in-training, David Bawden also remembers his mad crush on a female counsellor. "Can you imagine," he asked, years after, "being sent out on [a] three-day canoe trip as her CIT?" See David Bawden, e-mail interview by author, 31 January 2001.

185 In one case, the geographical clustering of camps allowed one teenage camper to carry out his own devious plan. In the early 1930s, "he, with another camper, visited a girls' camp, posed as counsellors from Ahmek, borrowed a canoe from a visitor at the camp without the owner's permission, and went out paddling with a maid who worked at the camp." See Dimock and Hendry, *Camping and Character*, 193.

186 Sherman, "Girls of Summer," 103.

187 OCA, "Directory of Member Camps," 1949; OCA Guide, 2000. An interesting shift also occurred in the relative number of single-sex camps. In 1949, half of the total number of camps were for boys only, and roughly one-third accommodated girls. By 2000, this had reversed itself to a mere 10 percent for boys only and one-fifth for girls only. To explain this shift I would offer, again, that more recent child-rearing methods, influenced by feminist thought, look positively on the notion of educating girls "on their own," while, in contrast, boys are still regarded as benefiting from the "civilizing" influence of girls. The weight of tradition also helps explain the persistence of certain single-sex camps as many are from among the oldest camps in the province.

188 TUA, OCA Papers, 78-004/002/31, Bert Danson, transcript of interview by J. Budge, 15 February 1973.

Chapter 6: Totem Poles, Tepees, and Token Traditions

1 As far as Edgar's Indian name goes, the camp claimed it translated as "friend of children." See Trent University Archives [hereafter TUA], Ontario Camping Association [hereafter OCA] Papers, 72-007/5/16, Mary S. Edgar, "Our Indebtedness to Our Indian Friends," c. 1971. For the remainder of this chapter I use the term "Indian," without the cumbersome quotation marks, to refer to the white-manufactured notion this represented. Otherwise, I use the terms "Aboriginal" and/or "Native" to refer to actual First Nations peoples. My sincere thanks to the four anonymous reviewers from the *Canadian Historical Review* for their comments on an earlier version of this chapter.

2 On Pauline Johnson, see Veronica Strong-Boag and Carole Gerson, *Paddling Her Own Canoe: The Times and Texts of E. Pauline Johnson (Tekahionwake)* (Toronto: University of Toronto Press, 2000); Cecilia Morgan, "'A wigwam to Westminster': Performing Mohawk Identity in Imperial Britain, 1890s-1990s," *Gender and History* 15, 2 (2003): 319-41. On Native participation in fairs, rodeos, and Buffalo Bill shows, see Keith Regular, "On Public Display," *Alberta History* 34, 1 (1986): 1-10; Glen Mikkelsen, "Indians and Rodeo," *Alberta History* 34, 1 (1986): 13-19; L.G. Moses, *Wild West Shows and the Images of American Indians, 1883-1933* (Albuquerque: University of New Mexico Press, 1996); and Bobby Bridger, *Buffalo Bill and Sitting Bull: Inventing the Wild West* (Austin: University of Texas Press, 2002). On Grey Owl, see, among others, Donald B. Smith, *From the Land of Shadows: The Making of Grey Owl* (Saskatoon: Western Producer Prairie Books, 1990). On other "wannabee Indians," see Donald B. Smith, *Long Lance: The True Story of an Imposter* (Toronto: Macmillan, 1982); Shari Huhndorf, *Going Native: Indians in the American Cultural Imagination* (Ithaca: Cornell University Press, 2001).

3 C.A.M. Edwards, *Taylor Statten* (Toronto: Ryerson Press, 1960), 88.

4 In addition to exploring racial play-acting in its "Indian" forms, Paris also traces the fascinating history of blackface minstrelsy at summer camp. See Leslie Paris, "Children's Nature: Summer Camps in New York State, 1919-1941" (PhD diss., University of Michigan, 2000). For other accounts of the use of Native imagery at camp, see also Nancy Mykoff, "A Jewish Season: Ethnic American Culture at Children's Summer Camp, 1918-1941" (PhD diss., New York University, 2002), 89-96.

5 Peter Stallybrass and Allon White, *The Politics and Poetics of Transgression* (Ithaca: Cornell University Press, 1986), 4.

6 Hartmut Lutz, "Cultural Appropriation as a Process of Displacing Peoples and History," *Canadian Journal of Native Studies* 10, 2 (1990): 167-82. For more on the late 1980s-90s discussion surrounding the controversial issue of cultural appropriation in Canadian literature and culture, see Joanne Cardinal-Shubert, "In the Red," *Fuse*, Fall 1989, 20-28; Lee Maracle, "Native Myths: Trickster Alive and Crowing," *Fuse*, Fall 1989, 29-31; Richard Hill, "One Part Per Million: White Appropriation and Native Voices," *Fuse*, Winter 1992. For a history of white appropriation of Native culture in Canada, see Daniel Francis, *The Imaginary Indian: The Image of the Indian in Canadian Culture* (Vancouver: Arsenal Pulp Press, 1992). For American studies, see also Thomas Parkhill, *Weaving Ourselves into the Land: Charles Godfrey Leland, "Indians," and the Study of Native American Religions* (Albany: State University of New York Press, 1997; and Ward Churchill's highly polemical *Indians Are Us? Culture and Genocide in Native North America* (Monroe: Common Courage Press, 1994).

7 Philip Deloria, *Playing Indian* (New Haven and London: Yale University Press, 1998); Huhndorf, *Going Native*; Rayna Green, "The Tribe Called Wannabee" *Folklore* 99 (1988): 30-57; Mark C. Carnes, "Middle-class Men and the Solace of Fraternal Ritual," in *Meanings for Manhood: Constructions of Masculinity in Victorian America*, ed. Mark C. Carnes and Clyde Griffen, 37-52 (Chicago/London: University of Chicago Press, 1990). Gillian Poulter, "Becoming Native in a Foreign Land: Visual Culture, Sport and Spectacle in the Construction of National Identity in Montreal, 1840-1885" (PhD diss., York University, 1999). Also useful in this context is Robert F. Berkhofer, Jr., *The White Man's Indian: Images of the American Indian from Columbus to the Present* (New York: Vintage Books, 1979 [1978]).

8 Edwards, *Taylor Statten*, 88. For more on Seton, see Introduction, note 20. On Seton's influence on American summer camps, see Deloria, *Playing Indian*, 95-110; Jay Mechling, "Playing Indian," *Prospects* 5 (1980): 18-21. On Seton at Ahmek, see TUA, OCA Sound/Tape Collection, 83-002/10/9, Adele Ebbs, interview by Jack Pearse, 22 May 1986.

9 Bert Danson, "The History of Camp Winnebagoe," unpublished paper, May 2000.

10 Family Service Association of Toronto Archival Collection [hereafter FSATA], Neighbourhood Workers' Association [hereafter NWA], "The Story of Bolton Camp," in booklet entitled "After Twenty Years: A Short History of the Neighbourhood Workers' Association," 1938, 43; Hedley S. Dimock and Charles E. Hendry, *Camping and Character: A Camp Experiment in Character Education* (New York: Association Press, 1929), 74. For more detail on the general set-up of Indian council rings, see W.J. Eastaugh, "Indian Council Ring," booklet (Taylor Statten Camps, n.d.).

11 TUA, OCA Papers, 98-019/13/6, series E, Adele Ebbs Papers, Mary L. Northway, "Canadian Camping: Its Foundation and Its Future," address given to the Manitoba Camping Association Annual Meeting, May 1946, 1.

12 Dimock and Hendry, *Camping and Character*, 74-75.

13 In the end, she was proud to declare: "Tanamakoon is a salutation meaning, in the Indian tongue, 'Hail fellow, well met.'" See Mary G. Hamilton, *The Call of Algonquin: Biography of a Summer Camp* (Toronto: Ryerson Press, 1958), 14; On Glen Bernard Camp, see TUA, OCA Sound/Tape Collection, 83-002/5/8, Barbara Gilchrist, interview by Jack Pearse, 6 November 1986.

14 TUA, Northway Family Fonds – Additions, 90-016/1/34, "Northway Recollection of Glen Bernard Camp," 16 May 1982; Northway, "Canadian Camping."

15 Barbara Gilchrist, interview by Jack Pearse, 6 November 1986.

16 Eastaugh, "Indian Council Ring," 12, 21.

17 FSATA, NWA, "Fresh Air Report – Season of 1933," 7.

18 Robert Berkhofer makes this argument with regard to the writings of James Fenimore Cooper, but his landmark study also stands as a general history and critique of white creation of the undifferentiated "Indian." See Berkhofer, *White Man's Indian*. See also Mechling, "Playing Indian." On Bolton's Indian programming, see FSATA, NWA, "Bolton Camp: Report of Operation, 1937." On Ahmek's council ring, see Dimock and Hendry, *Camping and Character*, 73-75. On Ahmek's Indian village, see TUA, Ronald H. Perry Fonds, "The War Whoop," *Canoe Lake Camp Echoes* 4, 3 (June 1931): 53.

19 Eastaugh, "Indian Council Ring," 30.

20 On the trend towards secularization, see Ramsay Cook, *The Regenerators: Social Criticism in Late Victorian English Canada* (Toronto: University of Toronto Press, 1985); David B. Marshall, *Secularizing the Faith: Canadian Protestant Clergy and the Crisis of Belief, 1850-1940* (Toronto: University of Toronto Press, 1992).

21 While scholars debate the timing, causes, nature, and ultimate impact of this transition, they generally agree that evangelicalism gave way to liberal Protestantism in the first half of the twentieth century. See Richard Allen, *The Social Passion: Religion and Social Reform in Canada, 1914-18* (Toronto: University of Toronto Press, 1971); Cook, *The Regenerators*; Nancy Christie and Michael Gauvreau, *A Full-orbed Christianity: The Protestant Churches and Social Welfare in Canada* (Montreal/Kingston: McGill-Queen's University Press, 1996); Catherine Gidney, *A Long Eclipse: The Liberal Protestant Establishment and the Canadian University, 1920-1970* (Montreal/Kingston: McGill-Queen's University Press, 2004); Gary Miedema, *For Canada's Sake: Public Religion, Centennial Celebrations, and the Re-making of Canada in the 1960s* (Montreal/Kingston: McGill-Queen's University Press, 2005).

22 United Church Archives/Victoria University Archives [hereafter UCA/VCA], 85.095C, box 30, file 3, "Seventh and Eighth Ontario Camp Council," 1934; "The Significance of a Christian Decision," *The Torch* 4, 4 (1928): 56; Marjorie Trotter, "A Girls' Religion," *The Torch* 9, 2 (1933): 38.

23 FSATA, NWA, "Camp as an Educational Opportunity: The Story of Bolton Camp for 1936," 12; FSATA, NWA, "Log of Bolton Camp, 1941," 1.

24 Hedley S. Dimock and Taylor Statten, *Talks to Counselors* (New York: Association Press, 1939), 77; Dimock and Hendry, *Camping and Character*, 138-39.

25 Edwards, *Taylor Statten*, 18. This ratio of religious to secular camps is based, again, on the *Ontario Camping Association 1949 Directory of Member Camps.*

26 Dimock and Hendry, *Camping and Character*, 141-42. Elsewhere it was stated: "The spirit of Bolton Camp denotes kindness and consideration and thoughtfulness for others and whenever there is that, there is God." See FSATA, NWA, "Log of Bolton Camp, 1941."

27 Dimock and Hendry, *Camping and Character*, 129, 141-42.

28 Seton, quoted in Mechling, "Playing Indian," 20. Longfellow, quoted in Helen Carr, *Inventing the American Primitive: Politics, Gender and the Representation of Native American Literary Traditions, 1789-1936* (New York: New York University Press, 1996), 135.

29 FSATA, NWA, "After Twenty Years," 43.

30 Dimock and Hendry, *Camping and Character*, 141.

31 Eastaugh, "Indian Council Ring," 1.

32 FSATA, NWA, "New Interests at Bolton Camp in 1935," 8; Edgar, "Our Indebtedness," 2.

33 Eastaugh, "Indian Council Ring," 7; TUA, Ontario Camp Leadership Centre, Bark Lake Fonds, 98-012/1/1, "Notes on Programme – Bark Lake," 1948.

34 "Five Years of Drudgery Bring Proud, Brave Family to End of Their Resources," *TDS*, 30 August 1927, 21. A 1952 issue of *Saturday Night* remarked, "This outdoor activity hardens muscles, tans the skin, and develops appetites one can only ... regard with awe." See Nancy Cleaver, "An Old Canadian Custom – Sending the Kids to Camp," *Saturday Night*, 19 April 1952, 17. Deloria points out that "a brown face ... demonstrated one's contact with the out-of-doors and nature, but it also signified a step back into a pre-modern time zone," while Paris notes the tan's "usefulness as a symbol of short-term, regenerative primitivism." See also Deloria, *Playing Indian*, 106; Paris, "Children's Nature," 243.

35 Bark Lake Fonds, "Notes on Programme – Bark Lake," 1948; Dimock and Hendry, *Camping and Character*, photo, 74; FSATA, Bolton Camp Photo Albums, 1920s-1950s.

36 Dimock and Hendry, *Camping and Character*, 139-40.

37 Eastaugh, "Indian Council Ring," 1.

38 A. Eustace Haydon, "Memorial Talk Delivered to Camp Ahmek – Founders' Day," 12 July 1959, quoted in Donald Burry, "A History of the Taylor Statten Camps" (MSc thesis, University of Saskatchewan, 1985), 27. Emphasis in original.

39 UCA/VUA, 85.095C, box 30, file 3, "Report of the Fifth Ontario Camp Council, 1931," 15.

40 W.A. Milks, ed. *The Camp Director's Manual* (Ontario Boys' Work Board, n.d.), 21-22. For the use of Indian imagery in promoting CGIT camping, see Helen E. D'Avignon, "Planning the Rally for Camp Promotion," *The Torch* 1, 5 (1925): 70; UCA/VUA, CGIT Collection, 85.095C, box 31, file 3, "Ontario Leadership Camp, 1927," brochure. On Pine Crest, see TUA, Camp Pine Crest Fonds, 78-009/2/1, Camp Pine Crest, "Annual Report," 1940.

41 Hamilton, *Call of Algonquin*, 4.

42 Edgar, "Our Indebtedness," 2.

43 On the borrowing of Indian culture to establish "Canadian" traditions, see Gerta Moray, "Wilderness, Modernity and Aboriginality in the Paintings of Emily Carr," *Journal of Canadian Studies* 33, 2 (1998): 1-23; Douglas Cole, "The Invented Indian/The Imagined Emily," *BC Studies* 125/26 (2000): 147-62; Terry Goldie, *Fear and Temptation: The Image of the Indigene in Canadian, Australian, and New Zealand Literatures* (Montreal/Kingston: McGill-Queen's University Press, 1989); Poulter, "Becoming Native in a Foreign Land"; Francis, *Imaginary Indian*, 190. Others who have researched whites playing Indian argue that distancing Euro-North Americans from the truth of their colonial past was its main function. See Deloria, *Playing Indian*; Huhndorf, *Going Native*. For two examples and also for the socio-political impact of the salvage paradigm in Canadian anthropology, see Peter Kulchyski, "Anthropology in the Service of the State: Diamond Jenness and Canadian Indian Policy," *Journal of Canadian Studies* 28, 2 (1993): 21-50; Andrew Nurse, "'But now things have changed': Marius Barbeau and the Politics of Amerindian Identity," *Ethnohistory* 48, 3 (2001): 433-72.

44 TUA, Ronald H. Perry Fonds, 82-016/2/8, *Canoe Lake Camp Echoes* 4, 3 (1931): 18.

45 "Pale-faced City Tikes Taught Indian Lore by Expert Woodsmen," *TDS*, 7 June 1950, 25; UCA/VUA, 85.095C, box 39, file 4, "Calling All Campers," newsletter, 1952.

46 Brian Back, *The Keewaydin Way: A Portrait, 1893-1983* (Temagami: Keewaydin Camp Ltd., 1983), 37.

47 For histories of blackface, see David Roediger, *The Wages of Whiteness: Race and the Making of the American Working Class* (London/New York: Verso, 1991), 115-32; Eric Lott, *Love and Theft: Blackface Minstrelsy and the American Working Class* (New York: Oxford University Press, 1993); Michael Rogin, *Blackface, White Noise: Jewish Immigrants in the Hollywood Melting Pot* (Berkeley: University of California Press, 1996). According to Leslie Paris, at American summer camps, black Others were similarly presented in grotesque forms, but the performance of nostalgic minstrel songs recalling southern homes may also have offered an emotional container for campers' own feelings of homesickness. See Paris, "Children's Nature," 261.

48 McKay, *Quest of the Folk*, 12.

49 On Western primitivism, see Adam Kuper, *The Invention of Primitive Society: Transformations of an Illusion* (London/New York: Routledge, 1988); Marianna Torgovnick, *Gone Primitive: Savage Intellects, Modern Lives* (Chicago: University of Chicago Press, 1990); Julian Stallabrass, "The Idea of the Primitive: British Art and Anthropology 1918-1930," *New Left Review* 183 (Fall 1990): 95-115; Bederman, *Manliness and Civilization*, 112-17; Carr, *Inventing the American Primitive*.

50 Back, *Keewaydin Way*, 142.

51 *TDS*, "Pale-faced City Tikes," 25.
52 Back, *Keewaydin Way*, 141.
53 This same tendency is noted in analyses of Canadian literature. According to Terry Goldie, "the canoe [was] made to seem a simplistic evocation of nature in opposition to white technology." See Goldie, *Fear and Temptation*, 21.
54 This is how the founder of Camp Keewaydin compared the Native people of Northern Ontario with the Native people in the United States: "Not reservation Indians, but Indians living freely, trapping, guiding, building their own canoes. Real Indians!" See Back, *Keewaydin Way*, 41.
55 FSATA, NWA, "Bolton Camp: Report of Operation, 1937," 8.
56 *TDS*, "Pale-faced City Tikes," 25.
57 Eastaugh, "Indian Council Ring," 7.
58 This phrase is borrowed from the title of Roediger's book, cited above.
59 Dimock and Hendry, *Camping and Character*, 75.
60 As Gail Bederman has pointed out, this meant that white boys were regarded as "the evolutionary equivalents of 'primitive' savages" and were to be encouraged in giving full expression to their "savage" impulses. See Gail Bederman, "'Teaching our sons to do what we have been teaching the savages to avoid': G. Stanley Hall, Racial Recapitulation, and the Neurasthenic Paradox," in her *Manliness and Civilization: A Cultural History of Gender and Race in the United States, 1880-1917*, 77-120 (Chicago and London: University of Chicago Press, 1999).
61 Eastaugh, "Indian Council Ring," 3. On games of "scalping," references to "scalps" (made of hemp rope) on display in council ring, and to Native "tribes" as "mortal enemies," see Eastaugh, "Indian Council Ring," 26, 31.
62 FSATA, NWA, "New Interests," 15. Upper Canada College Archives [hereafter UCCA], Ann Hall, "Arthur Lewis Cochrane: A Biographical Sketch," Queen's University, Kingston, 1964. The reference to "pioneers" instead of the usual "cowboys" was, perhaps, meant to distinguish the game from its American counterpart. My thanks to Gillian Poulter for suggesting this distinction. However, if pioneers were the kinder, gentler, *Canadian* version of cowboys, the "Indians" remained just as savage, as these passages reveal.
63 FSATA, NWA, "New Interests," 8, 10.
64 Eastaugh, "Indian Council Ring," 2-4, 26
65 Mary G. Hamilton, *The Call of Algonquin: Biography of a Summer Camp* (Toronto: Ryerson Press, 1958), 149. Deloria has noted a similar gendering of the phenomenon in the American Camp Fire Girls, who used Indian programming to inculcate a domestic vision of womanhood. See Deloria, *Playing Indian*, 111-15. On the other hand, the attempt to portray Aboriginal people in less "savage" ways may have been due to other postwar changes in thinking regarding racial tolerance (discussed later in this chapter).
66 Hamilton, *Call of Algonquin*, 22.
67 Edwards, *Taylor Statten*, 96. With perhaps less hoopla and flair, the CGIT planned its own information evenings with a "tribal theme" to interest urban girls in the prospect of camp. See Helen E. D'Avignon, "Planning the Rally for Camp Promotion," *The Torch* 1, 5 (1925): 70.
68 TUA, OCA Papers, 84-019/1/1, Newsclippings Scrapbook, "Canada's Summer Indians Hit the Trail," *Star Weekly Magazine*, 11 June 1960; TUA, Adele and Harry Ebbs Papers, 80-014/1/8, "The Taylor Statten Camps," brochure, c. 1950; UCA/VUA, 85.095C, box 31, file 3, "Ontario Leadership Camp, 1927," brochure.

69 Edwards, *Taylor Statten*, 88.
70 Barbara Gilchrist, interview by Jack Pearse; Burry, "A History of the Taylor Statten Camps," 33. As a non-profit camp, Bolton was forced to rely on the good will of the Canadian Progress Club – to the tune of $600 – for funds to construct its council ring in 1926. See FSATA, NWA, minutes, Bolton Camp Committee, 17 June 1926.
71 Eastaugh, "Indian Council Ring," 9.
72 Edgar, "Our Indebtedness," 1-5.
73 Hamilton, *Call of Algonquin*, 8; Back, *Keewaydin Way*, 42.
74 TUA, Ronald H. Perry Fonds, 82-016/2/8, "The Fine Art of Canoeing," *Canoe Lake Camp Echoes* 4, 3 (1931): 37.
75 Back, *Keewaydin Way*, 53; UCCA, A.L. Cochrane, "Camp Timagami," *College Times*, Easter 1924, 44.
76 Douglas Creelman, interview by author, 23 June 2000; Robert Foster to Sharon Wall, 8 September 2000; TUA, OCA Sound/Tape Collection, 83-002/7/1, Nora Cochrane and Billie (Aileen) Nesbit, interview by Keith Rumble, 22 February 1974.
77 Patricia Jasen cites an Ojibway guide working in the Fort Frances area in the early years of the century, who stated: "I loved working as a guide because, once I left camp, I was the boss. The tourists had to depend on me, on what I knew about fishing, about not getting lost, and about surviving in the bush if anything went wrong." Quoted in Patricia Jasen, *Wild Things: Nature, Culture, and Tourism in Ontario, 1790-1914* (Toronto: University of Toronto Press, 1995), 140. In his exploration of white men who acted as guides in Maine, Nathan Lowrey explains they were partly drawn to the work for the prestige value of mingling with and gaining the respect of members of elite society. As with the Aboriginal case, they were also paid more than the typical lumberman. See Nathan S. Lowrey, "Tales of the Northern Maine Woods: The History and Tradition of the Maine Guide," *Northeast Folklore* 28 (1989): 69-110.
78 These numbers are based on what Robin Jarvis Brownlie has found in the Georgian Bay area. See R.J. Brownlie, *A Fatherly Eye: Indian Agents, Government Power, and Aboriginal Resistance in Ontario, 1918-1939* (Don Mills: Oxford University Press, 2003), 20-28.
79 Cecilia Morgan, "Performing for 'Imperial Eyes': Bernice Loft and Ethel Brant Monture, Ontario, 1930s-1960s," in *Contact Zones: Aboriginal and Settler Women in Canada's Colonial Past*, ed. Katie Pickles and Myra Rutherdale, 67-89 (Vancouver: UBC Press, 2005); FSATA, NWA, "Bolton Camp: Report of Operation, 1937," 6.
80 Olive Dickason describes the Six Nations as "the largest and wealthiest Native group in the country," while Veronica Strong-Boag and Gerson refer to them as "a showpiece of both Native talent and the supposed success of Canadian Indian policies." Although the group did also contain traditionalists who were less inclined to adopt Western ways, it was Christian "progressives" – Johnson's and Loft's families among them – who controlled Six Nations' councils during this period. For more on the Six Nations, see Strong-Boag and Gerson, *Paddling Her Own Canoe*, 19-58; Olive Patricia Dickason, *Canada's First Nations: A History of Founding Peoples from Earliest Times* (Oxford: Oxford University Press, 1992), 355-59; Sally M. Weaver, "The Iroquois: The Grand River Reserve in the Late Nineteenth and Early Twentieth Centuries, 1875-1945," in *Aboriginal Ontario: Historical Perspectives on the First Nations*, ed. Edward S. Rogers and Donald B. Smith, 213-57 (Toronto/Oxford: Dundurn Press, 1994).
81 For more biographical information on Loft, see Robert Stacey, Donald Smith, and Bryan Winslow, "Introduction," in Dawendine, *Iroquois Fires: The Six Nations Lyrics and Lore of*

Dawendine (Ottawa: Penumbra Press, 1995), 11-21; Cecilia Morgan, "Private Lives and Public Performances: Aboriginal Women in a Settler Society, Ontario, Canada, 1920s-1960s," *Journal of Colonialism and Colonial History* 4, 3 (2003), available at http://muse.jhu.edu/journals/journal_of_colonialism_and_colonial_history/v004/4.3morgan.html; Morgan, "Performing for 'Imperial Eyes.'"

82 In the days of Cartier and Champlain, heralding the birth of the "civilized" world's hunger to see Indians in their "savage" state, various Native individuals were taken to Europe, often forcibly, and put on display. See Christian F. Feest, ed., *Indians and Europe: An Interdisciplinary Collection of Essays* (Aachen: Edition Herodot, Rader Verlag, 1987); Green, "Tribe Called Wannabee," 33. For commentary on Cartier's capturing of Donnaconna and his time in Europe, see Jacques Cartier, *The Voyages of Jacques Cartier*, intro. Ramsay Cook (Toronto: University of Toronto Press, 1993).

83 Morgan, "Private Lives." See also her "Performing for 'Imperial Eyes'"; Cecilia Morgan, "'A wigwam to Westminster': Performing Mohawk Identity in Imperial Britain, 1890s-1990s," *Gender and History* 15, 2 (2003): 319-41; H.V. Nelles, *The Art of Nation-building: Pageantry and Spectacle at Quebec's Tercentenary* (Toronto: University of Toronto Press, 1999), 164-81; Deloria, *Playing Indian*, 122; Paige Raibmon, "Theatres of Contact: The Kwakwaka'wakw Meet Colonialism in British Columbia and at the Chicago World's Fair," *Canadian Historical Review* 81, 2 (2000): 157-90. For more on Aboriginal performance, see S. Elizabeth Bird, ed. *Dressing in Feathers: The Construction of the Indian in Popular Culture* (Boulder, CO: Westview Press, 1996); Robert Cupido, "Appropriating the Past: Pageants, Politics, and the Diamond Jubilee of Confederation," *Journal of the Canadian Historical Association* 8 (1998): 156-97; Wade A. Henry, "Imagining the Great White Mother and the Great King: Aboriginal Tradition and Royal Representation in the 'Great Pow-wow' of 1901," *Journal of the Canadian Historical Association* 11 (2000): 87-108; Ian Radforth, "Performance, Politics and Representation: Aboriginal People and the 1860 Royal Tour of Canada," *Canadian Historical Review* 84, 1 (2003): 1-32. Certain historians of blackface have offered up similar arguments, suggesting that marginalized peoples could create liberating contexts out of white-instigated racial play. Though his appears to be something of a minority viewpoint, W.T. Lhamon argues that blackface represented a "complex attempt to understand racial mixing." His work, while recognizing the racist elements of the genre, also explores "the way blackface actions have often contradicted what was expected of them." See W.T. Lhamon, Jr., *Raising Cain: Blackface Performance from Jim Crow to Hip Hop* (Cambridge: Harvard University Press, 1998).

84 On Loft/Dawendine at Bolton, see FSATA, NWA, "Bolton Camp: Report of Operation, 1937," 6. On Loft at Glen Bernard, see Lennox and Addington Historical Society Museum, Celia B. File Papers, box 3, file 5.28, Mary S. Edgar to Celia B. File, 4 November 1935. My thanks to Cecelia Morgan for sharing this research with me. On Loft's interactions with Camp Temagami, see UCCA, copy of Ann Hall, "Arthur Lewis Cochrane: A Biographical Sketch," unpublished paper, Queen's University, Kingston, 1964.

85 On guides at Keewaydin, see Back, *Keewaydin Way*, 108, 141-44.

86 This phrase is borrowed from Francis, *Imaginary Indian*, 97-108.

87 FSATA, NWA, "Bolton Camp: Report of Operation, 1937," 6.

88 Edgar, "Our Indebtedness," 4.

89 Quoted in Morgan, "Performing for 'Imperial Eyes.'" To add to her discomfort, Loft and her father were sometimes criticized by members of their own Six Nations community for their involvement with white society, with one local woman apparently accusing Loft of "selling her race." See Ibid.

90 These are the terms by which Bunny McBride has analyzed the life of Molly Nelson, a Penobscot Indian from Maine who became a popular stage performer during the interwar period and whom McBride describes as a woman who wrestled with the issue of her "two-pronged identity." See Bunny McBride, "The Spider and the WASP: Chronicling the Life of Molly Spotted Elk," in *Reading beyond Words: Contexts for Native History*, 403-27 (Toronto: Broadview Press: 1996). Veronica Strong-Boag alludes to similar issues of double identity in her reading of the stage career of Pauline Johnson. See Strong-Boag, *Paddling Her Own Canoe*, esp. chap. 3.

91 Quoted in Morgan, "Performing for "Imperial Eyes."" For Loft's correspondence with Celia B. File, see Lennox and Addington Historical Society Museum, Celia B. File Papers, box 3, file 5.28. My thanks to Cecelia Morgan for sharing this research with me.

92 Jasen, *Wild Things*, 133-45; Tina Loo, "Of Moose and Men: Hunting for Masculinities in British Columbia, 1880-1939," *Western Historical Quarterly* 32, 3 (2001): 296-319. Even in the case of white guides, Lowrey notes that they routinely shouldered all the work of hunting – preparing, packing, planning routes, paddling, unpacking, cooking, and ensuring general safety – save delivering the final shot. See Lowrey, "Tales of the Northern Maine Woods."

93 Douglas Creelman, interview by author, 23 June 2000; Robert Foster to Sharon Wall, 8 September 2000. Nancy Forestell's observation that these racial outsiders, who ran restaurants and laundries in the service of white miners, were never regarded as fully "men" in the public eye might, to some extent, have applied here, even if mitigated by images of Native men as physically masculine. See Nancy M. Forestell, "Bachelors, Boarding-houses, and Blind Pigs: Gender Construction in a Multi-ethnic Mining Camp," in *A Nation of Immigrants: Women, Workers and Communities in Canadian History, 1840s-1960s*, ed. Franca Iacovetta with Paula Draper and Robert Ventresca, 251-90 (Toronto: University of Toronto Press, 1998).

94 Douglas Creelman, interview by author, 23 June 2000, Toronto.

95 Ibid., 144.

96 The tendency to draw parallels between Aboriginal peoples and animals is also noted by Terry Goldie in the context of Canadian literature. He argues that "their sense of belonging to place" is presented, "not [as] a matter of human choice but animal genetics." See Terry Goldie, *Fear and Temptation: The Image of the Indigene in Canadian, Australian, and New Zealand Literatures* (Montreal/Kingston: McGill-Queen's University Press, 1989), 25-26.

97 At Bolton Camp, staff members were praised in 1933 for offering "co-operation ... in the effort to drastically cut down Camp expenses," suggesting, perhaps, that they also had pay cuts demanded of them. See FSATA, NWA, "The Gateway to Health and Happiness: Bolton Camp Speaks Again, 1933," 1.

98 Brian Back describes the nature of the guide/administration relationship in his *Keewaydin Way*, 146-47. He explains that this transition to white labour was possible with improvements in road conditions and with access to better-quality maps. Ultimately, Aboriginal knowledge of the area had been passed on to whites.

99 Borrowing from Mary Louise Pratt, Karen Dubinsky profitably applies the notion of "contact zone" to the case of tourists encountering Native peoples at Niagara Falls. See Karen Dubinsky, "Local Colour in the 'Contact Zone': The Spectacle of Race," in *The Second Greatest Disappointment: Honeymooning and Tourism at Niagara Falls* (Toronto: Between the Lines, 1999), chap. 3. For the original reference, see Mary Louise Pratt, *Imperial Eyes: Travel Writing and Transculturation* (New York: Routledge, 1992).

100 Raibmon, "Theatres of Contact," 170.
101 "Indian Boy, 7, Is Pining in Squalid City Home," *TDS*, 27 June 1936, 1, 3.
102 Edgar, "Our Indebtedness," 5.
103 FSATA, NWA, Bolton Camp Publicity Scrapbook, "Big Businessmen Enjoy Visit to Camp at Bolton," *TDS*, 9 July 1937. For camper memory, see Susan Houston, conversation with author, 11 November 2003. On Statten and Seton, see Adele Ebbs, interview by Jack Pearse; Edwards, *Taylor Statten*, 88. *Camping and Character* explains that the Gitchiahmek Order eventually came to include campers deemed worthy of the honour. Meeting "after the camp itself was asleep" (in the manner of most secret orders), its activities included a ritualistic membership process with the bestowing of Indian names. See Dimock and Hendry, *Camping and Character*, 139-40.
104 FSATA, NWA, "After Twenty Years," 43; FSATA, NWA, "Bolton Camp: Report of Operation, 1938," 11.
105 TUA, OCA Sound/Tape Collection, 83-002/5/1, Ron Perry, interview by Bruce Harris, 2 December 1981.
106 Shirley Ford, interview by author, 20 June 2000, Toronto.
107 Dimock and Hendry, *Camping and Character*, 321; Camp Pine Crest, "Director's Report," 1950, 78-009/2/1, TUA, Camp Pine Crest Fonds.
108 TUA, OCA Papers, 88-006/3/7, transcript of interview with Adele Ebbs, 1986, 20.
109 TUA, "Northway Recollection of Glen Bernard Camp."
110 Jane Hughes, interview by author, 26 June 2000.
111 James Buchanan, interview by author, 26 July 2000, Toronto.
112 For a history of the repression of the potlatch, see Douglas Cole and Ira Chaikin, *An Iron Hand upon the People: The Law against the Potlatch on the Northwest Coast* (Vancouver: Douglas and McIntyre, 1990). On state responses to Native participation in rodeos and fairs, see Regular, "On Public Display"; and Mikkelsen, "Indians and Rodeo."
113 Anne McClintock, *Imperial Leather: Race, Gender, and Sexuality in the Colonial Contest* (New York: Routledge, 1995), 52; Constance Backhouse, *Colour-coded: A Legal History of Racism in Canada, 1900-1950* (Toronto: University of Toronto Press, 1999), 8. Two scholars who explicitly reject the concept of race as a category of social analysis are Kenan Malik, *The Meaning of Race: Race, History and Culture in Western Society* (Basingstoke: McMillan, 1996); and Robert Miles, *Racism after "Race Relations"* (New York: Routledge, 1993). As is now well known, Indian status was a condition both bestowed and revoked according to the dictates of state legislation. At different points in time, legal definitions of Indian status were made through appeals not only to "bloodlines" but also to intermarriage, adoption, "reputation," and "mode of life," making the category of "Indian" particularly shifting and unstable. See Backhouse, *Colour-coded*, 21-27.
114 The coercive approach of Indian policy – with regard to pressing land claims, hunting and fishing rights, education and traditional celebrations – intensified in the 1920s. See Miller, *Skyscrapers Hide the Heavens*, 217, 219-220; Cole and Chaikin, *Iron Hand*.
115 Bruce W. Hodgins and Jamie Benidickson, *The Temagami Experience: Recreation, Resources, and Aboriginal Rights in the Northern Ontario Wilderness* (Toronto: University of Toronto Press, 1989), 210-28. For more on the twentieth-century history of Native/white relations in northern Ontario, see J. Garth Taylor, "Northern Algonquians on the Frontiers of 'New Ontario,'" in *Aboriginal Ontario: Historical Perspectives on the First Nations*, ed. Edward S. Rogers and Donald B. Smith, 344-73 (Toronto, Oxford: Dundurn Press, 1994).
116 In the 1970s, camp director and scholar Bruce Hodgins began researching his *Temagami Experience* (cited above), which took a sympathetic view of Aboriginal rights in Temagami.

During the late 1980s, former Keewaydin camper and, later, camp historian Brian Back served as director of the Temagami Wilderness Society (precursor to Earthroots), which fought for environmental protection and a just settlement for the Temagami peoples. In 1989, the society's eighty-four-day blockade of the Red Squirrel Road in Temagami brought national and international attention to the region. See articles in Matt Bray and Ashley Thomson, eds., *Temagami: A Debate on Wilderness* (Toronto and Oxford: Dundurn Press, 1990).

117 Back, *Keewaydin Way*, 132, 143-44; UCCA, Gordon Deeks and Richard B. Howard, "Temagami Magic," *Old Times*, Summer 1995, 38. TUA, OCA Sound/Tape Collection, 83-002/7/1, Nora Cochrane and Billie (Aileen) Nesbit, interview by Keith Rumble, 22 February 1974. On the broader history of relations between the Aboriginal community and recreational interests in Temagami, see again Hodgins and Benidickson, *Temagami Experience*.

118 UCA/VUA, 85.095C, box 30, file 3, "Report of the Fourth Ontario Camp Council," 1930, 6.

119 TUA, OCA Papers, 98-019/13/10, Taylor Statten, "Developing the Program on a Group Basis," address given to the Conference of the Pacific Camping Association, 16-19 March 1939.

120 Hamilton, *Call of Algonquin*, 66. Mary Edgar, director of Glen Bernard, founded a separate camp – Shangrila – for young British war guests just down the road from her first camp and then arranged for these campers to meet with Glen Bernard campers several times a week. See Shirley Ford, interview by author, 20 June 2000, Toronto.

121 UCA/VUA, 85.095C, box 14, file 6, CGIT Camps, National Girls Work Board, "Morning Watch," 1941, 15; Hamilton, *Call of Algonquin*, 63; FSATA, NWA, "Bolton Summer Camp, 1944."

122 Franca Iacovetta, *Gatekeepers: Reshaping Immigrant Lives in Cold War Canada* (Toronto: Between the Lines Press, 2006). On the new rhetoric of tolerance, see also Mariana Valverde, "Building Anti-delinquent Communities: Morality, Gender, and Generation in the City," in *A Diversity of Women: Ontario, 1945-1980*, ed. Joy Parr (Toronto: University of Toronto Press, 1995), 20.

123 Hamilton, *Call of Algonquin*, 150; Bert Danson, interview by author, 12 June 2000; FSATA, NWA, "Bolton Summer Camp, 1944."

124 Olive Dickason, *A Concise History of Canada's First Nations* (Toronto: Oxford University Press, 2006), 230-31.

125 Hamilton, *Call of Algonquin*, 22.

126 Adele Ebbs, transcript of interview, 20.

127 Liz Lundell, *Summer Camp: Great Camps of Algonquin Park* (Toronto: Stoddart Publishing, 1994), 104-6. In a 1995 guide to Canadian summer camps, no Ontario camps listed Native or Indian lore as among their activities, but the influence of these programs lives on in the offering of archery, campfires, canoeing, and, in one case, paddle-making. Many camps also retain their quasi-Indian names. See Ann West, *Summer Camps in Canada: A Complete Guide to the Best Summer Camps for Kids and Teens* (Vancouver: Polestar Press, 1995). On Bolton Camp, see Fred Okada, conversation with author, 15 December 1998; FSATA, NWA, Dale Callendar, "History of Bolton Camp," unpublished paper, Summer 1997, 11.

Conclusion

1 Cronon notes that this view has been strangely resilient, shaping the thinking of modern environmentalism well into the late twentieth century. He argues that the tendency continues to be to judge environments according to "a set of bipolar moral scales in which the human and the non-human, the unnatural and the natural, the fallen and the unfallen, serve as [the] conceptual map for understanding and valuing the world." See William Cronon, "The Trouble with Wilderness; or, Getting Back to the Wrong Nature," *Environmental History* 1, 1 (1996): 25.

2 Tina Loo uses this term in her study of twentieth-century wildlife conservation, describing it as "a knowledge about the natural world circulated by mass-marketed products." See Tina Loo, "Making a Modern Wilderness: Conserving Wildlife in Twentieth-century Canada," *Canadian Historical Review* 82, 1 (2001): 94.

3 Keith Walden, *Becoming Modern in Toronto: The Industrial Exhibition and the Shaping of Late Victorian Culture* (Toronto: University of Toronto Pres, 1997), 188.

4 T.J. Jackson Lears, *No Place of Grace: Antimodernism and the Transformation of American Culture, 1880-1920* (Chicago: University of Chicago Press, 1981), xii, 237, 263.

5 The reference to psychology is by Clarence Hincks and is quoted in Jocelyn Motyer Raymond, *The Nursery World of Dr. Blatz* (Toronto: University of Toronto Press, 1991), 30.

6 Ian McKay, *Quest of the Folk: Antimodernism and Cultural Selection in Twentieth-century Nova Scotia* (Montreal/Kingston: McGill-Queen's University Press, 1994), 37.

7 Dean MacCannell, *The Tourist: A New Theory of the Leisure Class* (New York: Schocken Books, 1976), 8.

8 Ibid.

9 Berman was speaking here of twentieth-century responses. As he argues, "Modernity is either embraced with a blind and uncritical enthusiasm, or else condemned with a neo-Olympian remoteness and contempt." See Marshall Berman, *All That Is Solid Melts into Air: The Experience of Modernity* (New York: Simon and Schuster, 1982 [New York: Penguin Books, 1988]), 24-29.

Bibliography

Primary Sources

Archival Collections

Algonquin Park Museum Archives
Camp Collection
Archives of Ontario
National Council on Physical Fitness: RG-2-75 and RG-2-73
Legislative Press Clippings: MS-755
Northway Papers
Ronald H. Perry Papers
Ontario Camping Association Papers
Ontario Camping Association Directories File
Ontario Camping Association Sound/Tape Collection
Ontario Camp Leadership Centre, Bark Lake
Trent University Archives
Adele Ebbs Papers
Adele and Harry Ebbs Papers
Camp Pine Crest Papers
United Church Archives/Victoria University Archives
Ontario CGIT Collection
Toronto CGIT Collection

Private Collections

Family Service Association of Toronto
Ontario Camp Leadership Centre: Files in possession of Dorothy Walter, Toronto, Ontario
Upper Canada College Archives

Interviews by Author

Anonymous Arawhon camper, by e-mail, 27 July 2000.
Barford, Ralph, 23 August 2000, Toronto.
Bawden, David, by e-mail, 31 January 2001.
Buchanan, James W., 22 July 2000, Toronto.
Cashia, Eugene, 22 August 2000, Toronto.
Creelman, Douglas, 23 June 2000, Toronto.
Danson, Bert, 12 June 2000, Toronto.
Felstiner, James, by e-mail, April 2001.
Ford, Shirley, 20 June 2000, Toronto.
Foster, Robert, response to interview questionnaire, 8 September 2000.
Hughes, Jane, 26 June 2000, Toronto.
Moses, Joan, 26 July 2000, Toronto.
Murphy, Mary, 7 June 2000, Toronto.
Royce, Marjorie, 24 August 2000, Toronto.
Shapiro, Elizabeth, by e-mail, 17 February and 25 February 2001.
Silbert, Sylvia, 16 June 2000, Toronto.
Warnock, Leila, 2 June 2000, Toronto.
Wirsig, Kathryn, by e-mail, 30 January 2001, Toronto.

Other Interviews (on file in Trent University Archives)

Blackstock, Blackie, interview by Harry Ebbs, n.d., OCA Sound/Tape Collection, 83-002/4/9.

Blackstock, Blackie, interview by Ontario Camping Association, 1 November 1978, OCA Sound/Tape Collection, 83-002/5/25.

Cochrane, Nora, and Billie (Aileen) Nesbit, interview by Keith Rumble, 22 February 1974, Ontario Camping Association [hereafter OCA] Sound/Tape Collection, 83-002/7/1.

Ebbs, Adele, interview by Jack Pearse, 22 May 1986, OCA Sound/Tape Collection, 83,002/10/9.

Ebbs, Adele, interview by Eugene Kates, 13 August 1985, OCA Sound/Tape Collection, 83-002/6/5.

Ebbs, Harry, interview by Bert Danson, Toronto, January 1982, OCA Sound/Tape Collection, 83-002/5/27.

Gilchrist, Barbara, interview by Jack Pierce, 6 November 1986, OCA Sound/Tape Collection, 83-002/5/8,

Haladner, Irwin, interview by Adele Ebbs, 4 May 1982, OCA Sound/Tape Collection, 83-002/5/5.

Kates, Eugene, interview by Adele and Harry Ebbs, 13 August 1985, Toronto, OCA Sound/Tape Collection, 83-002/6/5.

Northway, Mary, interview by Cathy Stuart and Warren Anderson, 21 January 1975, OCA Sound/Tape Collection, 83-002/2/5.

Northway, Mary, interview by Jocelyn Palm, 17 November 1981, OCA Sound/Tape Collection, 83-002/005/024.

Passmore, Jack, Memories of Bark Lake Camp, Bark Lake, 8 May 1982, OCA Sound/Tape Collection, 83-002/8/10.

Perry, Ron, interview by Bruce Harris, 2 December 1981, OCA Sound/Tape Collection, 83-002/5/1.

Stewart, Helen, interview by Bruno Morawetz, 12 January 1983, OCA Sound/Tape Collection, 83-002/5/3.

Government Documents

Algonquin Park Leaseholders Association/Ontario Department of Lands and Resources, *Algonquin Park: A Park for People.* Ontario: Algonquin Park Leaseholders Association, 1969.

"Algonquin Provincial Park: Advisory Committee Report." Government Policy, 16 July 1973.

Canadian Youth Commission. *Youth and Recreation: New Plans for New Times.* Toronto: Ryerson, 1944.

Dominion Bureau of Statistics. *Ninth Census of Canada, 1951.* Vol. 1. Ottawa: Minster of Trade and Commerce, 1951.

Leacy, F.H., ed. *Historical Statistics of Canada.* 2nd ed. Ottawa: Statistics Canada, 1983.

Province of Ontario, *Education Report.* 1948-55.

Newspapers and Periodicals

College Times (Toronto): 1920 to 1955.

Toronto Daily Star (Toronto): 1 June-31 August for every year from 1920 to 1951.

Books and Articles

Cleaver, Nancy. "An Old Canadian Custom: Sending the Kids to Camp." *Saturday Night*, 19 April 1952.

Dimock, Hedley S. *Administration of the Modern Camp.* New York: Association Press, 1948.

Dimock, Hedley S., and Charles E. Hendry. *Camping and Character: A Camp Experiment in Character Education.* New York: Association Press, 1929. Reprinted 1931.

Dimock, Hedley S., and Taylor Statten. *Talks to Counselors.* New York: Association Press, 1939.

Hamilton, Mary G. *The Call of Algonquin: Biography of a Summer Camp.* Toronto: Ryerson Press, 1958.

Lundell, Liz, *Fires of Friendship: Eighty Years of the Taylor Statten Camps.* Toronto: Fires of Friendship Books, 2000.

Newman, Peter. "Junior's $10 Million Adventure in the Pines." *Financial Post*, 5 June 1954.

Northway, Mary L. *Appraisal of the Social Development of Children at a Summer Camp.* Toronto: University of Toronto Press, 1940.

–. "Security Pegs for Campers," *Camping Magazine* 14, 4 (1942): 3-7.

–. "Sustaining Interests," *Camping Magazine* 11, 9 (1939).

–. "Tools for the Job." *Parent Education Bulletin* 13 (1941): 1-6.

–. "What Are the Camps Achieving," *Camping Magazine* 9, 8 (1937).

Northway, Mary L., and Flora Morrison, "Adventuring by Canoe in 1941: Part 2," *Camping Magazine* 14, 2 (1942): 2-8.

Ontario Camping Association, *Ontario Camp Bulletin* 1, 2 (1946).

Seeley, John R., R. Alexander Sim, and Elizabeth W. Loosley. *Crestwood Heights: A Study of the Culture of Suburban Life*. Toronto: University of Toronto Press, 1956.

Statten, Taylor. *Talks to Counsellors*. Taylor Statten Camps, 1928.

Trudeau, Pierre. "Exhaustion and Fulfilment: The Ascetic in a Canoe." In *Wilderness Canada*, ed. Borden Spears, 1-5. Toronto/Vancouver: Clarke, Irwin, 1970. First published in *Jeunesse Etudiante Catholique,* November 1944.

Secondary Sources

Books

Abella, Irving, and Harold Troper. *None Is Too Many: Canada and the Jews of Europe, 1933-1948*. Toronto: Lester and Orpen Dennys, 1982.

Adams, Mary Louise. *The Trouble with Normal: Post-war Youth and the Making of Heterosexuality.* Toronto: University of Toronto Press, 1997.

Addison, Ottelyn. *Early Days in Algonquin Park.* Toronto: McGraw-Hill Ryerson, 1974.

Allen, Richard. *The Social Passion: Religion and Social Reform in Canada, 1914-29.* Toronto: University of Toronto Press, 1973.

Anderson, H. Allen. *The Chief: Ernest Thompson Seton and the Changing West.* College Station: Texas A&M University Press, 1986.

Anderson, Kay. *Vancouver's Chinatown.* Montreal: McGill-Queen's University Press, 1993.

Arnup, Katherine. *Education for Motherhood: Advice for Mothers in Twentieth-century Canada.* Toronto: University of Toronto Press, 1994.

Axelrod, Paul. *Making a Middle Class: Student Life in English Canada during the Thirties.* Montreal/Kingston: McGill-Queen's University Press, 1990.

Back, Brian. *The Keewaydin Way: A Portrait, 1893-1983*. Temagami: Keewaydin Camp Ltd., 1983.

Backhouse, Constance. *Colour-coded: A Legal History of Racism in Canada, 1900-1950.* Toronto: University of Toronto Press, 1999.

Bailey, Beth L. *From Front Porch to Back Seat: Courtship in Twentieth-century America.* Baltimore: Johns Hopkins University Press, 1988.

Barman, Jean. *Growing Up British in British Columbia: Boys in Private School.* Vancouver: UBC Press, 1984.

Bederman, Gail. *Manliness and Civilization: A Cultural History of Gender and Race in the United States, 1880-1917.* Chicago and London: University of Chicago Press, 1999.

Benidickson, Jamie. *Idleness, Water, and a Canoe: Reflections on Paddling for Pleasure.* Toronto: University of Toronto Press, 1997.

Berger, John. *Ways of Seeing: A Book Made by John Berger (and others).* New York: Viking Press, 1972.

Berkhofer, Robert F., Jr. *The White Man's Indian: Images of the American Indian from Columbus to the Present.* New York: Vintage Books, 1979 [1978].

Berman, Marshall. *All That Is Solid Melts into Air: The Experience of Modernity.* New York: Simon and Schuster, 1982. Reprint, New York: Penguin, 1988.

Berton, Pierre. *The Great Depression.* Toronto: McClelland and Stewart, 1990.

Billinghurst, Jane. *Grey Owl: The Many Faces of Archie Belaney.* Vancouver: Greystone Books, 1999.

Blumin, Stuart. *The Emergence of the Middle Class: Social Experience of the American City, 1760-1900.* New York/Cambridge: Cambridge University Press, 1989.

Bradbury, Bettina. *Working Families: Age, Gender, and Daily Survival in Industrializing Montreal.* Toronto: Oxford University Press, 1993.

Bray, Matt, and Ashley Thomson, eds. *Temagami: A Debate on Wilderness.* Toronto: Dundurn Press, 1990.

Breines, Wini. *Young, White and Miserable: Growing Up Female in the Fifties.* Boston: Beacon Press, 1992.

Broadfoot, Barry. *Ten Lost Years, 1929-1939: Memories of Canadians Who Survived the Great Depression.* Toronto: Doubleday, 1973.

Brumberg, Joan Jacobs. *The Body Project: An Intimate History of American Girls.* New York: Vintage Books, 1997.

Carr, Helen. *Inventing the American Primitive: Politics, Gender and the Representation of Native American Literary Traditions, 1789-1936.* New York: New York University Press, 1996.

Cavallo, Dominick. *Muscles and Morals: Organized Playgrounds and Urban Reform, 1880-1920.* Philadelphia: University of Pennsylvania Press, 1981.

Christie, Nancy, and Michael Gauvreau, *A Full-orbed Christianity: The Protestant Churches and Social Welfare in Canada, 1900-1940.* Montreal/Kingston: McGill-Queen's University Press, 1996.

Churchill, Ward. *Indians Are Us? Culture and Genocide in Native North America.* Monroe: Common Courage Press, 1994.

Clarkson, Stephen, and Christina McCall. *Trudeau and Our Times.* Vol 1: *The Magnificent Obsession.* Toronto: McClelland and Stewart, 1990.

Clement, Wallace. *The Canadian Corporate Elite: An Analysis of Economic Power.* Toronto: McClelland and Stewart, 1975.

Cleverley, John, and D.C. Phillips. *Visions of Childhood: Influential Models from Locke to Spock.* New York: Teachers College Press, 1986.

Cohen, Sol. *Challenging Orthodoxies: Towards a New Cultural History of Education.* New York: Peter Lang Publishing, 1999.

Cole, Douglas. *Captured Heritage: The Scramble for North West Coast Artifacts.* Vancouver: Douglas and McIntyre, 1985.

Cole, Douglas, and Ira Chaikin. *An Iron Hand upon the People: The Law against the Potlatch on the Northwest Coast.* Vancouver: Douglas and McIntyre, 1990.

Comacchio, Cynthia. *Nations Are Built of Babies: Saving Ontario's Mothers and Children.* Montreal/Kingston: McGill-Queen's University Press, 1993.

Conable, Charlotte Williams. *Women at Cornell: The Myth of Equal Education.* Ithaca: Cornell University Press, 1977.

Cook, Ramsay. *1492 and All That: Making a Garden out of a Wilderness.* North York: Robarts Centre for Canadian Studies, 1993.

–. *The Regenerators: Social Criticism in Late Victorian English Canada.* Toronto: University of Toronto Press, 1985.

Coontz, Stephanie. *The Way We Never Were: American Families and the Nostalgia Trap.* New York: Basic Books, 1992.

Copp, Terry. *The Anatomy of Poverty: The Condition of the Working Class in Montreal, 1897-1929.* Toronto: McClelland and Stewart, 1974.

Crocker, Ruth Hutchison. *Social Work and Social Order: The Settlement Movement in Two Industrial Cities.* Chicago: University of Chicago Press, 1992.

Cronon, William, ed. *Uncommon Ground: Toward Reinventing Nature.* New York: W.W. Norton and Company, 1995.

Cross, Gary. *Kids' Stuff: Toys and the Changing World of American Childhood* Cambridge: Harvard University Press, 1997.

Dean, Malcolm. *Censored! Only in Canada: The History of Film Censorship – The Scandal off the Screen.* Toronto: Virgo Press, 1981.

Deloria, Philip. *Playing Indian.* New Haven and London: Yale University Press, 1998.

de Martino, Stefano, and Alex Wall. *Cities of Childhood: Italian Colonies of the 1930s.* London: Architectural Association, 1988.

Dickason, Olive Patricia. *Canada's First Nations: A History of Founding Peoples from Earliest Times.* Oxford: Oxford University Press, 1992.

Dickson, Lovat. *Wilderness Man: The Strange Story of Grey Owl.* Toronto: Macmillan, 1973.

Dodds, Gordon, Alvin Esau, and Russell Smandych, eds. *Dimensions of Childhood: Essays on the History of Children and Youth in Canada.* Winnipeg: Legal Research Institute, University of Manitoba, 1991.

Doherty, Thomas. *Teenagers and Teenpics: The Juvenilization of American Movies in the 1950s.* Boston: Unwin Hyman, 1988.

Drummond, Ian M. *Progress without Planning: The Economic History of Ontario from Confederation to the Second World War.* Toronto: University of Toronto Press, 1987.

Dubinsky, Karen. *Improper Advances: Rape and Heterosexual Conflict in Ontario, 1880-1929.* Chicago: University of Chicago Press, 1993.

–. *The Second Greatest Disappointment: Honeymooning and Tourism at Niagara Falls.* Toronto: Between the Lines Press, 1999.

Dyhouse, Carol. *No Distinction of Sex? Women in British Universities, 1870-1939.* London: UCL Press, 1995.

Edwards, C.A.M. *Taylor Statten.* Toronto: Ryerson Press, 1960.

Eells, Eleanor. *History of Organized Camping: The First 100 Years.* Martinsville: American Camping Association, 1986.

Ehrenreich, John. *The Altruistic Imagination: A History of Social Work and Social Policy in the United States.* Ithaca: Cornell University Press, 1985.

Feest, Christian F., ed. *Indians and Europe: An Interdisciplinary Collection of Essays.* Aachen: Edition Herodot, Rader Verlag, 1987.

Fingard, Judith. *The Dark Side of Life in Victorian Halifax.* Porter's Lake: Pottersfield Press, 1989.

Fishman, Robert. *Bourgeois Utopias: The Rise and Fall of Suburbia.* New York: Basic Books, 1987.

FitzGerald, James. *Old Boys: The Powerful Legacy of Upper Canada College.* Toronto: Macfarlane, Walter and Ross, 1994.

Francis, Daniel. *The Imaginary Indian: The Image of the Indian in Canadian Culture.* Vancouver: Arsenal Pulp Press, 1992.

Giddens, Anthony. *Modernity and Self-identity: Self and Society in the Late Modern Age.* Stanford: Stanford University Press, 1991.

Gleason, Mona. *Normalizing the Ideal: Psychology, Schooling, and the Family in Postwar Canada.* Toronto: University of Toronto Press, 1999.

Goldie, Terry. *Fear and Temptation: The Image of the Indigene in Canadian, Australian, and New Zealand Literatures.* Kingston/ Montreal: McGill-Queen's University Press, 1989.

Gordon, Linda. *Heroes of Their Own Lives: The Politics and History of Family Violence.* New York: Penguin Books, 1988.

Gossage, Carolyn. *A Question of Privilege: Canada's Independent Schools.* Toronto: Peter Martin Associates Ltd., 1977.

Grace, Sherrill E. *Canada and the Idea of North.* Toronto: University of Toronto Press, 2002.

Gregory, Derek. *Geographical Imaginations.* Cambridge: Blackwell, 1994.

Griswold, Robert. *Fatherhood in America: A History.* New York: Basic Books, 1993

Grygier, Pat Sandiford. *A Long Way from Home: The Tuberculosis Epidemic among the Inuit.* Montreal/Kingston: McGill-Queen's University Press, 1994.

Hall, Stuart, David Held, Don Hubert, and Kenneth Thompson, eds. *Modernity: An Introduction to Modern Societies.* Malden, Oxford: Blackwell Publishers, 1997.

Harkness, Ross. *J.E. Atkinson of the* Star. Toronto: University of Toronto Press, 1963.

Harvey, David. *The Condition of Post-modernity: An Enquiry into the Origins of Cultural Change.* Cambridge: Blackwell Publishers, 1990.

Hodgins, Bruce W., and Margaret Hobbs, eds. *Nastawgan: The Canadian North by Canoe and Snowshoe.* Weston: Betelgeuse Books, 1985.

Hodgins, Bruce W., and Jamie Benidickson. *The Temagami Experience: Recreation, Resources, and Aboriginal Rights in the Northern Ontario Wilderness.* Toronto: University of Toronto Press, 1989.

Hodgins, Bruce W., and Bernadine Dodge, eds. *Using Wilderness: Essays on the Evolution of Youth Camping in Ontario.* Peterborough: Frost Centre for Canadian Heritage and Development Studies, 1992.

Horn, Michiel, ed. *The Dirty Thirties: Canadians in the Great Depression.* Toronto: Copp, Clark, 1972.

Houston, Stuart C. *R.G. Ferguson: Crusader against Tuberculosis.* Toronto: Hannah Inst./ Oxford: Dundurn, 1991.

Howard, Richard B. *Upper Canada College, 1829-1979: Colborne's Legacy.* Toronto: Macmillan, 1979.

Huhndorf, Shari. *Going Native: Indians in the American Cultural Imagination.* Ithaca: Cornell University Press, 2001.

Humble, A.H., with J.D. Burns. *The School on the Hill: Trinity College School, 1865-1965.* Port Hope: Trinity College School, 1965.

Ignatiev, Noel. *How the Irish Became White.* New York: Routledge, 1995.

Jackson, Kenneth T. *Crabgrass Frontier: The Suburbanization of the United States.* New York and Oxford: Oxford University Press, 1985.

Jackson, Peter A. *Maps of Meaning: An Introduction to Cultural Geography.* London, Winchester: Academic Division, Unwin Hyman, 1989.

Jasen, Patricia. *Wild Things: Nature, Culture, and Tourism in Ontario, 1790-1914.* Toronto: University of Toronto Press, 1995.

Jervis, John. *Exploring the Modern: Patterns of Western Culture and Civilization.* Oxford: Blackwell Publishers, 1998.

Kilbourn, Craig. *Adirondack Furniture and the Rustic Tradition.* New York: Harry N. Abrams, 1987.

Killan, Gerald. *Protected Places: A History of Ontario's Provincial Parks System.* Toronto: Dundurn, 1993.

Korinek, Valerie J. *Roughing It in the Suburbs: Reading* Chatelaine *Magazine in the Fifties and Sixties.* Toronto: University of Toronto Press, 2000.

Kuper, Adam. *The Invention of Primitive Society: Transformations of an Illusion.* London/New York: Routledge, 1988.

Ladd-Taylor, Molly. *Mother-work: Women, Child Welfare, and the State, 1890-1930.* Urbana: University of Illinois Press, 1994.

Lake, Marilyn. *Getting Equal: The History of Australian Feminism.* St Leonard's: Allen and Unwin, 1999.
Lears, T.J. Jackson. *No Place of Grace: Antimodernism and the Transformation of American Culture, 1880-1920.* Chicago: University of Chicago Press, 1981.
Leslie, John F., and Ron Maguire, eds. *The Historical Development of the Indian Act.* Ottawa: Indian and Northern Affairs, 1978.
Lhamon, W.T., Jr. *Raising Cain: Blackface Performance from Jim Crow to Hip Hop.* Cambridge: Harvard University Press, 1998.
Little, Margaret Hillyard. *No Car, No Radio, No Liquor Permit: The Moral Regulation of Single Mothers in Ontario, 1920-1997.* Toronto: Oxford University Press, 1998.
Lopez, Barry. *Arctic Dreams: Imagination and Desire in a Northern Landscape.* New York: Scribner, 1986.
Lott, Eric. *Love and Theft: Blackface Minstrelsy and the American Working Class.* New York: Oxford University Press, 1993.
Lundell, Liz, and Beverley Bailey. *Summer Camp: Great Camps of Algonquin Park.* Toronto: Stoddart Publishing, 1994.
MacCannell, Dean. *The Tourist: A New Theory of the Leisure Class.* New York: Schocken Books, 1976.
MacDonald, Robert H. *Sons of the Empire: The Frontier and the Boy Scouts Movement, 1890-1918.* Toronto: University of Toronto Press, 1993.
MacKay, Niall. *By Steam Boat and Steam Train: The Story of the Huntsville and Lake of Bays Railway and Navigation Companies.* Erin: Boston Mills Press, 1982.
MacLeod, David. *Building Character in the American Boy: The Boy Scouts, YMCA, and Their Forerunners, 1870-1920.* Madison, University of Wisconsin Press, 1983.
Mahar, William J. *Behind the Burnt Cork Mask: Early Blackkface Minstrelsy and Antebellum American Popular Culture.* Chicago: University of Illinois Press, 1999.
Malik, Kenan. *The Meaning of Race: Race, History and Culture in Western Society.* Basingstoke: McMillan, 1996.
Marshall, David B. *Secularizing the Faith: Canadian Protestant Clergy and the Crisis of Belief, 1850-1940.* Toronto: University of Toronto Press, 1992.
May, Elaine Tyler. *Homeward Bound: American Families in the Cold War Era.* New York: Basic Books, 1988.
McClintock, Anne. *Imperial Leather: Race, Gender, and Sexuality in the Colonial Contest.* New York: Routledge, 1995.
McCuaig, Katherine. *The Weariness, the Fever, and the Fret: The Campaign against Tuberculosis in Canada, 1900-1950.* Montreal/Kingston: McGill-Queen's University Press, 1999.
McDonald, Robert A.J. *Making Vancouver: Class, Status, and Social Boundaries, 1863-1913.* Vancouver: UBC Press, 1996.
McDougall, Heather. *Activists and Advocates: Toronto's Health Department, 1883-1983.* Toronto: Dundurn Press, 1990.
McKay, Ian. *Quest of the Folk: Antimodernism and Cultural Selection in Twentieth-century Nova Scotia.* Montreal/Kingston: McGill-Queen's Press, 1994.
McKinsey, Elizabeth. *Niagara Falls: Icon of the American Sublime.* Cambridge: Cambridge University Press, 1985.
McLaren, Angus. *Our Own Master Race: Eugenics in Canada, 1885-1945.* Toronto: McClelland and Stewart, 1990.
Merchant, Carolyn. *The Death of Nature: Women, Ecology, and the Scientific Revolution.* San Francisco: Harper and Row, 1979.

Metcalfe, Allan. *Canada Learns to Play: The Emergence of Organized Sport, 1807-1914*. Toronto: McClelland and Stewart, 1987.

Meyerowitz, Joanne. *Not June Cleaver: Women and Gender in Postwar America, 1945-1960*. Philadelphia: Temple University Press, 1994.

Miles, Robert. *Racism after "Race Relations."* New York: Routledge, 1993.

Miller, J.R. *Skyscrapers Hide the Heavens: A History of Indian-white Relations in Canada*. Toronto: University of Toronto Press, 1989.

Mishler, Paul C. *Raising Reds: The Young Pioneers, Radical Summer Camps and Communist Political Culture in the United States*. New York: Columbia University Press, 1999.

Morton, Suzanne. *Ideal Surroundings: Domestic Life in a Working-class Suburb in the 1920s*. Toronto: University of Toronto Press, 1995.

Moses, L.G. *Wild West Shows and the Images of American Indians, 1883-1933*. Albuquerque: University of New Mexico Press, 1996.

Nash, Roderick. *Wilderness and the American Mind*. New Haven: Yale University Press, 1973.

Nelles, H.V. *The Art of Nation-building: Pageantry and Spectacle at Quebec's Tercentenary*. Toronto: University of Toronto Press, 1999.

–. *The Politics of Development: Forests, Mines and Hydro-Electric Power in Ontario, 1849-1941*. Toronto: Macmillan, 1974.

Newman, Peter. *The Canadian Establishment*. Vol. 1. Toronto: McClelland and Stewart-Bantam, 1979.

Norton, Wayne. *"A whole little city by itself": Tranquille and Tuberculosis*. Kamloops: Plateau, 1999.

Oelschlaeger, Max. *The Idea of Wilderness: From Prehistory to the Age of Ecology*. New Haven: Yale University Press, 1991.

Ontario Camping Association. *Blue Lake and Rocky Shore: A History of Children's Camping in Ontario*. Toronto: Natural Heritage/Natural History, 1984.

Owram, Doug. *Born at the Right Time: A History of the Baby Boom Generation*. Toronto: University of Toronto Press, 1996.

Parkhill, Thomas. *Weaving Ourselves into the Land: Charles Godfrey Leland, "Indians," and the Study of Native American Religions*. Albany: State University of New York Press, 1997.

Parr, Joy, ed. *Childhood and Family in Canadian History*. Toronto: McClelland and Stewart, 1982.

–, ed. *A Diversity of Women: Ontario, 1945-1980*. Toronto: University of Toronto Press, 1995.

–. *The Gender of Breadwinners: Women, Men, and Change in Two Industrial Towns, 1880-1950*. Toronto: University of Toronto Press, 1990.

–. *Labouring Children: British Apprentices to Canada, 1869-1924*. Toronto: University of Toronto Press, 1980, 1994.

Patrias, Carmela. *Relief Strike: Immigrant Workers and the Great Depression in Crowland, Ontario, 1930-1935*. Toronto: New Hogtown Press, 1990.

Peiss, Kathy. *Cheap Amusements: Working Women and Leisure in Turn-of-the-Century New York*. Philadelphia: Temple University Press, 1986.

–. *Hope in a Jar: The Making of America's Beauty Culture*. New York: Metropolitan Books, 1998.

Perry, Adele. *On the Edge of Empire: Race, Gender, and the Making of British Columbia*. Toronto: University of Toronto Press, 2001.

Pierson, Ruth Roach. *"They're still women after all": The Second World War and Canadian Womanhood.* Toronto: McClelland and Stewart, 1986.

Piva, Michael J. *The Condition of the Working Class in Toronto, 1900-21.* Ottawa: University of Ottawa Press, 1979.

Porter, John. *The Vertical Mosaic: An Analysis of Social Class and Power in Canada.* Toronto: University of Toronto Press, 1965.

Pratt, Mary Louise. *Imperial Eyes: Travel Writing and Transculturation.* New York: Routledge, 1992.

Prentice, Alison, Paula Bourne, Gail Cuthbert Brandt, Beth Light, Wendy Mitchinson, and Naomi Black, eds. *Canadian Women: A History.* Toronto: Harcourt, Brace, 1988

Rawlyk, George A., ed. *The Canadian Protestant Experience, 1760-1990.* Montreal/Kingston: McGill-Queen's University Press, 1990.

Raymond, Jocelyn Motyer. *The Nursery World of Dr. Blatz.* Toronto: University of Toronto Press, 1991.

Rea, K.J. *The Prosperous Years: The Economic History of Ontario, 1939-1975.* Toronto: University of Toronto Press, 1985.

Richardson, Theresa R. *The Century of the Child: The Mental Hygiene Movement and Social Policy in the United States and Canada.* Albany: State University of New York Press, 1989.

Roediger, David. *The Wages of Whiteness: Race and the Making of the American Working Class.* London. New York: Verso, 1991.

Rogers, Edward S., and Donald B. Smith, eds. *Aboriginal Ontario: Historical Perspectives on the First Nations.* Toronto, Oxford: Dundurn Press, 1994.

Rogin, Michael. *Blackface, White Noise: Jewish Immigrants in the Hollywood Melting Pot.* Berkeley: University of California Press, 1996.

Rooke, P.T., and R.L. Schnell. *Discarding the Asylum: From Child Rescue to the Welfare State in English Canada, 1800-1950.* Llanham: University Press of America, 1983.

–. *No Bleeding Heart: Charlotte Whitton, a Feminist on the Right.* Vancouver: UBC Press, 1987.

Rome, David. *Clouds in the Thirties: On Antisemitism in Canada, 1929-1939: A Chapter on Canadian Jewish History.* Montreal: [s.n.], 1977.

Rosenzweig, Roy. *Eight Hours for What We Will: Workers and Leisure in an Industrial City, 1870-1920.* Cambridge: Cambridge University Press, 1983.

Rosenzweig, Roy, and Elizabeth Blackmar. *The Park and the People: A History of Central Park.* Ithaca: Cornell University Press, 1992.

Ross, Ellen. *Love and Toil: Motherhood in Outcast London, 1870-1918.* New York/Oxford: Oxford University Press, 1993.

Rotundo, E. Anthony. *American Manhood: Transformations in Masculinity from the Revolution to the Modern Era.* New York: Basic Books, 1993.

Ruffo, Armand Garnet. *Grey Owl: The Mystery of Archie Belaney.* Regina: Coteau Books, 1996.

Rutherford, Paul, ed. *Saving the Canadian City: The First Phase, 1880-1920.* Toronto: University of Toronto Press, 1974.

Rutman, Leonard. *In the Children's Aid: J.J. Kelso and Child Welfare in Ontario.* Toronto: University of Toronto Press, 1981.

Sangster, Joan. *Regulating Girls and Women: Sexuality, Family, and the Law in Ontario, 1920-1960.* Toronto: Oxford University Press, 2001.

Saunders, Audrey. *Algonquin Story.* Toronto: Ontario Department of Lands and Forests, 1963.

Schmidtt, Peter. *Back to Nature: The Arcadian Myth in Urban America.* Baltimore: Johns Hopkins University Press, 1990.

Scott, Joan Wallach. *Gender and the Politics of History.* New York: Columbia University Press, 1988.

Shaw, Bernard S. *Canoe Lake, Algonquin Park: Tom Thomson and Other Mysteries.* Burnstown: General Store, 1996.

Shi, David E. *The Simple Life: Plain Living and High Thinking in American Culture.* New York, Oxford: Oxford University Press, 1985.

Shields, Rob. *Places on the Margin: Alternative Geographies of Modernity.* London: Routledge, 1991.

Sklar, Robert. *Movie-made America: A Social History of American Movies.* New York: Random House, 1975.

Skocpol, Theda. *Protecting Soldiers and Mothers: The Political Origins of Social Policy in the United States.* Cambridge: Belknap Press of Harvard University Press, 1992.

Smith, Donald B. *From the Land of Shadows: The Making of Grey Owl.* Saskatoon: Western Producer Prairie Books, 1990.

–. *Long Lance: The True Story of an Imposter.* Toronto: Macmillan, 1982.

Strange, Carolyn. *Toronto's Girl Problem: The Perils and Pleasures of the City, 1880-1930.* Toronto: University of Toronto Press, 1995.

Strickland, Dan, Russ Rutter, and Heather Lang-Runtz, eds. *The Best of the Raven: 150 Essays from Algonquin Park's Popular Newsletter – A Centennial Collection.* Whitney: Friends of Algonquin Park, 1993.

Strong-Boag, Veronica. *The New Day Recalled: Lives of Girls and Women in English Canada, 1919-1939.* Toronto: Copp Clark Pittman, 1988.

Strong-Boag, Veronica, and Carole Gerson, *Paddling Her Own Canoe: The Times and Texts of E. Pauline Johnson (Tekahionwake).* Toronto: University of Toronto Press, 2000.

Struthers, James. *"No fault of their own": Unemployment and the Canadian Welfare State, 1914-1941.* Toronto: University of Toronto Press, 1983.

Sutherland, Neil. *Children in English-Canadian Society, 1880-1920: Framing the Twentieth-century Consensus.* Toronto: University of Toronto Press, 1976. Reissued by Wilfrid Laurier University Press, 2000.

–. *Growing Up: Childhood in English Canada from the Great War to the Age of Television.* Toronto: University of Toronto Press, 1997.

Thelan, David, ed. *Memory and American History.* Bloomington and Indianapolis: Indiana University Press, 1990.

Thomas, Keith. *Man and the Natural World: Changing Attitudes in England, 1500-1800.* London: Allen Lane, 1983.

Thompson, E.P. *Making of the English Working Class.* London: Victor Gollancz, 1963. Reprint, New York: Penguin Books, 1980.

Thompson, John Herd, and Allen Seager. *Canada, 1922-1939: Decades of Discord.* Toronto: McClelland and Stewart, 1985.

Thompson, Paul. *The Voice of the Past: Oral History.* Oxford: Oxford University Press, 1978.

Tillotson, Shirley. *The Public at Play: Gender and the Politics of Recreation in Post-war Ontario.* Toronto: University of Toronto Press, 2000.

Tomkins, George S. *A Common Countenance: Stability and Change in the Canadian Curriculum.* Toronto: Prentice-Hall, 1986.

Torgovnick, Marianna. *Gone Primitive: Savage Intellects, Modern Lives.* Chicago: University of Chicago Press, 1990.

Tulchinsky, Gerald J. *Taking Root: The Origins of the Canadian Jewish Community.* Toronto: Lester Publishing, 1992.

Turner, James. *Without God, Without Creed: The Origins of Unbelief in America.* Baltimore: Johns Hopkins University Press, 1985.

Ursel, Jane. *Private Lives, Public Policy: 100 Years of Intervention in the Family.* Toronto: Women's Press, 1992.

Valverde, Mariana. *The Age of Light, Soap, and Water: Moral Reform in English Canada, 1885-1925.* Toronto: McClelland and Stewart, 1991.

Wadland, John Henry. *Ernest Thompson Seton: Man in Nature and the Progressive Era, 1880-1915.* New York: Arno Press, 1978.

Walden, Keith. *Becoming Modern in Toronto: The Industrial Exhibition and the Shaping of Late Victorian Culture.* Toronto: University of Toronto Press, 1997.

Wall, G., and J. Marsh, eds. *Recreational Land Use: Perspectives on Its Evolution in Canada.* Ottawa: Carleton University Press, 1982.

Wetherell, Donald, with Irene Kmet. *Useful Pleasures: The Shaping of Leisure in Alberta, 1896-1945.* Edmonton: Alberta Culture and Multiculturalism, 1990.

Williams, Raymond. *The Country and the City.* London: Chatto and Windus, 1973.

Wills, Gale. *A Marriage of Convenience: Business and Social Work in Toronto, 1918-1957.* Toronto: University of Toronto Press, 1995.

Wilson, Alexander. *The Culture of Nature: North American Landscape from Disney to the Exxon Valdez.* Toronto: Between the Lines, 1991.

Zelizer, Viviana A. *Pricing the Priceless Child: The Changing Social Value of Children.* New York: Basic Books, 1981.

Articles and Book Chapters

Adams, Mary Louise. "Almost Anything Can Happen: A Search for Sexual Discourse in the Urban Spaces of 1940s Toronto." *Canadian Journal of Sociology* 19, 2 (1994): 217-32.

Altmeyer, George. "Three Ideas of Nature in Canada, 1893-1914." *Journal of Canadian Studies* 11, 3 (1976): 21-36.

Anderson, H. Allen. "Ernest Thompson Seton and the Woodcraft Indians." *Journal of American Culture* 8, 1 (1985): 43-50.

Arnup, Katherine. "Raising the Dionne Quintuplets: Lessons for Modern Mothers." *Journal of Canadian Studies* 29, 4 (1994-95): 65-84.

Baillargeon, Denyse. "'If you had no money, you had no trouble, did you?' Montreal Working-class Housewives during the Great Depression." *Women's History Review* 1, 2 (1992): 217-37.

Balmori, Diane. "Architecture, Landscape, and the Intermediate Structure: Eighteenth-century Experiments in Mediation." *Journal of the Society of Architectural Historians* 50, 1 (1991): 38-56.

Barman, Jean. "'Oh no! It would not be proper to discuss that with you': Reflections on Gender and the Experience of Childhood." *Curriculum Inquiry* 24 (Spring 1994): 53-67.

Bator, Paul Adolphus. "The Health Reformers versus the Common Canadian: The Controversy over Compulsory Vaccination against Smallpox in Toronto and Ontario, 1900-1920." *Ontario History* 74, 4 (1983): 348-73.

–. "'The struggle to raise the lower classes': Public Health Reform and the Problem of Poverty in Toronto, 1910 to 1921." *Journal of Canadian Studies* 14, 1 (1979): 43-49.

Bennet, Paul W. "Taming 'Bad Boys' of the 'Dangerous Class': Child Rescue and Restraint at the Victoria Industrial School, 1887-1935." *Histoire Sociale/Social History* 21, 41 (1988): 71-96.

–. "Turning 'Bad Boys' into 'Good Citizens': The Reforming Impulse of Toronto's Industrial Schools Movement, 1883 to the 1920s." *Ontario History* 78, 3 (1986): 209-27.

Berger, Carl. "The True North Strong and Free." In *Nationalism in Canada,* ed. Peter Russell, 4-14. Toronto: McGraw-Hill, 1966.

Bordo, Jonathan. "Jack Pine: Wilderness Sublime or Erasure of the Aboriginal Presence from the Landscape." *Journal of Canadian Studies* 27, 4 (1992-93): 98-128.

Bradbury, Bettina. "Pigs, Cows and Boarders: Non-Wage Forms of Survival among Montreal Families, 1861-1891." *Labour/Le Travail* 14 (Fall 1984): 9-46.

Brannigan, Augustine. "Mystification of the Innocents: Crime Comics and Delinquency in Canada, 1931-1949." *Criminal Justice History* 7 (1986): 111-44.

Bullen, John. "Hidden Workers: Child Labour and the Family Economy in Late Nineteenth-Century Urban Ontario." *Labour/Le Travail* 18 (Fall 1986): 163-87.

–. "J.J. Kelso and the 'New' Child-savers: The Genesis of the Children's Aid Movement in Ontario." *Ontario History* 82, 2 (1990): 107-28.

–. "Orphans, Idiots, Lunatics, and Historians: Recent Approaches to the History of Child Welfare in Canada." *Histoire Sociale/Social History* 18, 35 (1985): 133-45.

Burke, Sara Z. "'Being unlike man': Challenges to Co-education at the University of Toronto, 1884-1909." *Ontario History* 93, 1 (2001): 11-31.

Callan, Eamonn. "John Dewey and the Two Faces of Progressive Education." In *Canadian Education: Historical Themes and Contemporary Issues,* ed. E. Brian Titley, 84-94. Calgary: Detselig, 1990.

Cameron, Ross D. "Tom Thomson, Antimodernism, and the Ideal of Manhood." *Journal of the Canadian Historical Association* 10 (1998): 185-208.

Cardinal-Shubert, Joanne. "In the Red." *Fuse*, Fall 1989, 20-28.

Carnes, Mark C. "Middle-class Men and the Solace of Fraternal Ritual." In *Meanings for Manhood: Constructions of Masculinity in Victorian America,* ed. Mark C. Carnes and Clyde Griffen, 37-52. Chicago and London: University of Chicago Press, 1990.

Cole, Douglas. "Artists, Patrons and Public: An Enquiry into the Success of the Group of Seven." *Journal of Canadian Studies* 13, 2 (1978): 69-78.

Comacchio, Cynthia. "Dancing to Perdition: Adolescence and Leisure in Interwar English Canada." *Journal of Canadian Studies* 32, 3 (1997): 5-35.

–. "'The history of us': Social Science, History, and the Relations of Family in Canada." *Labour/Le Travail* 46 (Fall 2000): 167-220.

–. "'A post-script for father': Defining a New Fatherhood in Interwar Canada." *Canadian Historical Review* 78, 3 (1997): 386-408.

Conwill, Joseph D. "Back to the Land: Pennsylvania's New Deal Era Communities." *Pennsylvania Heritage* 10, 3 (1984): 12-17.

Coulter, Rebecca. "The Working Young of Edmonton, 1921-31." In *Childhood and Family in Canadian History,* ed. Joy Parr, 143-59. Toronto: McClelland and Stewart, 1982.

Cronon, William. "The Trouble with Wilderness, or, Getting Back to the Wrong Nature." *Environmental History* 1, 1 (1996): 1-23.

Cruickshank, Marjorie. "The Open-air School Movement in English Education." *Paedagogica Historica* 17, 1 (1977): 62-74.

Danylewycz, Marta. "Domestic Science Education in Ontario, 1900-1940." In *Gender and Education in Ontario: An Historical Reader,* ed. Ruby Heap and Alison Prentice, 129-47. Toronto: Canadian Scholar's Press, 1991.

Davies, Stephen. "'Reckless walking must be discouraged': The Automobile Revolution and the Shaping of Modern Urban Canada to 1930." *Urban History Review* 18, 2 (1989): 123-38.

Dawson, Michael. "'That nice red coat goes to my head like champagne': Gender, Antimodernism and the Mountie Image, 1880-1960." *Journal of Canadian Studies* 32, 3 (1997): 119-39.

Deeks, Gordon, and Richard B. Howard, "Temagami Magic." *Old Times*, Summer 1995, 34-38.

Dehli, Kari. "'Health Scouts' for the State? School and Public Health Nurses in Early Twentieth-century Toronto." *Historical Studies in Education* 2, 2 (1990): 247-64.

d'Emilio, John. "The Homosexual Menace: the Politics of Sexuality in Cold War America." In *Passion and Power: Sexuality in History,* ed. Kathy Peiss and Robert A. Padgug, 226-40. Philadelphia: Temple University Press, 1989.

Dirks, Patricia. "'Getting a grip on Harry': Canada's Methodists Respond to the 'Big Boy' Problem." *Canadian Methodist Historical Society Papers* 7 (1990): 67-82.

Dummitt, Chris. "Finding a Place for Father: Selling the Barbecue in Postwar Canada." *Journal of the Canadian Historical Association* 9 (1998): 209-23.

Dyer, S.W. "Back to the Land: Settlement Schemes for Adelaide's Unemployed, 1930-35." *Labour History* 31 (1976): 30-37.

Forestell, Nancy. "Bachelors, Boarding-houses, and Blind Pigs: Gender Construction in a Multi-ethnic Mining Camp, 1909-1920." In *A Nation of Immigrants: Women, Workers, and Communities in Canadian History, 1840s-1960s*, ed. Franca Iacovetta with Paula Draper and Robert Ventresca, 251-90. Toronto: University of Toronto Press, 1998.

Fox, John J. "First Readers: Five Introductions to Oral History." *Oral History Review* 25, 1-2 (1998): 119-28.

Francis, Daniel. "Great White Hope: Myth of the North." In *National Dreams: Myth, Memory, and Canadian History*, 152-71. Vancouver: Arsenal Pulp Press, 1997.

Frisch, Michael H. "The Memory of History." *Radical History Review* 25 (1981): 9-23.

Gad, Gunter, and Deryck W. Holdsworth. "Streetscape and Society: The Changing Built Environment of King Street, Toronto." In *Patterns of the Past: Interpreting Ontario's History*, ed. Roger Hall, William Westfall, and Laurel Sefton MacDowell, 174-205. Toronto and Oxford: Oxford University Press, 1988.

Gleason, Mona. "Embodied Negotiations: Children's Bodies and Historical Change in Canada, 1930 to 1960." *Journal of Canadian Studies* 34, 1 (1999): 112-38.

–. "Race, Class, and Health: School Medical Inspection and 'Healthy' Children in British Columbia, 1890-1930." *Canadian Bulletin of Medical Health* 19 (2002): 95-112.

Goldin, Grace. "Building a Hospital of Air: The Victorian Pavilions of St. Thomas' Hospital, London." *Bulletin of the History of Medicine* 49, 4 (1975): 512-35.

Golz, Annalee. "Family Matters: The Canadian Family and the State in the Postwar Period." *Left History* 1, 2 (1993): 9-49.

Grant, S.D. "Myths of the North in the Canadian Ethos." *Northern Review* 3/4 (1989): 15-41.

Green, Rayna. "The Tribe Called Wannabee." *Folklore* 99 (July 1988): 30-55.

Hall, M. Ann. "Rarely Have We Asked Why: Reflections on Canadian Women's Experience in Sport." *Atlantis* 6, 1 (1980): 51-60.

Harris, Richard. "A Working-class Suburb for Immigrants, Toronto, 1909-1913." *Geographical Review* 81, 3 (1991): 318-32.

Harris, Richard, and Matt Sendbuehler. "The Making of a Working-class Suburb in Hamilton's East End, 1900-1945." *Journal of Urban History* 20, 4 (1994): 486-511.

Harvey, Fernand. "Children of the Industrial Revolution in Quebec." In *Readings in Canadian History: Post-confederation.* Vol. 2, ed. R. Douglas Francis and Donald B. Smith, 195-204. Toronto: Holt, Rhinehart and Winston, 1982.

Heald, Carolyn. "Documenting Disease: Ontario's Bureaucracy Battles Tuberculosis." *Archivaria* 41 (1996): 88-107.

Heron Craig. "The High School and the Household Economy in Working-class Hamilton, 1890-1940." *Historical Studies in Education* 7, 2 (1995): 217-59.

Hill, Richard. "One Part Per Million: White Appropriation and Native Voices." *Fuse*, Winter 1992, 12-22.

Hobday, R.A. "Sunlight Therapy and Solar Architecture." *Medical History* 41, 4 (1997): 455-72.

Hurl, Lorna. "Restricting Child Factory Labour in Late Nineteenth-century Ontario." *Labour/Le Travail* 21 (Spring 1988): 87-121.

Hurwitz, David. "How Lucky We Were." *American Jewish History* 87, 1 (1999): 29-59.

Iacovetta, Franca. "Gossip, Contest, and Power in the Making of Suburban Bad Girls: Toronto, 1945-60." *Canadian Historical Review* 80, 4 (1999): 585-623.

–. "Making 'New Canadians': Social Workers, Women and the Re-shaping of Immigrant Families." In *Gender Conflicts: New Essays in Women's History,* ed. Franca Iacovetta and Mariana Valverde, 261-302. Toronto: University of Toronto Press, 1992.

Jean, Dominique. "Family Allowances and Family Autonomy: Quebec Families Encounter the Welfare State, 1945-55." In *Canadian Family History: Selected Readings,* ed. Bettina Bradbury, 401-37. Toronto: Copp, Clark, Pitman, 1992.

–. "Le Recul de travail des enfant au Quebec entre 1940 et 1960: Une explication des conflits entre les familles pauvres et l'etat profidence." *Labour/Le Travail* 24 (Fall 1989): 91-129.

Jessup, Lynda. "Prospectors, Bushwhackers, Painters: Antimodernism and the Group of Seven." *International Journal of Canadian Studies* 17 (1998): 193-214.

Kinsmen, Gary. "Character Weakness and 'Fruit Machines': Towards an Analysis of the Anti-homosexual Security Campaign in the Canadian Civil Service." *Labour/Le Travail* 35 (1995): 133-61.

Lacombe, Michele. "'Songs of the open road': Bon Echo, Urban Utopians and the Cult of Nature." *Journal of Canadian Studies* 33, 2 (1998): 152-67.

Lathrop, Anna H. "'Strap an axe to your belt': Camp Counselor Training and the Socialization of Women at the Margaret Eaton School (1925-1941)." *Sport History Review* 32, 2 (2001): 110-25.

Lenskyj, Helen. "Femininity First: Sport and Physical Education for Ontario Girls, 1890-1930." *Canadian Journal of History of Sport* 13, 2 (1982): 4-17.

–. "Training for 'True Womanhood': Physical Education for Girls in Ontario Schools, 1890-1920." *Historical Studies in Education* 1, 2 (1990): 205-23.

Lewis, Nora. "Creating the Little Machine: Child-rearing in British Columbia, 1919-1939." *BC Studies* 56 (Winter 1982/83): 44-60.

–. "Physical Perfection for Spiritual Welfare: Health Care for the Urban Child, 1900-1939." In *Studies in Childhood History: A Canadian Perspective*, ed. Patricia T. Rooke and R.L. Schnell, 135-66. Calgary: Detselig, 1982.

Loo, Tina. "Making a Modern Wilderness: Conserving Wildlife in Twentieth-century Canada." *Canadian Historical Review* 82, 1 (2001): 92-121.

–. "Of Moose and Men: Hunting for Masculinities in British Columbia, 1880-1939." *Western Historical Quarterly* 32, 3 (2001): 296-319.

Lowrey, Nathan. "Tales of the Northern Maine Woods: The History and Tradition of the Maine Guide." *Northeast Folklore* 28 (1989): 69-110.

Lutz, Hartmut. "Cultural Appropriation as a Process of Displacing Peoples and History." *Canadian Journal of Native Studies* 10, 2 (1990): 167-82.

MacLaren, I.S. "Cultured Wilderness in Banff National Park." *Journal of Canadian Studies* 34, 3 (1999): 7-58.

MacLeod, David. "A Live Vaccine: The YMCA and Male Adolescence in the United States and Canada, 1870-1920." *Histoire Sociale/Social History* 11, 2 (1978): 5-25.

Mann, Jean. "G.M. Weir and H.B. King: Progressive Education or Education for the Progressive State?" In *Schooling and Society in Twentieth-century British Columbia*, ed. Donald Wilson and David C. Jones, 91-117. Calgary: Detselig, 1980.

Maracle, Lee. "Native Myths: Trickster Alive and Crowing." *Fuse*, Fall 1989, 29-31.

Marr, M. Lucille. "Church Teen Clubs, Feminized Organizations? Tuxis Boys, Trail Rangers, and Canadian Girls in Training, 1919-1939," *Historical Studies in Education*, 3, 2 (1991): 249-67.

Marshall, Dominique. "The Language of Children's Rights, the Formation of the Welfare State, and the Democratic Experience of Poor Families in Quebec." *Canadian Historical Review* 78, 3 (1997): 409-41.

Matters, Diane L. "The Boys' Industrial School: Education for Juvenile Offenders." In *Schooling and Society in Twentieth-century British Columbia*, ed. J. Donald Wilson and David C. Jones, 53-70. Calgary: Detselig, 1980.

Maynard, W. Barksdale. "'An ideal life in the woods for boys': Architecture and Culture in the Earliest Summer Camps." *Winterthur Portfolio* 34, 1 (1991): 3-29.

McCombs, Douglas W. "Therapeutic Rusticity: Antimodernism, Health and the Wilderness Vacation, 1870-1915." *New York History* 76, 4 (1995): 409-28.

McDonald, Robert A.J. "'Holy Retreat' or 'Practical Breathing Spot'? Class Perceptions of Vancouver's Stanley Park, 1910-1913." *Canadian Historical Review* 65, 2 (1984): 127-53.

McIntosh, Robert. "The Boys in Nova Scotia Coal Mines, 1873-1923." *Acadiensis* 16 (Spring 1987): 35-50.

–. "Constructing the Child: New Approaches to the History of Childhood in Canada." *Acadiensis* 28, 2 (1999): 126-40.

–. "The Realm of Uncertainty: The Experience of Work in the Cumberland Coal Mines, 1873-1927." *Acadiensis* 16 (Autumn 1986): 3-57.

McLaren, Angus. "The Creation of a Haven for 'Human Thoroughbreds': The Sterilization of the Feeble-minded and the Mentally Ill in British Columbia." *Canadian Historical Review* 67, 2 (1986): 127-50

Mechling, Jay. "Playing Indian." *Prospects* 5 (1980): 17-33.

Mergen, Bernard. "The Discovery of Children's Play." *American Quarterly* 27, 4 (1975): 399-420.

Mikkelsen, Glen. "Indians and Rodeo." *Alberta History* 34, 1 (1986): 13-19.

Miller, Peter J. "Psychology and the Child: Homer Lane and J.B. Watson." In *Studies in Childhood History: A Canadian Perspective*, ed. Patricia T. Rooke and R. L. Schnell, 57-79. Calgary: Detselig, 1982.

Mitchinson, Wendy. "The YWCA and Reform in the Nineteenth Century." *Histoire Sociale/Social History* 12, 24 (1979): 368-84.

Morgan, Cecilia. "Performing for 'Imperial Eyes': Bernice Loft and Ethel Brant Monture, Ontario, 1930s–1960s." In *Contact Zones: Aboriginal and Settler Women in Canada's Colonial Past*, ed. Katie Pickles and Myra Rutherdale, 67-89. Vancouver: UBC Press, 2005.

–. "Private Lives and Public Performances: Aboriginal Women in a Settler Society, Ontario, Canada, 1920s-1960s." *Journal of Colonialism and Colonial History* 4, 3 (2003): available at http://muse.jhu.edu/journals/journal_of_colonialism_and_colonial_history/v004/4.3morgan.html.

–. "'A wigwam to Westminster': Performing Mohawk Identity in Imperial Britain, 1890s-1990s. *Gender and History* 15, 2 (2003), 319-41.

Morris, Brian. "Ernest Thompson Seton and the Origins of the Woodcraft Movement." *Journal of Contemporary History* 5, 2 (1970): 183-94.

Mott, Morris. "Confronting 'Modern' Problems through Play: The Beginning of Physical Education in Manitoba's Public Schools, 1900-1915." In *Schools in the West: Essays in Canadian Educational History*, ed. Nancy M. Sheehan, J. Donald Wilson, and David C. Jones, 57-71. Calgary: Detselig, 1986.

Myers, Tamara. "The Voluntary Delinquent: Parents, Daughters, and the Montreal Juvenile Delinquents' Court in 1918." *Canadian Historical Review* 80, 2 (1999): 242-68.

Nasaw, David. "Moving Pictures in the Early Twentieth Century." In *Small Worlds: Children and Adolescents in America, 1850-1950*, ed. Elliott West and Paula Petrikk, 14-25. Lawrence: University Press of Kansas, 1992.

Paris, Leslie. "The Adventures of Peanut and Bo: Summer Camps and Early Twentieth-century American Girlhood." *Journal of Women's History* 12, 4 (2001): 47-76.

–. "'A home away from home': Brooklyn Jews and Interwar Children's Summer Camps." In *The Jews of Brooklyn*, ed. Ilana Abramovitch and Seán Galvin, 242-49. Hanover: University Press of New England, 2002.

–. "'Please let me come home': Homesickness and Family Ties at Early Twentieth-century Summer Camps." In *The American Child: A Cultural Studies Reader*, ed. Caroline Levander and Carol Singley, 246-61. New Brunswick, NJ: Rutgers University Press, 2003.

Patterson, R.S. "The Canadian Experience with Progressive Education." In *Canadian Education: Historical Themes and Contemporary Issues*, ed. E. Brian Titley, 95-110. Calgary: Detselig, 1990.

Pederson, Diana. "'Building today for the womanhood of tomorrow': Businessmen, Boosters, and the YWCA, 1890-1930." *Urban History Review* 15, 3 (1987): 225-42.

–. "'Keeping our good girls good': The YWCA and the 'Girl Problem,' 1870-1930." *Canadian Women Studies* 7, 4 (1986): 20-24.

Pitsula, James. "The Emergence of Social Work in Toronto." *Journal of Canadian Studies* 14, 1 (1979): 35-42.

Pogue, Gail, and Bryce Taylor, "History of Provincial Government Services of the Youth and Recreation Branch, Part 1: 1940-1950." *Recreation Review* (November 1972): Supplement no. 1.

–. "History of Provincial Government Services of the Youth and Recreation Branch, Part 2: 1950-1960." *Recreation Review* (March 1973): Supplement no. 2.

Powell, T.J.D. "Northern Settlement, 1929-1935." *Saskatchewan History* 30, 3 (1977): 81-98.

Prang, Margaret. "The Girl God Would Have Me Be: The Canadian Girls in Training, 1915-1939." *Canadian Historical Review* 66, 2 (1985): 154-183.

Reiter, Ester. "Secular Yiddishkait: Left Politics, Culture, and Community." Labour 49 (2002): 121-46.

Robinson, Daniel J., and David Kimmel. "The Queer Career of Homosexual Security Vetting in Cold War Canada." *Canadian Historical Review* 75 (1994): 319-45.

Rodgers, Daniel. "The Antimodernist Critique of Capitalist Culture." *Radical History Review* 28-30 (1984): 464-71.

Rodwell, Grant. "Australian Open-air School Architecture." *History of Education Review* 24, 2 (1995): 21-41.

Rooke, Patricia T. "The 'Child-institutionalized' in Canada, Britain and the United States: A Trans-Atlantic Perspective." *Journal of Educational Thought* 11, 2 (1977): 157-71.

Rooke, Patricia T., and R.L. Schnell. "Child Welfare in English Canada, 1920-1948." *Social Service Review* 55, 3 (September 1981): 484-506.

–. "Childhood as Ideology." *British Journal of Educational Studies* 27 (February 1979): 7-28.

Rutherdale, Robert. "Fatherhood and Masculine Domesticity during the Baby Boom: Consumption and Leisure in Advertising and Life Stories." In *Family Matters: Papers in Post-Confederation Canadian Family History*, ed. Lori Chambers and Edgar-André Montigny, 309-27. Toronto: Canadian Scholars' Press, 1998.

Rutherford, Paul. "Tomorrow's Metropolis: The Urban Reform Movement in Canada, 1880-1920." Canadian Historical Association, *Historical Papers* 6, 1 (1971): 203-24.

Rutty, Christopher J. "The Middle-class Plague: Epidemic Polio and the Canadian State, 1936-37." *Canadian Bulletin of Medical History* 13, 2 (1996): 277-314.

Sackett, Andrew. "Inhaling the Salubrious Air: Health and Development in St. Andrews, NB, 1880-1910." *Acadiensis* 25, 1 (1995): 54-81.

Sanford, Barbara. "The Political Economy of Land Development in Nineteenth-century Toronto." *Urban History Review* 16, 1 (1987): 17-33.

Schwager, Sally. "Educating Women in America." *Signs: Journal of Women in Culture and Society* 12, 2 (1987): 362-65.

Setliff, Eric. "Sex Fiends or Swish Kids? Gay Men in Hush Free Press, 1946-1956." In *Gendered Pasts: Historical Essays in Femininity and Masculinity in Canada*, ed. Kathryn McPherson, Cecilia Morgan, and Nancy Forestell, 158-78. Toronto: Oxford University Press, 1999.

Sherman, Geraldine. "The Girls of Summer." *Toronto Life*, September 2001, 100-6.

Smith, Allen. "Farms, Forests, and Cities: The Image of the Land and the Rise of the Metropolis in Ontario, 1860-1914." In *Old Ontario: Essays in Honour of J.M.S. Careless*, ed. David Keane and Colin Read, 71-94. Toronto: Dundurn Press, 1990.

Smith, Donald B. "Grey Owl." *Ontario History* 63, 3 (1971): 160-76.

Smith, Michael. "The Ego Ideal of the Good Camper and the Nature of Summer Camp." *Environmental History* (January 2006). http://www.historycooperative.org/journals/eh/11.1/smith.html.

Smith, Michael J. "Dampness, Darkness, Dirt, Disease: Physicians and the Promotion of Sanitary Science in Public Schools." In *Profiles of Science and Society in the Maritimes Prior to 1914*, ed. Paul A. Bogaard, 200-3. Halifax: Acadiensis Press, 1990.

Spears, Betty. "Mary, Mary, Quite Contrary, Why Do Women Play?" *Canadian Journal of History of Sport* 18, 1 (1987): 67-75.

Stacey, Robert, Donald Smith, and Bryan Winslow. "Introduction." In Dawendine, *Iroquois Fires: The Six Nations Lyrics and Lore of Dawendine.* Ottawa: Penumbra Press, 1995.

Stallabrass, Julian. "The Idea of the Primitive: British Art and Anthropology, 1918-1930." *New Left Review* 183 (Fall 1990): 95-115.

Stamp, Robert. "Canadian High Schools in the 1920s and 1930s: The Social Challenge to the Academic Tradition." *Historical Papers* (1978): 76-93.

–. "Education for Democratic Citizenship." In *The Schools of Ontario, 1876-1976*, ed. Robert Stamp, 164-82. Toronto: University of Toronto Press, 1982.

–. "Teaching Girls Their 'God-given place in life': The Introduction to Home Economics in the Schools." *Atlantis* 2, 2, pt. 1 (1977): 18-34.

Strange, Carolyn. "From Modern Babylon to a City upon a Hill: The Toronto Social Survey Commission of 1915 and the Search for Sexual Order in the City." In *Patterns of the Past: Interpreting Ontario's History*, ed. Roger Hall, William Westfall, and Laurel Sefton MacDowell, 255-77. Toronto: Dundurn Press, 1988.

Strickland, Charles E., and Andrew M. Ambrose. "The Baby Boom, Prosperity, and the Changing Worlds of Children, 1945-1963." In *American Childhood: A Research Guide and Historical Handbook,* ed. Joseph M. Hawes and N. Ray Hiner, 533-66. Westport: Greenwood Press, 1985.

Strong-Boag, Veronica. "Home-Dreams: Women and the Suburban Experience in Canada, 1945-60." *Canadian Historical Review* 72, 4 (1991): 471-504.

–. "Intruders in the Nursery: Childcare Professionals Reshape the Years One to Five, 1920-1940." In *Childhood and Family in Canadian History,* ed. Joy Parr, 160-78. Toronto: McClelland and Stewart, 1982.

–. "'Wages for housework': Mothers' Allowance and the Beginnings of Social Security in Canada." *Journal of Canadian Studies* 14, 1 (1979): 24-34.

Struthers, James. "'In the interests of the children': Mothers' Allowance and the Origins of Income Security in Ontario, 1917-30." In *The Limits of Affluence: Welfare in Ontario, 1920-1970*, 19-49. Toronto: Ontario Historical Studies Series, 1994.

–. "'Lord give us men': Women and Social Work in English Canada, 1918 to 1953." Canadian Historical Association, *Historical Papers* (1983): 96-112.

–. "A Profession in Crisis: Charlotte Whitton and Canadian Social Work in the 1930s." *Canadian Historical Review* 62, 2 (1981): 169-85.

Sulman, Michael. "Humanization of the American Child: Benjamin Spock as a Popularizer of Psychoanalytic Thought." *Journal of the History of the Behavioral Sciences* 9 (1983): 258-65.

Sutherland, Neil. "The Triumph of 'Formalism': Elementary Schooling in Vancouver from the 1920s to the 1960s." *BC Studies* 69-70 (Spring/Summer 1986): 175-210.

–. "'We always had things to do': The Paid and Unpaid Work of Anglophone Children between the 1920s and the 1960s." *Labour/Le Travail* 25 (Spring 1990): 105-41.

Synge, Jane. "The Transition from School to Work: Growing Up Working Class in Early Twentieth-century Hamilton, Ontario." In *Childhood and Adolescence in Canada,* ed. K. Ishwaran, 249-69. Toronto: McGraw-Hill Ryerson, 1979.

Tennant, Margaret. "Children's Health Camps in New Zealand: The Making of a Movement, 1919-1940." *Social History of Medicine* 9, 1 (1996): 69-87.

Turmel, A. "Historiography of Childhood in Canada." *Pedagogical Historica* 33, 2 (1997): 509-20.

Turner, David. "The Open Air School Movement in Sheffield." *History of Education* 1, 1 (1972): 58-80.

Valverde, Mariana. "Building Anti-delinquent Communities: Morality, Gender, and Generation in the City." In *A Diversity of Women: Ontario, 1945-1980,* ed. Joy Parr, 19-45. Toronto: University of Toronto Press, 1995.

Van Nus, Walter. "The Fate of City Beautiful Thought in Canada, 1893-1930." Canadian Historical Association, *Historical Papers* (1975): 191-210.

Weiss, Nancy Pottishman. "Mother, the Invention of Necessity: Dr. Benjamin Spock's Baby and Child Care." In *Growing Up in America: Children in Historical Perspective,* ed. N. Ray Hiner and Joseph M. Hawes, 283-303. Urbana and Chicago: University of Illinois Press, 1985.

West, D.A. "Re-searching the North in Canada: An Introduction to the Canadian Northern Discourse." *Journal of Canadian Studies* 26, 2 (1991): 108-19.

Wilmot, Frances. "In Search of Birmingham's Open-air Schools." *Local Historian* 29, 2 (1999): 102-13.

Wolfe, Roy I. "The Summer Resorts of Ontario in the Nineteenth Century." *Ontario History* 54, 3 (1962): 149-61.

Wright, Cynthia. "'Feminine trifles of vast importance': Writing Gender into the History of Consumption." In *Gender Conflicts: New Essays in Women's History,* ed. Franca Iacovetta and Mariana Valverde, 229-60. Toronto: University of Toronto Press, 1992.

Wright, Donald A. "W.D. Lighthall and David Ross McCord: Antimodernism and English-Canadian Imperialism, 1880s-1918." *Journal of Canadian Studies* 32, 2 (1997): 134-53.

Unpublished Theses and Dissertations

Burry, Donald. "A History of the Taylor Statten Camps." MSc thesis, University of Saskatchewan, 1985.

Ketchum, John Anthony Cheyne. "'The most perfect system': Official Policy in the First Century of Ontario's Government Secondary Schools and Its Impact on Students between 1871 and 1910." EdD thesis, University of Toronto, 1979.

Miller, Susan A. "Girls in Nature/The Nature of Girls: Transforming Female Adolescence at Summer Camp, 1900-1939." PhD diss., University of Pennsylvania, 2001.

Mykoff, Nancy. "A Jewish Season: Ethnic American Culture at Children's Summer Camp, 1918-1941" PhD diss., New York University, 2002.

Paris, Leslie. "Children's Nature: Summer Camps in New York State, 1919-1941." PhD diss., University of Michigan, 2000.

Poulter, Gillian. "Becoming Native in a Foreign Land: Visual Culture, Sport and Spectacle in the Construction of National Identity in Montreal, 1840-1885." PhD diss., York University, 1999.

Rutty, Christopher. "'Do something! ... Do anything!' Poliomyelitis in Canada, 1927-1967." PhD diss., University of Toronto, 1996.

Smith, Michael B. "'And they say we'll have some fun when it stops raining': A History of Summer Camp in the United States." PhD diss., Indiana University, 2002.

Toerpe, Kathleen. "Small Fry, Big Spender: McDonald's and the Rise of a Children's Consumer Culture, 1955-1985." PhD diss., Loyola University of Chicago, 1994.

Van Nus, Walter. "The Plan-makers and the City: Architects, Engineers, Surveyors and Urban Planning in Canada, 1890-1939" PhD diss., University of Toronto, 1977.

Unpublished Papers and Addresses

Danson, Bert. "The History of Camp Winnebagoe." Unpublished paper, May 2000.

Dodge, Bernadine. Address to the Friends of the Bata Library. Trent University, Peterborough, February 1992.

Forbes, Susan L. "'Nothing but a rag between you and the sky': Northway Lodge Girls' Camp and the Wilderness Experience." Paper presented to the Canadian Historical Association Conference, Edmonton, 24-29 May 2000.

Hall, Ann. "Arthur Lewis Cochrane: A Biographical Sketch." Queen's University, Kingston, 1964.

Wall, Sharon. "'Canada is a camping country': Cultural Nationalism and the Ontario Summer Camp, 1920-1955." Paper presented to the British Association for Canadian Studies, University of Edinburgh, 12 April 2000.

Index

Note: Camps are listed by name first, followed by "Camp," e.g., Ahmek, Camp; (m) after a page number indicates a map and (p), a photograph.